SCIENCE FICTION/HORROR

A Sight and Sound Reader

Edited by Kim Newman

bfi Publishing

First published in 2002 by the
British Film Institute
21 Stephen Street, London W1T 1LN

The British Film Institute is the UK national agency with
responsibility for encouraging the arts of film and television
and conserving them in the national interest.

Cover image: Jennifer Jason Leigh in *eXistenZ* (David Cronenberg, 1999)
Set by Design Consultants (Siobhán O'Connor)
Printed in the UK by St Edmundsbury Press, Suffolk

British Library Cataloguing-in-Publication Data
A catalogue record for this book is available from the British Library

ISBN 0-85170-897-8 (pbk)
ISBN 0-85170-896-x (hbk)

Contents

Section 6: Case Study – Stanley Kubrick

Introduction

This Reader is the fourth in a series which draws contents almost entirely from articles and reviews published in *Sight and Sound* since 1991. That year, the British Film Institute relaunched its flagship magazine, and combined it with its sister publication, *Monthly Film Bulletin*. The earlier readers cover *Action/Spectacle Cinema* (edited by José Arroyo), *American Independent Cinema* (edited by Jim Hillier) and *Film/Literature/ Heritage* (edited by Ginette Vincendeau). It is symptomatic of the fluid boundaries of genre that each of the other books includes pieces which might have found an equally welcome home here, while I have used articles that could almost as easily have been accommodated in one (or more) of them. 1990s action/spectacle cinema overlapped to a great extent with the science fiction film of the same era (hence a slight bias towards the horror end of the spectrum in this selection), many important contributors to horror and sci-fi cinema have emerged from the American independent sector (Quentin Tarantino has argued that without George A. Romero there could be no Steven Soderbergh), and a surprising percentage of horror and science fiction films are either direct adaptations from pre-existing literary works or draw on traditions (satire, utopia, gothic, fairytale, ghost story) that predate the cinema. I am sure my experience in compiling this Reader was shared by the earlier editors, of having to assess not only whether I thought any given piece of more than passing interest but of whether or not it truly fit the remit of this specific volume.

The articles republished here were originally commissioned, mostly by *Sight and Sound* editors Philip Dodd and Nick James, to make up the balance of the topical (what's out this month), the retrospective (what's worth looking at again) and the whimsical (what's worth saying) necessary in any monthly film publication. This means there are a subtle variety of approaches on offer. The coverage of contemporary films, overwhelmingly published at about the time of their UK release, has to tread a wary path between giving too much away (in her piece on *Fight Club*, 1999, Amy Taubin does not reveal the big twist), delivering a verdict in advance of all the evidence (it takes a few years and a couple of viewings to sort out an individual reaction to a complex film, let alone arrive at anything like a critical consensus) or merely trotting out enough story details to slake the inescapable reader's question of 'what's it about?' As a magazine whose review section provides full synopses of every film theatrically released in the United Kingdom, *Sight and Sound* is paradoxically free in articles and the reviews themselves from the tiresome need to work in enough story details to support the analysis.

Generally, these articles and reviews were originally intended to be read by people who haven't yet seen the film under discussion but are quite likely to do so soon – and may feel impelled to join in the argument by writing to the magazine. Almost uniquely, *Sight and Sound* offers not only a letters page forum for further debate but also a section of errata and corrigenda. In his BFI Classic booklet on *The Night of the Hunter*, Simon Callow credits Mr Peter Richards of Bridgend, a particularly vehement *Sight and Sound* correspondent (Callow characterises his tone as 'breathtaking rudeness and arrogance') with forcing him to do further research on the authorship of that film's screenplay, and to revise his original view of the issue. From a critic's point of view, think pieces on new films are the hardest to write. It's like making a snap decision about a person you've just met, delivering a verdict at the end of an evening rather than after a long acquaintanceship. Written between the press screening and the monthly deadline, they are not informed by a body of criticism and often seem personal or subjective, suggested approaches rather than definitive dissections. A revisionary piece, such as the analyses of *A Clockwork Orange* (1971) or *It's a Wonderful Life* (1947) by Kevin Jackson and Jonathan Romney included here, is only possible after a film has been in the public domain for decades and already inspired whole volumes of in-depth study.

The tone of the pieces on older films (a term which inevitably but not entirely comfortably means made before 1991) is different. Here, the assumption is that the readership is already familiar with *The Night of the Hunter* (1955), *The Shining* (1980) or *The Curse of the Cat People* (1944). The authors of the articles explore the films in detail as if revisiting the maze of the Overlook Hotel, pointing out features of interest that have been missed for all these years or wiping away some cobwebby assumption that has gone unchallenged for too long. In these pieces, we move away from topicality, towards the controversial pantheon-building necessary as an adjunct to the map-making impulse that drives us to draw boundaries of genres or compose Venn diagrams that allow for such subsets as the science fiction horror movie (*Alien*, 1979) or the teenage postmodern slasher picture (*Scream*, 1997). I have included articles which are purely analysis-based, but also studies which delve into the historical context or even production circumstances of enduring work – note Thomas Elsaesser's examinations of the Dr Mabuse films and *Nosferatu: eine Symphonie des Grauens* (1922). It is worth remembering, though, that these articles may still have a date-tied element: keyed in to a re-release, a retrospective or a remake. The *Nosferatu* piece was originally run in the month that Elias Merhige's *Shadow of the Vampire* (2000), a film about the production of Murnau's *Dracula* movie, was in release.

Less interesting in the long run, I feel, are interview-based pieces on upcoming or current films. It strikes me that no matter how much critics may flounder when confronted with a challenging movie, they manage on the whole to contribute more to an understanding of it than any statement by the director, writer or stars. It may be that the circumstances of promoting a film are not conducive to useful self-analysis, or it may be that creative people feel that explanations are unnecessary even as they recognise the need to get out and tub-thump the product (these days, contracts include commitments to giving interviews), which too frequently leads to the awkward sidestepping of probing questions. There are fewer interview-based articles here than in earlier Readers, not least because strong pieces about David Cronenberg (*Naked Lunch*, 1992; *Crash*, 1996), Mary Harron (*American Psycho*, 2000) and Abel Ferrara (*The Addiction*, 1994) have already been reprinted in the Hillier and Vincendeau volumes. However, I have found room for a sidebar from Michael Tolkin, about his directorial debut, *The Rapture* (1992).

The first question this Reader sets out to explore, as opposed to answer, is one of definition. What is or are horror and science fiction? Here, as often, the two genres are lumped together at a stroke in a way other compatibles rarely are. Genre-definers would hesitate to stake out continent-sized areas labelled musical/comedy or cowboy/cop or romance/porno. It is sometimes felt by practitioners of science fiction, that this Siamese twinning does a disservice to their sacred field. Sci-fi writers and film-makers like to think of themselves with their eyes on the stars, alive to the thrilling possibilities of science and exploration, made pure by the rigour of their adherence to strict principles of possibility and likeliness, contributing something more useful than passing entertainment. Meanwhile, the misshapen lump of the horror genre clings to their backs, dragging them down into a neurotic morass of doubts and fears, polluted by unhealthy desires and appetites, intent on seeing decay and collapse and death to the exclusion of rationality, progress and credibility, freed by the contrivance of fantasy to make up anything without so much as a single theorem to justify it. Then again, sci-fi enthusiasts sometimes look down on horror in much the same spirit that the Gene Hackman character's dirt-poor share-cropper father in *Mississippi Burning* (1988) joins the Ku Klux Klan because 'if I ain't better than a nigger who am I better than?'

Here, science fiction and horror are yoked together like the convicts in *The Defiant Ones* (1958) or Robert Donat and Madeleine Carroll in *The 39 Steps* (1935). Though genre insiders may complain, horror and sci-fi are perceived outside the fields as the same sort of thing. They both offer worlds separate or even remote from our accepted reality (whether Mars or Castle Dracula), more often than not feature monsters (i.e. special effects and make-up), can be caricatured as at once childish in their commitment to the unreal and unsuitable for children by virtue of gruesomeness or luridness, and have fandoms which overlap to a great degree (though with as much internal dissent as the Balkans in 1912). Authors and directors often work in both fields, recognising – to borrow a metaphor from a work that has to be classified as both s-f and horror – that the rational Dr Jekyll and the brutish Mr Hyde share a single body. Each is free to pursue a unique path but the pair are conjoined in the lizard brainstem. It may be that sci-fi can only look at the stars because horror regards the grave, and the repeated discovery that horrors may come from science or the future or outer space as easily as from magic or the past or Transylvania is matched by that rare, sublime, transcendental streak in horror that finds the wonder in the heart of madness, as Jack Nicholson freezes to crystal perfection in the maze of *The Shining* or Lillian Gish fills in the harmonies that make a real hymn of the hateful chant of Robert Mitchum in *The Night of the Hunter*.

It only seems easy to recognise a science fiction or horror film. At the centres of the genres are cases it's impossible to argue: *2001: A Space Odyssey* (1968) and *Blade Runner* (1982) are science fiction films, while *Dracula* (1931, 1958, 1979, etc.) and *The Mummy* (1932, 1959, 1999) are horror films. Except that *Blade Runner* is also a *film noir* (and a literary adaptation) and the latest remake of *The Mummy* is more of an Indiana Jones/ Rider Haggard-style action adventure or a Ray Harryhausen effects fantasy than a horror film. Different versions of Dracula have been swashbucklers (Christopher Lee's cloak-swishing and Peter Cushing's crucifix-waving are clearly in a Rathbone–Flynn duel tradition), bodice-rippers (the Frank Langella–Kate Nelligan take), literary adaptations (there's a section on *Bram Stoker's Dracula*, 1992, in the *Film/Literature/ Heritage* Reader), political allegories (*Jonathan*, 1971), comedies (*Love at First Bite*, 1979), porno (the inevitable *Dracula Sucks*, 1972), musicals (the Indian *Bandh Darwaza*, 1990) or auteur works (Elsaesser discusses *Nosferatu* in terms of its relationships with Murnau's other movies) and pick-and-mix any-of-the-above efforts (Werner Herzog's *Nosferatu – Phantom der Nacht*, 1979). Even a genre cornerstone such as *2001* makes as much sense as a Stanley Kubrick movie as sci-fi, and its final section ('Beyond the Infinite') demands that we, like Bowman and Arthur C. Clarke, leave behind our understanding of sci-fi as a genre of rational debate and qualified prophecy to embrace something very like literal pantheon-building.

As we travel outwards from genre central, all assumptions blur. Are non-supernatural stories such as *Peeping Tom* (1959) and *Psycho* (1959) horror films or psychological thrillers? In these cases, does approach – the deployment of literal shock tactics – get a film into the club? If so, does that make movies that share their subject matter but *don't* incline to gothic mists or hand-through-the-window scares also eligible? *Fight Club*, which is discussed here, is a logical extension of the arguments of both *The Strange Case of Dr Jekyll and Mr Hyde* and *Psycho*, but director David Fincher, who has never worked outside the horror field without ever making something that would be classified straight-off as a horror picture, develops a style so at odds with anything that might be considered generic that it seems like a radical mutation rather than a continuance of tradition. Conversely, some films which would never be listed as horror movies make deliberate use of the visual tropes of horror to reveal monstrousness. In Alexander Mackendrick's *Sweet Smell of Success* (1957), cinematographer James Wong Howe (*Mark of the Vampire*, 1935) lights the evil gossip columnist played by Burt Lancaster to make him look like Boris Karloff and shadows barroom or press-den lairs like a 1930s Universal horror picture shot by Karl Freund.

Some of my inclusions are designed to test the limits – hence pieces on *Beauty and the Beast* (1946, 1991), *The Rapture*, *The Truman Show* (1998), *Wisconsin Death Trip* (1999) and the Sinclair-Petit *Asylum* (2000). All these films might be considered footnotes to genre, and can profitably be read as questioning or even attacking straighter horror/s-f films. Clearly, *The Rapture* and *Wisconsin Death Trip* are working very different games than *The Omen* (1976) and *The Texas Chain Saw Massacre* (1973), but they have thematic overlaps. *The Rapture* takes seriously the theology that is just a mcguffin for *Rosemary's Baby* (1968), a feminist Catholic horror created by Jewish men (Ira Levin, Roman Polanski); while *Wisconsin Death Trip*, which would have to be classified as some species of poetic documentary, comes at the dark heart of America so often visited by the horror film since *Psycho* from a startling new angle and may well inform future readings of the earlier films.

The classification of works like this as horror or sci-fi often sets fans' blood boiling and gets angry messages posted on Internet newsgroups, but it needs to be stressed that inclusion here does not mean these films should be considered only as genre pieces. In asserting that profitable horror and/or s-f readings can be pursued, we are echoing a moment from that most hotly debatable movie, David Cronenberg's *Crash*, when Vaughan concedes (of the suggestion that the Kennedy assassination be interpreted as a car accident) that 'the case could be made'. Often, our job is to make the case. It's up to others to respond to it. One of the central tensions explored in this collection is between the critic's need to make cages and the artist's impulse to find files in cakes. Some of our cagers (Iain Sinclair, Jonathan Coe, Paul Mayersberg, Michael Eaton) are also escape artists – screenwriters, novelists, film-makers. Meaning shifts, and various writers come at their subjects from different angles – locating a specific film or film cycle in psychohistory or psychogeography, as in the pieces that reassess Cold War sci-fi from objective (J. Hoberman) or subjective (Howard Waldrop) perspectives or in Iain Sinclair's explorations of the by-ways of London as haunted by the cinema's ghosts; considering films as symptoms of deep political, psychological or scientific trains of thought, which even ropes in the audience as a co-creator because their willingness to accept a message is every bit as significant as a studio's willingness to deliver it; discovering in a given movie a development or mutation of one of the several primal stories (*Beauty and the Beast*) or traditions (the vampire legend) of genres old before Méliès first invented the film special effect; making connections by applying a cross-disciplinary approach (as Christopher Frayling and Eduardo Paolozzi do by assessing sci-fi film in design terms) or focusing on a single trope (Linda Ruth Williams's look at eye-abuse in horror).

This Reader does not speak with one voice. The 'house style' of *Sight and Sound* is loose enough to accommodate a great many individual and individualist styles and approaches. I have assembled the articles into general sections on Themes, Films, and People and Stories, with more specific case studies on an auteur (Kubrick), a sub-genre (the teenage horror film) and a zeitgeist (Rubber Reality). I have made use of reviews (in the *Monthly Film Bulletin* format of synopsis followed by analysis) to lend context to some of the articles. Two of the case studies are primarily collations of reviews, affording a month-by-month account of the development of trends that shaped horror and sci-fi in the late 1990s. To answer questions that come up surprisingly often: yes, the credited reviewer is also responsible for writing the synopsis and, yes again, it is often the trickiest part of working for the magazine.

Kim Newman, January 2002

Section I:
Themes

A question often raised in connection with horror cinema is 'Why do people like to be scared?' Implicit in this is a different wording 'Why do sickos like you enjoy this stuff which normal folk like me find at best puerile and at worst abhorrent?' Horror cinema is supposed to be unruly, transgressive, upsetting, 'not for everyone'. Often, the makers and audiences of horror films pride themselves on bad reviews in the 'straight' press. Who would want to listen to a rock band that their parents liked? As far back as *Frankenstein* (1931), horror has been written off by the short-sighted, often with a kind of desperate graveyard gaiety, as impossible to take seriously and probably unhealthy. Fantasy and science fiction excite less extreme reactions, but it is still possible for people who are supposedly open to all manner of popular or high arts to write the fields off as entirely without interest. A few select works have been allowed into the academy, but often as a way of excluding everything else – a fatal error in genre, where often it is the coral-like accumulation of film upon film that makes the point.

In this section, writers (and one artist) take the surprisingly uncommon but eminently sensible path of assessing the specifics not of a single film but of clutches of films, sometimes rooted in specific historical moments and the fantasies they shaped (as in the contrasting and complementary pieces by J. Hoberman and Howard Waldrop on science fiction in the shadow of nuclear brinkmanship), sometimes in the assessment of a single trope (Linda Ruth Williams' assessment of the recurring image of gouged eyes) or mutation of an old, old story (Amy Taubin on a small group of mid-90s vampire movies). What these pieces share is an understanding that it is impossible to locate the fantastical entirely in the realms of fantasy. The question often asked here is 'Why did we dream these dreams?' It is asked of film-makers, who might find unexpected uses in the forms of fantasy, and of audiences, whose acceptance of these visions might lead us to conclusions about their lives and times.

A frequent accusation against any kind of analysis of film beyond the simplest synopsis-and-star-rating-plus-gossip level is that critics 'read too much into' material intended as mere entertainment. I am of the opinion that it's almost impossible to read too much into anything, and even the most meretricious movies or cycles of movies are complex works, confused tangles of intentionality and accident, of serendipity and canniness. That does not, of course, make them good, admirable or even interesting – though there are often, good, admirable and interesting things to say about them. The author Howard Waldrop (*Howard Who?*, 1986, *All About Strange Monsters of the Recent Past*, 1987, *Night of the Cooters*, 1990) reports, from an adult perspective, on the precise associations two films and three pieces of music had for him in 1959, offering personal testimony; while the critic J. Hoberman comes at similar material almost from an archaeologist's viewpoint, decoding the messages left in films serious and trivial. Meanwhile, the novelist and poet Iain Sinclair (*Downriver, Radon's Daughters*) explores the psychogeography of a London haunted by the ghosts of crimes, movie characters and moods, which linger in the brickworks (cf: Nigel Kneale's teleplay *The Stone Tape*) like Waldrop's memories. These are pieces which tell us where we have been.

WHEN DR NO MET DR STRANGELOVE

J. Hoberman

America's politics would now be also America's favourite movie, America's first soap opera, America's best-seller.

Norman Mailer, 'Superman Comes to the Supermarket' (1960)

The thousand-day reign, which came to be called nostalgically after *Camelot*, a Broadway musical that opened two months after the 1960 election and ran into 1963, was America's first and most compelling mini-series. Born in manufactured glamour and ending in televised catastrophe, it has slowly fissured in an endlessly syndicated half-life of docudramas, factoid novels, revisionist biographies and conspiracy theories.

Watcher of movies, lover of actresses, reader of best-sellers, John F. Kennedy was both the subject and object of American mass culture. His administration was a form of social science fiction. A specialist in crisis, Kennedy rode the missile gap of the 'Sputnikchina' – that dread period when the Soviets seemed to challenge US techno superiority – into Cuba, Berlin and Vietnam, living a high-style melodrama of cynical realpolitik, grand ambition and apocalyptic betrayal. It was a period of glamour and anxiety embodied by another ruthless and exciting new hero, James Bond.

The revelations that emerged a dozen years after Kennedy's assassination only confirmed the surplus of innuendo and rumour. But the intuition, or perhaps the desire, existed even then. Kennedy and his court inspired a number of movies – several based on popular novels, most made by men who had served their apprenticeships in television rather than in Hollywood. These Kennedy scenarios – *The Manchurian Candidate, Seven Days in May, Dr Strangelove* and *Fail Safe* among them – represented American politics as the province of demagogues, blackmailers and conspirators, placing one president after another in the terrifying light of some personal or public Armageddon.

JFK, as the new president had reconfigured his identity after his election, wasted little time in establishing himself as an icon. His youthful image, hatless and without an overcoat, beamed out on the freezing morning of his inauguration, had as much impact as his speech – the only one since Roosevelt's first to add a koan to the golden anthology of American rhetoric: 'Ask not what your country can do for you...'

Over the next few weeks, the president would dazzle his subjects with a series of unrehearsed, televised press conferences. He had barely taken office before one ABC news commentator told the *TV Radio Mirror* that JFK 'has discovered he's a new television idol' and would be using the medium as FDR did radio. Nevertheless, Kennedy lost his first global spectacular when the Soviets upstaged the first scheduled Mercury flight and orbited the cosmonaut Yuri Gargarin.

The nightmarish 'Sputnikchina' was not yet over. On 12 April 1961, Kennedy found himself in the same hapless role in which he'd cast Eisenhower. A force of 1,400 CIA-trained Cuban exiles landed at the Bay of Pigs. 'Even Hollywood would not try to film such a story,' Castro sneered when, receiving neither US air support from above nor Cuban popular support on the ground, the abortive invasion fizzled out.

The Bay of Pigs was no glorious Alamo – on the contrary. JFK became obsessed with his fiasco, which would set the course of his administration down to its last day. Although the president's approval rating shot up, he felt betrayed – set up by Eisenhower, the CIA, the Joint Chiefs, even his own state department. And so JFK delivered a second State of the Union address in May, requesting more marines, helicopters and personnel carriers, asking for a greater emphasis on civil defence – promising, in return, to land an American on the moon by 1970.

The US was hurtling headlong into the future. The president linked his political comeback to the space race. He virtually inducted the NASA astronauts into his administration, inviting them to the White House as exemplary new frontiersmen. In late May the show went on the road as President and Mrs Kennedy visited Paris, London and Vienna, where he held his first summit with Nikita Khrushchev. The tour made for sensational television, but after a tense meeting during which he and the Soviet premier had exchanged threats over Berlin, Kennedy told advisors that the US and Soviet Union were 'very close to war'. Abruptly, he appeared on television in late July to announce that he'd be fortifying Berlin, calling up reserves and requesting funds for a massive fallout shelter programme. The effect was startling: no previous president had so openly raised the possibility of nuclear attack.

As schoolchildren took cover beneath their desks and black and yellow 'Shelter' signs blossomed like pressed-metal sunflowers in the stairwells of public buildings, *Life* ran a laudatory cover 'How You Can Survive Fallout. 97 Out of 100 Can Be Saved', while *US News and World Report* advised its readers that 'If Bombs Do Fall' it would still be possible to write cheques on an incinerated bank account. Presidential advisor McGeorge Bundy would recall that season as 'a time of sustained and draining anxiety'. On television, *The Twilight Zone* dramatised the end of the world no fewer than three times.

In September of that year, Frank Sinatra – the most widely publicised of the president's friends – was a weekend guest at the Kennedy compound in Hyannis Port. Among other things, Sinatra used his visit to secure the president's approval for the movie that he, writer George Axelrod and director John Frankenheimer hoped to adapt from Richard Condon's lurid thriller *The Manchurian Candidate*. Sinatra had a deal with United Artists, but UA president Arthur Krim – who was also the national finance chairman for the Democratic Party – felt that the project was political dynamite. Published in April 1959, *The Manchurian Candidate* had posited the outrageously paranoid premise that the Russians and Chinese had infiltrated the highest levels of American electoral politics with brainwashed dupes. It was a comic version of the John Birch Society's so-called 'Black Book' a samizdat that had been circulating among the true believers since the summer of 1958 – in which Birch Society founder Robert Welch identified President Eisenhower as the dedicated agent of a vast Communist conspiracy, who had been painstakingly manoeuvred by his Kremlin handlers into the White House.

Kennedy and James Bond

Throughout the 1960 Primary campaign Kennedy was popularly associated with Sinatra; during the 1960 Democratic Convention, Mailer had paid the candidate the compliment of comparison with Brando; once elected, JFK seemed to prefer Ian Fleming's fictional secret agent James Bond. After a March 1961 *Life* article listed *From Russia with Love* just ahead of Stendhal's *The Red and the Black* among the president's ten favourite books, Fleming's entrée to the White House was regularly invoked – particularly once United Artists put its first 007 thriller into production a year later in still-colonial Jamaica. While *Dr No* was being shot, UA's Arthur Krim organised another presidential bash the Madison Square Garden rally where presidential brother-in-law Peter Lawford served up Marilyn Monroe to serenade JFK with a suitably steamy 'Happy Birthday'. Frank Sinatra, then completing *The Manchurian Candidate*, was conspicuous by his absence.

James Bond was one more triumph for the image. Replete with colourful Third World atmosphere, *Dr No* bespeaks a time when foreign travel was exotic and airports seemed glamorous. The half-German, half-Chinese villain may run his island 'like a concentration camp', but his white sand beaches are magnificently secluded and his palace a bachelor pad worthy of a six-page feature in *Playboy*. *Dr No* was not the most extravagant of Bond novels, but it was surely the most timely in its concern with a malevolent island despot and secret missile base in the Caribbean. (Even as *Dr No* was on location Khrushchev was vacationing on the Black Sea, brooding over the Jupiter missiles the US had placed in Turkey and wondering whether he should plant a few of his own in Cuba.)

Paying lip service to the fantasy that Britain was still a major world power, cementing a de facto North Atlantic alliance to make the hemisphere safe for an American moon rocket, James Bond was to be a new frontiersman who was neither ugly nor an American. UA executives were unimpressed by Scottish actor Sean Connery. As staunch Kennedy supporters, they preferred Peter Lawford – who turned down the part and thus lost the sinecure of a lifetime. Lawford's smarminess might have capsized the cycle before it began, but it is Kennedy's open identification with Bond that gives pause for thought. Suave, cynical, untroubled by doubts, the secret agent inhabited a daydreamer's paradise of beautiful women, high-stakes gambling and narrowly avoided danger, amplified by the twangy and sinister surf music that underscores his private moments.

Bond was Sinatra writ large and playing for keeps. He made his own rules, but he was hardly a social rebel. Without being aggressively youthful or overtly anti-authoritarian, Bond embodies a new permissiveness. In *Dr No* women are fascinated by him – he always gets a reaction shot, if not a date. (The most active boudoir scene, however, has him killing the – no doubt female – tarantula planted in his bed.) Thoroughly professional in a suit and stingy-brimmed fedora, Bond is best at beating up people. He endures the vaporisation of a native colleague without a thought, coolly shoots an unarmed adversary (a professor, no less) point blank, sadistically delivering an extra shot to make the corpse twitch in a visual equivalent of the various jokes about dead bodies delivered with British understatement.

Bond was licensed to kill and he enjoyed it. In spring 1961 Joseph Alsop reported in *The Saturday Evening Post* that the president had 'quietly discarded' the American policy against launching a nuclear first-strike policy. (After the article was published the Kremlin put Soviet forces on special alert, while Khrushchev berated Pierre Salinger, Kennedy's press officer: 'This warmonger Alsop – is he now your Secretary of State? Not even Eisenhower or Dulles would have made the statement your President made.') Fleming had once suggested to JFK that the Americans took Castro too seriously – they should institute a covert way to deflate his authority through ridicule and innuendo. Did Fleming's ideas inspire Operation Mongoose, the secret anti-Castro campaign initiated in January 1962, when Attorney General Robert Kennedy told the CIA's Richard Helms that to get rid of Castro was top priority – no money, effort or manpower was to be spared? The Kennedy brothers wanted to have Castro out by October 1962, in time for the mid-term elections, which would be a referendum on their administration.

Cuban blockade and paranoia

That autumn, the various scenarios came to fruition. ABC premiered a half-hour series based on *Mr Smith Goes to Washington*. Irving Berlin opened what would be his last Broadway musical, *Mr President*. And, even as the *New York Times* reported a widening breach between the Pentagon and Hollywood studios, a novel about a military coup against a pro-disarmament president was climbing the best-seller list.

Seven Days in May, written by Fletcher Knebel and Charles N. Bailey, the Washington correspondents for the *Des Moines Register*, was conceived in the aftermath of the Bay of Pigs fiasco and written during the anxious autumn of 1961. Scarcely had the novel been published than a liberal coalition was assembled to bring it to the screen, perhaps in time for Kennedy's projected 1964 race against right-wing militarist senator Barry Goldwater. Movie rights were purchased by Kirk Douglas, who hired *Twilight Zone* creator Rod Serling to write the adaptation and John Frankenheimer, fresh from *The Manchurian Candidate*, to direct. Meanwhile, the year's other best-selling political thriller *Fail Safe*, the story of an inadvertent nuclear war, was serialised in *The Saturday Evening Post*. The president was reported to have read both, as well he might.

Dr No had its London premiere in October. 'It is almost a certainty,' *Time* reported, 'that one evening next winter, at perhaps 19.30 hours, the President of the United States will enter a small room. For two hours a machine will play with his emotions. He may groan, but he will not be physically hurt. If he is disappointed when he leaves, he will at least emerge into a world where his job seems relatively tame, for he will have seen *Dr No*, the first attempt to approximate on film the cosmic bravery, stupefying virility, six-acre brain, and deathproof nonchalance of Secret Agent James Bond – the President's favorite fictional hero.'

In fact, even as *Time*'s prediction went to press, the president was straining his own six-acre brain, pondering two-day-old aerial reconnaissance pictures of Soviet missile sites in Cuba. This was the moment of truth. Some advisors, including Secretary of State Dean Rusk and the Joint Chiefs, recommended a surprise air attack. Monday morning's *New York Times* reported 'an air of crisis in the capital', the 'almost constant conference all weekend, imparting serious agitation and tension to official Washington'. By noon, US forces had been placed on worldwide alert. For the first time ever, all Strategic Air Command aircraft were armed with nuclear weapons. That evening, amid reports of impending military action, Kennedy delivered the most frightening television address ever given by a US president.

Announcing the presence of offensive missile sites in Cuba, Kennedy imposed a blockade around the island and prepared for a showdown with the Soviets. The next day's papers buzzed with references to Pearl Harbor and D-Day. In New York, where the UN Security Council had gone into a televised emergency session, the dean of City College said that he found the faculty members reacting with an 'air of unreality'. Meanwhile, the CIA detected an unprecedented concentration of Soviet submarines in the Caribbean. It was a week, Norman Mailer would write, 'when the world stood like a playing card on edge ... One looked at the buildings one passed and wondered if one was to see them again.'

Variety had previewed *The Manchurian Candidate* in late September, a month before the crisis, and predicted blockbuster results. According to director John Frankenheimer, however, the first public preview was 'hysterical'. The film was denounced by the American Legion and the Communist Party; the day before it opened, it was attacked by a widely syndicated Catholic film critic as 'anti anti Communism gone crazy, like a fox. Like a red fox.' It had its premiere on 24 October, even as Strategic Air Command heightened its alert posture and Soviet ships headed towards the edge of the US quarantine. (So did *We'll Bury You!*, a newsreel compilation distributed by Columbia Pictures. 'It was a grim experience,' the *New York Times* reported, 'to sit in a darkened theatre, watch a chillingly convincing documentary on the spread of Communism and wonder, meanwhile, what was developing on the high seas.')

The Manchurian Candidate

Politics as spectacle, *The Manchurian Candidate* is the quintessential Kennedy-era thriller, a movie which conflates right-wing demagogues and the international Communist conspiracy, mind control and assassination, uncorking a plot which, as one conspirator brags, would 'rally a nation of television viewers to sweep us into the White House with powers that make martial law look like anarchy.' *The Manchurian Candidate*, which permitted its star to engage in the first-ever karate fight in an American movie, was Bond-like in its futuristic technology, robotic hit-men, sinister Asians (one played by Khigh Dhiegh, a member of New York's avant-garde Living Theater) and jocular violence. But given its deadpan non-sequiturs and matter-of-fact integration of dreams, flashbacks and waking reality (modelled, according to screenwriter Axelrod, on Alain Resnais's *Hiroshima Mon Amour*), it was far crazier. What was one to make of the continual identification of Communists with motherhood, a costume party to which a McCarthy-like senator comes dressed as Lincoln to nibble on an American flag made out of Polish caviar, or the use of the national anthem to forestall the hero's preventing the climactic assassination?

Andrew Sarris would point out that *The Manchurian Candidate* reflected 'a new conception of America as dangerously "sick"'. But *The Manchurian Candidate*'s cynical, absurdist tone was itself 'sick' – in the sense with which the word had been applied to a form of American humour since the 'Sputnikchina'. (Indeed, the jokey headlines occasioned by the failure of the Vanguard rocket – Flopnik, Kaputnik, Stayputnik – in what Tom Wolfe called a 'hideous cackle of national self-loathing' were an earlier popular manifestation of the sick.)

Like the John Birch Society 'Black Book', *The Manchurian Candidate* offered a retrospective of Cold War concerns, from television image-building to Communist infiltration of the government. Unlike the mildly futuristic novel, the movie is a period piece that has its climax at the 1956 Republican Convention. In addition to speculating on how a McCarthy might have been nominated, it took an extremely literal and highly fanciful view of behavioural modification, or 'brainwashing'. Associated with Chinese propaganda, the term was in common usage by the end of the Korean War. Indeed, *The Manchurian Candidate* became an explanation for brainwashing – so much so that a 1979 ABC documentary on DIA 'mind control' used clips from the movie to illustrate its thesis. By that time, *The Manchurian Candidate* had been out of circulation for almost a decade, withdrawn by Sinatra in the early 1970s.

Sinatra's alleged reasons for suppressing *The Manchurian Candidate* have become incorporated in the film's meaning. He was, it was said, disturbed at having produced so prophetic a vision. (At the same time that Sinatra pulled *The Manchurian Candidate* from circulation, he also withdrew *Suddenly* – an obscure 1954 movie in which he played a would-be presidential assassin and which Marina Oswald told the Warren Commission her husband had seen on Dallas television shortly before Kennedy was shot.) When *The Manchurian Candidate* was finally re-issued, after a well-publicised showing at the 1987 New York Film Festival, it was explained that Sinatra had taken the movie out of circulation in a dispute with United Artists over money. But although it has since become a part of *The Manchurian Candidate*'s mythology that it was a popular failure, the movie had supplanted *The Longest Day* as the national box-office champion by Election Day 1962. Nor was it critically misunderstood. The *New Yorker* seconded *Variety*'s enthusiasm, beginning a rave review with 'many loud hurrahs'. The *New York Times* was less than amused, charging Sinatra with 'a grave sort of irresponsibility'. Referring to other, unnamed Sinatra films where 'truth has been distorted and angled to get wild effects', the *Times* compared his technique with that of 'the "big lie"', concluding that 'this does not do credit to American films'. When *The Manchurian Candidate* opened in Paris in December, the critic for *L'Express* wrote that she left the theatre praying that something of Europe would be able to survive the impending clash between the two superpowers. *Le Monde* concurred. Although the movie was 'incoherent', it would certainly help to fuel 'anti-American propaganda'.

The missile crisis was resolved on 28 October, one day after an American U-2 was shot down over Cuba (while another strayed over Siberia) and one day before the planned US air strike. When the Joint Chiefs were informed that Khrushchev had agreed to remove the missiles, General Curtis LeMay reportedly pounded the table and bellowed, 'It's the greatest defeat in our history … *We should invade today!*' (LeMay, the former chief of the Strategic Air Command, was virtually acting out the role which had already been scripted for him or rather for Burt Lancaster – in *Seven Days in May*.) Secretary of Defense Robert McNamara remembers looking at Kennedy and noticing 'he was absolutely shocked. He was stuttering in reply.'

Although the US maintained its forces at the highest state of alert until 20 November, the anxiety that had gripped the country since the summer of 1961 began to dissipate. In the aftermath of the missile crisis, the US and the Soviet Union negotiated a ban on atmospheric testing and established an emergency 'hot line'. There were, nevertheless, two remarkably similar movies in production on the subject of accidental nuclear war.

The first, announced in May 1962, was *Dr Strangelove; or, How I learned to Stop Worrying and Love the Bomb*, adapted by Stanley Kubrick from *Red Alert*, a 1958 pulp novel by former RAF pilot Peter George. The second was based on the far better known *Fail Safe*. Max Youngstein, a UA vice-president and founding member of the Hollywood chapter of the Committee for a Sane Nuclear Policy, read *Fail Safe* while it was still in manuscript and acquired the movie for his first picture as a producer, hiring formerly blacklisted Walter Bernstein to write the screenplay.

There was a sense in which the movie industry was operating as if it were still mobilised, but was unsure which part of the government – the Pentagon or the president – to obey. Armed with the knowledge that two films about accidental nuclear warfare were in preparation, General LeMay encouraged a Universal producer Sy Bartlett to make *A Gathering of Eagles*, which, dedicated to the Strategic Air Command, introduced the iconography of vast B-52 phalanxes, flashing alerts and ominous red telephones, and reportedly included a scene shot in the war room itself. Although ostensibly a celebration of American nuclear readiness, the movie did not fully achieve the intended result when it opened in mid-1963. 'Take Rock Hudson out [as SAC commander] and imagine Rod Steiger or Richard Widmark in the part,' *Newsweek* wrote. 'Without the distraction of Hudson's preternatural charm, it is appallingly clear that only a maniac can run a SAC wing properly.' Or, as the *Washington Post* titled its pan, 'Lifelike Jets, Robot People'.

Kennedy's death

The shock of Kennedy's murder threw the continuity of his cinema into disarray. The very day of the assassination, there was a full-page advertisement in the *New York Times* announcing the release of *Seven Days in May*. The movie's opening was necessarily delayed until the following January, as was that of *Dr Strangelove*.

Having evolved from straightforward thriller to daring black comedy, *Dr Strangelove* was at once austerely didactic in its demonstration of (largely invented) military codes, procedures and chains of command, and implacably farcical in its slapstick. To the image of the Pentagon war room the movie added the icon of bombers over the snowy Siberian tundra, the idea of the government fallout shelter, and the premise of the Doomsday machine – a negative version of what would be conceptualised 20 years later as the Strategic Defense Initiative.

In the novel, the bomb is too damaged to detonate. But *Dr Strangelove* took its premise all the way to Doomsday. *New York Times* critic Bosley Crowther called it 'the most shattering sick joke I've ever come across,' expressing unhappiness with the film's 'contempt for our whole defense establishment, up to and even including the hypothetical Commander in Chief'. (Peter Sellers' balding, reasonable and ineffectual president unmistakably suggested Adlai Stevenson, who as neither Crowther nor

Kubrick had any way of knowing – was subject through the Kennedy years to nightmares of Holocaust and 'the end of life on this planet'.) Once *Seven Days in May* opened, Crowther complained that 'it's beginning to look as though the movies are out to scare us all to death with dire and daring speculations on what might happen any day in Washington.' No less than *Dr Strangelove*, *Seven Days in May* offered a 'fearsome prospect of the crisis that might occur if another Air Force general planned to seize control of the Government.'

Although producer Edward Lewis would get to rework this conspiracy, with Lancaster again as the heavy, in the 1973 *Executive Action*, *Seven Days in May* seemed designed to offer a rhetorical preview of the 1964 campaign. (Like JFK, the incumbent Democrat risks signing a test ban treaty with the Soviets – offending Lancaster's chairman of the Joint Chiefs, who appears at Senate hearings to deliver the Goldwater-LeMay line.) *Dr Strangelove*, by contrast, dramatised the catastrophe which America had been dreading since spring 1961 and expected during October 1962. During the Cuban missile crisis, an air-force psychiatric officer characterised the mood on the base where he was stationed as one of exhilaration. The mounting tension and the constant simulation of combat preparedness had finally given way to an actual alert. With the assassination of JFK the worst had occurred – or at least one version of it. *Dr Strangelove* was another exorcism. Lewis Mumford wrote to the *Times* to praise the movie as 'the first break in the catatonic cold war trance that has so long held our country in its rigid grip' and in the *New York Review of Books*, Robert Brustein called it 'extraordinarily liberating'. Antonin Artaud, he thought, would surely have admired it. *Dr Strangelove* 'released, through comic poetry, those feelings of impotence and frustration that are consuming us all'.

Dr Strangelove had been extensively previewed in New York in autumn 1962. Then, according to Susan Sontag in *Partisan Review*, liberals wondered whether such political daring might not trigger riots – that *Dr Strangelove* would be *The Iron Curtain* in reverse, with 'American legion types storming the theatres, etc. But, as it turned out, everybody, from the *New Yorker* to the *Daily News*, had had kind words for *Dr Strangelove*; there are no pickets and the film is breaking records at the box office. Intellectuals and adolescents both love it. But the 16-year-olds who are lining up to see it understand the film and its real virtues, better than the intellectuals, who vastly overpraise it.'

Indeed Brustein had embraced *Dr Strangelove* in strikingly regressive terms. It was, he thought, a particularly American movie. It overwhelms 'the weary meanderings of Resnais, Fellini, and Antonioni'. It is 'fun – this is its one debt to Hollywood. It is enjoyable for the way it exploits the exciting narrative conventions of the Hollywood war movie – say, *Air Force* or *Thirty Seconds over Tokyo* – and even more for the way it turns these upside down.'

What was new, at least in movies, Brustein thought, was *Dr Strangelove*'s 'wry, mordant, destructive, and, at the same time, cheerful, unmoralistic' tone. This attitude – most apparent in the smutty, desecratory humour of the title and the names of the principal characters (Generals Jack D. Ripper and Buck Turgidson, Premier Dmitri Kissoff and President Merkin Muffley) – was familiar from 'comic novels, cabaret acts, satiric revues, living rooms, and dreams'; it had 'rumbled a little bit under the conventional noises of *The Manchurian Candidate* [but] has never before fully entered the mass media.' Brustein hailed *Strangelove* as the 'first American movie to speak truly for our generation,' noting that Kubrick had 'managed to explode the right-wing affirmation: the odour of the 30s [has] finally been disinfected here.'

What was really new, perhaps, was the mixture of Kennedy cynicism and post-Kennedy euphoria. As the Soviet youth of the mid-20s experienced a sense of cultural liberation following Lenin's death, so did American teenagers. Mourning became electric; Bond was supplanted by the Beatles. 'I Want to Hold Your Hand' was released the day after Christmas, went to No. 1 on 1 February and remained there for seven weeks – during which time the Beatles appeared twice on *The Ed Sullivan Show*. 'I Want to Hold Your Hand' was succeeded at No. 1 by 'She Loves You', which held the top spot for two weeks before being displaced by 'Can't Buy Me Love', which remained the nation's No. 1 song for another five weeks, well into May.

Nukes and Ronald Reagan

When *Fail Safe* went into production in 1963, it was suggested that the Kennedy administration would not look kindly on a movie that showed an American president – even Henry Fonda – nuking New York. Producer Max Youngstein was not only turned down for Pentagon assistance, but was unable to obtain the necessary stock footage from a number of film libraries which had been cautioned against co-operation. Nevertheless, the film served the Democrats well. The Gulf of Tonkin notwithstanding, the new president Lyndon Johnson was running as the peace candidate. *Fail Safe* had its world premiere at the New York Film Festival only nine days after the Democrats bought time during NBC's *Monday Night at the Movies* to air the notorious spot known as 'The Daisy', which linked Republican candidate Senator Goldwater to the nuclear obliteration of a five-year-old child.

In late September, shortly before *Fail Safe*'s general release, Democratic vice-presidential candidate Hubert Humphrey brought the movie to the attention of presidential press officer Bill Moyers – 'the more millions of people who might see it in these next few weeks, the better will be their understanding of the crucial role of the Chief Executive in preserving the peace.' Moyers sent a memo on to LBJ reiterating *Fail Safe*'s favourable impact 'since it deals with irresponsibility in the handling of nuclear weapons'. After the outrageous *Dr Strangelove*, *Fail Safe* could not but appear anti-climactic. The sober absence of music, the over-articulated fear that technology was developing its own (unelected) logic, the relatively staid resident mad scientist, the humanist SAC general who wakes up sweating from a nightmare about a bullfight (JFK's preferred metaphor for the pressures of his own job) were hopelessly square. War room and B-52s notwithstanding, *Fail Safe* suggested a turgid Antonioni film – with the sophisticates at a DC party arguing over nuclear war until dawn. (*La notte*, in fact, *had* opened in New York during the missile crisis.)

Yet *Fail Safe* remains a prototype for subsequent disaster films and did manage to dramatise one of Norman Mailer's more radical suggestions, proposed in *Village Voice* soon after the missile crisis. Perhaps inspired by the novel, Mailer had written an open letter to the president, requesting Mrs Kennedy as a hostage: 'The moment an invasion is let loose, and you as the Commander in Chief go to your deep bomb shelter, why not send us your wife and children to share our fate in this city?' (In the midst of the missile crisis, Kennedy had asked his wife if she wanted to go to the government shelter in the Virginia hills.)

As *Fail Safe*'s JFK-surrogate, Henry Fonda was more resolute. Despite its tepid box office, this last of the Kennedy films was Fonda's apotheosis – 25 years after playing *Young Mr Lincoln*, president at last. When Otto Preminger's *Advise and Consent* – the first of the Kennedy-era melodramas – opened in mid-1962, Andrew Sarris thought it 'perverse' to cast Fonda as the ambitious liberal with a guilty past. Fonda's forte, Sarris explained, 'has always been truthfulness and virile sincerity, and yet he has served also as one of the heroic paladins of the New Deal – Popular Front Left … He fought the Fascists in Spain in *Blockade*, fought organised society in Fritz Lang's *You Only Live Once* and embodied the aspirations of the rural proletariat in *The Grapes of Wrath.* There is something a bit wicked in casting our most truthful actor as a liar.'

What was wicked, rather, was the fate of the old Popular Front. For Fonda did track the trajectory of tormented liberalism – forged in the crucible of the 1930s, tested under fire in the Second World War – as he failed upward in his JFK trilogy. Defeated in his bid to become Secretary of State in *Advise and Consent*, he appeared in that position in *The Best Man*; rejected there as a presidential nominee (too neurotic), he returned as the agonised president – as elitist and anti-democratic and idealistically manipulative as one might have feared – who lets loose Armageddon. Afterwards Fonda became a post-apocalyptic liberal. Thanks to his crazy kids, Peter and Jane, he wound up the 1960s as the personification of the generation gap.

Fail Safe was the climax of the Kennedy scenario. Soon after its release, three weeks before the 1964 American election, Kennedy's great adversary was gone. The Soviets lost their human face, although NBC's *The Man from U N C L E*, the show with which Bond went network, gave its secret agent hero a cute Russian sidekick (played by a Scottish actor with a Beatle haircut). Khrushchev's fall was the sound of the last shoe dropping, but there was one postscript. A series based on Kennedy's book *Profiles in Courage* premiered – programmed on Sundays opposite *Lassie* and *Mr Ed* – five days after Johnson swamped Goldwater. The only solace hip Republicans could take was the sensational election eve presentation, billed as 'A Thoughtful Address by Ronald Reagan'.

Stressing that he was speaking without a script, the then host of the television show *Death Valley Days* insisted that there was no more left and right, only up or down: 'We're at war with the most dangerous enemy that has ever faced mankind on his long climb from the swamp to the stars… Freedom has never been so close to slipping from our grasp… this is the last stand on earth.' Thus paraphrasing Kennedy's 1960 campaign rhetoric, Reagan attacked the Democrats as 'socialists' and accused them of making the presidential election a contest of personalities. One star-politician had died, another was about to be born.

AN EYE FOR AN EYE

Linda Ruth Williams

'Once upon a time', we are told, a man sharpens his cut-throat razor. We see his hands purposefully perform the task, his intent face as he tests the blade on his thumb. The man goes to the balcony and watches a cloud move towards the full moon; a woman's eye is held wide open. The cloud crosses the moon; the razor passes across the eyeball, slitting it open, right there on screen, and liquid oozes out. This opening two minutes of Buñuel's *Un chien andalou* (1928) is one of the most shocking sequences in cinema history. No one struggles, there is no apparent pain or flinching, the act is as dispassionate as it is grotesque. Victim and aggressor seem entirely inappropriate terms of judgment; certainly one person is injured while another wields a razor, but it is perhaps the viewer who occupies the most painful position. What taboos are violated in this spectacle, what tensions are released? What is at stake in showing the obscene act, which ought to be kept to the margins between cuts?

Contrast this classic scene of violent spectacle with a more recent one involving a less vulnerable body part. *Un chien andalou* has long been an art-house favourite, and has just been released on video. But at the nastiest (and wittiest) moment in Quentin Tarantino's *Reservoir Dogs* (which has so far been refused a video certificate by the BBFC), we see nothing but a bare wall, and the muffled screams as knife meets flesh are drowned by Stealer's Wheel's 1974 'Dylanesque pop bubble-gum favourite' 'Stuck in the Middle with You'. While the sound and sight of Mr Blonde slicing off Nash's ear are central to Tarantino's movie (making this the film's most notorious scene), what we actually see and hear is but a cinematic conceit: at the crucial moment the camera looks demurely away, sliding to the left with a wicked humour that does the censoring for us, only to look back once the deed is done. ('Was that as good for you as it was for me?' asked Mr Blonde.) The impression is of breathtaking explicitness, an audacious transgression which combines a singalong soundtrack, on-screen dancing and awesome sadism, demanding that we laugh and be sick at the same time in the time-honoured tradition of full-frontal schlock, yet the violence takes place elsewhere and nowhere. Apart from a few unforgettable examples, this kind of implied violence has often been the cinematic fate of the eye – sliced, gouged and pierced at the edges of the frame or off-screen. What is it about violence to this particular organ that pushes the limits of on-screen spectacle?

At the other end of the century and cultural scale, Buñuel's scene is replayed by Arnold Schwarzenegger as the Terminator. Having already performed an operation on his injured cybernetic arm, he – almost unwatchably – deals with a battle-damaged eye. The instruments of injury (or surgery) are carefully displayed, the scalpel recalling the razor of *Un chien andalou*. In each case, before the blade goes in, a face (Buñuel's woman and Cameron's Terminator) is fixed for a second as its left eye is held open by fingers, the face each time occupying roughly the same space at the centre of the frame. Buñuel cuts to the moon cut by clouds before returning to the eye at the point of violence (a strategy which catches us horribly off guard), while Cameron's camera keeps looking as the scalpel penetrates the exposed eye. We expect one cut and get another: the edit away doesn't happen and instead we see the knife go in.

Hideous as this would be in long shot or by implication (we could, perhaps, just see the hand picking up the instrument and then those heavy drops of blood in the sink which come later), the problem isn't simply the close-up which offers us the injured eye centre frame. The key is the *movement*, the *process* of violation which doesn't end where it ought, doesn't cut before knife meets eye (the sequence viewed in freeze-frame has nothing of the same impact). Only after witnessing this act of violation do we cut to profile and the removal of the false humanoid cornea. The wound is patted with a dry white towel, and we move to an extreme close-up of the vulnerable socket encasing the Terminator's camera-eye, its 'pupil' redder and more responsive than the flesh which surrounds it (it dilates, it swivels). The famous Terminator sunglasses are then donned to create the iconic Raybanned image which is now so familiar that we forget the reason for the shades: to mask the evidence of ocular violence.

Eyes have been subject to a range of cinematic violation which few other body parts have had to endure. They are pecked out or penetrated with pins and splinters (*The Birds, Suspiria, Zombie Flesh Eaters, Opera*), mirror fragments are wedged into them (*Manhunter*), they are sliced by knives (*New York Ripper, Un chien andalou*), sucked half way out of their sockets (*Total Recall*), forced open with metal brackets (*A Clockwork Orange*). Damage to eyes recurs as a symbol of the worst possible violence, a spectacular last straw in horror far more disturbing even than representations of fatal injuries to vital organs.

Those few moments when the camera not only looks but looks closely and unswervingly have presented a fascinating problem, bound up with the difficult pleasures at the heart of the spectator's response. Why can we see these actions so graphically when a robotic android is their subject, as in *The Terminator*, or a surreal (and therefore unreal?) heroine, as in *Un chien andalou*, when similar representations involving more identifiably 'real' humans are marginalised? These are scenes which offer a number of scrambled visual satisfactions: the thrill of being there when something goes 'too far', a straightforward indulgence of transgression, the breaking of (here, the eye's) taboo, as well as the complex pleasures of mixed identification. Given the correspondence between on-screen eyes and the viewing organs of the spectator, are these pleasures primarily masochistic? How does the dispassionate tone of some of these scenes disrupt the sense that the spectacle of violent injury must be resolved into a drama of violator and violated? What is it *not* to flinch, to keep looking, or else to be caught unawares when the camera fails to look away? Any response to screen violence must address the question of identification: in looking, are we the eye that is broken or the hand that wields the knife? There are clearly moments when screen violence is anything but a violation, and our response must take on board the pleasures and consent involved.

Rather than trying to resolve these questions with an all too neat moral response, we would be better to look for a way of describing how the rhetoric of these films shapes our involvement image by image, looking closely at scenes which plot the movement of the spectator's reaction. While the power, poetics and perversion of the gaze are now a staple concern of film theory, the cinematic life – and protracted death – of the organ of vision is less well documented. And while the eye and the (sexualised) gaze are not synonymous, clearly something interesting is taking place on the level of identification when the organ through which the image is seen is spectacularly sacrificed on screen, in view, for our eyes only.

Cameras may be weapons (*Peeping Tom*) or surrogate weapons, as in the surveillance equipment deployed by countless cinema psychos, fixing their victims until they are ready for the gun. Overtly murderous gazes abound, not just in Hitchcock but across a range of gothic and exploitation flicks, film noir, horror: *Rear Window*, *Eyes of Laura Mars*, *Videodrome*, you name it. That the sights of a gun mark out a target like a camera frames its image has offered rich cinematic and theoretical pickings – as US Defense Secretary W. J. Perry said, 'once you can see the target, you can expect to destroy it.' This is quoted by Paul Virilio in *War and Cinema*, which focuses on the historical synchronicity of the technology of warfare and that of cinema, 'the eye's function being the function of a weapon'. But what of the eye's function as the target – the 'bull's eye' of violence?

Newly bereaved relatives are known to be more reluctant to consent to cornea donations than to donations of any other organ – even the heart – and though this must certainly be bound up with a sense that the eye is the prime site of a loved one's identity, it also comes from a peculiar squeamishness which only the eye, and any notion of violent injury to it, can provoke. The eye is the supreme organ of violation not just because of what it does but because of what it is: grotesquely penetrable, soft, liable to cry, bleed, respond with discharge, exquisitely sensitive to light and touch. In the world of schlock horror, the eye is asking for it. But while the camera might dwell long and hard on scenes of decapitation, disembowelment or the surreal ways in which a body can be turned inside out on screen, the eye, in its violable vulnerability, constitutes a limit of what audiences can and cannot tolerate. Is this because violence to the eye is the image most immediately felt as visual violence 'done to' the spectator?

For Georges Bataille (author of that marvellous work of ocular porno-horror *Story of the Eye*, as well as of the 1929 essay 'Eye', written partly in response to Buñuel's film), the repulsion of the violated eye is bound up with its seductiveness, for 'extreme seductiveness is probably at the boundary of horror'. Certainly the violated eyes in the work of Dario Argento are profoundly seductive, and *Opera* (sometimes known as *Terror at the Opera*), described by Argento as an 'aria of violence beyond imagination', abounds with them. The most resonant image of the film is that of its heroine Betty as she is forced to witness a series of murders after a row of needles is strapped to her lower lids so that she must look if she is to avoid impaling her eyes by blinking. Her eyes bleed a little, but the real violence comes from the fact that she cannot close them. Who is the focus of the violence is not clear: others are being killed, but Betty's violation is primary – she is made to watch, on penalty of losing her eyes themselves, which is worse than the deaths taking place before her.

This image is reinforced by the instruments of vision which litter the film: video monitors, opera and magnifying glasses, the sights of a gun, a raven's eye blinking like a camera shutter through the opening credits, irised views through keyholes, even eye drops that magnify and blur the eye's surface. The camera moves through a number of peculiar positions: it looks up from a plug-hole as liquid is poured on it (and us), savours the beauty of instruments of destruction as the killer's box of tricks is opened, and most notoriously follows a bullet in slow motion close-up as it spins through a keyhole to meet Mira's peeping eye.

One of the horrific things about this scene is that it takes so long: from the moment Mira kneels down to keyhole level (again, in Betty's sight) and we see with her through the keyhole that the killer is there with a gun, the vulnerability of her eye is signalled. The keyhole is an opening for the killer, not her, even though she is the one who looks. First we see her seeing in profile, then we cut to the irised image through the keyhole, only to see a hand turning the gun until the barrel points towards us. In the space of a second we look with her into the eye of the gun, see the white flash of the bullet's release, and watch the oblique side view of it spinning to its destination. We then cut back to Mira in profile, still looking at the point of impact, and for around 11 seconds a slow-motion female death is constructed, first through a profile shot that shows the back of her head coming away, then a long shot, held for seconds, as she collapses in slow motion.

Clearly Argento subscribes to the Poe philosophy that the death of a beautiful woman is the most poetic – and cinematic – of topics, and clearly the deaths of his female characters need to be read with the history of feminist reactions to sexualised screen violence in mind. But as the camera fixes Mira again, lying face-up on the floor with only her bloody eye as evidence of her death, the importance of this scene as a key to the film's ocular obsessions, its role as a central moment of transgressive violence, are apparent. Here Argento not only takes us into the moment of violence as it happens; he also presents the spectacle of that violence in motion in its absurd impossibility.

This is a difficult scene to watch, not least because it is so flagrantly unrealistic. Argento revels in exquisitely contorted violations of the body, a gothic-baroque *mise-en-scène* forever signalling its own artifice, washed by a supremely unnatural palette and preyed upon by a camera that signals its presence with a restless, prowling motion. The film refuses to serve up the innocently, impotently witnessed scenes of everyday sadism that horror's critics claim and castigate; here the neat scopic division of watcher and watched as violator and victim collapses in a protracted experiment with artifice carried out on both sides of the keyhole.

Argento's is just the most focused example in a whole history of such images. Certainly these scenes are bloody, but graphically gory techniques are hardly synonymous with realism, especially in the context of 'impossible' cinematography and special effects which only make you wonder how they were effected: it is as if a correlation between the extravagance of an image and its unreality is emerging. Neither are the sexual discourses which underpin these scenes a clear index of the gratifications which might be provoked: read the Terminator's mutilation alongside Mira's death, or that of Buñuel's woman alongside the spectacular death of Mira's killer later in *Opera* (his eye is pecked out and then eaten by ravens, in the Japanese version at least, before he is killed not once but twice). It is hard to confront the anxieties of these disparate scenes without alluding to castration anxiety, or even to some vaguer fear of penetrability, but the codes and sexual contexts offer no clear image of this either. These are ideas made flesh, elements of a violent visual theory played out like a mystery play – no less politically problematic for all that, but also no less a fantasy, plotted with a macabre meticulousness which obsessively marks its difference from the real.

PARANOIA AND THE PODS

J. Hoberman

Currently in its second official remake, *Invasion of the Body Snatchers* has a title that suggests nothing so much as Hollywood's boundless capacity to feed upon itself. But then, as much as it was anything, the original 1956 *Body Snatchers* – produced by Walter Wanger, directed by Don Siegel, and written (mainly) by Daniel Mainwaring from the novel by Jack Finney – has been a source of outrageous simile. The most famous B-movie allegory of the 1950s, it gave the familiar Cold War fantasy of extra-terrestrial conquest an additionally paranoid twist. Drifting down from the sky, seed pods from outer space replicate human beings and replace them (as they sleep) with perfect, emotionless, vegetable doubles – thus successfully colonising the earth with the asexual other-directed drones of a harmoniously single-minded mass society.

Ever since the Truman administration began stoking up the Red Scare in 1947, Communism had been visualised as a disease, a germ, a form of alien mind-control. By the time *Invasion of the Body Snatchers* appeared, however, there was also the soothing presence of President Eisenhower, the psychologically homogenising combination of Miltown and Levittown. Which was which? 'As the newcomers to the middle class enter suburbia, they must disregard old values, and their sensitivity to those of the organization man is almost systematically demonstrable', noted William Whyte in his 1957 tract *The Organization Man.* And in his 1958 bestseller *Masters of Deceit*, FBI chief J. Edgar Hoover was warning Americans to 'remember, always, that there are thousands of people in this country now working in secret to make it happen here.'

Winston Churchill and 'The Body Snatchers'

If *High Noon* (1952) attacked Hollywood cowardice while providing justification for America's Cold War foreign policies, *Invasion of the Body Snatchers* offered an all-purpose metaphor for the nation's domestic life. Like *High Noon*, also set in a nondescript western town, *Invasion of the Body Snatchers* lent itself to both right- and left-wing readings – alternatively a drama of Communist subversion or of suburban conformity unfolding in a hilariously bland atmosphere of hyper-vigilance. The script originally ended with a close-up of the distraught pod-fighter Dr Miles Bennell (Kevin McCarthy), screaming at the audience: 'There's no escape ... no time to waste. Unless you do, you'll be next!'

Given its maximally lurid title (Finney simply called his work *The Body Snatchers*), the movie is all the more enjoyable for the podlike quality of its impressive performances and its cheap, open-air *noir* naturalism. Nor is this the only source of deadpan humour. An innocuous small town is the very fount of contagion; the cops have become criminal. Love is a source of terror; tranquillisers must be prescribed by creatures from another planet. Psychology is identified with brainwashing; adjustment is made synonymous with conformist coercion. The family has been infiltrated by inhuman enemies; the telephone is an instrument of surveillance. This transformation of ordinary Americans into soullessly Sovietised Babbitts was a pop *1984* complete with the notion of subversive sex crime. Normality was sinister. A sense of overwhelming anxiety inspires a desire for security, a longing to merge with the group, whether in suburbs or party cells – yet the urge to merge is a threat to the self. *Invasion of the Body Snatchers* showed America alienated from itself. The 'good' motherland is experienced as a nearly identical 'bad' one.

First appearing as *The Body Snatchers* in the 26 November, 10 December and 24 December 1954 issues of *Collier's* magazine, Finney's pods had been anticipated by the eponymous 'puppet masters' of Robert Heinlein's novel, serialised in the September 1951 issue of *Galaxy*. In the Heinlein scenario, giant slugs from Saturn's moon Titan travel to earth via a flying saucer and attach themselves to American citizens, whom they transform into zombies controlled by an unfeeling communal mind.

Although set after the Third World War, *The Puppet Masters* was totally contemporary – resembling in some respects a two-fisted, kisser-mashing Mike Hammer thriller. There is even a suggestion that the slugs have already conquered Russia (thus making it, in effect, its own puppet regime). Back in the US, these disgusting aliens actively seek to take over government officials, army brass and congressmen. Civil liberties must be suspended. The question of the hour (are you now or have you ever been a slug-zombie spy?) is superseded by the moral articulated by the book's intelligence-agent hero: 'The price of freedom is the willingness to do sudden battle, anywhere, any time, and with utter recklessness.'

Finney's novel is less overtly McCarthyite, particularly as it has been revised several times: first when it was published as a Dell paperback in February 1955 and again, 23 years later, when it was re-issued to coincide with Philip Kaufman's remake of the Siegel movie. As originally published in *Collier's*, *The Body Snatchers* was set during the summer of 1953, soon after the execution of Julius and Ethel Rosenberg capped a six-year hunt for Communist traitors and immediately following the Korean armistice – a moment when the American press was preoccupied with stories of GIs subjected to Communist 'brainwashing'. There are other Cold War markers as well. Going into battle, Miles Bennell invokes Winston Churchill: 'We shall fight them in the fields, and in the streets... we shall never surrender.' In *Collier's*, the story has a happy ending: the FBI successfully beats back the invasion.

As imagined by Finney, the collectivised pods suffer from apathy, letting the town they infiltrate fall into a state of seedy decline, the stores as empty of produce as those in a drab Eastern European city. ('You can hardly even buy a Coke in most places,' a travelling salesman complains to Miles. 'Lately, this place has been out of coffee altogether, for no reason at all, and today when they have it, it's just lousy, terrible.') Still, for Finney's hero, the pods suggest more than just Communists. As Glen M. Johnson pointed out some years ago in *The Journal of Popular Culture*, Finney's *The Body Snatchers* provides an even more comprehensive catalogue of topical anxieties than

Siegel's film. At one point in the book, Miles compares the pods' false human person-alities to the exaggerated servility of the middle-aged black man who runs the town shoeshine stand; elsewhere he refers to himself as a 'puppet' married and divorced as if devoid of will. America is already a land of masked rage and zombie automatons.

Sorting out the politics of the men who filmed *Invasion of the Body Snatchers* is not easy. Siegel has described himself as a liberal, although his oeuvre is more suggestive of a libertarian belief in rugged individualism. Wanger, a producer with an interest in topically political material, was responsible for both the crypto-fascist *Gabriel Over the White House* (1933) and the prematurely anti-fascist *Blockade* (1938), as well as for such New Dealish genre exercises as *You Only Live Once*, *Stagecoach* and *Foreign Correspondent*. A brief stretch in prison for shooting his wife Joan Bennett's agent, resulted in the reformist *Riot in Cell Block 11*, directed by Siegel, and perhaps the anti-capital punishment *I Want to Live*.

From pulp to classic

Although working on a budget of less than $400,000, Wanger treated *Body Snatchers* as an important production. Scarcely had *Collier's* finished running Finney's serial than Wanger, Siegel and Siegel's erstwhile collaborator Daniel 'Geoffrey Homes' Mainwaring met with the author to discuss the movie. Mainwaring, a man of left-wing associations who had begun his career writing socially conscious journalism and pulp fiction in the depths of the Depression, is credited with Miles's speech about the changes he has noted in American society: 'People have allowed their humanity to drain away... only it happens slowly rather than all at once. They didn't seem to mind.' Mainwaring's previous scripts included hard-hitting exposés such as Joseph Losey's *The Lawless* and Phil Karlson's *The Phenix City Story*. During the Korean War, however, he wrote two topical cavalry Westerns – *The Last Outpost*, a key film in the construction of the 'new' action-oriented, gun-toting Ronald Reagan, and *Bugles in the Afternoon*, both stressing the importance of white antagonists uniting to fight a common Indian enemy. His anti-Communist crime-drama *A Bullet for Joey*, a relentlessly perfunctory tale of atomic chicanery, served to 'clear' A. I. Bezzerides and Edward G. Robinson.

As a further complication, once *Invasion of the Body Snatchers* went into production in late March 1955, the script was reworked by Richard Collins, author of *Riot in Cell Block 11* and one of the most ambiguous figures of the blacklist era. A former Communist Party functionary, co-author of the once notorious *Song of Russia* (1943), an announced unfriendly witness first subpoenaed by the House Un-American Activities Committee in autumn 1947 among the original Hollywood Nineteen, Collins subsequently reversed field – first as an FBI informer and then as the namer of 26 names before HUAC on 12 April 1951.

Having wrapped after a brisk 23-day shoot, *Invasion of the Body Snatchers* further evolved over the course of a lengthy post-production debate on how best to position the narrative. Wanger thought to preface the movie with a recent quote from Winston Churchill and, as he had in *Foreign Correspondent*, to add a didactic final warning. The necessity for a framing story, to be set up by an on-screen narrator, was perceived as increasingly urgent after a series of unsuccessful previews during the summer of 1955.

Wanger's first choice for narrator was Orson Welles, drawing an obvious line to *The War of the Worlds* which had been filmed as an allegory of US-Soviet war in 1953. The alternatives were a trio of Second World War radio correspondents: Edward R. Murrow, Lowell Thomas and Quentin Reynolds.

A framing story was ultimately shot, sans celebrity narrator, in late September, thus providing the movie with a marginally more optimistic ending. And finally, the title also presented a problem. *The Body Snatchers* was too similar to Val Lewton's 1945 *The Body Snatcher*. The distributor, Allied Artists, proposed the generic *They Came from Another World*. Siegel objected strongly, offering instead *Sleep No More* and *Better Off Dead* – titles that suggested the familiar Cold War metaphor of sleep versus wakefulness and the mantra 'Better dead than Red' – before the idea of 'invasion' was affixed to the threat of 'body snatchers'.

Even without Welles, Wanger was committed to the movie's liberal interpretation. In November he told the American Booksellers Convention that his still unreleased *Invasion of the Body Snatchers* was a picture on the subject of 'conformity', showing 'how easy it is for people to be taken over and to lose their souls if they are not alert and determined in their character to be free'. Just as European commentators were quick to recognise *High Noon*'s foreign policy implications, so the Italian critic Ernest G. Laura was apparently the first to link *Invasion of the Body Snatchers* to the harder anti-Communist rhetoric of J. Edgar Hoover and *Reader's Digest*. Two years after the movie's release, the anti-Stalinist leftist Seymour Stern wrote programme notes for a revival at LA's Coronet Theater that took its epigram from a recent item in the *Los Angeles Times*: 'India's communists today began a crucial special congress called primarily to perfect their new political technique – the attainment of absolute power through respectability.' Tracing the film's lineage back to D. W. Griffith's *The Flying Torpedo* (1916), Stern gave the movie an unambiguously anti-totalitarian reading: 'Long ago, the natives whose bodies are snatched by the pods had cancelled or forfeited their own birthright of sexual freedom based only on mutual consent; they had lost their liberty in meek submission to their own conservative authority. If all brands of sovietization seem here, then all forms of Fascism are here, too – clerical fascism, economic fascism, political fascism, sexual fascism, social fascism, name-the-brand.'

Counterculture crack-up

An instant staple of low-budget sci-fi, the 'body snatcher' premise informed two great 1960s cheapsters, *Creation of the Humanoids* and *Night of the Living Dead*, was given a feminist twist in the mid-70s with *The Stepford Wives* and Valie Export's avant-garde *Invisible Adversaries*, and was finally celebrated for itself with Kaufman's 1978 remake. While the original opened on a double bill with *The Atomic Man* (a British pick-up) and was deemed too disreputable to warrant a *New York Times* review, the remake was released for Christmas and hailed by Pauline Kael in the *New Yorker* as 'the American movie of the year – a new classic'.

Of course, Siegel's *Invasion of the Body Snatchers* is so intrinsically 1950s that Kaufman felt compelled to link his own version to the epic revival that began around the time of Richard Nixon's re-election (and continued, almost unabated, through the middle of Ronald Reagan's second term). 'We were all asleep in a lot of ways in the Fifties, living conforming, other-directed types of lives. Maybe we woke up a little in the Sixties, but now we've gone back to sleep again,' he told one interviewer, referring to the self-involvement and political disorientation that followed the counterculture's crack-up. Transposed to San Francisco, Kaufman's *Invasion of the Body Snatchers* reeks of local colour and urban alienation, populated by a gaggle of smart-mouthed free spirits, ex-hippies employed by the Department of Health, and smooth, hustling guru-therapists forever asking each other about their 'feelings'. San Francisco was still the capital of American non-conformism – even if Siegel himself had visualised it as Dirty Harry's playground. Indeed, thanks to two recent sensational post-counterculture tragedies, the movie's setting imbued it with additional resonance. Less than a month before *Invasion of the Body Snatchers'* premiere, a deranged former member of the San Francisco Board of Supervisors assassinated both the city's mayor and its most public homosexual activist, supervisor Harvey Milk, while members of the People's Temple, formerly of San Francisco, committed mass suicide in the Guyana jungle at the behest of their leader, the Reverend Jim Jones.

Each in its way suggested that the wages of lifestyle might be death. Rather than *The Lonely Crowd*, the pop-sociological context for this second *Invasion of the Body Snatchers* was Christopher Lasch's *The Culture of Narcissism*, published just as the movie was released. Unlike the original, Kaufman's mannerist, alternately self-conscious and rhapsodic remake made little argument in favour of podification. Banality has no place in San Francisco. (Kael called the film 'a surreal variant of Simone Weil's thesis that the people who resisted the Nazis weren't the good, upright citizens – they were the dreamers and outcasts and cranks'. What was at stake was 'the right of freaks to be freaks – which is much more appealing than the right of "normal" people to be normal'.) Less concerned with the threat of political subversion and the comfort of the lonely crowd than with the struggle against creeping psychobabble and the need to protect the environment, Kaufman's *Invasion of the Body Snatchers* is the *cri de coeur* of the ageing yuppie.

Abel Ferrara's 1993 version, by contrast, is fast-paced, impersonal and completely imagistic. As a second remake, Ferrara's film isn't hide-bound by cultural guilt – the original has already been snatched. This latest *Body Snatchers* appropriates several aspects of the Kaufman version (both were produced by Robert H. Solo), and elaborates on Kaufman's splashier special effects. The transformation from human to pod – invisible in Siegel – is even more visceral in Ferrara than in Kaufman, with tendrils descending on sleeping humans and snaking into their various orifices. And expanding on Kaufman's punchline, Ferrara explores the capacity for pod-people to transform themselves into banshee alarm systems.

Although a more expensive production than Kaufman's, Ferrara's returns the material to its B-movie roots, re-imagining it as a tough-talking action flick set not among the hot-tubs of California but on an Alabama military base. Macho is the ultimate social construction, as exemplified in an unmistakable Ferrara touch: when a military pod wants to check the status of a passing-for-pod, he tells him, 'Just so you know, I fucked your girlfriend.'

Delusion and illness

So familiar has the 'body snatchers' metaphor become that it's worth noting that back in 1956 *Variety* found the original sometimes 'difficult to follow due to the strangeness of its scientific premise'. As film theorist Noel Carroll has pointed out, however,

Invasion of the Body Snatchers offers a near textbook illustration of a condition called Capgras syndrome – the delusional belief that close relatives or associates, sometimes including one's pets or oneself, have been replaced by sinister doubles. (Indeed, despite considerable evidence to the contrary, Finney has described his novel in similar terms: 'For years now, I've been amused by the fairly widely held notion that *The Body Snatchers* has anything to do with the cold war, McCarthyism, conformity ... It does not. I was simply intrigued by the notion of a lot of people insisting that their friends and relatives were impostors.') *I Married a Monster from Outer Space* (1958) and the original *Invaders from Mars* (1953) are related examples of Capgrasoid sci-fi, and a study of the syndrome's case histories shows that imagined Communist conspiracies were scarcely unknown during the heightened suspicion of the Cold War.

Capgras syndrome has been variously analysed as a paranoid projection (if a familiar person no longer elicits the same affective response, the person must have changed rather than the subject's feelings) and as the denial of certain negative traits in one with whom the subject has stong emotional ties. As Capgras syndrome suggests the need to idealise a particular individual, it makes sense that the original *Invasion of the Body Snatchers* would appear soon after the 1948–53 period of maximum mobilisation – once it was safe to dramatise the recent hysteria and meditate on the Pod That Failed. Capgras syndrome has also been theorised as a defensive manoeuvre that allows the subject to handle erotic or aggressive feelings towards a parental figure, and it is in this sense that Ferrara's *Body Snatchers* is most vivid. Almost devoid of children, Kaufman's 1978 film focuses exclusively on mature heterosexual relationships. Ferrara's current version, though, concerns the nuclear family. The protagonist Marti Malone is an estranged teenage stepdaughter – for her, mother has long since been replaced by the soulless pod of the second Mrs Malone. The big chill here is a daycare centre where the children produce identical finger paintings; the key sequence has Mrs Malone disintegrate in her sleep, then reappear naked and impassively witchy before her five-year-old son ('That isn't my mommy!'), who is subsequently trapped between zombie daycare and imposter mom.

No more crying

To grow up and join society is *a priori* to become a conformist pod. While this is at least implicit in the Siegel version – at one point podified parents place an alien spore in their baby's crib with the comment that 'there'll be no more crying' – it is Ferrara's subject. His movie feeds on the tension between father and daughter, pitting Marti and her off-limits soldier boyfriend against the rest of the family. That Mr Malone works for the Environmental Protection Agency is a red herring – although, unlike both previous movies, Ferrara makes the resident shrink (Forest Whitaker) a heroic pod-fighter. The army base is at once an updated suburbia, a prison camp and a toxic waste dump. Indeed, Ferrara turns the Capgras syndrome into a universal principle: given the demands of military discipline, how can you tell when a soldier is a pod? The klaxon blare of the base's full-alert only amplifies the individual's need to protect his or her ego by remaining awake.

As the troubled Malone family is a transplant from *Rebel without a Cause*, so the base commander is played by R. Lee Ermey, promoted from his tour of duty as marine drill sergeant in *Full Metal Jacket*. Explicitly post–Desert Storm (the war commanded by the most severely pod-like of recent US presidents), and featuring a complete panoply of firefighters, choppers and bombing raids, as well as a story of adolescent sexual acting out, the movie collapses the whole of baby-boomer history – from the Cold War through Vietnam to the New World Order – into a single package. Ferrara even manages to evoke Oliver Stone: pod subversion is envisioned as a military coup.

And yet if this latest *Body Snatchers* leaves less of a residue than Kaufman's, the fault is less Ferrara's than history's. (One wonders whether Disney's belated adaptation of *The Puppet Masters*, due later this year, will have any resonance at all.) Bucking the positivist trend of the late 1970s, Kaufman deliberately positioned his remake in direct opposition to the current feel-good space invasion of *Close Encounters of the Third Kind* – although within a year one of his ideas had been co-opted in Steven Spielberg and George Lucas's supremely soulless *Raiders of the Lost Ark*. Ferrara, by contrast, can only position his remake in opposition to the inflated B-movie ethos that Spielberg and Lucas have long since established.

Looking back on the Cold War from the post-McCarthy period, Siegel and company not only naturalised the Red Scare, but imbued it with Darwinian angst – the fear that Communism might actually be a higher stage on the evolutionary ladder. The original *Invasion of the Body Snatchers* provided an imaginative visualisation of the national security state and reckoned its psychic cost to America's self-image. At this point – and this may be the point – Americans no longer even have that identity left to lose.

LONDON: NECROPOLIS OF FRETFUL GHOSTS

Iain Sinclair

Patrick Keiller's *London* is not your London, not the ersatz moon base ceded to you by the image merchandisers, not cinema as we have come to know it. His locations are pedestrian. Literally so. The metropolis, its shrines and suburbs, rivulets, parks, ceremonies and literary mementos are investigated by pilgrims bearing a second-hand Éclair Cameflex, that most nostalgic of instruments. Keiller's concentration is so steady, we sweat for it: the steadiness of the out-patient, the 'care in the community' psycho outstaring rush-hour headlights. The film is a quiet provocation – provoking reverie, honouring accidental survivals (like the London Stone) which we have never quite got around to visiting. Postcards so familiar we can choose to ignore their origins. His journal is as honest in its fictions as Defoe's, conjuring a voice out of silence, an interior monologue, ironic but insistent – a nail of clear water boring into the brain. We are guided backwards and forwards across the sacred diagonals of a city we have ceased to deserve. The film is the only evidence of its existence.

The documentary in its present debased form (not a journey of discovery, but the justification of a script-approved argument) is franchise fodder, a trade-off between consenting production companies: television. 'Steam on the glass,' as East London novelist Emanuel Litvinoff describes it. *Laissez-faire* accumulations of meaningless evidence or the personality-led essay. Print journalism with jump-cuts. The world is explained (censored) as it is revealed, with language reduced to the function of cement – holding together disparate elements. Keiller's method, in which text and picture are independent, posthumously 'married' in the cutting room, is therefore a notable curiosity.

London has the meandering form of an epistolary novel, a fabulation backed by congeries of face. The narrator, returning from a seven-year exile, takes a leisurely inventory of the city's consciousness, makes expeditions, bears witness to public events, the aftermath of violent political acts, fantasies of escape.

Paul Scofield, that most pared-down, Xanaxed of Lears, is the whisperer, the voice in the head, the syrup keeping authorial distemper in check. He is describing an absence, a necropolis of fretful ghosts, a labyrinth of quotations: not so much the ruin of a great city as the surgical removal of its soul. The casting of Scofield signals a weary integrity; it is so clear that he is *not* the narrator. It's a performance – tired, slightly camp, detached. (The barber, out of the stage version of *Staircase*, a keeper of secrets, dispenser of healing unguents.) The man is too old for the adventures he is claiming, too careful; he uses English with such absurdist precision – a second language. 'Bezaar,' he says. And bizarre it is. Anecdotes rinsed, then swallowed.

'A journey to the end of the world.' That's how it begins, reversing expectations. An immediate invocation of Louis-Ferdinand Céline, the unacknowledged laureate of last-gasp Britain, present but rarely named, the blitz-culture Betjeman in a beret. *Voyage au bout de la nuit.* ('The greatest French movie ever made.' Jack Kerouac. On the book.)

Keiller's narrator, a ship's photographer, is coming back to spend time with his reclusive and possibly dying, former lover, Robinson, who is marooned (Crusoed) in a solidy built redbrick hulk in Vauxhall. ('His income is small, but he saves most of it.') Robinson, of course, is never seen; we take him on trust – Harry Lime without the shadow. He's a rumour corrupting complacency, a virus. The cruise liner, a creamy berg of threat (cabins: £4,000 per week) completes its stately progress through Tower Bridge and into the archives of London cinema.

The incoming vessel (no visible crew) is always a threat (Dracula at Whitby), while the downriver cruiser (Bob Hoskins in *The Long Good Friday*) is merely boastful and self-deluding. He's there to show off the Olympia & York skyline. No way out. Tower Bridge, like so much of London, is now a museum of itself, held together by frequent coats of paint. You buy a ticket to watch waxworks operate the gleaming Victorian machinery. The bridge is also the most convenient of establishing shots – anything beyond it is wasteland, unworthy of comment. It opens Jules Dassin's *Night and the City*. It salutes Hitchcock's return from exile in *Frenzy* – one of the last films to draw on the rich midden of London sub-culture fiction, the swift narratives of lives at once on the margin and at the centre – based on Arthur La Bern's novel *Goodbye Piccadilly, Farewell Leicester Square*.

Perhaps the optioning of Alexander Baron's *The Lowlife* as a vehicle for Harry H.

Corbett (never made) was the end of it, this flirtation between a subversive (cheap to buy) literature and the chew 'em up/spit 'em out world of mainstream cinema. Or perhaps the Roeg/Cammell *Performance* was the final flare, the defiant burn-out: an original screenplay using authentically subterranean material transmitted by David Litvinoff, a novelist *manqué*. Litvinoff wrote nothing, he made tapes. His life was the book, the forerunner of an age of ghosted gangland memoirs.

Hitchcock struck an eminently practical attitude towards all this. 'I don't read novels, or any fiction. I would say that most of my reading consists of contemporary biographies and books on travel,' he informed Truffaut. Jack Trevor Story, the backbone of the Sexton Blake Library, never recovered from Hitchcock's transfer of his first book, *The Trouble with Harry*, from its original scrubby heathland to autumnal Vermont. The paltry sum for which he let the property go remained a grievance to the end. But when producers grew bored with proletarian fables, publishers lost their nerve and simply airbrushed certain areas from the map. (The North, wherever that is, was still OK. Exotic, raw. Cab the proofs around to Woodfall. But London? Forget it.) Emanuel Litvinoff (David's half-brother) only managed to bring out his Whitechapel sketch *Journey through a Small Planet* by agreeing to follow it with a 'serious' East European trilogy.

Tower Bridge: Hitchcock's camera swoops through the span and along the river in a conspicuous display of budget. (A prophetic summary of the *News at Ten* credit sequence?) Keiller's Cameflex, asserting the modesty of its status, never moves, moves only *between* shots—the unrecorded trek to the next set-up. The long-focus stare is mesmeric, healing, a charm against frenzy (both the culture of speed *and* Hitchcock's malign virtuosity). Movement becomes a function of voice, voice an instrument. It's a mode utterly estranged from industrial cinema, with its basis in montage: Hitchcock's time-travel is revealed as nostalgia for the London of the silk-tie strangler.

Frenzy, exploiting the last rites of Covent Garden as a working market, is infected by a Europhobic terror of alien cuisines, trays of unwashed immigrant fruit. The leather elbow patches of La Bern's ex-bomber pilot—a tribute to his faded gentility— once filmed become a badge of raffish style, the retro fashion of Camden Lock. Anna Massey, fleeing from the career-threatening crisis of Michael Powell's *Peeping Tom*, distrait, nibbled to her essence like a Giacometti maquette, is cast perversely against type as a perky barmaid, a one-night-stand victim.

The silence of things that can no longer be said, locations stripped of their resonance. ('I had lunch with Hitch in his office.' Michael Powell, *A Life in Movies*. 'Silent movies are a dead duck, Micky.') The silence of Powell's film within a film, the diary, the snuff movie shot by the cameraman with the bayonet tripod. London as a labyrinth, a closed system.

Keiller perceptively defines this silence, the absence of debate, as a conspiracy of the suburbs, an attack on metropolitan life and all its amenities by small-minded provincials, careerists distrustful of the liberties of the café-bar, the aimlessness of the *flâneur*. He quotes Alexander Herzen, his 'motivating source', who saw London life as a discipline of solitude. ('One who knows how to live alone has nothing to fear.') The city offers itself up to poets and exiles, men of silent watchfulness, visionaries (Rimbaud and Verlaine) wandering through the docks, opium smokers, dreamers, dowsers of invisible energy patterns. A dystopia run by uniformed enforcers, like the Victorian prisons, like Pentonville, on The Silent System. The soul of the place opposes cinema, the light. Its bureaucratic weather is against it. Skies like a hangman's hood. The scuttle of wife-killers in starched collars, eyes in the dirt. Backstreet chemists doling out paraquat.

Not since the 1960s has government demonstrated any practical interest in film, beyond inviting Michael Caine around for a snifter. And, even in the days when the Social Democrats were falling for the glamour of photo opportunities, the memorable images were being captured by foreigners, visitors with work permits: Losey, Polanski, Skolimowski (Munich for London), Antonioni. It took an Italian to track down the mysteries of Maryon Park in Charlton, a perfectly ambiguous site for the crime discovered by the photographer in *Blow-up*. A site which film-maker Christopher Petit (Polaroid in hand?) visited, as he recounts in an essay on Julian Maclaren-Ross, in an act of homage. The London he was beginning to imagine, and which he later described in his novel *Robinson* and his television films, was a geography of disconnected locations.

Any future urban cinema, wanting to learn from Keiller and Petit, should become a cinema of vagrancy. There's no longer time for the laying of tracks, the crane, the cherry-picker: obsolescent industrial terminology. The truth of a city, divided against itself, can only be revealed, so Keiller believes, through a series of obscure pilgrimages, days spent crawling out on to the rim of things. The transcendent surrealism of airport perimeter roads, warehouses and reservoirs. J. G. Ballard. Shepperton.

London cinema in its pomp was in any case a creature of the suburbs – that's where the studios were. That's where a phantom metropolis could be built, civic dignity reduced to plasterboard. (Canary Wharf is the contemporary version.)

Monsters of paranoia, menageries of blood beasts – Fu Manchu, Jack the Ripper, Jekyll and Hyde – stalked from these sheds like a regiment of escaping battery hens. A second London, the floating capital of Swedenborg's visions, was laid out. A monochrome principality with no sky. A day-for-night mirror world where sweet tea was served in cups the size of slopping-out buckets. A busy thoroughfare of dripping raincoats, greasy trilbies, paste teeth. A polis devised for the convenience of voyeurs – where speech is meticulously coded, and the social classes divided by the strictest of faultlines. Even the clippies articulate like debutantes on laughing gas. Pocket watches can be checked against the regular nine o'clock toppings.

The city of cinema, born of low-life fiction, is a place of flight. It is defined by the distance a man can run in trying to escape from it. Arthur Woods's *They Drive by Night* (based on a novel by the admirably intransigent James Curtis) is a paradigm of the genre. Sniffling Emlyn Williams, looking like an unfixed mutation somewhere between Charlie Chaplin and Nigel Lawson, is the innocent on the run, determined to prove that the countryside is never more than a few fake tussocks, a clapboard truckers' shack and perpetual rain.

The city as a self-cannibalising system. Pursuit: elegant tracking shots into clubs (linking interior and exterior), wrestling matches, the flats of chorus girls. Hatchet alleyways like lesions in the brain. Gerald Kersh's *Night and the City* is the apotheosis of this mode (both book and film). ('He saw London as a kind of Inferno – a series of concentric areas with Piccadilly as the ultimate centre.') Jules Dassin's translation of

Kersh's novel into spatial terms is dynamic and exemplary, mixing psychologically perceptive set design with an extraordinarily vivid account of the geography of post-war London: the open city of docks, rubble mounds, bridges.

Pursuit summons once again the figure of the Shroudy Stranger, the genealogy of Céline's Robinson, who slides, covertly, from the American poet Weldon Kees (and his parasite, Simon Armitage), through Burroughs and Kerouac, to Patrick Keiller, Jonathan Meades (*Pompey*), and Christopher Petit. Petit's assumption of *Robinson* (the novel) is an unmatched (and largely unnoticed) act of cinematic and literary retrieval: the junction point where the lost fiction engages with the new cinema. (On television, Petit's film *London Labyrinth* conceives of a city of memory shards, an accumulation from theatrical and documentary sources. Pathological modernism: the art of the dustbin, the skip thief.) *Robinson* exploits and celebrates the Soho of Maclaren-Ross, Mark Benney, Kersh. Then allows it to be colonised by Orson Welles (actor as much as director, gourmand most of all) and Fassbinder (claustrophobia, misogyny, camera working close as a rectal thermometer).

Petit's astute cultural truffling doesn't stop there. He pays his respects in *Robinson* to the legendary *habitué* of the Coach and Horses, Robin Cook. ('Robin behaved badly before anyone else did.' Jonathan Meades.) Cook, between wives in the South of France, one career as a novelist nuked, decided to give it another shot, reinventing the London of the Edgar Wallace films and dosing it with Krafft-Ebing. His name had been pinched in his absence by an airport shelf-spoiler, so he became Derek Raymond. His Factory novels – psychopaths on the loose in millennial weather – were acclaimed as the ultimate mapping of the posthumous dream city. A geography much closer to Céline's *Guignol's Band* than to the *London A–Z*. They were filmed, naturally, in France.

Where Cook and Petit, romantics, are drawn inwards to the heart of the labyrinth, Keiller resolutely explores the banks of the River Brent. Had he been a poet, he confesses, Brent Cross shopping centre would have been his inspiration. At last the camera *moves*, travelling upwards on an escalator, gazing on plashy fountains, a crowd numbed by the muzak of the spheres. Keiller's narrator speaks of noticing a 'small intense man' reading Walter Benjamin, for all the world like a card-carrying Cambridge poet. The instant of sympathy is illusory. The fetch vanishes into Willesden. Could it have been Petit himself? Or Dennis Nilsen?

Beyond the vast hangars of consumerism the city gives up. Keiller can wait, crouching in fields, watching the calligraphy of wind on water. He has already told us so much. But he can never tell it all. The multitude of solitary lives lived within the circuits of the crowd. There is more history than any one man can bear. So the film-makers pass through Mortlake without noticing the estate of Dr John Dee (his Angel Magick): the point of departure for Derek Jarman's punk deconstruction *Jubilee*.

Keiller knows that London is finally an absence, a congregation of provincials. Having no culture of the centre, that is what we have become. Eliot's sleepwalkers commuting to a city of silence, a marketing device, the excuse for an anthology from some disgraced politician. The only cinema appropriate to this London is the cinema of surveillance. (Petit again. Eleven minutes on *The Late Show*.) Unedited mute, riverine; menacing in its boredom. Diaries kept by machines. The home movies of multi-story car parks. Be noticed and you're dead. A cinema that requires no audience.

BLOODY TALES

Amy Taubin

Every cinephile has her/his own litany of blood movies. A mere mention of certain titles summons up the image of red; spurting, gushing, suffusing the screen. Pulsing veins, severed limbs, flayed bodies float before the mind's eye. It's our visceral response to such images that fixes them in memory. But even the most intensely visceral images fade unless they also embody other kinds of meaning. Not that there isn't guilty pleasure in gore for its own sake. I thrilled at the moment in the otherwise anaemic *Interview with the Vampire: The Vampire Chronicles* when Tom Cruise squeezed the blood from a rat's body into a wine glass and offered it to a revolted Brad Pitt; six months from now, I will probably have forgotten it entirely.

For the record, my own list of blood movies includes *The Red Shoes* (1948), *Window, Water, Baby Moving* (1959), the Zapruder footage of JFK's assassination (1963), *Weekend* (1967), *Bonnie and Clyde* (1967), *The Wild Bunch* (1969), *The Act of Seeing with One's Own Eyes* (1971), *The Texas Chain Saw Massacre* (1974), *Taxi Driver* (1976), *Carrie* (1976), *Alien* (1979), *The Shining* (1980) and *Scanners* (1980). It is perhaps worth mentioning that both *Taxi Driver* and the Zapruder footage were recently added to the list of films designated by the National Registry of the Library of Congress as 'historically and culturally significant and worthy of preservation'. Only 150 films have been chosen in the six years the Film Registry has been in operation.

My choices are obviously conditioned by my personal history and reflect my politics, my aesthetic sensibility and my psycho-sexual predilections. If I had been an adult when I saw *The Red Shoes*, I might not have been transfixed by the sight of Moira Shearer's white tights stained with red (which doesn't mean I think the film should be off-limits for children). *Weekend, Bonnie and Clyde* and *The Wild Bunch* all spoke to the violence in Vietnam; the red which dappled the movie screen was what was missing from the nightly news, as transmitted to black and white TVs. The body horror of *Carrie, Alien* and even *Scanners* emerged from a patriarchy shaken up about feminism and gender. *The Shining* was Kubrick's distillation of the horror film, the happening genre of the 1970s which continued to reign in the home-video market of the 1980s and 1990s. The blood that washes from the elevator in *The Shining* is a terrifying metaphor for nuclear-family violence, Kubrick's misogynist subtext notwithstanding.

Taxi Driver is the most prescient of these films, not only because it made violence, rather than sex, an art-house hook, but also because it defines psychosis as the condition of relating to the world as if it were a movie. The windshield of Travis's cab is his camera lens; through it, he sees, framed and at a distance, 'all the animals [that] come out at night: whores, skunk pussies, buggers, queens, fairies, dopers, junkies, sick, venal'. At the climax of the film, when he leaves the cab, armed to the teeth, on an insane mission of rescue and revenge, he walks into a movie of his own making, complete with spinning overhead shots, blasted bodies and buckets of blood.

From *Taxi Driver*, it's a short step to the 1990s self-referentiality of Quentin Tarantino's

Reservoir Dogs and *Pulp Fiction.* Tarantino's aestheticising of violence is a version of Warholian cool in which an image of splattered brains is an image of splattered brains is an image of splattered brains. Tarantino's films are interesting not for what they have to say about the construction of masculinity, or for what they refuse to admit about race relations, but for the way they force their audiences to confront the sado-masochistic pleasure they derive from images of violence. In *Reservoir Dogs*, our position mirrors that of the hapless cop; like him, we're tied to our seats, mesmerised by the homicidal menace of the dancing Mr Blonde. In *Pulp Fiction* we're exhilarated by the power of the movies to reverse time – thereby triumphing over death – so that the loveable gangster who's blown away half way through the film is resurrected to dance across the screen at the final fade.

Tarantino's aesthetics of cool are the postmodern twist on (some would say a parody of) the modernist version of aesthetic distance. In *Pulp Fiction*, when we find ourselves gasping at the sight of a needle poised to penetrate a woman's heart, we re-establish our cool by laughing at ourselves for reacting as if the image were real. On the other hand, when Stan Brakhage fretted, during the editing of *Window, Water, Baby Moving*, about whether an image of the placenta plopping out of his wife's vagina would cause an irreparable breach of aesthetic distance, he was acknowledging the realist potential of the photographic image that Tarantino is desperate to deny. Brakhage's *Window, Water, Baby Moving* and *The Act of Seeing with One's Own Eyes* are among the greatest blood movies because they are simultaneously meditations on the body and on its representation. (The politics of Brakhage's films, on the other hand, leave something to be desired – witness his facile assumption in *Window, Water, Baby Moving* of his wife's labours as his own.)

Bloodstream and mainstream

The reader may have noted that the most recent film on my list was released in 1980. Frankly, I'm not sure if, at that point, I simply lost my taste for cinematic blood or if movies themselves became less visceral as they became more violent. Or perhaps the proliferation of schlock horror has had a desensitising effect. In video stores, blood is cheap. And while such directors as De Palma, Kubrick and Oliver Stone never lost interest in showing bodies that bleed, the image seemed exhausted.

By the late 1980s, however, the Aids crisis had given blood a new meaning. *Near Dark, Alien³, Bram Stoker's Dracula, Wolf* and *Interview with the Vampire* are all metaphoric Aids-anxiety movies. Blood functions in their various narratives as the medium for a network of contamination. It means death from without, even as it circulates within living bodies.

Along with souped-up blood imagery, a wide array of sado-masochistic discourses and practices has made its way into the mainstream. Pierced and scarified bodies have surfaced as fashion statements in shopping malls and high schools across America. S&M clubs are said to be for the 1990s what swinging-singles retreats were for the 1960s. The most successful US television drama series of autumn 1994 is Michael Crichton's *E.R.*, set in the casualty department of a big-city hospital and featuring a non-stop stream of profusely bleeding trauma victims, as well as patients suffering from a wide range of minor and major ailments and psychiatric disorders. In general, *E.R.* speaks to American anxiety about healthcare (aggravated by the Clinton healthcare-reform debacle). But the image of doctors and nurses sheathed in latex to protect them from contact with potentially deadly fluids brings the Aids crisis home to even the most naïve couch potatoes.

Blood made the headlines in the art world as well. Even before the election that gave them a congressional majority, right-wing conservatives launched a renewed attack on the National Endowment for the Arts for indirectly funding (with a lavish $150) a performance art event at the Walker Art Center in which artist Ron Athey used a scalpel to carve a design on the back of fellow performer Darryl Carlton, blotted the blood with paper towels and then hung the towels on a line that stretched across the audience. Athey is HIV positive; Carlton is not. Athey followed safety procedures, wearing latex gloves and using disposable instruments. Nevertheless, one audience member complained to the state health board that he had been subjected to the risk of HIV infection, the story was whipped up in the press to epic proportions by the Christian right, and Congress punished the NEA by reducing its budget by several million dollars.

With the victory of the Republicans, the discourse of S&M – and, more specifically, of vampirism – dominates the political landscape. The triumphant right wing immediately proclaimed that the time had come to discipline all those welfare mothers and their children who have drained the economy and corrupted family values. Vampirism is as apt a metaphor for the power relations within an increasingly desperate capitalism and the not unrelated culture of victimisation as it is for 'Tainted Love' in the age of Aids. Vampirism involves a symbiotic relationship of unequal power in which the powerful (the vampire) projects its own guilt (for being inhuman, undead, evil corrupt, murderous, or whatever) on to its powerless victim, blaming the victim for being complicit in his or her own destruction (since the victim is now evil, less than human, corrupt and so on). Moreover, the vampire regards the victim as a drain on its own energy since the victim's blood is never sufficient to slake its thirst.

Blood buddies

If Neil Jordan is aware of these dynamics, he certainly doesn't allow them to surface in his film adaptation of Anne Rice's best-selling novel. Nor does he incorporate what is most compelling in Rice's text. Published in 1976, *Interview with the Vampire* is the first of the author's supernatural pot-boilers. (Rice has also written several porno-graphic novels; published under a pseudonym, they take a less veiled approach to the pleasure of S&M.) Written nearly a decade before Aids was identified – although the HIV virus was already, secretly, on the move – the novel was inspired by her intimate knowledge of another disease of the blood. Her daughter had died of leukaemia at the age of five. Rice's *Interview with the Vampire* is haunted by the image of the mother/child dyad and by the mother's feelings of guilt, rage, loss, and powerlessness, in not being able to give her child eternal life.

The Hollywood version of *Interview with the Vampire* is an inert, heavily atmospheric costume drama, devoid of eroticism, emotion and ideas. Although the narrative is framed in the first person (Louis, the 200-year-old reluctant vampire, tells his story to a magazine writer whom he picks up in a San Francisco back alley), the film lacks any sense of subjectivity. And what use is a vampire film that never lets you see through undead eyes?

Brad Pitt as the petulant Louis and Tom Cruise as the desecrated Lestat give callow though enthusiastic performances. Both actors are encumbered by make-up (chalky white powder, a tracing of blue veins) that deprives them of the charm of their good looks, without transforming them into creatures capable of inspiring awe or terror. One longs for the slow-burn seduction of John Malkovich in *Dangerous Liaisons* or, more to the point, of Gary Oldman in *Bram Stoker's Dracula*. Lacking such charismatic performers, *Interview with the Vampire*, quickly deteriorates into a series of barely animated tableaux in which one or other of the vampires cosies up to his victim, rattles off a few lines of dialogue and wham-bam goes for the jugular.

The film is erratically edited, either because of the need to cut around the performances or because the powers-that-be couldn't figure out how much languor they could afford in a product aimed at the mass market. Or perhaps the overall shapelessness signals a failure to come to terms with the film's blatant, though not necessarily intentional, contradictions. But if *Interview with the Vampire* is dull to watch, it's not uninteresting to mull over as a cultural object. In the matter of the mainstreaming of blood, there's probably as much red stuff drunk and spilt in Jordan's film as there is filling the elevator room in *The Shining*—though Jordan's imagery is more about gross-out than grandeur.

In fact, the fetishising of blood functions as a shield, distracting attention from the film's greater though only partially realised transgression. *Interview with the Vampire* is the story of an exceedingly longtime companionship, of a marriage between two men which begins in the heat of passion (when Lestat first sinks his teeth into Louis' neck, they fly heavenward locked in each other's arms) and which then settles into a daily routine of naggings, recriminations and betrayals without ever losing its symbiotic pull. Furthermore, these homosexuals – who are played by one major star and one stud-like upcomer – are the only characters in the film with whom the audience can identify.

But the film could hardly be said to embrace homosexuality. Except in their initial moment of contact, Louis and Lestat seem devoid of all sexual desire. The homoeroticism implicit in the narrative is totally repressed on the screen. And don't forget, these are a couple of vampires – meaning they're evil perverts who carry the plague in their tainted blood. So are they supposed to be good guys or bad guys?

Femmes with fangs

The film's evasiveness leaves the audience high and dry – and word of mouth has been mixed. *Interview with the Vampire* took $36.4 million in its opening weekend, which placed it fifth on *Variety's* list of all-time biggest openings. The following weekend, however, the gross dropped by over 50 per cent, the third weekend being even worse. The film is now expected to gross no more than $110 million in the US. However, although such lukewarm business may put paid to plans for a sequel, Hollywood is hardly lacking for other blood-sucker projects.

While *Interview with the Vampire* drowned its metaphors in blood, two independently produced vampire films, both scheduled for 1995 release, allow their subtexts to flow by keeping gore to a minimum. Pulp-meister Abel Ferrara is currently editing *The*

Addiction, which stars Lili Taylor as a New York University doctoral candidate who vampirises an entire philosophy department plus a few downtowners without advanced degrees. Michael Almereyda's lyrical *Nadja*, executive-produced by David Lynch, stars Elina Lowensohn as Dracula's daughter, an exotic interloper who wreaks havoc in the East Village scene. Both films can be read as Aids-anxiety fantasies constructed from a male heterosexual position, with the vampire as a femme fatale who lures both men and women to their doom. Emulating Hitchcock's restraint in making *Psycho*, both film-makers shot in black and white, with the result that blood is abstracted, suggesting a state of mind rather than body. Nevertheless, the two films could not be more dissimilar in visual and narrative style.

Almereyda combines Pixelvision video with richly detailed 35mm, shooting the East Village as it if were the Paris of the Surrealists (he takes inspiration as much from Breton's *Nadja* as Dreyer's *Vampyr*). The Pixelvision image, simultaneously sharp-edged and soft-focused, suggests the vampire point of view. When the film cuts from 35mm to Pixelvision, it's as if the world were sliced open and we see from the inside out. The vampire's presence destabilises time, space, desire. Marriages dissolve bloodlines are severed. Dracula's daughter seduces Lucy on the floor of the railroad flat where she lives with her husband. Later, in the midst of chaos, Lucy plaintively asks: 'Maybe we should have a baby.' That murderous stranger who we recklessly invite in for the night, the vampire is also a doppelgänger who kills from within.

The Addiction (which I've seen only in rough cut) is one of Ferrara's twisted genre-combinations. It could be a sequel to his rape-revenge thriller *Ms .45* or a companion piece to the sordid but inescapably moral *Bad Lieutenant*. In *The Addiction*, Aids is not a metaphor but a fact of life, the environment in which addiction flourishes; and the febrile, tensile-strengthened Lili Taylor is high not only on blood but also on junk, power, knowledge, seduction, and on evil itself. Unlike *Interview with the Vampire*, which pays only lip service to its first-person narration, *The Addiction* presents the vampire's as the *only* subjectivity. 'Tell me to leave you alone. Tell me with authority,' says the vampire to her victim, but she might as well be talking to us. If we don't withdraw we risk becoming complicit with her point of view. And if we don't quite grasp the seriousness of the situation – how close we are to being dominated, possessed even, by 'the other' – it's because Ferrara is expert at using parody to keep us off guard. After all, who could fall for a vampire who mangles her Husserl with her Nietzsche?

For all its blood-letting, *Interview with the Vampire* keeps the undead at a safe distance, removed to a faux nineteenth century and sheathed in big-budget respectability. *Nadja* and *The Addiction* let us know that vampires are here and they are us.

EDUARDO PAOLOZZI'S MACHINE DREAMS

Christopher Frayling

Sculptor, print-maker and graphic artist Sir Eduardo Paolozzi has said of his work that 'art is a long word which can be stretched'. 'The interesting thing,' he has added, 'is that one comes back to original obsessions, or perhaps the original obsession always lies under the surface … parts of an experience which is previous work pressing through.' One of Paolozzi's most enduring obsessions – from his earliest collages dating from 1946, via his portrait sculptures, to his huge public art projects of the 1980s – has been with the robot and the automaton. His work has referred, again and again, to Vaucanson's digesting duck, a mechanical cow, the metallic Maria from Lang's *Metropolis*, Robby the Robot from Fred Wilcox's *Forbidden Planet* (who was used, in person as it were, as part of the 'This is Tomorrow' exhibition of 1956), tin robot toys from Japan and latterly, Sebastian's replicant workshop from Ridley Scott's *Blade Runner*.

* * *

Christopher Frayling: Where does this fascination with robots – especially with human bodies which transmute into machines, and vice versa – come from?

Eduardo Paolozzi: I think a lot of it comes from the early days of childhood. I mean, every child – may I say, particularly if you are a boy – is involved with machines. In my era you started off with aeroplanes and motor cars and even railway engines. It's part of one's childhood to draw these things, so there's all that kind of world rather than the artist's concern with the portrait or the landscape or the still-life. It has been an endless fascination for me to think of robots as a kind of metaphor: the mechanical man. In a strange way, without quoting Mary Shelley, it might, when I was young, have been like a taboo world. Being brought up as a Christian, they would much rather you drew Christian subjects: the fact that you were drawing a mechanical man was almost as if you were making the man yourself. A deep theme.

Christopher Frayling: Like the Futurists' celebration of technology, in Italy?

Eduardo Paolozzi: Also a symbol of modernism, in a sense. A kind of existence which couldn't have happened in the past. A new history. And you are making a kind of identity for yourself, a mechanical identity. In the mid-1920s and 1930s, it fascinated a whole culture – all those World's Fairs had robots, it was a fever of the time. Like Einstein in New York and the craze for relativity.

Christopher Frayling: What was your first experience of robots in cinema?

Eduardo Paolozzi: Gog and Magog must have been very early. I didn't see the early classic ones – *The Golem, Metropolis* – until much later. *Metropolis* wasn't available in Scotland when I was young. I think I saw *Just Imagine*, a musical which included a vision of New York of the future. Certainly popular magazines like *Modern*

Mechanix all had robots and there were the serial and popular literature robots – the awful ones you might find in Abbott and Costello or the Three Stooges, made out of painted cardboard. They were still quite convincing, though.

Christopher Frayling: Even in your early collages, you have B52 bombers and human heads put next to each other: you are already exploring the visual connections between machines and people. There are Arcimboldo-style heads made up of cogwheels and mass-produced consumer goods rather than fruit.

Eduardo Paolozzi: That's right. That was after I had gone through Edinburgh College of Art and the Slade and it was like clawing back my childhood, going back to things I could identify with. Making a face out of bits of motor cars seemed much more my cup of tea than trying to draw in the style of Vuillard.

Christopher Frayling: Presumably a lot of your contemporaries were doing 'still-life with wine bottle and a piece of Camembert' while you were turning to industrial imagery.

Eduardo Paolozzi: Exactly. But going back to these things was helped by going to Paris after the Slade and seeing the Dada magazines and even the Surrealist journal *Minotaure*, which renewed one's faith in bad movies and bad photographs. There was a tremendous white-collar disdain in England for B movies – the same kind of disdain as prevented people from shopping in Woolworths – and a horror of going near flea-pits. In fact, London was full of flea-pits showing flea-pit type films – within walking distance of the Slade there was the Tolmer, which showed all kinds of interesting films. But a lot of these cinemas were dependent on the local housing, on the estate people who lived nearby. Bethnal Green had flea-pits which showed American adventure films to people who were not particularly interested in books.

Christopher Frayling: The kinds of cinematic robots which have got to you seem to be very different. If you compare the serial robots of the 1930s with Robby in *Forbidden Planet*, which opened in London in June 1956, the mechanical man has changed his meaning. Robby is like a consumer's dream, a walking, talking all-electric kitchen. Some critics writing about your work of this period have called it 'the aesthetics of plenty' – the view from austere England of all those well-stocked fridges and consumer goodies on the other side of the Atlantic.

Eduardo Paolozzi: *Forbidden Planet* was a beautifully made film in CinemaScope. It had that MGM gloss, and the same kind of palette as *National Geographic* Magazine – pale lavenders and blues and greys – beautiful colouring for the planet. Hollywood at that time had wound itself up like a beautifully made music box – great set-designers and craftsmen and orchestras, with a curious harmony about it all. This was before the decline of a wonderful *industry* – except that it has all been revived now by the special effects studios which have taken over. But there was a time in the late 60s when the decline seemed quite serious. Television had taken over.

Christopher Frayling: What was it about Robby that earned him a place in the Whitechapel Gallery?

Eduardo Paolozzi: He was a wonderful piece of humanoid machinery and he was also a gentle, nice creature with a friendly relationship with Anne Francis, who played the Miranda figure. Gentle, helpful and indestructible. He was so popular he spawned a sequel, teaming up a year later with a little Sears Roebuck boy in *The*

Invisible Boy. I think Robby was a reflection of the idea of innocence in Hollywood – the innocence of Frank Capra's films, for example. When there was still good and bad. Like when Korda was trying to enter the American market. *The Thief of Bagdad*, which was one of John Kobal's favourite films, is a wonderful use of cinema to tell a lovely, elaborate, almost Arthur Rackham fairy story. But after Robby, the robot starts to get more sinister and evil, which is a reflection of novels of the time, which were more critical of society. It's the world of Burt Lancaster and Tony Curtis and *The Sweet Smell of Success*, where you start to get psychological penetration. There's some of this in *Forbidden Planet*, too, with the Prospero figure whose greatest enemy is his own libido – the monster from his Id who is melting the steel door, the impregnable door.

Christopher Frayling: By the late 1960s, with *2001*, the concept of the robot has become much more problematic, much darker, as in the battle of wits between the astronaut and the computer HAL over who is to control the spaceship.

Eduardo Paolozzi: I think for the modern child the notion of the computer has taken over from the idea of 'things being put together'. I don't think the idea of the mechanical man fascinates people so much. Kids still enjoy the serials I saw – *Flash Gordon* and so on – which are full of innocence: when they are travelling through space they are all standing there holding on to the steering wheel. The whole American idea of the robot begins with the influence of Europe on American literature, then there is a magic point when the genre starts to become all-American. You could never do serials like that in England, nor could you have made pulp magazines like the ones I read; there's a kind of industrialisation of the imagination in America. An English film-maker could never have created Robby the Robot. The wonderful American magazines called *Popular Mechanics* were full of American know-how and a belief in modernity, and the robot runs right through that. *Popular Mechanics* and *The Wizard of Oz*: with the Tin Man, there is a whiff of the fact that small American towns had to have a blacksmith and a hardware store – all that world of *Oklahoma!* and *Carousel*. The robot became as American as apple pie. I'm skipping around the idea not only of the differences between American culture and English culture in the 30s – that hybrid culture I grew up in – but also the degree of industrialisation in America, with mechanisation taking command, which led to an overflowing of energy back into Europe.

Christopher Frayling: Not just to Europe, I remember we both went into a huge toy shop in Tokyo a few years ago, and in the corner was a glass case full of tin robots – many of them Robby clones. A museum of the mechanical man.

Eduardo Paolozzi: Way back in 1971 I did a print called B.A.S.H., which has a mechanical robot going 'ha, ha'. And that was from a *Japanese* source. The Japanese seemed to go crazy about robots, and in the end made more tin robots than the Americans. Very bizarre. I bought a lot of them, and they are now in the V&A in the *Krazy Kat Archive*, where they share space with the American pulps and science fiction books of the 30s with their wonderful covers and drawings. With the Americans at that time, the robot became part of popular imagery, almost part of folkcraft, like the Tin Man. At the New York World's Fair in 1939, for the General Motors tyre division, they had an incredibly expensive robot just pushing its foot up and down on a rubber tyre. I don't think it would catch people now – the modern version would have 25 television screens all doing different things, computer controlled. Then between these images, or metaphors, you have wonderful hybrids like *Star Wars*, which has an image I just love – the crazy bar, with its semi-mechanistic wall decoration. Pure comic-strip – robots, animals, humans and machines. Layers and layers of iconography.

Christopher Frayling: An artificial environment, with artificial people in it. And in walks a clean-cut American actor.

Eduardo Paolozzi: In the print *B.A.S.H.* I have a robot together with an image out of *Scientific American* of a monkey from an animal experiment who is behind a big metal sheet which looks like a mask. The monkey's eyes stare through the mask, and its hand comes out from behind it. If one is thinking of robots, one might also be thinking of artificiality: in the same print, there is a Marilyn Monroe with her skirt blown by the updraft from the New York subway which came out of the Hollywood wax museum, the best wax museum I've ever seen. There's also a smiling Jack Kennedy who comes from the same place. In the print is this idea of the American way of making icons – and that's a form of artificiality too. A little after *B.A.S.H.* I did a series of prints for Olivetti called *Science and Fantasy in the Technological World* where in almost every print there is a Robby or some metal vertebrae, sometimes with a kind of dreamed-up space girl, and beside them the architecture of nuclear installations or of TWA aeroplanes. And sometimes there is a boy of yesterday standing in wonder at it all or dreaming in his bedroom. There's some *Lost in Space* as well, and American airmen in their survival suits, who are becoming semi-robotic in order to survive. There are animals, too, but they are the real thing because scientists practised what happens when you go into outer space by using animals because they didn't know what would happen to humans.

Christopher Frayling: In some of your 'Science and Fantasy' images, the robot looks like a sexual predator or a fantasy figure of that kind. And at the entrance of the 'This is Tomorrow' exhibition, the friendly and amiable Robby was redrawn for a poster as a bug-eyed monster carrying off a hapless blonde B-movie actress, King Kong style. In the introduction to your 'Science' portfolio you wrote that 'the schism that separates Space Age Engineering, technical photography, film-making and types of street art from fine art activities is for many people/artists unbridgeable.' Evidently for you, though, these images of automation had already become absorbed into your visual language.

Eduardo Paolozzi: Yes – and the morality of the robot has certainly altered since then. There's a shop called Forbidden Planet where you get these horrible machines which look like something from Dungeons and Dragons – monsters used for counters in games, from a grotesque world of four-headed giants with clubs. And there are strange parallels and crossovers: there are also kits of Japanese mechanical robots and variations on *The Terminator* made by little workshops in Enfield and Essex, cottage industries of people putting together variations for an insatiable market. A rich mix: a *Terminator* model with layers of other cultures as well – a medieval skull, mechanistic parts, some genetic engineering. This is an image people understand now. Robby is nice, but this is indestructible and nasty, like some devil worked by electronic magic.

Christopher Frayling: When we went to see *Blade Runner*, the sequence that struck you most forcibly was the one where the replicant-maker J. F. Sebastian first enters his workshop. As he arrives, a three-foot-high Kaiser Wilhelm figure with a mouth clamp marches forward, saying 'home again, home again, jiggidy jig'. There are bits of replicants lying around in the background, too. You turned to me and said, 'That's just like my studio.'

Eduardo Paolozzi: It's true. The events in that film are so full of paradoxes. Although it's the future, you've somehow got the world of Raymond Chandler. I think that was very perceptive – much more convincing than the H. G. Wells kind of modernism in *Things to Come*, with its age of innocence and idea of a Brave New World and that incredible speech about technological optimism as the rocketship takes off; as Norah's Ark leaves the earth. There's something about the confidence of the American rich in that film, although it's superimposed on an English set of ethics and hierarchy. The Americans were getting muscular enough to assume that their morality was superior to that of the Europeans, as in that debate between the American and the 'little man' of Europe.

Where *Blade Runner* is concerned, there was recently a very complex TV film on Philip K. Dick. I hadn't realised until then that he was, I think, a genuinely tortured psychotic. It really comes through in the film transcription of his book – a tortured man with immense imagination and knowledge. You know in the first few minutes of *Blade Runner* that you are going to be absorbed: the flames belching out of those chimneys hundreds of feet up and the endless cityscape through the pollution. And the strong moments: the one at the end when the replicant could have destroyed the detective, but he has that flash of humanity; the strange *gloss* on the girl who is dressed in that 30s outfit like a walking mannequin; the private detective who wears mid-west, *Northern Exposure* clothes. Running through it, there is this unpredictability. The way violence is portrayed is extraordinary and quite theatrical: as theatrical as you might find in a sequel to *Macbeth* or *The Changeling*. The pursuit of the snake-woman, which I thought was a brilliant piece of cinematic cutting, also picked up on some ancient and archaic threads: I mean, she was a goddess who had the power to destroy, like Medusa. Her end is beautifully choreographed – where this superb goddess crashes through a series of plate-glass windows surrounded by flashing neon signs. It's like something you would expect in some ancient tale: the snake-woman destroyed.

Christopher Frayling: *Blade Runner* has a lot of *Metropolis*, which in turn is full of references to ancient myths. There's the mouth of Moloch, swallowing the underground workers and of course the creation of the robot Maria in Rotwang's laboratory. In your collection of prints 'General Dynamic Fun', 1970, the image called *20 Traumatic Twinges* is of the mechanical Maria standing in front of the skyscrapers of the above-ground Metropolis.

Eduardo Paolozzi: It's a 60s kind of sketchbook of images we love, images we treasure and images the younger generation might not have heard of. The Independent Group exhibitions were all about the counter-play of images against each other, of which the robotic image was an important one. All these images, like back-up X-rays, were a kind of footfall. They still fascinate me, and in a strange way they still fascinate the public, although the boyish enthusiasm of the 50s has turned into something more reflective. Take *Robocop*, where the perfect policeman is in fact mostly a machine. It's an illusion, but people might suggest that things are going that way.

Christopher Frayling: We've come a long way since the mid-50s, when Ernie the premium-bond random-number robot was introduced, and automation was seen as a lot of fun. In *Robocop*, automation – plus surgery – is digitalised, and the story revolves around which corporate group can control it for its own selfish ends. In one sequence, a law-enforcement robot is tested out in front of the corporate bosses, and the demonstration turns into a massacre. As the robot tries to get up the stairs, in a later sequence, I thought 'there's a Paolozzi in action.' Your lifetime's fascination seems to have been picked up by the movie-makers; Paolozzi robots have turned into movie robots and the circle is complete.

Eduardo Paolozzi: Absolutely.

A SUMMER PLACE, ON THE BEACH, BEYOND THE SEA

Howard Waldrop

In my 13-year-old mind, it was all tied together: a movie I didn't see for 40 years, and its theme song; a movie everyone saw; and a song by an Italo-American lounge lizard. By the time you finish this article, it'll all be inseparable in your mind, too. Or, maybe, my confusion will have been made more real and logical-like to you, and I will get to live out my rapidly approaching 'golden years' without benefit of tastefully barred windows and supervised outings to the therapeutic trout pond...

The short version: the movie I didn't see (till last night) was *A Summer Place*. It was 1959 and you could not go anywhere without 'Theme from *A Summer Place*' by Percy Faith and His Orchestra playing; on the radio, at the municipal swimming pool, every prom and party, every jukebox (the record sold 9 jillion give or take a bazillion copies).

The movie me and everyone saw was *On the Beach*: I had my first date to see it (Linda Rodden, where are you now?). Among other things, it showed the world would end in 1964... ('Welcome to the future, kid' as Gahan Wilson would later say in the comic strip *Nuts*.)

The other song that played everywhere that year, when 'Theme from *A Summer Place*' wasn't playing and poking melodic holes in the air, was Bobby Darin's version of 'Beyond the Sea'.

Stick with me: I lived it, you only have to read about it.

*   *   *

A Summer Place. A movie with Richard Egan, Dorothy McGuire, Arthur Kennedy, Troy Donahue and Sandra Dee. Everybody was talking about it (over the theme music played everywhere): I mean everybody. It was adapted and directed by Delmer Daves from a Sloan (*Man in the Grey-Flannel Suit*) Wilson middlebrow novel. The movie is jam-packed with adultery, alcoholism, passion, pre-marital sex and teen pregnancy, divorce scandal, repression and a Frank Lloyd Wright house: in other words, 1959 in a nutshell. Plus, it had a great Max Steiner score, with the aforementioned theme. (He went from *King Kong*, which figures heavily in a dialogue section of *A Summer Place*, to *Casablanca* to this in only 26 years...)

All my friends went with their older brothers and sisters and their girlfriends and boyfriends to see it at the drive-in. Me? My parents worked two jobs each all the time; the Arlington Theater wouldn't let kids in unless they paid the full adult price (and 65 cents was more money than I saw in three weeks, unless it was summer – it wasn't and I was mowing 100' x 200' yards for a buck-fifty a time...). So, as was my wont, I grilled all my friends (and some pretty much total strangers at school) for details. They made it sound a lot hotter than it seemed to be as I watched it on tape last night. (Although, for 1959, it's cranked pretty high, you do not, as my friends implied, Get To See The Whole Thing...)

So, it was the year of 'Theme from *A Summer Place*', also *On the Beach* (more later). And 'Beyond the Sea'.

*   *   *

The Bobby Darin song had, to me, the same haunting melancholy as Nevil Shute's novel, and Stanley Kramer's movie made from it. (Give me a break, I was a kid. Or guy. Mannish boy. Teenager in love. With death, and the atomic bomb, at least. Joe Dante's film *Matinee*, set during the Cuban Missile Crisis of 1962, has some of that same fatalistic melancholy feel, and is at the same time hilarious, and has some deep insight into the times... his time, my time.)

In 'Beyond the Sea', there's this guy, looking out towards the ocean, singing about the love he knows is there, but has left. Over the horizon, but close, and on the way. I saw Darin staring out into that same irradiated air of the West Coast of the US from *On the Beach*.

Darin sings of his love, across the ocean, knowing, just knowing, they'll meet again...

I mean, this is the Bobby Darin of the *Ed Sullivan Show* – Vegas days, before his 'If I Was A Carpenter' – relevant days...

It's all tied together, the movies and the songs.

I've had the words to 'Waltzing Matilda' (the theme song adapted for *On the Beach*) in every wallet I've owned from the time I was 13, clipped out of a magazine article (*Life*) about the Kramer film.

The words are by A. B. (Banjo) Paterson, the unofficial poet laureate of the Land Down Under (most of his work reads like a mix of Rudyard Kipling and Robert W. Service). I was in Perth, Australia, in January of 1997, as guest-of-honour at Swancon, a science fiction convention, on Australia Day. I was on a panel at 2 p.m. when suddenly, everybody at the convention came into the room and they all sang 'Waltzing Matilda' to me. I was moved beyond tears.

The words and music to 'Beyond the Sea' are by a Frenchman, Charles Trenet (its original title is 'La Mer'); the English words are by Jack Lawrence. Though it became a big hit in 1959, the year of *A Summer Place* and *On the Beach*, it was written in 1945, the year of Hiroshima and Nagasaki.

And it wasn't just me, evidently, caught up in this swirling maelstrom of aural and visual emotion, connections and resonances. A year later, Bobby Darin of 'Beyond the Sea' married Sandra Dee of *A Summer Place*.

I started early, being the avatar of the zeitgeist.

∗   ∗   ∗

On the Beach was released late in 1959.

There's been either World War III or some accident that led to the mutual exchange of atomic and hydrogen bombs, and the Northern Hemisphere is devoid of life. The radioactive cloud is drifting south, across the equatorial calms, and Australia and the rest of the Southern Hemisphere awaits its turn.

The movie opens with the USS *Sawfish* nuclear submarine entering an Australian harbour. It's been heading southward since whatever happened happened, and it's commanded by Dwight Towers (Gregory Peck). We meet the rest of the cast of characters: there's Anthony Perkins playing an Aussie naval lieutenant; Moira Davidson (Ava Gardner) as a good-time woman who knows and feels a lot more than she lets on; Julian (Fred Astaire), an embittered nuclear physicist whose hobby is racing dangerous cars (there's a lot more about this character in the novel than the movie); there's Donna Anderson as Perkins's young wife and they've just had a baby. There are lots of finely realised character bits: two old guys at a stuffy club trying to drink up all the fine wines before they're wasted on the dead; an Australian admiral and his aide; a really good bit by an actor, playing a doctor, late in the movie as the first symptoms of radiation sickness show up.

These people await the end of life on Earth in the bright Australian sun; what they do with the time left makes up the movie.

Half-way through, the *Sawfish* goes back to the West Coast of the US. There's a theory some of the radioactivity may have been washed from the air by winter rains, which proves to be wrong, and there have been messages, received in Australia, on the short-wave in Morse code, mostly gibberish, from somewhere near San Diego, that may indicate survivors, possibly children.

The only full words that have come through so far are 'water' and 'connect'. (Shades of E. M. Forster. The title of Shute's novel and the movie are from T. S. Eliot's 'The Hollow Men', the one that ends 'not with a bang but a whimper'.)

The messages, it turns out when a sailor in a CIMP suit leaves the sub to explore – it's at a refinery, the generators are still going – are caused by a Coke bottle, caught in the pull-ring of a window shade, blowing in the wind so that the neck of the bottle occasionally touches a live telegraph key.

It's a great scene. It was in 1959; it still is.

Just a little earlier, one of the crewmen had deserted when the sub was off his home town, San Francisco. In one of those bits of reverse casting, there's A. Perkins playing an Australian, while Aussie John Meillon is the Californian (he's Mike's pal in the

Crocodile Dundee movies made in the 1980s). There's a scene where the sub rises to conning-tower depth and Peck talks to him through the loudspeaker next morning, while he's fishing. All the fish are dead by this time, too. It's too late to take him back in; he'll be dead in a few days. They have a conversation that says much of what the movie was trying to say: it all comes down to people.

There are things wrong with the movie: it was, after all, a Stanley Kramer Film. Everybody's stiff-upper-lip, even though these are supposed to be 1964 Aussies and Americans. There are no riots, no ghost dances in the streets, no bonfires of money and vanities. (The closest we get is the Grand Prix of Australia, where there are crashes galore – it doesn't matter, they're all going to be dead in a few weeks anyway – that Julian, the Astaire character, wins.) Everything's keyed so low that Donna Anderson's breakdown (packing for a trip to the England that no longer exists, instead of facing the inevitability of death, or suicide by Government Prescription #24768, which she'll also have to give the baby with its milk) seems out of place, as if the character is pitched too high for the movie she's in.

There's a great deal of quiet heartbreak in the film; instead of Dwight sliding it into Moira at first invitation, he holds out some hope that his family is still alive in Mystic, Connecticut. He's got a BB gun on the sub for his son, which would have been a belated Christmas present, if the duty tour had not been interrupted by World War III.

Dwight and Moira start the big kiss and become lovers, in a mountain resort, among drunken revellers at a disastrous early-opening trout season, in a rainstorm. Drunks are singing in other rooms, at the pub downstairs, everywhere. The scene is a great one (despite what Bill Warren, a man I admire inordinately, says in his entry on the movie in *Keep Watching the Skies*). The drunks are singing 'Waltzing Matilda', endlessly and off-key; a window blows open, rain comes in; the couple jump up to close it, touch, and, as they kiss, and the camera (which has been still as a stump for most of the movie) swirls around them in a 360° circle, the voices downstairs turn into a single smooth baritone, who sings the final verse of the song perfectly, with its line 'you'll never catch me alive, says he'...

The things which work in the movie really work: cheerful resignation; small grumblings about how nuclear war plays hell with the cricket and fishing seasons; people going through motions they always have (when Dwight returns from the futile Coke bottle-telegraph mission, he comes across a field Moira and her father are ploughing, sowing a crop that will never be harvested). Julian, who helped invent the hydrogen bomb, only wants to live long enough to run in the Grand Prix of Australia; when it is time for everyone to die, he closes up his garage, climbs behind the wheel of the machine and guns the motor, thick clouds of exhaust (and carbon monoxide) rising around him; he's made a very personal choice of how he wants to go. There are endless lines of people waiting to receive the suicide pills, like people getting swine flu shots or the polio vaccine, while the Salvation Army, under the giant banner 'There Is Still Time, Brother', plays endlessly to thinner and thinner crowds.

The butler at the gentlemen's club, all gentlemen gone forever, brings himself a drink and starts to play billiards. The lights go out. We assume nobody's running them anymore, either.

After the Perkins, Anderson and Astaire characters are gone, the only actors left are

Gardner and Peck. She, Moira, already fevered and throwing up, on the beach, watching the *Sawfish* sail away, scarf blowing in the wind, beside her car, which she's taken out for the last time; he, Towers, takes one last look at the noon sun and goes down the hatch; the *Sawfish* submerges (a reverse of the opening) on its last trip back to America so the crew can die there. There's a cut to all the major cities of the world deserted, a few newspapers blowing in the streets, no movement anywhere except that from the radioactive wind. The movie ends with three close-ups of the Salvation Army banner in Australia.

*   *   *

What all this has to do with is the same feeling Darin got in 'Beyond the Sea'. It's like, in the old French phrase, nostalgia for the future. In this case, a future closed off to all the possibilities. An imagined future, without anyone around to imagine it, like thoughts hanging in the air.

On the Beach can almost make you see and feel and yearn for it; for the story to go on after everyone's gone.

I had my first date to go see *On the Beach*; this was the future waiting for me, for everyone my age, for everyone everywhere. Only five years away, maybe, said the movie. Or less...

Or more. It's 40 years later now; we're still here, lots of us.

It was a future we didn't have to live, because someone imagined it for us; had shown us the face of extinction (without mutants, without showing a single bomb going off, without fights with someone over a can of beans, without fuss and bother, not with a bang: but not exactly a whimper, either).

And the music tied it all together. 1959–60 was the year of 'Theme from *A Summer Place*' and 'Waltzing Matilda'. And as Bobby Darin married Sandra Dee, so were alpha and omega linked: a movie about the end of the world and a song written at the very start of the Atomic Age.

Now, it all doesn't seem so dumb, does it?

Fight Club (David Fincher, 1999)

Section 2:
Films

Though genre is cyclical, and often makes sense when considered in terms of groupings and clutches rather than individual films, there are also tentpoles – films which stand out in the crowd. They might gain their position through commercial and/or critical success, instant or long-term influence on other film-makers, a lucky shot that hits precisely the zeitgeist (who could have foreseen *The Blair Witch Project*, 1999), or even obvious artistic achievement. This section considers those films, whether classic (i.e.: made before 1991, though that's not a definition which will have much currency outside this book) or modern (i.e.: released during the lifetime of the current incarnation of *Sight and Sound*).

While reviewing what came out this week could as easily be called 'viewing', the writers here literally review – going back to look again at a film that has already been written about by dozens of others, been through its commercial run and settled into its place in the history of cinema and of its creators. Films like *It's a Wonderful Life* (or *'It's a Wonderful Life'*, as Jonathan Romney insists), *Blade Runner* and *Psycho* have been the subject of whole books (single-author studies, collections of essays, in-depth making-ofs) and almost drowned under printer's ink. Often, a first reaction to articles like these is 'What, again?' But these films wouldn't have attained their status if there weren't many things to say about them.

Many films we take seriously now were unpopular with audiences and critics on their original release, but eventually make it into the pantheon because their qualities become obvious with the passing years. When a commercial flop is remade as a bank or jeans commercial, it has entered if not the zeitgeist then at least the video collections of ad execs. Some attract small, devoted audiences and become so-called 'cult movies', like *Blade Runner* (if everybody who now rates it as a masterpiece paid for a ticket on its original release it wouldn't have flopped), *Les yeux sans visage* (a pulp-poetic effort from an art-inclined director working for a change in a commercial frame) *Peeping Tom* (a career-killer for Michael Powell) or *Night of the Hunter* (its reception was so bad that Charles Laughton never directed another movie). There are even back doors to mainstream appeal: the Capra film became an institution through the copyright quirk of falling into the public domain and becoming a staple of US TV stations around Christmas.

Of the contemporary films discussed here, *The Rapture*, *Lost Highway* and *Wisconsin Death Trap* were scarcely box-office blockbusters. *Wisconsin Death Trap* played a week at the National Film Theatre, not even enough of a release to qualify it for a regular *Sight and Sound* review. *Fight Club* was widely perceived as a commercial disappointment, though its box-office returns strike me as surprisingly respectable for such an extreme work. They may in time accrue cults of their own: *The Rapture* and *Fight Club*, which are about cults, are well on their way . Delving into dark matters is a risky business, and homing in on subjects audiences don't realise they're afraid of yet is not always a winning proposition. These films, arguably tangential to genre, strike me as looking a lot like what the horror films of the 2010s might be.

Also here are movies everyone saw when they came out, box-office hits from major directors, based on popular novels, with big stars – *Psycho, Rosemary's Baby, Don't Look Now* (which is based on a story called 'Don't Look Now'). Not all high-profile horror or s-f films last (when was the last time you read an article on *Willard*, 1970, or *Superman – the Movie*, 1978). These three may owe their continuing high profile to interest in the work of their directors as much as for the now-passé once-cutting edge sexual, horrific or theological content. Interestingly, the commentators here choose mostly to write about the films as films, not building blocks in the reputations of Hitchcock, Polanski and Roeg. We were intrigued by these films because of their stories, and the fears they tapped into – not because of their pedigree.

My article on *The Curse of the Cat People* should be considered an addendum (or sequel) to the BFI Classic I wrote about *Cat People* (1942). The films were re-released on a double bill at about the time the book came out, and I thought it made sense to do a sort of mini-BFI Classic on the often-overlooked sequel. Its representation here in juxtaposition with David Thomson's piece on *Night of the Hunter* and, in the 'People and Stories' section, my look at 'The Legend of Sleepy Hollow', illuminates the connections between films that come out of a terror-in-childhood tradition and a specific American locale.

BLADE RUNNER: TELLING THE DIFFERENCE

Philip Strick

Accidentally rediscovered, so the story goes, when the wrong print was sent from the Warner archives to a Beverly Hills cinema, the original 'director's cut' of *Blade Runner* went on to break the house record during a special San Francisco re-run in October 1991. Audiences were reported to be delighted by the film's soundtrack, no longer cluttered with an intrusive voiceover, and by the 'symphonic strings' which were said to have replaced the 'jarring' compositions of Vangelis. Encouraged by such enthusiasm, Warner Bros announced an international relaunch of the film. This was to be the director's re-cut of his own version and would incorporate a dream sequence and a new, bleaker ending.

The promise of a revitalised *Blade Runner*, fuelled by rumours of extra footage, has prepared the way for a gala show at the London Film Festival and nationwide exposure to follow. What is to be revealed at these screenings, however, unless the Warner vaults contain further variants not yet shown to the press, is a distinctly and splendidly familiar, if slightly abbreviated *Blade Runner*. The only obvious differences from the form in which we have known it for the past decade are that it has been shorn of its narration, cropped of its ending and enhanced by the glimpse of a unicorn. Happily, the Vangelis score remains intact.

Arguments over which version we should prefer of such phenomena as *Lawrence of Arabia, Fatal Attraction, Aliens,* or *Hear My Song*, are mischievously nurtured by the video market, which has everything to gain from selling a title several times over. Certainly the claim that a film should be seen as its director intended offers a reasonably reliable principle, but it makes no allowance for the possibility that the director might have had second thoughts or not enough thoughts in the first place, or was several directors plus a producer, or has simply been misreported. In practice, it seems sensible to judge each version of a work in isolation, disregarding what it was 'supposed' to be: the only useful criterion is whether it functions efficiently in its existing form. But things aren't so easy. The knowledge of alternative footage creates distractions, affecting our response to what we see. How is it possible, having once watched Cameron's deleted episode of a space-colonist family under attack, to recall *Aliens* without it? How do we now judge *Pat Garrett and Billy the Kid* in any version which omits the grim introduction – added years later – in which Garrett is ambushed? Or *Andrei Rublev*, without the recently restored balloon sequence?

Adding to the confusion, the press kit for *Blade Runner* describes the original ending to the film (now deleted) as the 'chase-and-escape' version, a poor label for the sequence as filmed and edited, with its soaring aerial shots, untroubled landscapes, and promise of at least temporary release. Surely the whole point of *that* ending was that the lovers would *not* be hunted down, that they were gambling on a reasonable life span of hard-won contentment far beyond city limits? The idea of the 'chase', in fact, came from the shooting script – in its penultimate form – in which the rival blade runner Gaff (Edward James Olmos) was to be shown hot on the heels of the fleeing couple. It never happened, and now the panoramic aerial shots, a startling burst of space and sunlight and relief, don't happen either. 'I was never quite comfortable with that,' explains Scott. So in the 'director's cut', the two exiles leave their apartment and retreat into an abrupt darkness, their prospects cruelly curtailed. Ringing in their ears and ours is an unwelcome repeat of Gaff's parting shot: 'It's too bad she won't live – but then again, who does?'

The curious effect of this premature conclusion is not only that it leaves us to make our own guesses, but also that it gives Gaff the last word, along with almost the final image, the tiny tinfoil unicorn. Previously dismissed (by way of the commentary) as a signal that the snooping cop has generously allowed his prey to survive, this discarded scrap suddenly acquires a heightened significance, given the film's other main interpolation, a 'living' unicorn. Arriving as Deckard dreams listlessly by his piano just before analysing one of the replicant snapshots, the unexplained (and unscripted) image of a unicorn galloping through misty woodland has no obvious link with anything. The shot was lifted from *Legend* (Scott's next film after *Blade Runner*), whose opening titles explain that 'light is harboured in the souls of unicorns ... They can only be found by the purest of mortals.' In the *Blade Runner* context, its main implication is that Deckard, who has hitherto shown little inclination towards the poetic, is again drinking too hard or has taken leave of his senses.

More kindly interpreted, the vision might hint at a quest of which Deckard is only faintly aware – the hunt for a fabled beast that might be the replicant superbeing, might be himself, or might be his own elusive past, pictured in fragmentary poses across the piano top. As the moment passes, we can only leave it there, particularly as the process of exploring the discovered photograph for clues remains the most fascinating piece of cinematic detection since *Blow-up*. But with the linking of the unicorn to Gaff, several new implications are on offer. Is the surviving replicant, Rachael, now the love of Deckard's life, being likened to the unicorn, and, in keeping with this emblematic symbol, being doomed to regal extinction? The shooting script describes the tinfoil figure as 'Gaff's gauntlet', but while it could indeed be the sort of challenge to which Scott's duellists would briskly respond, it hints more of collusion than of malice – and collusion of a notably perceptive kind.

How would Gaff be aware that Deckard has, in his time (and ours), dreamed of unicorns? It could, of course, be mere coincidence. Gaff's other sculpted contributions to the case have been a paper-tissue chicken and a well-endowed matchstick man, and if these, too, are supposed to be symbolic (other than, at best, not inappropriate), we would have inexhaustible material for unhelpful speculation. What they do establish, incontrovertibly, is that Gaff is a model-maker like Chew (who makes eyeballs), Sebastian (who makes animated dolls) and Tyrell (who makes androids). A seedy but ambitious puppet-master, angling for promotion, Gaff haunts the edges of Deckard's life as if secretly in control of it. Playes by Olmos in satanic beard and uneasy contact lenses, he makes a chilly attendant who, like the android medical officer in Scott's *Alien*, knows and manipulates more than he will admit to.

What might be guessed from Gaff's presence, imagination running wild, is that he has Deckard's real identity at heart, that he knows Deckard's programming, and that Deckard, of course, is also a replicant. Admirers of Philip K. Dick, the science fiction writer whose novel *Do Androids Dream of Electric Sheep?* is closer to *Blade Runner* in spirit than his fans would generally like to acknowledge (the interrogation of Rachael, for example, has been transferred almost intact), cheerfully support this theory on the basis of Dick's conviction that *most* people are replicants and consequently unreliable, dangerous and pathetic. In their book, maybe even Gaff is a replicant – and why not? But in the affair of Deckard, the film offers more substantial clues, partly by accident and partly by design – and these have been subtly enhanced by the 'director's cut', unicorn and all.

The accident, which remains uncorrected in the film's new version and is becoming known as 'Ridley's deliberate mistake', throws into question exactly how many Nexus-6 replicants are at large in the streets of Los Angeles in 2019. Summoned to the office of his former boss Bryant (M. Emmet Walsh), the 'retired' blade runner (i.e. specialist in identifying and destroying illegal androids) is informed that, like it or not, he is back in service. Four replicants have arrived in the city – Pris, Zhora, Leon and their leader Roy Batty (Rutger Hauer) – and Deckard has to deal with them. Minutes later, Bryant describes how six replicants ('three male, three female') hi-jacked a space shuttle back to Earth, and one of these has since been killed during a break-in at the Tyrell Corporation headquarters. Which leaves five.

A look at the shooting script reveals that almost to the last moment of casting, the replicant team was to include another female, Mary. A sad, petulant figure decaying fast in the final stages of her four-year life span, she dies in Sebastian's apartment shortly before Deckard arrives for his battles with Pris and Roy. Raging at her fate, she has some splendid lines: "I hate this place – streets full of little people scurrying and wiggling. We weren't made for this ... We were made to be injured or wounded or slaughtered. We were meant to be torn apart by C-Beam-hits or burned up in Hydrogen fires." Of the group, it was to be Mary who gave the clearest picture of android existence, part slave, part conquistador, alongside Roy's melancholy boast: 'We've seen things you people wouldn't believe.' But Mary, too, never happened.

Instead, her ghost haunts *Blade Runner* in the shape of one replicant unaccounted for. And if we are to confine our reading of the film strictly to the information it provides, the 'missing' replicant conveniently suggests a hidden identity for Deckard, who, disconsolate and solitary, his family ties represented merely by an unreliable jumble of photographs, might indeed have only recently fallen to Earth. In casual confirmation, a glimpse of him beside Rachael, whose eyes shine with a metallic android gleam, shows his eyes, too, as reflective surfaces. Or is this just another minor error (like the incorrect serial number, the stuntperson in a wig, the unsynchronised interrogation of the snake-maker)? Nonsense, surely, that Deckard could be anything but human, with his long-established reputation as a blade runner and his obvious lack of the superhuman strength shown by his opponents? But the point is made that the replicants rely desperately on photographs to reinforce their 'memories', while Scott matches Deckard visually with both Leon (they are intercut in identical positions after Zhora's death) and Roy (they pause at the same time to repair their hands during the final confrontation). And with the disappearance of the commentary, Deckard is no longer able to talk his way out of suspicion.

Added as an afterthought following preview tests of *Blade Runner* in 1982, the commentary has always proved a controversial device. 'Both Harrison Ford and I objected to it,' says Scott, 'but it seemed to be required by the audience, so we put it in.' With its world-weary, dismissive tone, the narration has few defenders. The first reaction to the 'director's cut', however, by anyone already familiar with the film, is to replace the missing phrases from memory. More Spillane than Chandler, they conveyed – as in the hardboiled thrillers they dully echoed – a jaded reassurance in their use of the past tense, as if this vividly predestined future had already been assimilated into the past. Now that many of *Blade Runner*'s images are confirmed as very much a matter of the present, revisited by Scott himself for *Someone to Watch Over Me* and *Black Rain*, the words are fully superannuated. And yet they cling in our memory, whispers too strong to be ignored. 'All he wanted,' Deckard was once heard to say, 'were the same answers everybody else wanted. Where do I come from? Where am I going? How long have I got?' It was ungraciously delivered, but it certainly focused the attention.

Without his assurances in our ears, Deckard loses a definition; no longer in control of events, he experiences them at *our* speed. He becomes an ambiguous, uncertain stumbler, as vulnerable and desperate, as much a face in the crowd, as the (other?) androids. Since the narration told us little that is not covered by the opening title and then clarified by all subsequent dialogue, its deletion exposes its special weakness – that it explained nothing at all. For at least half the plot, in which Deckard has no part to play, it had no relevance. Without such distraction, the real strength of the film is that its images do the explaining. And while we may in hindsight be tempted to 'read' *Blade Runner* as a paraphrase by screenwriter David Peoples of his script for *Unforgiven* (veteran manhunter, bullied from retirement, shoots down undeserving fugitives), those images remain beyond words, a triumphant vindication of Scott's technique. They contain, too, the arguments that continue to perplex him – questions of seniority, of symmetry, of the ageing process, and of a compulsive struggle between darkness and light. 'What is light without dark?' cried his spectacular adversary in *Legend*, speaking from unicorn country for all replicants everywhere. 'I am a part of you all! You can never defeat me. We are brothers eternal.'

I AM A BELIEVER

Michael Eaton

Brothers and sisters, the time has come for me to make my testimony, to share with you my witness of an event which changed me for good and all. Only last year I was walking down Broadway with no direction to my life when I stopped before a movie house displaying a poster for *The Rapture*. Now friends, I have to confess that I had never heard the name of Michael Tolkin, believe me when I tell you I had not yet read his novel, *The Player*. I did not even know that it was Robert Altman's next movie – but then neither, to judge from the one other, loudly snoring, customer in that tiny downtown theatre, did anybody else in Manhattan. But something bigger than me drew me inside with a force I still do not understand and I thank Providence I was so drawn for I saw upon that screen something I was searching for and had expected never to find: an American film that takes religion at its word. When I came out into the pale light of an October evening I felt compelled to testify.

An overwhelming majority of the US population believes in the Christian God and a sizeable number of them subscribe to the doctrine that these are the Latter Days. Each one of them is a born-again semiotician, scouring the visible for evidence of the signs and wonders which, foretold in the (admittedly polysemic) Apocalypse of St John, precede the second coming of Jesus Christ, when the souls of the righteous will be taken to meet their Lord in the middle of the air. This event is known as the Rapture and there is a well-known painting, much reproduced on posters and postcards, which gives, in an effectively primitive style, a pictorial embodiment of this moment which all of the saved await with faith: a freeway running through a modern American city, flanked by tall buildings of glass and steel; presumably the Seventh Seal has just been broken, Gabriel's trumpet has sounded and the Lord has returned, because trucks, cars and motorbikes, previously piloted by the righteous, career destructively into hapless vehicles driven by we damned sinners who cast aside our chance at repentance but now are condemned to live through the thousand-year reign of the Anti-Christ. Eschatological specifics differ from group to group, but as anyone who has spent any time in the United States will tell you, this is a belief held throughout all classes and races and, seemingly, has little to do with the mainstream practices and ideologies of the various Protestant strands in Western Europe. (Which is why, incidentally, Tolkin's reference in his accompanying article to Bresson as a spiritual film-maker, despite a possible similarity in their unmoralising, undirective styles, is ultimately untenable.) Even the previous incumbent of the White House, we are told, determined his geo-political strategies via the Book of Revelations: Armageddon was not just a reality, it was a divine obligation, Gorbachev's birthmark was the mark of the Beast.

Perhaps the only sectors of society in which such doctrines are not axiomatic are the Jews, Communists and homosexual intellectuals who make up the Hollywood film community. On the evidence of the movies, we might think that America's metaphysics grants credence, on the one hand, to serial child killers who refuse to lie down when they're killed, or, in a rosier perspective, to sidetracked yuppies who can only re-centre once they've learned to embrace the innocent child within us all. The American film industry, in short, refuses to turn its gaze on the country's most widespread and insidious belief system: that fundamentalist Christianity which is the unofficial state religion. And this is why Michael Tolkin's film is so important.

When I was watching the movie, innocently unprepared by any of the advance publicity (of which, I guess, this piece has to be seen as an instance) I was entirely unable to fathom exactly where it was coming from until the very last scene, when all was made clear. To see it again a second time, or to have seen it prepped with a knowledge of Tolkin's other work or with the insights his accompanying article provide, would not re-create the scary frisson I felt living through my first viewing – for a moment there, I thought that somebody was trying to convert me, for a moment there I felt that I might be as unsafe in a picture house as I was out on the street.

It is not my purpose here to outline the plot of *The Rapture*; my role is only to urge you to see it because, unlike most movies, it is about something. However, it is necessary to say that a contributory reason to explain the uncomfortable viewing experience is that it is, to an extent, structured like a Christian film. Although Christianity is the dominant mental map of most Americans, Christian films remain sub-cultural. Occasionally, say in the pre-Vatican Two anti-socialist work of Leo McCarey, such as *Going My Way* or *Satan Never Sleeps*, the voice of the pulpit coincides with the screen, but Hollywood's religion has usually been of the sentimental feel-good variety which corresponds not a jot to the mystical terror of most believers' faith. Fundamentalist features, which bear many structural similarities to the official Chinese films made during the Cultural Revolution, in that their aim is to convert rather than to entertain, usually circulate not in cinemas, but in Mission Halls and evangelical gatherings. These are films which exist to show you the error of your ways, to bring you to God, and as such they are as highly structured as that moment in a camp meeting when one of the born-again is wheeled out to present their autobiographical witness, their testimony.

Invariably this involves a highly coloured and rather unbelievable elaboration of the witness's sinful and decadent lifestyle before they saw the light. (Somebody trying to convert me once told me how before he had met Jesus he had 'dabbled' with drugs. The reaction he had expected was one of shock, but unfortunately I could only express a connoisseur's interest: 'Which drugs?' I asked, 'Well ... illegal drugs!' was his unilluminating reply.) In *The Rapture*, we are forced to witness the degradation of Sharon's life as a 'swinger' – a life which, naturally, leaves her feeling only emptiness. Then, of course, at the end of Act One comes the moment of revelation – she accepts God.

The discomfort this film engendered in this seeker-after-truth is perhaps a result of the matter-of-fact way these scenes of sinning and repenting are presented. For example, there is nothing in the flat *mise-en-scène* which allows us the security of adopting a moral position towards Sharon's mundane foursome couplings. We may well be in the airless terrain of cheap pornography; we may well have stumbled into the wrong cinema. But when two besuited bicycling evangelists arrive at Sharon's apartment and convince her of the imminence of hell-fire, the presentation is equally uncontoured. I trust it is not simply because this is a writer's first outing at the helm that the film lacks the formal stridency which is the usual rhetoric of contemporary American cinema. For a while here we do not know how we are supposed to feel – it makes us as vulnerable as a potential convert.

The next step in the narrative of the conversion text is that belief doesn't come easy. Act Two is usually concerned with testing, possibly though the death of a loved one or by contracting some debilitating disease – this movement ends with a crisis of faith. In *The Rapture*, this stage of the tale is almost programmatic: Sharon's wonderful Christian home is shattered when her husband is murdered. Act Three you can write yourself. You know how it has to end: through the Slough of Despond and on to the Heavenly City.

Not so, my friends, in *The Rapture*.

The great shock of this film is that when Sharon (and it must be said here that one of the great delights of this picture is Mimi Rogers's entirely convincing performance) does receive a much awaited sign, she is told that it is hers alone, and therefore may well not be a gift of God, but a snare of Satan. At this point the film, which had hitherto been uncomfortable, spirals into brilliance, making all that has gone before retro-spectively brilliant – the allure of being one of the chosen runs headlong into the fear that belief is nothing more than paranoia.

During the course of *The Rapture* there are few arguments for and against fundamentalism which are not demonstrated honestly. Tolkin's strength is that he never belittles belief. Having seen the film for a second time, two questions remain: if God does exist, is He responsible for the idiocy of His believers? And, if it is His plan to crucify us on the internal contradictions of His wayward design, then who will forgive God's sins? Follow my path into the desert, friends: see this film.

Ecstatic States

Writer of *The Player*, Michael Tolkin reflects on directing his first movie, *The Rapture*

I was given the choice by *Sight and Sound* to write about 'either the shift from screenwriter or about the making of *The Rapture*, or about the subject of faith and the cinema'. Can we see if they connect?

The most difficult passage in the shift from screenwriter to director is the astonishing gift of responsibility, something that is more profoundly important than the lessons learnt about technical issues surrounding the translation of the written to be filmed. In some ways, it's probably easier to make the adjustment from novelist to director, since in the novelist's control over the lives of his characters, and his isolation from the world, there develops the kind of megalomania necessary to control a production. The screenwriter, accustomed to a life of serving various masters who will always betray him, has some advantage in his reservoir of rage, but most screenwriters (and I was typical) are innocent of the real struggles involved in making a film, and perhaps have traditionally been shielded from the battle, in order to protect them from making things too easy for the company. Once, late in the fourth or fifth day of night-shooting on The Rapture, I swore to myself that I would never again type 'EXT. LOCATION – NIGHT'. Most good shots have a little blood in them, and a writer should not know what he's asking of people.

A little of the movie's history. *The Rapture* began as a twenty-two page script for a short film. I was sick of screenwriting, *and The Player* was barely forty pages long, when I finished, for the first time in twelve years and six or seven scripts, my first screenplay without a writing partner. It was called *Cowboy Heaven*, and the story is pitched in *The Player*, or at least, in the novel. (Perhaps we should now call it the pre-novelisation.) It's a sweet story, and one of my last attempts at writing something directly for the studios. I was still trying to write for Spielberg. (There's talk now of finally getting it made, which doesn't completely thrill me, since in some ways *The Rapture* was my response to the *Cowboy Heaven*'s failure.)

When I finished *Cowboy Heaven* I took a drive in the Mojave, and saw a bumper sticker that said 'Warning, In Case Of Rapture, This Car Will Be Unmanned'. The driver of the car was a born-again Christian, and the bumper-sticker announced his faith in the imminent confirmation of Biblical prophecy, that he knows without doubt that these are the last days, and that before the Battle of Armageddon is fought on Earth, he will become spirit, transported, in an instant, into Heaven, to meet Christ in the air.

Sometime later that day I go stopped for speeding by a San Bernadino county sheriff, an Officer Foster, whose name and job are now in the movie, and then I continued on, in a terrible frenzy, driving around the high desert for three days, incapable of stopping anywhere for more than half an hour. When I got home, I threw myself into my office, and for a month literally beat myself around the head, trying to tease a few images into a story. For a long time I had carried a shelf full of ideas about movies, about religion, about California, and finally they had congealed into twenty-two pages.

When I was eleven I wrote a paper for a class assignment in which I said I wanted to be a director when I grew up. Now I was thirty-five, and I'd never looked through a camera, and I had these twenty-two weird pages. I showed the script to friends, family and a few studio executives, one of whom said that if I wanted any kind of career 'in this town', I should put the script in a drawer and never show it to anyone again. Fortunately, Nick Wechsler read it, and said there was no sense in making a short, and promised that if I could write a full-length feature, he would produce it and I would direct. Five years later, his promise was fulfilled.

On the first day of shooting I walked onto a set with a crew of forty-five, ten actors, sixty extras and four producers. We shot that day in a church, where a mysterious child, the Boy, tells Sharon (Mimi Rogers), that the call she hears, telling her to go to the desert, is hers alone, and she will have no company. (In my original draft, everyone went, but we didn't have it in the budget.) It was an amazing day, like skiing well, or like seeing the light after a long meditation. Every second sparkled with feeling. The privilege was overwhelming. I wanted to cry.

The next morning, I woke up calculating the cost to my life if I got on a plane to Baja California. After a night's rest, I was miserable, scared. Nothing the day before had gone really well. What was I doing? My wife had to coax me into my clothes, and out of the door, and into my car, and when I came to the location, a neighbourhood in Hollywood, for the exterior of Sharon's apartment, I sat in the car for fifteen minutes, afraid of everything. Finally I dragged myself to the set, where there was a problem with the camera, and we were three hours late getting our first shot, and by that time I was back in some control, but for another week those feelings of panic seldom left. Neither did the producers. Nick, Nancy Tanenbaum, Laurie Parker and Karen Koch were still there, telling me to fly, but staying in the nest.

After twelve days we arrived at the orgy, in which Sharon and Vic (Patrick Bauchau) take a couple of tourists back to his house. Something happened that night, another late start, and the dawn was fast approaching, and the producers were telling me to take charge, they had to leave. They did. Now there was no one behind me when I looked over my shoulders and things began to improve. The crew stopped telling me to ignore the producers. But I was still thinking about everyone's feelings.

Two weeks later, out in the desert, we were shooting the scene where Foster (Will Patton) visits Sharon's campsite at night. It was Will's first night on the set. He was the most intense actor in the production, and I needed to concentrate with him. The set was noisy. I got angry at the first AD. I told him it was his job to keep things quiet, and I wanted the set quiet. I didn't want to see anyone in my peripheral vision. I wanted to see only those people who absolutely needed to be near the camera. I had a small tantrum.

Five minutes later, everything was different, quiet, even solemn. No one shouted. Conversation was at a whisper. I think the scene is one of the best in the movie. Yes, I was finally learning a few simple tricks to make a scene cut together, but more than that, I was learning, like a novelist, that I was responsible for every detail. At that point, at the point that I had the tantrum which was respected, the day that I was not punished for being difficult, I stopped being a screenwriter.

When the movie came out we weren't sure what we had. As the film festivals accepted it, first Telluride and Toronto and then New York, we kept expecting someone to bring everyone to their senses and shuttle us straight to video. The critics were divided, although I was surprised how many mainstream critics supported the movie, when writers for the alternative press were dismissive, or worse. We were on a number of ten best lists, and some of the ten worst.

Whenever I showed the film at a festival, or at a college, or at the two screenings we had for Christian audiences, one in Atlanta (the buckle on the Bible belt) and one in Los Angeles, I would lead a question-and-answer period after the film. These discussions lasted from an hour to two hours, and were less about film than religion. There were four positions on the film. The film is great, because it shows the necessity to believe in Christ. The film is great, because it shows the futility of religion, the arrogance of God. The film, being Christian propaganda, is evil. The film, being blasphemous, is evil. Often in the discussions, people would argue with each other, one person defending, one attacking the film, while I moderated. When I showed *The Rapture* at a film school where they had also just seen *The Player*, I asked that we talk about movie-making, not God, but after a few minutes I was back to the familiar debate about the film's meaning.

One of my standard answers to all the questions was to say this: I was trying to take back from Spielberg the idea that a spectacle has to be positive. The spectacle films of the last ten years had turned the audience into a lynch mob united behind the hero against an arbitrarily chosen villain. I wanted something different, to leave the audience atomised, with everyone forced into themselves, alone, thinking. Now, negativity may be just as easy a device as the relentlessly happy ending that defies all plausibility, but a film teacher told me that his students today, when shown *Shampoo*, complain that it isn't fair for George not to get the salon and Julie Christie. They don't want to feel anyone's loss. They resent the film-makers for leaving them alone.

The question I heard most often from audiences were, 'What do you believe in?', and, 'What are you trying to say?' I never knew how to answer them. If I said, 'The film is the answer', then I was being coy, but I hated the arrogance of saying something like, 'Sharon rejects God at the end because she refuses to go along with the creator of such a dreadful universe' If I said 'I believe in peace', I sounded like a greetings card. At the New York Film Festival press screening, I was asked a question about the movie's view of religion, and I got a bit of a laugh, intentionally, when I said, to get out of the harsh light. 'Well, I live in California'. Later, a critic denounced the film, resorting to the French for his assistance, when he said, 'As the French would say, the film is *très très Californie*'.

Was I trying to make a spiritual film, or a film about spirituality? And I heard the word all the time, but what do we really mean by 'spiritual'?

It's obvious, and correct, to cite Bresson as a spiritual film-maker, but by that, do we mean that he increases our feelings of compassion, defuses our violence, and guides us to self-sacrifice, an end to materialism, jealousy and greed? Or can we find something awful in the implications of a spirituality whose only goal is a kind of useless revelation, some glimpse into an eternity terrifying in its indifference to our moral lives? And if eternity is not indifferent, if in our daily lives, in our pettiest decisions, we hold the cosmos in the balance, each of us, then the effect of seeing a spiritual film would have to be nothing less than dedication to the practice of complete attention to every consequence. So a movie would have to be part of a ritual, acting out a human drama that brought everyone to a point of attention where we could resonate with the angels. Or would a spiritual cinema lead to social action that was effective without violence? Or would a spiritual cinema lead to a self-consciousness that caused people whose actions were evil to see them in a clear light? For example, if someone, after seeing The Player, fulfils a vow to return all phone calls, would that make the film spiritual?

Some movies appeal to some of us, but we can't explain why. What is it about the ending of Antonioni's *The Eclipse* (1962) that's so beautiful? (If you agree with me, and think that it is.) We see something, we feel something. But when I saw Spielberg's *Close Encounters of the Third Kind* (1980) for the first time, I though then that I was seeing God. Now this embarrasses me, but at the time I was suffused with feelings of awe. Later I saw Fassbinder's *Fear Eats the Soul* (1973), and knew that if I wasn't seeing God, I was getting a peak into something that reflected Him, but if I say why, I'll start sounding like a Californian. So I'd better stop.

THE RAPTURE
USA 1991
Director: Michael Tolkin

Sharon works as a telephone information operator in Los Angeles. She cruises the bars at night with her friend, Vic, picking up other couples for casual sex. On one such occasion, she meets Randy and continues to sleep with him afterwards. Meanwhile, at work, Sharon overhears a group of her colleagues talking about a pearl, and about a boy. Later Sharon is visited by two evangelists who tell her that Judgment Day is imminent. During a group sex session, Sharon is fascinated by a strange tattoo of a pearl on the woman, Angie's, back. Sharon becomes increasingly depressed and disenchanted with her life. One day, she picks up a hitch-hiker, Tommy, and takes him to a motel, but then steals his gun and orders him to leave. In despair, she contemplates shooting herself, but finds a Bible and, as she reads it, experiences a vision of the pearl. Sharon tells Vic about her religious conversion, but he laughs at her and they part company.

Sharon discovers that her boss, Henry, is also a believer. He introduces her to a group led by a black boy prophet who predicts the end of the world in five or six years. She asks Randy to be her partner and, reluctant at first because he does not share her faith, he eventually agrees. Six years later, they have a daughter, Mary, and the whole family is dedicated to born-again Christianity. After Randy is murdered by a deranged employee, Sharon sees a vision which she interprets as a sign that she and Mary will be reunited with God and Randy in heaven if they go to the desert.

Sharon's friend Paula gives her a gun to protect herself. Sharon and Mary camp in the desert, where Sheriff Foster takes an interest in their welfare. After several days and nights waiting in vain, Mary pleads with Sharon to kill them both so they can join Randy in heaven. Sharon shoots Mary dead, but is unable to kill herself. After burying her daughter she takes to the road, where she sees visions of the Four Horsemen of the Apocalypse. She is stopped by Foster and confesses to Mary's murder.

In prison, Sharon finds herself in the same cell as Angie, who informs her that the Apocalypse has begun. Sharon responds that she no longer believes in God. The prison bars crumble and the prisoners walk free. Foster collects Sharon and they drive on his motorbike into the desert, where they come face to face with the Horsemen. Sharon's daughter materialises and offers them both a final chance of redemption. Foster affirms his faith in God and is saved, but Sharon refuses and is left alone in darkness forever.

* * *

The Rapture's director/writer Michael Tolkin has been quoted as saying that he wanted to create a film which left the audience 'thrown back into themselves'. He seems to have succeeded, since his audacious attempt to dramatise the end of the world certainly makes one wonder exactly what Tolkin himself believes. In the United States, the movie has received a mixed welcome, championed by some as confirming the need for faith in God, derided by others as religious propaganda. Tolkin may have had little trouble in his novel *The Player* scorning the perverse deities who run Hollywood, but he is more hesitant in declaring his feelings about the brand of religious fundamentalism consuming a disturbingly large number of Americans as the twentieth century draws to a close.

At first glance, *The Rapture* seems to belong with the recent wave of films (*The Fisher King, Grand Canyon*) featuring heroes in search of something to believe in. Here, a woman joins that disaffected company – not a high-flying lawyer or successful radio DJ, but a telephonist trapped in a boring and isolating job whose apartment, decorated in the style of an anonymous hotel room, is the perfect backdrop for her casual sexual encounters. The heroes of *The Fisher King* and *Grand Canyon* discover salvation in a personal mythology, while Sharon finds hers in off-the-peg Christian evangelism. Tolkin depicts this fundamentalism as a religion found in shopping malls and motels, sold door-to-door by men in suits who might as well be hawking double glazing.

Religion is seen as the valium of the people – a panacea for a depressed and frightened woman on the verge of insanity. Both Vic and Randy, Sharon's non-believing sexual partners, initially see her conversion this way, offering traditional secular explanations: 'It's just a drug ... Instead of doing heroin, you're doing God.' But Tolkin's direction and Mimi Rogers's compelling performance ensure the audience's sympathy for Sharon. Equal weight is given to her boss Henry's remark that 'The unbelievers make out that we're stupid, that there's something wrong with us.' However, the theological debate never rises above the level of the slogans found on evangelical posters decorating bus shelters.

Religion is seen to offer a haven to its followers – until it is tested. As converts, Sharon and Randy enjoy an affluent suburban lifestyle. This is certainly not a faith that eschews materialism: Sharon carefully chooses the dresses that she and Mary will wear for their meeting with God. But such details as this, or Sharon mistaking a car alarm for the clarion call, are not depicted with any irony. And Armageddon is similarly represented straight, via a series of singularly tacky images – the Grim Reaper and the Four Horsemen look like something out of a greetings card-style Book of Revelations. Obviously, budget restriction played some part in this (in Tolkin's original script, the rapture happens to a number of people who levitate from their cars up into the heavens). But this cheap, literal iconography, envisaging the end of the world in cartoon terms, is the stuff of evangelical TV programming, and is the imagery that Sharon, as a believer, would accept.

The Rapture could be seen as being primarily about Sharon's disturbed state of mind, with which, unnervingly, the audience becomes increasingly involved. Having achieved a kind of mental stability through religion, Sharon then finds it shattered by the violent death of her husband. Once again, she deals with the trauma through her faith, which sanctions her bizarre journey into the wilderness. But this, and the subsequent murder of Mary, are undeniably the actions of a psychotic. Sharon's madness might have been explored to provide a tragic, melodramatic core to the film. But Tolkin's distanced style refuses any emotional impact, even to the killing of a daughter by her mother.

Sharon's trials in the desert may have biblical and mythical overtones – as an inversion of the story of Abraham and Isaac, for instance – but ultimately they are seen as part of her drive to self-destruction. Even when she 'comes to her senses' and disavows God, it is too late: she is left alone in the darkness of limbo. This is an appropriately ambiguous metaphor with which to end an alienating film. *The Rapture* offers no easy redemptive resolution; rather it leaves us with an irritating sense that Tolkin wants to have his milk and honey and eat it too.

Lizzie Francke

SITTING INSIDE

Jenny Diski

There was a phrase in quite general use by male critics during the 1950s and 1960s to describe certain women writers (though not directors – but as far as I can remember only Agnès Varda had movies released back then). They were described as 'man haters'. The phrase comes back to me because something similar is cropping up these days in articles written by women about film directors (still largely men). Settle down to a piece by a woman about Peckinpah, De Palma, Altman or Tarantino and you're very likely to read that they 'don't like women'. (The language is slightly changed, but then women are different. They're nicer, aren't they?) 'He doesn't like women': it's a phrase that might be fine for dismissing a piece of work without merit or interest (though 'crap' would do better, taking up minimal space and leaving room to write about other things). But unless the desire is to dismiss an entire body of work, it's not a criticism that tells us very much or takes us very far.

Of all directors, Peckinpah is the least problematic: women are male accessories, pure and simple, sometimes allowing his men to feel a little sentimental (though they're better at doing that with other men), but usually no more than flesh for consumption. Tarantino might be Peckinpah's successor as regards his interest in women. De Palma and Altman come further along the line of complexity, directors whose women are at least sometimes given psychological and biological motivation and are gazed at with some thought by the camera.

Don't misunderstand me: I'm not suggesting that these directors, and others, *do* like women, I'm writing from a feeling that most men find the idea of women alarming in some way or other – and that their films, books, the way they sell us cabbages, can't help but reflect their ambivalence. To say that this is the case is to say nothing very remarkable – if used as a criticism in itself, it merely closes down further thought. Perhaps the real problem we have is that there are only two off-the-peg genders available for depiction (even allowing for alternative sexual choice), and that the relationship between them is inevitably suffused with the generalised tension which any paired oppositions must feel for one other. As a woman, I'm neither surprised nor necessarily personally offended by this state of affairs (though there are moments). Having acknowledged the inevitability, I reserve the right to be intrigued rather than outraged. In any case, it's better for my health.

Roman Polanski's view of women is nothing if not intriguing, ranging as it does from moments of remarkable sensitivity about their lives to pure and puerile pornographic depiction of their bodies. It's probably the range of understanding most men experience internally, but Polanski lays it down on film for us all to see. It is Polanski who expresses most clearly the ambiguity of his feelings – empathy and disgust – for the other sex. For this, at least, he deserves serious attention.

And in this respect, *Rosemary's Baby* is his richest film, centring as it does on the Other in her most esoteric condition. His earlier and later films address aspects of her predicament – neurosis, vulnerability, strangeness – but Rosemary herself is ground zero: the reproducing woman. Pregnancy is the state in which women are most alien to men. This is not unreasonable; it's also the state in which they may be most alien to themselves. Prior to pregnancy, and prior to the understanding of its linkage with reproduction, women's ability to bleed and remain healthy has always been under interdiction; the rhetoric has claimed that they are unclean, but, more essentially, it is evidence – to men who bleed only when injured – that women are beyond the ordinary human condition. You don't have to be a man to see that menstruation and pregnancy are likely to disturb those who do not experience them. You don't have to be a man to feel that the internal incubation of a life is alien. Very likely we would all have got along a lot better if we'd evolved to reproduce by laying eggs. That way the male, like the Emperor Penguin, could sit with them on his feet and feel he was an active participant in the process. Women too could benefit from the same reassurance. In exploring Rosemary's pregnancy, Polanski is not just looking at male resentment and envy at what is going on without their participation, he is also, and more interestingly, exploring the impotence of women themselves in the process of making life. Whether as a man he is fit to do so is perhaps arguable, though not by me. (One of the great disservices of the teaching of English today – and by extension any creative activity – is that children are told they must write only out of their own experience, as if reaching out to what is not known had no part in creativity.) Personally, I'm happy for Polanski to do his best, or worst, or just middling, with a woman's experience of pregnancy, and content to assess the results.

Viewed from the perspective of all the *Exorcists* and *Omens* – parts one to infinity – *Rosemary's Baby*, released in 1968, looks like the mother of modern satanic movies. As such, it's a fairly ordinary popular film with a better than average sense of humour. The motivation is simple: emotionally remote, ambitious actor husband (John Cassavetes) succumbs to the temptations of good roles offered by a neighbouring coven in return for the use of his painfully naïve and submissive wife's body (Mia

Farrow at her most anorexic) to incubate the son of Satan. The fun is in the detail: Ruth Gordon's intrusive busybody as modern urban witch (all those interfering neighbours who can no longer be denounced and burned); Ralph Bellamy as a latterday witch-doctor (what male gynaecologist isn't?); Rosemary's proto-yuppie snobbery ('They only have three matching plates') getting its come-uppance. But something else is going on which makes you suspect that the diabolical storyline is, after all, only a trope for something much more disturbing. The real subject of the film is child-bearing, not the devil's incarnation as Anti-Christ.

The all-pervasive use of the colour yellow (Rosemary's clothes, the flowered bedroom walls, the bed sheets, the nursery décor, the refrigerator; there's scarcely a frame without some tinge of yellow) whispers not of satanic hellfire but of Easter eggs, spring and birth. Red is saved for the outfit Rosemary wears on the night of impregnation, and if it carries overtones of the daddy incubus of them all, it also speaks of the menstrual cycle and the care with which Cassavetes, as husband Guy (good name), has ensured that the womb in question is nicely lined and receptive. It may not be the contaminated chocolate mousse that Ruth Gordon gives her to eat on baby-making night which renders Rosemary impotent in the matter of her own pregnancy, but Guy's assumption of control over the process at its earliest stages. Guy initiates the idea of making a baby and takes charge of the timing, appropriating Rosemary's menstrual cycle, marking the calendar on the kitchen wall, stabbing at it with his finger to point out to her the precise day of her peak fertility. By the following month, he, not Rosemary, knows that she is exactly two days overdue. Guys like to keep tabs on what they fear they can't control. The stiff little pre-impregnation dinner à deux inaugurates not lovemaking, but Rosemary's paralysis and rape by her husband and/or the Prince of Darkness. The apparently doctored mousse is a sufficient but not necessary condition for Rosemary's mental absence from the act of procreation; if we chose to set aside the satanic storyline, Guy's cold controlling formality would do just as well.

Rosemary dislikes the constant attention of her elderly neighbours, but the wilting of her already etiolated spirit seems to have more to do with Guy's neglect. For all I know, the symptoms she develops in early pregnancy may be classic signs of a woman bearing the son of Satan, but they must be just as common in women who through isolation feel that pregnancy is an illness. She loses weight (a horrible thing to see when the actress is Mia Farrow), she has pains 'as if a wire was being tightened inside me', she is fearful of something she can't name. If we didn't know we were watching a satanic movie, we wouldn't hesitate to call her increasing conviction that there is a conspiracy between her husband and the neighbours paranoia. Certainly, the good gynaecologist she escapes her flat to go uptown to consult sees it that way, as she sits in his office and tells him what's been going on. Indeed, it takes an enormous effort of will to see it any other way, even within the conventions of the movie we think we're seeing, because Mia Farrow's performance in that scene is so classically psychotic. This is Polanski having it, uncomfortably for us, both ways. Read Rosemary's fears as the terror of pregnancy, and all the devil-bearing stuff falls into place as the world viewed from her disturbed mind. The neighbours are filmed less and less realistically, and in the final scene, where Rosemary breaks through into the next door flat to find the coven and the black-draped cradle, the view is so distorted that the far end of the room vanishes into near-infinite distance and the people in it are virtual statues.

From an objective point of view, a nine-month pregnancy is a mysterious and fearful thing. How do you know what is going on inside you? It's an astonishing feat of (I suppose) evolution that women mostly get through the long uncertainty believing that something perfectly ordinary is happening to them. Even so, there can be few who haven't wondered to themselves that something *live*, something *not them* is sitting inside them, taking nourishment and coming to term. Pregnancy and alien implantation are only a thin, rational line apart, and Polanski teeters along it as he tries to imagine what such an experience must be like. It's a classic case study of *pre-partum* psychosis, not such a rare thing, and certainly not an entirely unreasonable response to such an unreasonable situation. Guys like to be in control, after all, so what must it be like for the half of the race who for months at a time are not in control at all? Men may envy women's capacity to bear life, but they must also feel some relief that they are not obliged to do so. *Rosemary's Baby* is an expression of that ambiguity.

DYING FOR ART

Peter Wollen

In 1827 Thomas De Quincey, famous as the English opium-eater, wrote his celebrated essay 'Murder Considered as One of the Fine Arts'. Although the theme of this essay is self-evident, it is treated somewhat ironically, and we can find a much balder and more provocative statement of the author's belief in his lesser-known article 'On the Knocking at the Gate in *Macbeth*', written two years earlier. Here he describes the notorious East London murderer John Williams in the following terms: 'At length, in 1812, Mr Williams made his debut on the stage of Ratcliffe Highway, and executed those unparalleled murders which have procured for him such a brilliant and undying reputation. On which murders, by the way, I must observe, that in one respect they have had an ill-effect, by making the connoisseur in murder very fastidious in his taste, and dissatisfied with anything that has been done since in that line. All other murders look pale by the deep crimson of his; and, as an amateur once said to me in a querulous tone, 'There has been absolutely nothing doing since his time, or nothing that's worth speaking of.' But this is wrong, for it is unreasonable to expect all men to be great artists, and born with the genius of Mr Williams.'

De Quincey set out to justify Shakespeare's perplexing stagecraft in *Macbeth* by referring the reader to Williams's stagecraft on the Ratcliffe Highway, explaining Shakespeare's dramatic genius by comparing his work to that of a recognised fellow-genius in the art of real-world murder. For De Quincey, 'everything in the world has two handles – murder, for instance, may be laid hold of by its moral handle, or it may also be treated aesthetically.' De Quincey once had the good fortune to meet the notorious Victorian serial killer Thomas Griffiths Wainewright, 'a murderer of a freezing class, cool, calculating, wholesale in his operations'. Wainewright was himself a poet, a painter, an aesthete and an art critic, a lover of Greek gems, Persian carpets, Florentine majolica and fine book-bindings, who carried his dandyism over into the sphere of crime not so long after De Quincey's article on murder was first published in *Blackwood's Magazine.* Needless to say, De Quincey was fascinated by his dinner companion.

Later, Oscar Wilde was to write a short essay on Wainewright, entitled 'Pen, Pencil and Poison'. 'There is no essential incongruity,' Wilde concluded, 'between crime and culture. We cannot re-write the whole of history for the purpose of gratifying our moral sense of what should be. Of course, he is far too close to our own time for us to be able to form any purely artistic judgement about him. It is impossible not to feel a strong prejudice against a man who might have poisoned Lord Tennyson, or Mr Gladstone, or the Master of Balliol. But had the man worn a costume and spoken a language different from our own, had he lived in imperial Rome, or at the time of the Italian Renaissance, or in Spain in the seventeenth century, or in any land or any century but this century and this land, we would be quite able to arrive at a perfectly unprejudiced estimate of his position and value.'

When Michael Powell's *Peeping Tom* was released in March 1960, it was greeted with a cascade of critical abuse and moral denunciation. It was in another land – France, needless to say – that its merits were first recognised and it was many more years before 'a perfectly unprejudiced estimate of [its] position and value' could be made in Britain. Today, of course, *Peeping Tom* is acknowledged as the final masterpiece of a director who in the opinion of many was England's greatest film artist, and who, after the disaster of *Peeping Tom*, was driven out of the British film industry to finish his professional career in television and, finally, in Australia. As Richard Maltby has pointed out, the London critics and censors have ritualistically denounced violent films that are made in Britain. The spiv films of the 1940s were consistently abused; and, after *Peeping Tom*, the next scapegoat was Sam Peckinpah's *Straw Dogs.*

Curiously, this position has its roots in the prejudices expounded in George Orwell's 1946 essay 'The Decline of English Murder', which draws a distinction between the artistic Victorian murders he cherished and the 'pitiful and sordid' Cleft Chin murder currently grabbing the headlines, 'a meaningless story, with its atmosphere of dance-halls, movie-palaces, cheap perfume, false names and stolen cars', lacking the dramatic structure and emotional depth displayed by the time-honoured classics of the genre. Orwell's essay, in which a nostalgic English aestheticism is affronted by a 'wanton' murder committed by a philistine 'americanized' couple, was published in *Tribune*, and it was in *Tribune*, too, that the most virulent attack on *Peeping Tom* was later made: 'The only really satisfactory way to dispose of *Peeping Tom* would be to shovel it up and flush it swiftly down the nearest sewer. Even then the stench would remain.'

Plainly, *Peeping Tom* triggered an intense outbreak of the moral panic which has traditionally greeted any striking display of violence in British cinema. By today's standards, *Peeping Tom* is not in fact an especially violent movie. Mark Lewis was much less brutal and bloody than De Quincey's hero, John Williams. He falls more closely into the category admired by Wilde and indeed Orwell, the middle-class aesthete gone terribly wrong. It has frequently been pointed out that Anglo-Amalgamated, which produced *Peeping Tom*, ventured into the horror genre because of the commercial success enjoyed by Hammer, which had turned to horror in the mid-1950s and managed to prise open the American market with Terence Fisher's *The Curse of Frankenstein*. Yet *Peeping Tom* is very different from the films of the Hammer horror cycle. Its terror is much colder and more intellectualised. It is an extremely knowing and sophisticated film, a kind of deviant art film

Essentially, *Peeping Tom* combines three distinct sub-genres – the serial killer film the film-about-film and the psychoanalyst or clinical psychologist film. The serial killer film has a long pedigree. Beginning obliquely in Weimar Germany with *The Cabinet of Dr Caligari* and *Pandora's Box*, it reached its culmination in Fritz Lang's *M*. It has included classics as weirdly diverse as Chaplin's *Monsieur Verdoux* and Laughton's *The Night of the Hunter*. It is a major force in contemporary cinema, encompassing Hollywood movies as different as Bigelow's *Blue Steel*, Demme's *The Silence of the Lambs* and Stone's *Natural Born Killers*, as well as midnight cult films such as *Henry, Portrait of a Serial Killer*, and off-beat documentaries such as Nick Broomfield's *Aileen Wournos: The Selling of a Serial Killer*. In this tradition, it seems significant that *Peeping Tom* was released in the same year as Hitchcock's *Psycho*, two films by the two greatest English directors, yet very different in their approach.

The film-about-film sub-genre has always been a favourite of cinephiles because it reflexively folds back their obsession with film on to film itself. For the same reason, it can be aligned with a kind of naïve modernism, a concentration of art upon its own materials and conditions of existence, both film and commentary on the nature of film. With *Peeping Tom* in mind, we might think of Vertov's *Man with a Movie Camera*, which celebrates the power of the camera and its ability to penetrate and see where the human eye cannot. Vertov makes a modernist hero out of the cameraman as he seeks out the truth in every avenue of life, filming women in childbirth in the hospital and chasing ambulances to the scene of violence. Another classic of the genre is Hitchcock's *Rear Window*, which, like *Peeping Tom*, dwells on the dialectic of the gaze, the intrusive look and its reciprocal engagement with the look of the other. The film-about-film, focusing on the camera as a crucial prop or even a virtual protagonist, necessarily becomes involved with the representation of voyeurism, at the moment it enters the field of violence and sexuality.

The psychoanalyst sub-genre also attracted Hitchcock – *Spellbound* was an early classic and *Psycho* too at least nods towards the form, although not until the end. In the English cinema proper, there was Compton Bennett's extraordinary melodrama *The Seventh Veil*, which came out in 1945, the same year as *Spellbound*, and the omnibus film *Dead of Night*, released the following year, which had an especially compelling episode directed by Alberto Cavalcanti. *Peeping Tom*'s roots are in this sub-genre. The scriptwriter, Leo Marks, had originally come to Powell with the idea of making a film about Freud himself, which had to be abandoned when they learned that John Huston had already embarked on his own Freud biopic. Essentially, *Peeping Tom* was a compromise formation, condensing the repressed Freud film with the surface Hammer horror film, by way of the voyeuristic implications of the film-about-film.

In *Peeping Tom*, as in *Spellbound*, the respected psychologist is himself the clinical case. Professor Lewis, like the psychiatrist in *Spellbound*, is an ambulatory psychotic whose pathology is socially acceptable and indeed socially honoured. It is only when it is transferred on to his son, its original victim, that it mutates into a psychosis which is socially condemned. Scientific scrutiny and veiled child abuse are transformed into voyeurism and murder, the penetrating gaze twinned with the penetrating switch-blade. Thus the respected psychologist mutates, in the next generation, into the serial killer. But whereas in *Psycho* Norman Bates has an aggressive mother and an absent father, Mark Lewis has an aggressive father and an absent mother. Norman Bates ends his career of murder by becoming his mother, by being absorbed into her; Mark Lewis by killing the father-in-himself, finally eliminating him in a bizarre self-execution. While both Norman Bates and Mark Lewis are voyeurs, Mark Lewis extends his voyeurism even further, into a magical involvement with the camera and with film-making.

This marks the transition into the film-about-film. Mark Lewis's film-making project is a mechanised yet intensely private activity of self-expression, really a kind of art-work. As his friend Helen recognises, at root he is an artist. In this sense, his relationship to murder, though mediated through voyeurism, is more like that of the dandy murderer in *Rope* than of the obsessive observer-of-murder in *Rear Window*. The serial killer has become radically aestheticised. Indeed, the cult status of *Peeping Tom* comes largely from this aestheticisation of death. Superficially, there is an identification with the serial killer as outlaw, the frontiersman who lives on the margins, transgresses the norms of normal society, crosses forbidden boundaries. But more profoundly, this entails a fascination with death itself, expressed in the last analysis by Mark's project of experiencing to the fullest the moment of his own self-inflicted death. The aestheticisation of murder, in the tradition of De Quincey and Wilde, is founded on a death-wish which can easily turn inwards on the tormented self. We find the same aestheticised compulsion-towards-death in the final suicidal leap of Victoria Page in Michael Powell's other masterpiece, *The Red Shoes*, as her commitment to her art leads inexorably to her death and mutilation.

Early critical accounts of *Peeping Tom* concentrated on the issue of sadism, probably because the French critics who first praised the film, in *Positif* and *Midi-Minuit*, were heavily influenced by Surrealism and hence by André Breton's own fascination with the Marquis De Sade. More recently, academic discussion of the film has been dominated by psychoanalytic interpretations, concentrating on voyeurism and the concept of the look – an approach which has come to be known as 'gaze theory' and owes its origin to Laura Mulvey's pioneering essay 'Visual Pleasure and Narrative Cinema'. In the case of *Peeping Tom*, psychoanalytic criticism is not simply imposed externally but is justified internally, from within the film itself. Not only was the collaboration between Powell and Marks initiated on the basis of their Freud project, but they allude directly to the concept of voyeurism in the film. The police assigned to Mark Lewis's murders bring in a psychoanalyst to help them with their investigations and he strikes up a conversation with Mark – the very murderer he is blindly seeking – which concludes with a discussion of Mark's father's own researches on the subject of scopophilia.

But sadism and voyeurism are not in themselves the central topics of *Peeping Tom*. Much more crucially, the film is about the pathological character of Mark's family. This explains not only his internalisation of his father's sadistic obsession with filming the spectacle of fear, but also his projection of sadism, through the medium of the camera, on to a succession of women who, in their willingness to be filmed, echo the sexual demonstrativeness of his hated stepmother. At the same time, in his relationship with the one woman he cannot and must not film, the shy and virginal Helen, he attempts to duplicate his relationship with his beloved mother. In fact, by chance, Helen is now sleeping in the same bedroom that was once his mother's room, and Helen's own mother is also the one person able to see his guilt – not literally, since she is blind, but intuitively through a kind of second sight. As Laura Mulvey points out in her audio-commentary on the Voyager video-disc of *Peeping Tom*, Helen's mother incarnates a visionary romanticism diametrically opposed to the positivist scientism of Mark's father. Like Mark, but for different reasons, she is an insomniac, a creature of the night whose solitary pleasure is to dream in the dark. Intuitively she understands the connection between cinema, the pathology of pornography and the burden of guilt and desire which drives Mark on his murderous career.

Mark's cruel father, however, is dead. He can no longer be harmed or punished by Mark. Except in an ingeniously roundabout way. Mark must first become his sadistic father and then punish himself, in retribution both for his father's guilt, which he has re-enacted in the form of his own serial murders, and for his own guilt at his parricidal desire. Thus Mark's final suicide is built into his scheme from the beginning. In his essay on 'Dostoevsky and Parricide', Freud comments on how, for Dostoevsky, the experience of his own death could be imagined as a 'moment of supreme bliss', the realisation of the death-wish he had originally directed at his own sadistic father. Now turned back on himself, it brings a glorious 'sense of liberation', an 'achievement of freedom', and thus of final triumph over the hated father. In the same essay (and also in his case study of Judge Schrebe, tormented by a sadistic father who used his son as an experimental subject for his quasi-scientific studies of child development) Freud also discusses the relationship between misogyny and male horror of feminisation and passivity, brought about by the abusive father. In the case of Mark Lewis, tormented by the paternal gaze, scopophilia is a secondary formation, a response to a more basic trauma and the instrument of a more basic desire.

For Mark Lewis, release from abject terror can come only with a return to sleep. When he himself becomes an adult, he both re-enacts his father's terroristic gaze and simultaneously must seek the unbreakable sleep which was denied him as a child. His suicide combines the two fantasies. He dies blinded by a repetition of the tormenting lights with which his father used to wake him and listening to his own childhood cries of fear, recorded by his father as research material. In his death, he experiences both ultimate possession by terror and ultimate blissful release. He has turned his father's murderous gaze upon himself in order to liberate himself from it, to escape it forever.

Just as Powell superimposes three sub-genres in *Peeping Tom*, he also superimposes the three looks which characterise the cinema (those of the spectator, the camera and the character in the film), simultaneously knotting together the three threads. When Mark, after filming his murders, sits at home in his private cinema to watch his 'documentary', we see exactly what he sees projected, from his point of view as the film's spectator. We also, of course, see exactly what the camera saw as the instrument of his directorial vision. Finally, we see what the principal character of the film, the murder victim, saw at the moment of her own death. For Mark Lewis not only kills his victims as he films them, with a kind of swordstick blade that projects out from the foot of his camera tripod, but he has also attached a mirror to this murderous instrument, so that the victim will see herself reflected in it at the moment of her death.

Thus we see exactly what she saw, with her final terrorised gaze. The first look is that of the serial killer, the second that of the scientific instrument, the third the point of view of the victim, folded back on itself within the film, as she is compelled to be the observer of her own death.

This extravaganza of scopophilia does not simply foreground the process of looking. It aestheticises the look. In the first instance, the murderer himself must enjoy the spectacle he has created, not simply as a documentary record, but as an ingeniously devised artefact. Second, the victim must not only be conscious of her own death, but must be conscious of her own consciousness of it. In the postscript which De Quincey added in 1854 to his 'Murder Considered as One of the Fine Arts', he recounted an incident which illustrates the 'ultra fiendishness' of John Williams. The killer, having just committed a series of bloody murders, comes across a sleeping servant girl. De Quincey explains that, as 'an epicure in murder', driven by 'pure aesthetical considerations', Williams must now wake the girl before he kills her. 'It would take away the very sting of enjoyment, if the poor child should be suffered to drink off the bitter cup of death without fully apprehending the misery of the situation.'

De Quincey goes on to note that, 'except for the luxurious purpose of basking and revelling in the anguish of dying despair, he had no motive at all, great or small, for attempting the murder of this young girl.' This instance of 'a murder of pure voluptuousness' provides a romantic model for Mark Lewis's enjoyment in *Peeping Tom*. Now, however, the moment of voluptuousness is given an aesthetic complexity undreamed of by De Quincey. The spectator in the cinema is made conscious of Mark Lewis's consciousness of his victim's consciousness of her own consciousness of death.

Michael Powell does all he can to make us think of *Peeping Tom* as an extremely personal film. As has often been noted, the film is full of in-joke allusions to Powell's own film career, such as a satirical attack on John Davis, long-time head of production for Rank at Pinewood, where he was bitterly hated by Powell. Powell even locates the house in which Lewis lives directly across the street from his own real-world home in Melbury Road. Notoriously, he also appears in the black and white film-within-a-film as Mark Lewis's film-maker father, the Professor, and cast his own young son, Columba, as the child Mark. Thus he chose to represent himself within his own film not only as director, but also as psychologist, sadist and voyeur.

Powell saw himself as a virtual incarnation of the cinema. He told *Midi-Minuit*, 'I am not a director with a personal style. I am simply cinema.' And, apropos of *Peeping Tom*, he observed, 'I felt very close to the hero, who is an 'absolute' director, someone who approaches life like a director, who is conscious of it and suffers from it. He is a technician of emotion.' Mark Lewis chose to die as the final aesthetic expression of his obsession. I still remember how, watching an *Arena* portrait of Michael Powell, I was electrified to hear Powell, while discussing *The Red Shoes*, chide Melvyn Bragg for not taking seriously the idea of dying for art. Powell turned away from his quizzical host towards the camera and re-affirmed his wildly romantic belief that the true artist – the 'absolute' director – must always be ready to die for art. He meant it.

HOMEOPATHIC HORROR

Iain Sinclair

As the credits roll, a night-darkened landscape is seen from a moving car. A middle-aged woman drives, looking at someone – or something – in her rear-view mirror. At last she stops the car and drags out a body to dump it in the river.

Professor Génessier, a famous plastic surgeon, is delivering a paper on skin grafts. He is called away to identify the body as his daughter Christiane (Edith Scob), who was disfigured in a car accident for which he blames himself. But the corpse is really that of another girl, kidnapped by Génessier so her face could be sutured onto Christiane (who for the moment must wear a moulded mask to disguise her disfigurement). Louise, Génessier's devoted assistant (on whom he once performed a similar operation), cons a Swiss student named Edna into coming out to the mansion. Bringing her to their private laboratory, they remove Edna's face and transplant it on to Christiane's. Edna commits suicide, and they bury her body in 'Christiane's' tomb. The graft doesn't take, and Christiane's new face starts to deteriorate. A friend of Edna's reports her disappearance to the police. Christiane phones her boyfriend Jacques (a doctor who works with Génessier), speaks only Génessier's name and hangs up. Suspicious, Jacques goes to the police, and they set a trap with a decoy. Génessier is about to operate on the decoy when they call him away. Christiane, driven mad, frees the decoy, stabs Louise in the jugular and liberates the many dogs and birds her father has experimented on. The dogs kill Génessier, tearing his face to shreds. In the final image, Christiane walks into the woods, doves hovering about her.

* * *

Eyes without a Face didn't hold much appeal for the British critical establishment on its first appearance at the end of the 1950s. Georges Franju, in Edinburgh for its launch, muttered darkly about hairy-kneed Scotsmen in skirts. The Scots could think themselves lucky. Franju had the reputation of being the Céline of conversationalists, a man of 'torrential vehemence' spitting out excremental expletives like a tracer-stream of olive pits. Confronted with a distasteful fable about a crazed surgeon giving new meaning to the term 'face lift', even *Sight and Sound* (according to Raymond Durgnat) 'bayed its utter scorn'. So it's refreshing to report that, in the wake of the

Cultural Studies boom that keeps so many semi-professional bullshitters afloat, fashion has shifted. 'Genre' is now a respectable term and Franju's ad hoc liposuction behind the garage can be read as a precursor of *The Silence of the Lambs*. The real problem is that the film might not be quite bad enough to be worth patronising. Edith Scob doesn't have the self-consciousness to be voted the Madonna of the New Universities. There's nothing camp about Franju. He's far too earnest. He never gives the impression that he's slumming. He's not going to make it, with Roger Corman and Terence Fisher, into that particular pantheon.

The *Sight and Sound* of the 1990s, with a much hipper agenda, was generous enough to lay on a screening to endorse the re-release of Franju's modest shocker. It was a rare privilege to test cinematographer Eugen Schüfftan's classically cold black and white images against my selective (and fading) memories of them. After a quarter of a century, the film in my head was a forensic collaboration: clusters of provocative stills, nightrides, the sound of a weir, Maurice Jarre's sinister soundtrack carousel. Narrative decays first, logic gives way to a poetic of the perverse. Accidentally captured weather is now unredeemable. We are free to co-author a dream version – like the cunningly butchered Jungle Girl epics the artist Joseph Cornell used to assemble for his chairbound brother. Worn-out cheapies rescued from junkshops, re-edited so that banal exchanges become, by repetition, magical. Cornell, an alchemist of trash, having no one to satisfy but himself, could afford to cut from one object of desire to the next; the temperature of excitement was the only continuity. Spontaneous composition: one image leading immediately and without censorship to the next.

But the two young women who were also at this BFI viewing were seeing the film for the first time. A period piece incapable of escaping its temporal limitations. They were not impressed. The surgical sequences were disgusting and the pacing funereal; all that plodding up endless staircases. Like Michael Winner having a pop at *Last Year in Marienbad*. But the cars and the clothes! They *loved* the shiny black Citroën DS. The fashions were unadulterated nostalgia. Their lives, they confessed, had been measured out in PVC flashbacks (available on prescription from Camden Lock market). On the retro level, Franju can still hack it. A film is certainly worth resurrecting when it is replete with styles that can be so effortlessly plagiarised.

Franju speaks of film as being a perpetual present tense, but the effect of viewing *Eyes without a Face*, even when it was a novelty, was of encountering a future memory, an auditioning nightmare. There was a somatic inevitability about the experience: a chill of recognition, familiar events that had not yet happened. An anaesthetic shock that floats between terror and boredom. The opening sequence, the night drive, is as haunting as the first dream of a dead man. The film's on a loop. It's happening backwards. The drift of light down the tree-lined road, the spasms of music, the headlights flaring in pursuit, they're tautologous. They are a staple of *film noir*. You'll catch them soon in *Psycho*. But that woman was running away. And she was alone. The way to 'justify' this loaded riff is to think of it as being seamlessly connected to the film's end, to Edith Scob wandering, like a blind woman, into the woods with her nimbus of doves. The kitsch poetry and obvious symbolism of the conclusion is underwritten by the ferocity of the start: Cocteau's decorative similes stomped by Mickey Spillane. To see the bare branches of these trees from the point of view of the travelling camera, you'd have to be inside an open coffin. The trees are their own negatives. They are watched through closed eyelids. The film feels as it it's been shot from the rear of a speeding car and then reversed. Sound is strangely amplified. The river is an overwhelming presence. The butch chauffeur's glossy black coat looks as if it's been tailored out of film stock. The dead passenger, nodding as if drunk has been strapped, childlike, into the rear seat. We gaze at the world with her slightly puzzled sense of wonder, when every posthumous detail is fresh and miraculous.

Arriving at the riverbank, we are made aware, by both the cutting and the performances, that these characters are controlled. They move like zombies. They sleepwalk. Alida Valli drags the girl's corpse to the water's edge as if she herself were being propelled, part of a human wheelbarrow. The concentration demanded is obsessive, fetishistic. Nothing in the narrative quite accounts for the significance of this costumed ceremony, the nude victim draped in a man's raincoat. (Why? Who does this garment belong to?) Tension is provoked by the accidental poetry that is aroused when the aesthetic of special-interest pornography is vitalised by a rush of pulp fiction: the ravaged disbelief found in Robert Aldrich's *Kiss Me Deadly*, another night drive, another naked woman in a trench coat stepping into the headlights. These spectral (and disposable) hitch-hikers, incidental to the plot, achieve their importance as mannequins of the irrational.

Christopher Petit has described *Eyes without a Face* as 'Hammer Films meets Georges Bataille'. And there is something in this. (Something also of Angela Carter collaborating with Simenon: the grown-up fairy story told as a police procedural, imprisoned daughters and detectives with bad tobacco habits.) Bataille's great moment in cinema came with Buñuel's razor across the eyeball in *Un chien andalou*. But he had that sense of cruel artifice necessary to penetrate the layers of Franju's film. 'It is clear,' he wrote in *The Solar Anus*, 'that the world is purely parodic, in other words, that each thing seen is the parody of another, or is the same thing in a deceptive form.' *Eyes without a Face* breaks down into self-contained stanzas that operate through repetition, as in a verse drama, the juxtaposition of visionary seizures with slower passages of exposition. But the process can easily be reversed: narrative explosions, plotting dispensed with, to make time for the predatory drives, the sepulchre at night when the plane passes slowly overhead, those vertiginous ascents chasing shadows up endless staircases. Society, when it is encountered, is satirised: insect woman attending Dr Génessier's lecture with their 'walkers'. Retread faces, stitches covered with make-up, listening to a talk on skin grafts. ('As to the future, Madame, we cannot wait that long.') Priests and Proustian vampires like the trapped guests of *The Exterminating Angel*. Even the crowd queuing for the Ionesco play look as if they've been dug up for the occasion, absurdist stiffs in cenotaph hats.

The setting, in keeping with the Hammer tradition, is somewhere just beyond the metropolis: a hospital, madhouse, private surgery. Franju's bleak poetic is documentary in impulse. The secret horrors take place in a real city: river, railways, bookshops, cafés, the Eiffel Tower. As they might be seen by Brassaï or Robert Doisneau. Student life, casually exploited by the *Nouvelle vague* directors, is seen here as a meat-market to be trawled for involuntary face-donors by Valli, the Sapphic succubus in her 2CV. (Juliette Mayniel, the provincial pick-up, will reappear in

Chabrol's *Les Cousins*.) The distance between the city and Dr Génessier's house of horror is the distance between London and the film studios at Bray. Franju is scrupulous in his delineation of that journey: one epiphany is a track-in on the level-crossing gates when Mayniel's fatal ride is interrupted by a passing express. Smoke hesitates over the damp ground. The camera holds fast on the 'safe' side of the barrier, letting the two women drive on into the land of the dead.

Inside Génessier's overblown mansion, with its Second Empire furniture and cellars of howling dogs, we shift from the detached documentation of the city to the Sadeian privacy of a closed set, where the director (medical or cinematic) can administer 'horror in homeopathic doses'. Suddenly, the fabulous has been domesticated: Beauty, in her chintzy, dove-filled boudoir, is also the Beast. The ingredients of the classic fairy story are present – the castle in the woods, the remote father, the 'wicked' stepmother – but they have been subverted. Actors carry with them not only the overspill of their public private lives (Ingrid Bergman in Rossellini's *Stromboli* and *Voyage to Italy*) but also their previous movie biographies. Valli, the 'foreigner' of *Eyes without a Face*, has to live up to the melancholy accretions of *The Third Man* and Antonioni's *Il grido*. A double past: the romantic exploitation of Génessier's house has to respect all that history.

Edith Scob, more than any other element, brings Franju's conceit to life. The name alone is enough, like the anagram of a wound. It carries more of a charge than the fictive 'Christiane' and its wimpish *Pilgrim's Progress* piety. Scob is a mesmerising presence, an arsenic-powdered kabuki doll, with a tensile, steel-skin fragility. A porcelain mask clipped over a carcinomic mess of flesh. Scob doesn't walk, she swims upright – arms at her side, stiff as twigs. She's covered, head to toe, in a stiff airfixed gown: the minotaur's bride. Her thin neck stretches like a stem out of the upturned collar. The convulsive gesture, lifting her hands to her throat, is echoed by Mayniel on her arrival at the house, as if it was a symbol of initiation into a sorority of masochists. Bandaged like a futurist chrysalis, Scob whispers her lover's name into the telephone – a tender communication from beyond the grave.

As in the opera, the women's clothes are unwearable signifiers of character. Valli's at-home dress is as thick as a carpet, tricked out with flaps and epaulettes like a military greatcoat. The claustrophobic cosiness of Christiane's bedroom, with its coal fire and fussy ornaments, is contradicted by the functionally spare basement in which the surgery takes place.

The climax of the whole performance, the operation itself, it taken head-on, with no tactful cutaways. The spare-parts virtuoso sweats and does the business – like Picasso in the Clouzot film, drawing directly onto glass. Génessier sketches with a pencil and blood oozes from his line. Franju is taking his inspiration from his recollections of Dr Thierry de Martel's *Trépanation pour crise d'épilepsie Bravais-Jacksonnienne*: a surgical documentary from which 20 people had to be carried out. 'An atrocious film but a beautiful and poetic one, because it was so realistic.'

The face, which should be the essence of the actor, is disallowed, replaced by a mask. Or the illusion of a mask – which only heightens our expectations for the dinner-table scene where Christiane's new face is revealed. Hidden, she had been free to wander among the cages of dogs, spontaneous in her gestures, knowing she was unobserved.

In her hallucinatory progress she spurned the kitsch of her mother's portrait, one of those expensive vanity numbers painted from a Polaroid, only for it to become the image at the end of the film, the walk into the woods. The very clip that the audience will carry away.

Much of the film's atmosphere is achieved by a carefully layered soundtrack: amplified rooks, doves, dogs, tyres on gravel, interspersed with Maurice Jarre's troubling music-box interludes, nails inside a tin drum, reducing the doctor's mansion to the dimensions of a doll's house. Sound is another present tense, a violation of immediacy that frets against the dreamtime of visuals so seductive that we want to retain them beyond their allotted span. Church bells intrude on Valli's reverie as she waits for Génessier to dispose of a body in the family vault (just as the striking of clock counterpoints the strokes of the butcher in *Le Sang des bêtes*. All the constituent parts combine to create a poetry of the paranoid, the bureaucratic – attic offices with thrift-store furniture, hospital corridors, mortuary hotels perched where the Métro runs out. Franju fetishises objects, arranges surreal collisions, insinuates his subversive strategies into a world of bland conformity, handshakes and stiff bows. With those qualities, it's quite possible that his time has come round again.

Tapping out this report on an unfamiliar machine, a word processor, I'm still timid about closing the thing down. A reassuring but peculiarly apposite message appears on the screen: 'It is now safe to switch off your Macintosh.'

LEARNING TO SCREAM

Linda Williams

Talk to psychoanalytic critics about *Psycho* and they will tell you how perfectly the film illustrates the perverse pleasures of cinema. Talk to horror aficionados about *Psycho* and they will tell you the film represents the moment when horror moved from what is outside and far away to what is inside us all and very close to home.

But talk to anyone old enough to have seen *Psycho* on its release in a movie theatre and they will tell you what it felt like to be scared out of their wits. I vividly remember a Saturday matinee in 1960 when two girlfriends and I spent much of the screening with our eyes shut listening to the music and to the audience's screams as we tried to guess when we might venture to look again at a screen whose terrors were unaccountably thrilling.

Most people who saw *Psycho* for the first time in a theatre have similarly vivid memories. Many will recall the shock of the shower murder and how they were afraid to take showers for months or years afterwards. But if it is popularly remembered that *Psycho* altered the bathing habits of a nation, it is less well recalled how it fundamentally changed viewing habits.

When the purposeful, voyeuristic camera eye investigating Marion Crane's love affair and theft of $40,000 'washed' down the drain in a vertiginous spiral after the shower murder, audiences took pleasure in losing the kind of control they had been trained to enjoy in classical narrative cinema. With *Psycho*, cinema in some ways reverted to what the critic Tom Bunning has described as the 'attractions' of pre-classical cinema – an experience that has more of the effect of a rollercoaster ride than the absorption of a classical narrative.

Anyone who has gone to the movies in the past 20 years cannot help but notice how entrenched this rollercoaster sensibility of repeated tension and release, assault and escape has become. While narrative is not abandoned, it often takes second place to a succession of visual and auditory shocks and thrills which are, as Thomas Schatz puts it in 'The New Hollywood', 'visceral, kinetic, and fast paced, increasingly reliant on special effects, increasingly "fantastic"... and increasingly targeted at younger audiences'. Schatz cites *Jaws* (1975) as the precursor of the New Hollywood calculated blockbuster, but the film that set the stage for the 'visceral, kinetic' appeal of post-classical cinema was *Psycho*.

From the very first screenings, audience reaction, in the form of gasps, screams, yells, even running up and down the aisles, was unprecedented. Although Hitchcock later claimed to have calculated all this, saying he could hear the screams when planning the shower montage, screenwriter Joseph Stefano counters, 'he was lying... We had no idea. We thought people would gasp or be silent, but screaming? Never.' Contemporary reviews were in no doubt that audiences were screaming as never before: 'So well is the picture made... that it can lead audiences to do something they hardly ever do any more – cry out to the characters, in hopes of dissuading them from going to the doom that has been cleverly established as awaiting them' (Ernest Callenbach, *Film Quarterly*, Autumn 1960).

But having unleashed such reactions, the problem Hitchcock and every theatre manager now faced was how to keep them from getting out of hand. According to Anthony Perkins, the entire scene in the hardware store following the shower murder, the mopping up and disposal of Marion's body in the swamp, was usually inaudible thanks to leftover howls from the previous scene. According to Stephen Rebello in *The Making of Psycho*, Hitchcock even asked Paramount to allow him to remix the sound to allow for the audience's reaction. Permission was denied.

Hitchcock's unprecedented 'special policy' of allowing no one into the theatre once the film had begun was one means both of encouraging, and handling, the mayhem. It also ensured that audiences would fully appreciate the shock of having the rug pulled out from under them so thoroughly in the surprise murder of the main character in the shower. Most importantly, however, it transformed the previously casual act of going to the movies into a much more disciplined activity of arriving on time and waiting in an orderly line.

Hitchcock's insistence that no one be admitted late to the film supposedly came to him during the editing: 'I suddenly startled my fellow-workers with a noisy vow that my frontwards-sidewards-and inside-out labors on *Psycho* would not be in vain – that everyone else in the world would have to enjoy the fruits of my labor to the full by seeing the picture from beginning to end. This was the way the picture was conceived – and this was how it had to be seen' (*Motion Picture Herald*, 6 August 1960). In a narrow sense, this simply meant that having worked so hard to set up the surprise of the shower murder, Hitchcock wanted to make sure that it was fully appreciated. In the larger sense, however, his demand that the audience arrive on time would eventually lead to the set show times, closely spaced screenings, elimination of cartoons and short subjects and patient waits in lines that are now standard procedure.

Critics obliged Hitchcock by promoting the new policy: 'At any other entertainment from ice show to baseball games, the bulk of the patrons arrive before the performance begins. Not so at the movies which have followed the policy of grabbing customers in any time they arrive, no matter how it may impair the story for those who come in midway' (*View*). Columnist Stan Delaplane describes in detail the experience of going to see *Psycho* and captures something of the psychological undertones of the new film-viewing discipline.

> There was a long line of people at the show – they will only seat you at the beginning and I don't think they let you out while it's going on . . . A loudspeaker was carrying a sound track made by Mr Hitchcock.
>
> He said it was absolutely necessary – he gave it the British pronunciation like 'nessary'. He said you absolutely could not go in at the beginning.
>
> The loudspeaker then let out a couple of female shrieks that would turn your blood to ice. And the ticket taker began letting us all in.
>
> A few months ago, I was reading the London review of this picture. The British critics rapped it. 'Contrived,' they said. 'Not up to the Hitchcock standards.'
>
> I do not know what standards they were talking about. But I must say that Hitchcock . . . did not seem to be that kind of person at all. Hitchcock turned us all on.
>
> Of all the shrieking and screaming! We were all limp. And, after drying my palms on the mink coat next to me, we went out to have hamburgers. And let the next line of people go in and die.
>
> Well, if you are reading the trade papers, you must know that *Psycho* is making a mint of money.
>
> This means we are in for a whole series of such pictures.
>
> *Los Angeles Examiner*, 9 December 1960

Obviously the audience described by Delaplane was docile. Their fun was dependent upon this docility. Yet we can see an element of playful performance at work in this evocation of the exhilaration of a group submitting itself to a thrilling sensation of fear and release. In this highly ritualised masochistic submission to a familiar 'master', we see shrieking and screaming understood frankly as a 'turn on', followed by a highly sexualised climax ('go in and die'), a limp feeling, and then a renewal of (literal and metaphorical) appetite. This audience, despite its mix of class (mink and hamburgers) and gender, has acquired a new sense of itself as bonded around certain terrifying sexual secrets. The shock of learning these secrets produces both a discipline and, around that discipline, a camaraderie, a pleasure of the group that was both new to motion pictures and destabilising to the conventional gender roles of audiences.

Another important tool in disciplining the *Psycho* audience were the promotional trailers. All three hinted at, but unlike most 'coming attractions' refrained from showing too much of, the film's secrets. In the most famous of these, Hitchcock acts as a house-of-horrors tour guide at the Universal International Studios set of the Bates Motel and adjacent house (now the Universal Studios Theme Park featuring the *Psycho* house and motel). Each trailer stresses the importance of special discipline: either 'please don't tell the ending, it's the only one we have', or the need to arrive on time.

But there was another trailer, not seen by the general public yet even more crucial in inculcating discipline into the audience. Called 'The Care and Handling of *Psycho*', this was not a preview but a filmed 'press book' teaching theatre managers how to exhibit the film and police the audience.

The black and white film begins with the pounding violins of Bernard Herrmann's score over a street scene outside the DeMille Theater in New York, where *Psycho* was first released. A long line waits on the sidewalk for a matinee. An urgent-sounding narrator explains that the man in the tuxedo is a theatre manager in charge of imple- menting the policy for exhibiting the film – a policy which has placed him out on the sidewalk directing traffic for the 'blockbuster'. The film then explains the key elements of the procedure, beginning with the broadcasting, in Hitchcock's own sly, disembodied voice, of the message that 'this queuing up is good for you, it will make you appreciate the seats inside. It will also make you appreciate *Psycho*.' The mixture of polite induce- ment, backed up by the presence of Pinkerton guards and a life-size lobby cardboard cut-out of Hitchcock sternly pointing to his watch, seem comical today because we have so thoroughly assimilated the lessons of punctuality and secret-keeping.

Part of the fun of the film is Hitchcock's playfully sadistic pose mixed with an over- solicitous concern for the audience's pleasure. He asks the waiting crowd to keep the 'tiny, little horrifying secrets' of the story because he has only their best interests in mind. (According to Rebello, the strategy succeeded – when shaken spectators leaving the theatre were grilled by those waiting in line, they answered only that the film had to be seen.) He then insists on the democracy of a policy that will not make exceptions for the Queen of England or the manager's brother.

Punctuated by short glimpses of a screaming woman (who isn't Janet Leigh – could it be her double?) [It is Vera Miles, a canny bit of misdirection (Editor's note).] and Herrmann's unsettling score, this training film is a fascinating record of the process by which film-going became both a more gut-wrenching experience and a more disciplined act. Exploiting his popular television persona of the man who loves to scare you, Hitchcock also went one better than television by providing the kind of big-jolt ride the small screen could not convey. And he obtained the kind of rapt attention that would have been the envy of a symphony orchestra from an audience more associated with the distractions of amusement parks than with the disciplines of high culture.

In *Highbrow/Lowbrow*, Lawrence Levine has written compellingly about the taming of American audiences during the latter part of the nineteenth century. Levine argues that while American theatre audiences in the first half of the century were a highly participatory and unruly lot, arriving late, leaving early, spitting tobacco, talking back to the actors, stamping feet and applauding promiscuously, they were gradually taught by the arbiters of culture to 'submit to creators and become mere instruments of their will, mere auditors of the productions of the artist'. Certainly Hitchcock asserts 'the will of the artist' to 'tame' his audience, but this will is in the service of producing visceral thrills and ear splitting screams rather than the passivity and silence Levine describes. Hitchcock's disciplining of the audience is a more subtle exercise of power, productive rather than repressive, in Michel Foucault's sense of the term, merging knowledge and power in the production of pleasure.

In the discipline imposed by Hitchcock, the efficiency and control demonstrated outside the theatre need to be viewed in tandem with the patterns of fear and release unleashed inside. And this discipline, not unlike that demanded by the emerging theme parks, was not based on the division of audiences into high and low, nor, as would later occur through the ratings system, was it based on the stratification of different age groups. In Hitchcock's assumption of the persona of the sadist who expects his submissive audience to trust him to provide a devious form of pleasure, we see a new bargain struck between artist and audience: if you want me to make you scream in a new way and about these previously taboo sexual secrets, then line up patiently to receive the thrill.

While the training film offers us a look at the audience for *Psycho* outside the theatre, photographs taken with infra-red cameras during screenings at the Plaza Theatre in London and issued in an oversized press kit by Paramount, the film's distributor, provide an insight into what went on inside. The intense-looking audience, jaws set, stares hard at the screen, with the exception of a few people with averted eyes. The somewhat defensive postures indicate anticipation – arms are crossed, while several people hold their ears, suggesting the importance of sound in cueing terror.

On the whole the men are looking intently, some with hands up towards their face or chin. One man is dramatically clutching his tie while holding it out from his body; another bites his fingers while the young man next to him both smokes a cigarette and grabs his cheek. It is women in these pictures who look down, including the woman whose hand covers her mouth sitting next to the cool male smoker.

How are we to interpret these images of an audience showing its fear? Is it possible that a discipline, albeit of a different kind, operated inside as well as outside the theatre? Of course, we have no way of knowing at what point in the movie these shots were taken. But we do know that the film's scariest moments occur before and during the appearances of 'Mrs Bates' and that these appearances result in the highly feminised terror first of Marion, then of subsequent victims.

The terrified female victim is a cliché of horror cinema: both the display of sexual arousal and the display of fear are coded as quintessentially feminine. As Carol J. Clover puts it in *Men, Women and Chain Saws*, 'abject fear' is 'gendered feminine'. The image of a highly sexualised and terrified woman is thus the most conventionally gendered of the film.

Much less conventional is the ostensible cause of this terror: 'Mrs Bates'. Apparently gendered feminine, yet equipped with a phallic knife, 'Mrs Bates' represented a new kind of movie monster. But Hitchcock's decision to turn the traditional monster of horror cinema into a son who dresses up as his own mummified mother was not so much about giving silent power to a castrating 'monstrous feminine' as about deploying the sensational pleasures of a sexually indeterminate drag.

'He's a transvestite!', says the District Attorney in a famously inadequate attempt to explain the roots of Norman's behaviour. Certainly Norman is no mere transvestite –

that is, a person whose sexual pleasure involves dressing up as the opposite sex – but rather a much more deeply disturbed individual whose whole personality, according to the psychiatrist's lengthy discourse, has at times 'become the mother'. Yet in the scene that supposedly shows us that Norman has 'become' the mother, what we in fact see is Norman, now without wig and dress, sitting alone and reflecting, in the most feminine of the many voices given 'Mrs Bates', on the evil of 'her' son. In other words, while ostensibly illustrating that Norman now 'is' the mother, the scene provides a visual and aural variation on Norman's earlier sexual indeterminacy. The shock of this scene is the combination of young male body and older female voice: it is not the recognition of one identity overcome by another that fascinates so much as the tension between masculine and feminine. The penultimate shot of Norman's face, from which briefly emerges the grinning mouth of Mrs Bates' corpse, drives this home.

The psychiatrist's contention that Norman is entirely his mother is therefore unproven. Instead, these variations of drag become an ironic, and by this point almost camp, play with audience expectations that gender is fixed. Norman is not a transvestite, but transvestism – an incomplete assimilation to one or the other pole of the gender binary – is an attraction of these scenes.

But if gender performance is a newly important element within the film, how does it also figure for the audience in viewing *Psycho*? I would argue that a destabilisation of gender roles takes place both on screen and in the theatre, and that even the most classic-seeming masculine and feminine forms of behaviour take on parodic elements of performance that destabilise gender-fixed reactions.

Thus while the men in the audience look conventionally masculine, while they appear to stay cool in the face of danger and to look steadily at the screen, there is something just a little forced about their poses. In the face of the gender-confused source of terror on screen, their dogged masculinity seems staged. The more masculine they try to appear – as with the man clutching his tie – the more it is clear that a threat of femininity has been registered.

The cringing and ducking women, on the other hand, assume classic attitudes of frightened femininity. Yet here, too, the exaggeration suggests a pleasurable and self-conscious performance. I once interpreted this classic women's reaction as a sign of resistance: that women resisted assault on their own gaze by refusing to look at the female victim of male monstrosity. However, this notion of resistance simply assumed a masculine monster and the displeasure of horror for female spectators. Now I am more inclined to think that if some of the women in the audience were refusing to look at the screen, then they were also, like my girlfriends and I, at the early stages of assimilating a discipline that was teaching us *how* to look – emboldening us to look as the men did, in the interest of experiencing greater thrills.

We also need to recognise what these photographs cannot show us: that these disciplines of gender performance evolved over time and, though they seem fixed here, were actually thrown into flux by *Psycho*. Male and female spectators who either stared stoically or clutched themselves, covered eyes, ears, and recoiled in fear at the shower murder may have been responding involuntarily, and quite conventionally, the first time, to an unexpected assault. But by the film's second assault, this audience was already begging to play the game of anticipation and to repeat its response in either gender conventional or gender transgressive – but in both cases increasingly performative – gestures.

By the time the game of slasher-assault had become a genre in the mid- and late 1970s, by the time a film such as *The Rocky Horror Picture Show* took on its own performative life, by the time the erotic thriller had become a newly invigorated genre in the 1980s and 1990s, this disciplined performing audience was to give way to the equivalent of the kids who raise their hands in rollercoaster rides and call out, 'Look Ma, no hands!'

The dislocations between masculine and feminine, between normal and psychotic, between eros and fear, even between the familiar Hitchcockian suspense and a new, gender-based horror were new in *Psycho*. And it is these qualities that make it the precursor to the kinds of thrill-producing visual 'attractions' that would become fundamental to the New Hollywood. After making *Psycho*, Hitchcock boasted of his power to control audience response, saying that if you 'designed a picture correctly in terms of its emotional impact, the Japanese audience would scream at the same time as the Indian audience'. It might seem that the photographs of the *Psycho* audience bear him out – certainly they exhibit his power to elicit response – yet there is reason to suspect a level of calculation behind his emotional engineering. We have seen that Hitchcock was in fact taken aback by the screams *Psycho* produced. Perhaps his elaborate attempts to stage the experience of the film's screenings were simply bids to regain control over an audience response which scared even him.

DESPERATION AND DESIRE

Leslie Dick

One of my favourite psychoanalytic concepts is *nachträglichkeit* – translated into French as *après-coup*, more obscurely into English as 'deferred action' or 'retroactive causality'. It means that the significance of past events or emotions is always re-configured according to the present context, retroactively; for example, a sexual event that takes place when a child is two years old may only become traumatic later, when the child is old enough to know what sex is. One of the results of this idea is that no psychoanalytic interpretation can ever be final – so if you undergo psychoanalysis when you're 25, and again when you are 50, the analysis will be very different, your reading of your own past will have been revised, and its meanings will have shifted. While this shift is never absolute (the insights of the first analysis will not be thrown out altogether), the idea of the meaning of the past being constructed within the present and therefore dependent on who you are, what you see and know, now, makes the psycho-analytic notion of time much more dynamic and lively than is generally acknowledged.

I saw *Don't Look Now* in 1974, when I was a college student in Brighton. I remember I went to see the film twice in the same week. It was necessary then to see films twice, or three times or more, in those dark days before video. It was necessary, in order to memorise the film. If you took film seriously, you had to memorise it as you watched. And if a film was complex and challenging, you went to see it again, and again.

Possibly because of this investment, I remember *Don't Look Now* vividly. I remember the opening sequence, where the photographic slide Donald Sutherland is studying starts to bleed liquid red across the image, obliterating it. Inexplicably he jumps up, and runs outside to find his daughter in her shiny red mac, drowned in the pond at the end of the garden. I remember his anguish, and the appalling loss the death of a small child represents. The rest of the film, as I remember it, is about that loss, about the ways a marriage might survive such a terrible blow, or not, and about the compelling power of the wish to have the lost child again, to make contact, to hold her in your arms once more. It's about desperation, and the crazed persistence, against all reason, of desire.

Watching the film again now becomes an experiment in *nachtraglichkeit*, like trawling for possible meanings, dragging ancient objects up from the bottom of the sea, scooping them up into one's net, every net a different weave, hauling up a different catch. I was 20 when I saw this movie, and I was tremendously moved by it, by the relationships it presented. Now I'm 41, and married, and I have a four-year-old daughter, who does not wear a shiny red raincoat, nor play alone near ponds, generally speaking. I'm very interested, in my own work, in investigating the experience of having a child as an experience of separation and loss. And I am fearful of watching *Don't Look Now*, on video, now; I think it will make me cry. Or worse, it won't, it won't work; it will seem baroque and over-elaborate, and I won't like it now. Now, when I'm closer to the characters' age and situation, now I fear it won't touch me the way it did when I was 20, and couldn't imagine myself in such a relationship, myself with a child.

I conduct my experiment in subjectivity, to measure what I've misremembered, to chart my own emotional susceptibility. To my delight, this film is all about time, and memory – as any film about loss and desire must be. It's even about *nachtraglichkeit*, sort of. Nicolas Roeg calls cinema a 'time machine': he's fascinated by the possibilities of undoing linear progression, locating meaning differently depending on spatial and temporal point of view. He was decisively influenced by George Polti's book *36 Dramatic Situations*, especially the 'situation' called the Enigma, a riddle that only death can solve. In *Don't Look Now*, it is only at the moment of his own death that the protagonist can make sense of the story; it is at the moment of closure that the narrative takes shape, retroactively.

In Venice, in winter, after the child's death, John Baxter (Sutherland) is working on the restoration of a Byzantine church. His wife Laura (Julie Christie) encounters two older English sisters in a restaurant ladies' room, where the blind sister tells her she sees Christine, the dead child, and she is happy, she's laughing, she's here. Laura is relieved of her grief, she feels OK for the first time in months, and wants more. Baxter is disturbed and disgusted, yet he himself cannot resist the lure of a small figure in a red hooded coat, apparently a manifestation of the dead child, who appears on three occasions, always out of reach, and running away. The small figure seems to be in danger, and a series of bloody murders provide the context for this set of relations. Baxter mistrusts the two sisters, regarding them as malevolent figures who increasingly gain ascendancy over Laura. Yet the film ends with Baxter's death, murdered by the small figure in the red hood, who turns out to be a terrifying dwarf with a big knife when he finally catches up with her.

Always running away

While his death is scary, a scene of unusual and extreme violence, it's also very moving, partly because he approaches the apparent child with such tenderness. It may not be his own lost girl, but it is a little girl in red, and he has to reach her. The murderous image, the knife slamming into the side of his neck, red blood spurting out, takes the tentative promise of reunion with the dead child and turns it inside out, into an emblem of death itself.

At the centre of the film is the sublime sex scene, where Sutherland and Christie make love in their hotel room in Venice. The scene was regarded as scandalously explicit at the time, and I know lots of people who remember it as one of the most erotic in cinema. It still works. In a *tour de force* of editing, Roeg presents an extended scene of ordinary, everyday undress – Christie takes a bath, Sutherland showers, brushes his teeth, sits naked at his drawing board – and then intercuts their intense and passionate sex with shots of them getting dressed afterwards, getting ready to go out to dinner. Roeg situates this sex in time, the time of anticipation (before) and reflection (after). It's the sex that people do who are married, who've been having sex with each other for years, and as such it is one of the only representations of 'married love' in the movies. But it's also difficult sex, sex about loss and impossible desire, and it carries an amazingly heavy emotional burden, the fact of their dead child.

Like *The Birds*, *Don't Look Now* is based on a Daphne du Maurier short story, and Roeg's project, cinematically, is visually to elaborate the narrative theme of the interconnectedness of past and future, life and death. Roeg uses the editing especially to connect disparate shots, through repetition of visual shapes, or objects, gestures or camera movements. Music is also a key device for linking otherwise discontinuous elements. In the opening sequence, the shots move between the two kids outside in the garden, the boy on his bike, the girl in her red mac by the pond, and Laura and Baxter by the fire inside. Jump cuts connect the girl throwing her red and white ball with Baxter throwing Laura her packet of cigarettes. The ball splashes on the surface of the pond as Baxter spills his glass of water, whereupon the red shape in the corner of the slide begins to bleed and run. The slide shows the interior of an Italian church, and the source of this red is hard to decipher, possibly a figure seated in a pew, seen from behind. The child's dead body, in her shiny red mac, which Baxter hauls out of the water moments later, fills the screen with the same curved red shape that obliterates the slide. It vaguely resembles the shape of a foetus, as if life and death were encompassed within this form.

Throughout, the colour red functions as a sign for this loss, and the wild hope that emerges out of it. The tiny red hooded figure in Venice is terrifying, an image of the ever-present possibility of sudden death. Baxter apparently has the gift of second sight, but he doesn't know it, he denies it, and so cannot take in the psychic's prophecy that his life in in danger as long as he remains in Venice. Laura believes this warning comes directly from their dead daughter, and the scene of confrontation is as intense as the love scene which precedes it. 'My daughter is dead, Laura,' Baxter states, with increasing anger. 'She does not come peeping with messages back from behind the fucking grave. Christine is dead; she is dead. Dead dead dead dead *dead.*' His wife flinches as he repeats the word, retreating to the wall as if battered. Their capacity to hurt each other – as when she suggests it was his idea to let the children play beside the pond – is palpable. His vehemence persuades her that maybe she's ill, deluded, in need of her doctor, her pills. She seems to comply, but secretly slips the pill under her cuff.

Ways of not seeing

After this row, a phone call in the middle of the night comes from England: their son has had an accident at school, and Laura decides to fly back immediately. After a poignant farewell, in which Roeg allows himself to present what proves to be their last embrace twice, from two different camera angles, Baxter goes to work. At the church, collapsing scaffolding leaves Baxter high above the nave on a wobbling cradle, suspended, in danger of falling to his death for seemingly interminable minutes, until finally hauled to safety. Hanging from a rope, the workman pushes his body with a pole to set him swinging so he can reach out to him: the horrifying comedy of this awkward rescue intensifies the error. The son's accident, his own near fall and the sight of the murdered corpse of a young woman being lifted out of the canal all increase the sense of terrible doom. At this point, Baxter sees Laura on a barge on the Grand Canal, standing all in black, the two sisters on either side of her. He shouts after her, but loses her, and remains convinced she is still in Venice, inexplicably, somehow at the mercy of these women.

The truth value of what we see is constantly called into question, as the issue of who is blind and who can see is repeatedly figured thematically and visually. Baxter's bulbous pale blue eyes are implicitly linked, again by jump cuts, to the huge blue eyes of the blind psychic. He is continually being watched, by the Italian workmen at the church, by unseen figures behind shutters or barred windows, finally by a cop instructed to shadow him. The desolate piazzas of Venice in winter appear like empty stages, where Baxter senses an invisible audience, the clapping of pigeons' wings mocking his anxiety. He is caught peeping through the keyhole of the sisters' hotel room, as the psychic, making contact with his dead daughter, shrieks yes! yes! yes! In a grotesque parody of orgasm. Light coming through shutters, light reflected on water then broken by elaborate Venetian windows and closed shutters, is another repeated image in the film, as if to signify the impediments to clear reflection. As in the opening shot of rain on the surface of the pond, which breaks the flat surface and prevents any clear mirroring, Roeg presents the visual complex of looking and being seen in the form of non-narrative details, fragmentary repetitions that call to mind the uncertainty of appearances.

Narrative theory proposes that the cinema has developed various markers to signify a shift away from the main narrative. Stories are told by presenting related events in linear sequence, unfolding in time as they occurred, and the task of editing is to join the segments one to the next, and to mask the inevitable ellipses. But almost all stories move away from this main line intermittently, events presented being shifted in time, forward or backward, or else into the imaginary or fantastic (as in dream sequences) – or they simply take the form of a parallel subplot subordinate to the main narrative line. Preliminary markers let you know which type of shift it is; classic examples of such markers are the protagonist gazing into the fire, to introduce a reverie, or the screen image wobbling as it dissolves into a fantasy sequence.

Roeg uses all three types of narrative shift, and he generally leaves out the markers that let us know where we are. The recurring shots of Christine's upside-down reflection in the pond are clearly flashbacks, and therefore marked as subjective, but is the red-hooded figure in Venice which echoes this image also therefore imaginary? When Baxter sees his wife on the Grand Canal after she's left Venice, is this a hallucination? (It is not until the very end that he understands this is a glimpse of the future: he has foreseen his own funeral.) The fact that past and future are areas of great uncertainty, subject to both the vagaries of recollection and the unpredictability of events, results in certain cultures using the same linguistic mode for statements about the past, the future, and the imaginary. Yet in the cinema, everything presented visually on the screen has equal claim to reality, and by leaving out crucial narrative markers, Roeg gives form to the larger, non-rational connections across time which the psychic sees and Baxter denies.

A rapid sequence of images floods the screen as Baxter dies; it is the trope of one's whole life flashing before one's eyes – although Roeg sensibly limits the 'whole life' to what the audience has already seen. It is here that the visual connection is finally made between the red shape on the slide at the beginning and the red hooded figure in Venice, through this connection, Roeg proposes that the whole narrative is somehow contained with a larger, inexplicable scheme, a scheme marked out formally, using the figure of the dead child, and by association, the colour red, to structure the events. It never makes sense: if there is a relationship between the evil dwarf and the death of the child, it is never elucidated, only surmised.

It is always deeply disconcerting when the protagonist dies suddenly; the structure of identification attaches our own wish to live to him, turning the screw an extra notch when we are presented with a scene of him agonisingly bleeding to death. His prone body shudders and heaves, his legs kick, recalling the psychic's epilepsy, or the jerking of a slaughtered animal. Roeg is clearly interested in putting death on the screen, sex and death. Violence is a way to figure the intensity of death in visual terms, and in this film, Roeg shows its terrible intimacy, when Baxter pulls the drowned child out of the water and staggers around, roaring with grief, clutching her limp body to him like a lover. The sex scene is itself so powerful partly because it takes place in the context of this unforgettable death, this unspeakable loss.

Stop making sense

The cascade of disparate images that cut across the shots of Baxter's dying body reconfigure the narrative, and situate his love for Laura at the centre of his existence. The images are partly flashback, partly parallel shifts (the psychic sister screams, a close-up of her neck suggesting she is simultaneously experiencing his death). At the very end there is a repetition of the flash forward, to the funeral, as his last moment of comprehension. This film exploits a fundamental fact of cinema, that the camera presents things from the outside, so that subjective and objective events require narrative markers to be distinguished. By leaving these out, Roeg presents a narrative in which inner and outer worlds are mixed up in a terrifying and tragic way. The film has such emotional impact partly because the intimate realism of key scenes of sex and death combines with this intimacy of identification with the central character. We see things through Baxter's eyes, we share confusion of his inner world, and our misunderstanding of the sequence of events coincides with his, until the moment of his death.

Yet despite this subjectivity, *Don't Look Now* is profoundly unpsychoanalytic in how it messes with time. At the moment of Baxter's death, the signifying elements move into some kind of meaningful relationship, with retroactive causality, *nachträglichkeit*. But Roeg goes further, using his cinematic time machine to throw the future in along with the past, confuse the dead with the living. The fundamental irrationality of the proposed structure, the Catholic-psychic continuum within which this story makes sense, has nothing to do with the relentless search for rational meaning that constitutes the psychoanalytic project. Psychoanalysis explains everything, it finds meaning everywhere, it's hooked on meaning. In *Don't Look Now*, these deaths are inexplicable, finally, like evil, and therefore fall outside meaning.

The only way that this narrative could be retrieved for psychoanalysis is to suggest that Baxter pursues the figure in red because unconsciously he knows it will kill him, as his guilt and his grief over his daughter's death propel him towards his own murder. Like Laura, he desires the dead child – and he gets her, so to speak, in all her horror. But that's my version of the story, it's not in the film, really, at all.

One of the real pleasures of this film, as with others by Roeg, lies in the details: the brilliant use of sound to frame a scene, or the moments when the camera remains after the scene is over, like a little excess, a sense of the margins on either side of the plot. Insignificant details become meaningful, and *Don't Look Now* is full of peripheral characters: the pensive chief of police, the anguished hotel concierge, the too too Catholic bishop, the archetypal minor-prep-school headmaster and his wife. There is a *grotesquerie* about all these figures which adds an uncanny dimension of deep dark humour to the film, a cold humour, as if, despite everything, *Don't Look Now* is indeed a machine, a very carefully calibrated clockwork structure which is heartless. As the film opens, Christine is playing by the pond, holding a talking Action Man, a little piece of high technology and gender disruption in this otherwise perfectly pastoral setting; she pulls its string and it makes grandiose military pronouncements, the most telling being 'Fall in!' This is hilarious, and appalling, and something you only notice if you watch on tape. Yet I would claim that this icy humour, like the precise interpolation of specific musical themes, like the sound of rain on water, or the use of blue to frame and counter the incessant, sudden red, or the camera movements across cuts, linking and separating disparate images, I would claim that all of these elements work to structure this film, and the devastating emotional impact of this love story is a direct result of a structure that is so tight, so cold and so true.

VOODOO ROAD

Marina Warner

The plot of *Lost Highway* binds time's arrow into time's loop, forcing Euclidian space into Einsteinian curves where events lapse and pulse at different rates and everything might return eternally. Its first and last shots are the same – the yellow markings of a straight desert road familiar from a thousand movies scrolling down as the camera speeds along low on the ground to the pounding soundtrack. But this linearity is all illusion, almost buoyantly ironic, for you can enter the story at any point and the straight road you're travelling down will unaccountably turn back on itself and bring you back to where you started. That emblem of pioneer America, the road ahead, that track to the future, collapses here into a changeling tale, in which contemporary phantasm about identity loss and multiple personality, about recovered memory, spirit doubles, even alien abduction, all unseat the guy in the driver's seat and lay bare his illusion of control. The film is made like a Moebius strip, with only one surface but two edges: the narrative goes round and round meeting itself, but the several stories it tells run parallel and never join up.

Two plots are braided together: Free Jazz saxophonist Fred Madison (Bill Pullman) and his elusive wife Renée (Patricia Arquette) double expert mechanic Peter Dayton (Balthazar Getty) and the dangerous blonde dollymop and gangster's moll Alice (Arquette again); somewhere in the middle, Fred is spirited away from a prison cell and Pete substituted and the film changes from an ominous Hitchcockian psycho-thriller to a semi-parodic gruesome gangster pic. Scraps of dialogue overlap; the male characters are pierced with excruciating flashes of memory from one another's lives; a puzzle seems to be forming, only to shatter again into an impossible theorem without issue.

The script, by David Lynch and Barry Gifford, mixes register and pitch, swerving between bizarre, semi-occult incidents, and a lowlife peopled by assorted high-tone pimps and heavies. The luscious – and affectless – blonde broad lures Pete into a life of crime, while her protector 'Mr Eddy' doubles as both porno racketeer and one of Lynch's trademark arch-conspirators, his shadow round every corner, his fingerprint on every surface, wiped. During a mountain drive in the Californian sunshine in his vintage Mercedes, Mr Eddy savages a tailgater: a kind of Tarantino vignette of unfettered random violence. This occult/mobster splice recalls *Twin Peaks*, of course, but it also looks back in style as well as narrative to the abrupt convergence of gangsters and initiates, of crime and magic, of external and internal world in *Performance*; *Lost Highway* gives a late millennial twist to Donald Cammell's fascination with switched identities, with dislocation and disorientation of the self. It also shares *Performance*'s Pinteresque manner of italicising such dialogue as does take place, though *Lost Highway* takes laconicism to aphasic extremes. But whereas for Cammell's cast the agents of disintegration are drugs and fame, Lynch's model of consciousness is a haunted house, invested by external, enigmatic forces, over which his protagonists can exercise no choice. 'This is some spooky stuff,' says one of the prison guards after Fred has been spirited from his cell.

American horror – Stephen King, the *Alien* movies – has long been interested in changing ideas about personality; *Lost Highway* similarly shifts its characters away from the humanist and Freudian unitary ego, safely mapped on a unique genetic blueprint and enriched with a lifetime of exclusive personal experiences. Instead Lynch and Gifford play here with a model of personality that far more closely resembles the belief of spirit religions as practised in Haiti, or elsewhere, among the Buissi people of the Southern Congo (as recorded this decade by the anthropologist Anita Jacobson-Widding). In such schemes of identity, the dream self can wander and perform independent acts or become possessed by the spirit and identity of a local stranger over whom the self has no authority. In Voodoo, as is well known, an animal spirit takes possession of the priestess or medium, and invites participants to 'ride' her, to *Tell My Horse*, as Zora Neale Hurston entitled her pioneering work of ethnography from the 1930s; the spirit can also evacuate personhood from a person, creating the walking shadow or 'zombie' so loved by the horror movie tradition. The Buissi, on the other hand, express a more tranquil acceptance of the plurality of the self. 'In the personal discourse,' writes Mary Douglas, 'metaphors for the person refer to body liquids and shadows. They evoke elusiveness, uncertainty, fluidity, ephemerality, ambiguity.' The Salem witch trials reveal how profoundly at risk Christians can feel when they think those shadows are closing in and that they are losing their grip on their sense of self.

Prowlers and intruders

David Lynch's characteristic flux of bizarre, lurid flashes and glimpses swims around the intrinsic instability of personality; his brooding images float and swivel in darkened rooms and mirror reflections from skewed vantage points – high above the action, crawling below it, until the camera itself becomes a plural narrator, a prowler as unpredictable and as knowing as the ghostly intruder who made the videotape that Fred Madison and his wife receive anonymously at the start of the film. There they find their house filmed, then themselves asleep in bed, and finally, in the sequence that brings the first story and Fred's life to a crisis, the savage murder of Renée in the same bedroom. Fred sees himself doing the butchery. But was it him, or was he swapped?

David Lynch does not say so in so many words – *Lost Highway* depends on its insolubility – but his plot assumes a form of shadow stealing or spirit doubling. For example, a 'Mystery Man' turns up at a party and hands Fred a cellular phone; he says that he's at Fred's house at that moment, and tells Fred to call him there. Fred does so, and the Mystery Man's voice, remote but unmistakable replies. The Mystery Man, played with sinister conspiratorial effectiveness by Robert Blake, grins. He has a satyr's pointed ears and eyebrows, and in whiteface and crimson lipstick looks Mephistophelian: he's a trickster figure, gifted with divine ubiquity and omniscience; he lives, we see later, in a desert hideout that spontaneously combusts only to reassemble perfectly, and it is he who is the source and master of the video camera that has anticipated – or perhaps prompted – the murder of Renée.

David Lynch is too committed to the principles of Surrealism to pitch for true thriller suspense; he'd rather catch its shadow after it's passed. He has often invoked

André Breton as a mentor and quoted Breton's axiom about *le merveilleux banal* (the mundane and its wondrousness) and *le hazard objectif* (daily coincidence). His films' eeriness grows from the everyday look of his characters, their suburban millieux and their inconspicuous lives; but *Lost Highway* does not gleam with hygienic and wholesome ordinariness to quite the same hallucinatory degree as *Blue Velvet* or *Twin Peaks*. This new film wears its strangeness with more baroque emphasis. But it does stage an anonymous Los Angeles of well-heeled houses and domestic values (Fred Madison is elegantly set up in a marital home, his doppelgänger Pete lives at home with Mom and Dad). It deploys a range of superfamiliar Californian-American paraphernalia along two axes: designer chic for Fred Madison, whose house is furnished in subdued and sparse Philippe Starck style (some of this being Lynch's own designs), and by contrast in Pete's life, a parodic LA of metallic light, big cars, lock-up cells, canyon roads, polished gold guns, underlit swimming pools, square suits – so that the spooky undependability of the film's storyline erupts more violently. One by one the rules of *film noir* and conventional narrative are laid down, only to be enigmatically set aside. Mr Eddy viciously threatens Pete for interfering with his girl, but thereafter the mobster's pursuit and revenge lose heat and energy. Patricia Arquette plays both Fred's wife and Pete's lover, changing wigs from an Uma Thurman heavy short fringe to a tousled fall of tinsel blonde. The plot confuses her identity beyond solution: she has already been murdered by Fred when she reappears in the bodywork repair shop where Pete works as a mechanic and thereafter vamps him into surrender and of course self-destruction. Or could the events be switched around, and her murder take place after their passionate affair? No, because in one photograph that Pete finds, as he's burgling her pimp's house at her order, she appears twice – side by side with herself.

Mesmerising vacancy

As usual where women are concerned in a David Lynch film, her mystery is as deep as the spectacle of her body and her face: that is, both impenetrable and yet as spectral and thin as the celluloid of which it's made. Peter Deming, the cinematographer, has been directed by Lynch to linger on her in fragments: Arquette's sturdy legs emphasised by shots of her from the back, stalking like some wader on stacked heels, her full mouth fetishistically incarnadined in close-up on a pink telephone, her hands fringed with black lacquered nails on her lovers' backs; she performs a striptease at gunpoint for Mr Eddy and the camera exposes her bit by bit to us, too, the whole manner of image-making effectively translating her substance into a thousand coloured shadows. Arquette sleepwalks with lazy lust through the role, a convincing phantom of desire within a circumscribed convention. Whereas the male doppelgängers whom she enthrals inspire an entirely different brand of scopophilia. Pullman as Fred and Getty as Pete frown, twitch, grow pale and sweaty, screw up lips and eyes in an orgy of expressive anguish that grants them an interiority the modern siren has been denied. Their dream selves have taken up multiple occupancy in their two bodies – and they pour all those recovered memories and unbidden desires into the mesmerising vacancy of Arquette's femme fatale, their fall underlined by such languorous standards as 'I Put a Spell on You', covered here by Marilyn Manson.

Robert Loggia as Mr Eddy brings a charge of cold evil to the part, but he doesn't suffuse the whole film with pent-up menace as Dennis Hopper did in *Blue Velvet*, and *Lost Highway* beats at a slower rate; its mysteries are schematic rather than visceral, those of a clever brainteaser rather than a spinechiller. The general verbal emptiness now and then erupts into a line of dialogue that seems to come from another movie ('That fucker's getting more pussy than a toilet seat'). But throughout, Lynch's interest seems to grasp at another kind of silence, another kind of vacancy: the gaps between sounds. *Lost Highway* has a soundtrack as quick and quivering as a newly shucked oyster or peeling sunburn: noise slashes and slices and shivers, thrums, hums, thrashes and explodes in cascades that suddenly come to a stop, leaving a hole where terror can only collect and deepen. He accompanies this clangour with flaring light – sudden white-outs on screen, foxfire flashes and ghostly shinings, and a climactic sex scene in the desert filmed in burned-out overexposure. In voiceover, such gothic bands as Nine Inch Nails and Smashing Pumpkins come to haunt the action, pacing its slow unfolding to a rhythm that is faster and hotter than the film's; sound effects that have been dubbed in later and have no explicable grounding in the action move in and out of the scenes, in and around the audience, coming and going in a dazzling aural equivalent of the prying and ubiquitous camera. Lynch's way of foregrounding his soundtrack calls attention to his film-making presence; significantly, it creates a faceless but insistent double who is masterminding the audience response. The conspicuous camera-work and flaring noise of *Lost Highway* don't enhance the story in a traditional thriller manner, but interrupt and disturb its flow, compelling the audience to see how film can take possession of your mind and estrange you from yourself, just as the characters in *Lost Highway* are estranged from themselves.

Invasive and distorting

As in Dziga Vertov's classic study of the cinema's way of looking, *Man with a Movie Camera*, *Lost Highway* is telling a story about the medium. But unlike Vertov's witty self-reflexive celebration, it expresses disquiet, distrust, even repudiation. Lynch may not be strongly invested in sincerity as a quality, but this latest movie certainly mounts an attack on film narrative's mendacity, showing deep alarm at its hallucinatory powers of creating alternative realities. Simultaneously, it also calls into question film's capacities to document and record: everything filmed is fabrication, but that fabrication has the disturbing power to supplant reality.

Fred's initial ferocious revulsion against the medium pulses through the whole film, dispersed among different characters: photography is totalising and invasive and distorting, its record of 'the way things happened' arbitrary and capricious and coercive; it replaces personal images and inhabits your head and takes it over. Fred's head bursts in agony with the pictures inside it; later Pete suffers a blow to his head and afterwards is crushed by migraines, as the memory of who he is crashes into phantasms of something other crowding his eyes. When Pete is breaking and entering the pimp's house a huge video screen hangs above the gilt and crystal living room, where a grimacing but mute Alice is being taken from behind (or perhaps buggered) in lumpy black and white. At first, it seems that she is in a room in the house somewhere at that moment, being forced; but then she comes down the marble flight upstairs, imperturbable. Lynch seems to want to clear space between his own kind of film-making and the porn industry: when Mr Eddy dies, his throat slit by Pete/Fred and a collar of gore seeping into his shirt, a pocket video monitor is thrust into his hand where the shooting of the porn film flickers; his murder is revenge for his debauch.

Yet Mr Eddy and his sidekick, the Mystery Man, may also embody Lynch's own alter egos, his shadow side. For their methods in *Lost Highway* replicate Lynch's process as a film-maker: he is the invisible eye that enters the bedrooms of his characters, who stages their sex acts, their crimes, their disintegration, who takes possession of their inner imaginary lives and moves them to his desire. And the plot of *Lost Highway* adapts narrative devices that film – and only film – can make actually visible, mines that potential to represent the uncanny that the medium had delightedly played with from its earliest years. *Der Student von Prag* (1913) first explored the theme of the doppelgänger, when its protagonist sells his shadow to the devil in return for a bottomless purse of gold, and then in a wonderfully shivery moment watches his identical double slide out of the door, smiling. Reversing action, slowing down time, replicating two different people in the same body (*The Double Life of Veronique* was a recent example of the genre) have almost become jaded cinema tricks, but still, prose storytelling can only assert they happen; film, in comic or eerie mode, can make them seem real. Lynch here has taken this further: his changelings imply the phantasmagoric but practical world of movie-making, in which actors alter appearance and behaviour from film to film, and stand-ins have to be indistinguishable from their 'originals'. Above all, though, his use of recovered memories extends the notion of flashback, as does indeed therapists' faith in them during analysis of previously forgotten abuse. Also, Lynch's handling of looped time mimics the fast-forward/reverse stasis of the editing booth, while his exploration of disassociated lives intermingling at random, and of switched identities, comments from one point of view on the relation between stars and audience and the projection the modern enterprise of fame overwhelmingly encourages in America – introducing a new aberration in iconoclasm, John Lennon's murder, Valerie Solanas's attempt on Andy Warhol.

Modern Narcissus

When Fred Madison declares, disclaiming the truth of the video record, 'I want to remember things my way – which is not necessarily the way they happened,' David Lynch is fingering a contemporary anguish about identity. Such contemporary artists as Sophie Calle have explored the autistic realm of the surveillance camera and its hosts of anonymous, zombie-like inhabitants; Tatsuo Miyajima's current show at the Hayward Gallery aestheticises digital signifiers in a poetic reverie that rescues ideas of symbolic time for metaphysics, reanimating automatically generated computerised data. Contemporary video installations, such as *Tall Ships* by Garry Hills or *The Messenger* by Bill Viola, conjure revenants and angels from the looped dreams of the camcorder. Those who fear to lose their souls to the image are desperately seeking to capture its unique mystery, somewhere stable and permanent amid the spate of duplicates and faked images and reflections. The modern Narcissus looks into the pool, and there are two of him there, maybe more; and he does not know which is which. *Lost Highway* touches on these concerns, but its handling remains oddly bland, ultimately hollow. The film asserts an all American, suburban-Puritan belief in the idiosyncratic eyewitness and the visionary, the truth of an individual viewpoint and even of messianic derangement, while all the while conveying almost wearily that such subjectivity as idealised elsewhere has entered terminal decline.

IT'S A WONDERFUL LIFE:
THE DARK END OF THE STREET

Jonathan Romney

Frank Capra's 1946 film *It's a Wonderful Life* has a place in American culture as a seasonal institution, as comfortingly indigenous as poinsettia garlands and fibreglass reindeer. Televised in the United States every Christmas, it offers a reminder of an imagined better time and place, and of that small-town benevolence of which Capra is generally considered the laureate. For many, the film can only be accepted now in the spirit of kitsch, as the ultimate hymn to mulled-wine nostalgia. In such ironic spirit, television sitcoms have rendered it homage: it has been sobbed over by the cast of *Cheers*, while Phoebe in *Friends* turned it off, traumatised, unaware that it had a happy ending.

But it can also be taken at face value as a heart-warmer. This year's London Film Festival brochure reprints Geoff Brown's *Time Out* review: 'an extraordinary unabashed testament to [Capra's] homely small-town moral values ... Capra enjoys ... a touching determination to believe that it is indeed a wonderful life.' A less charitable view is James Wolcott's, in the *New Yorker* in 1986: '*It's a Wonderful Life* is the perfect film for the Reagan era, celebrating the old-fashioned values of home and hearth that everyone knows deep down have eroded... Like Reagan, Capra is a blue-sky optimist who filters out bad news.' In fact, even on its release at Christmas 1946, the film was seen in similar terms. Bosley Crowther in the *New York Times* called it 'a figment of simple Polyanna platitudes', while the *New Republic* saw Capra as 'Hollywood's Horatio Alger [fighting]... to convince movie audiences that American life is exactly like the *Saturday Evening Post* covers by Norman Rockwell'.

We certainly deceive ourselves if we fondly imagine Capra's film to be a naïve expression of its time, the pure spirit of 1946. As these reviews suggest, it already seemed anachronistic in its day, and it was eclipsed at the box office by a far more sober anatomy of America's mood after World War II – *The Best Years of Our Lives* by William Wyler, Capra's partner in the independent Liberty Films.

But Capra's picture of nightmare duality should alert us to look further than the film's reassuring surface. Despite his antipathy, Wolcott hits the spot when he talks of Capra filtering out bad news, because the film is very much about that filtering – about the mechanisms that suppress frustration in order to make life bearable. Closing on an image of community and seasonal cheer, as its traumatised hero George Bailey (James

Stewart) is reunited with family and friends, *It's a Wonderful Life* may purport to leave us smiling, yet having unveiled life's underlying horrors, it can hardly hope to cover them up again so neatly. The film's seemingly utopian setting has its dark converse: convivial Bedford Falls has its nightmare mirror image in the hellish Pottersville, where George spends his dark night of the soul. The film's defining, irreducible bad news is that Pottersville is not a place apart from Bedford Falls, but contained within it.

Capra's own explanation of the film, however, was unequivocal. He saw it as a message of comfort and encouragement. In his autobiography *The Name Above the Title*, he called it 'a film that said to the downtrodden, the pushed-around, the pauper, "Heads up, fella."' He claimed that he himself had been on the receiving end of just such a brisk admonition: ill and depressed after the success of his 1934 film *It Happened One Night*, he was visited by a mysterious 'little man' who told him to use his film-making talent for the good of the community: 'When you don't use the gifts God blessed you with – you are an offence to God – and to humanity.'

Yet the film is far from being a straightforward parable. In the opening credit sequence, a fantasia of Christmas-card iconography, the title actually appears as *'It's a Wonderful Life'*. The inverted commas suggest that the expression is not the film's unqualified statement, but rather the citation of a proverb, a piece of common folk wisdom. The film will not simply illustrate that wisdom, but put it to the test. What is proposed is not a statement but a question: how wonderful is life, and under what conditions?

Another Good Sam

Based on a short story by Philip Van Doren Stern, the film tells a tale of sacrifice and reconciliation. George Bailey, as Capra put it, is 'a Good Sam who doesn't know that he is a Good Sam'. This young man with big dreams – to see the world, to build bridges – renounces his passions one by one and stays in his home town to do his familial and civic duty. The very first time we see him, in a flashback to his childhood, he saves his kid brother Harry from drowning in an icy pond, losing the hearing in his left ear in the process. As a man, he gives up travel, study and his honeymoon to step into his father's place running the town's Buildings and Loan company, all to save Bedford Falls from the clutches of the banker Potter (Lionel Barrymore). Potter, the sort of top-hatted capitalist you see only in old Soviet cartoons or Capra films, is a reincarnation of the manipulative demagogues in Capra's earlier *Mr Deeds Goes to Town* (1936), *Mr Smith Goes to Washington* (1939) and *Meet John Doe* (1941), just as George at first seems a simple avatar of those films' stand-up heroes.

But where those earlier Good Sams were yanked out of their home towns and con-fronted with cynical urban values, George Bailey is tested at home. His altruistic deeds are performed on sufferance – he knows only too well what he's giving up. Where Longfellow Deeds and Jefferson Smith, unimpressed by city ways, might happily have subscribed to the motto 'There's no place like home', George is not so sure: secretly, he views home as his chief torment. Having dreaded to languish in his father's 'business of nickels and dimes', he can only hold out for so long before he recognises Bedford Falls as his prison, and his home life – bedrock value the film appears to endorse – as his personal cell. One Christmas Eve, his Uncle Billy mislays $8,000, which falls into Potter's hands, and George is faced with ruin. Returning home to his wife Mary (Donna Reed) and boisterous children, George cracks up entirely. On the verge of suicide, he must be saved by heavenly powers, who intervene to remind him that his is a wonderful life, after all.

Their intervention is implicitly punitive. George is policed not only for flouting the prohibition against suicide, but also for seeing through the façade and recognising that the seemingly idyllic Bedford Falls has its hellish aspects. The town is ruled by the satanic Potter, who forever threatens townspeople with perdition; only George can redeem them, not through goodwill but with hard cash. And in this apparently good-neighbourly utopia, pettiness and malevolence threaten to erupt at any moment: an unidentified Iago figure lurks at the high-school hop, ready to whisper ideas of sabotage to Mary's spurned beau; tongues conspire against local sexpot Violet (Gloria Grahame); and George's flock of savings investors are so fickle that he constantly has to dole out bounty to keep them from straying to Potter.

Only George, apparently, can hold the fragile surface of things together. Just as his eventual lapse of faith threatens moral perdition, so in Bedford Falls every stable surface threatens an unexpected fall: thin ice that cracks, nearly killing George's brother Harry; the high-school dance floor that splits open to reveal a swimming pool; the river that invites George to a suicidal leap. If the film can be read in terms of America's disillusion and fatigue following World War II, it's worth pointing out that the war itself features as another of George's crises, again associated with falling and water: while his faulty hearing keeps him at home, Harry becomes a hero saving seaborne troops from drowning.

Sneaky scene shifting

Having crossed the barrier to despair, George must be brought back to the world, taught to accept and even enjoy his fate – not just the pleasures of home, but the full weight of the problems he faces. The agent sent to retrieve him is Clarence (Henry Travers), an angel who stands to win his wings if he succeeds in his mission. The film's framing sequence, in which two celestial nebulae summon Clarence for the job, is oddly reminiscent of *Mission Impossible* – before he sets out, Clarence is briefed on his target. The first half of the film, reviewing George's life, thus takes the form of Clarence's private screening of the George Bailey biopic.

Once Clarence has stepped in to George's story and saved him from jumping, he still has to persuade him back to a positive path. He does this by granting George's wish that he had not been born, and takes him round Bedford Falls as it would have been without him. This whole twenty-minute segment, known in production as the 'unborn sequence', is effectively the second of two films-within-the-film – it is a movie that has been laid on for George's benefit, and its genre is *film noir*.

Benevolent Bedford Falls has suddenly become dark Pottersville, its jolly, friendly Main Street a garish, starkly lit night drag of strip joints and cocktail bars, where police sirens blare and innocently saucy Violet is an unruly hussy dragged away by the cops. George's pals, the town's jolly cop and cabbie, have taken on the hard-bitten look of *film noir* heavies; erased from existence, George is unknown to his own mother, now a pinched-faced boarding-house keeper. George's ultimate shock – and this is where modern audiences tend to lose patience with the film's persuasive rhetoric – is to find that romantic, tender Mary is Pottersville's frosty librarian. Traumatised, George pleads to be restored to the world, and rushes in relief back to his home and his worries. The story's structure is effectively the same as Dickens' *A Christmas Carol*, but where Scrooge is shamed by the picture of an infinitely better future without him, George sees a world damned by his absence.

This spectacle terrorises George through its appeal to his concern for others, but, perversely from a Christian point of view, it also speaks directly to his narcissism. He is effectively shown that he is the centre of the universe. 'Each man's life touches so many other lives,' Clarence philosophises. 'When he isn't around, he leaves an awful hole.' So Bedford Falls collapses without George, and its dark twin town hangs around a George-shaped hole. Only he could have saved Bedford Falls: without him, Mary would have found no other man; his mother would have known no joy; and no one else could have measured up as an adversary of Potter.

It seems drastically out of proportion, this elevation of unsung small-town hero to universal redeemer. And the extraordinary excess of this argument reveals the 'unborn sequence' for what it is – a piece of persuasive rhetoric on both Clarence's part and the film's. It is targeted as much at the viewer as at George, as if to bolster the self-esteem of every undervalued Good Sam in the audience.

This excess is manifest in the whole style of the Pottersville sequence, which is so radically at variance with the rest of the film that we can't help suspecting its artifice. Pottersville is an elaborately fabricated scare, a shadow show laid on for George's benefit by Clarence (who after all stands to gain his wings if his rhetoric succeeds), a piece of stage work in which phenomenal feats of *mise-en-scène* have been pulled. The homely wooden sign announcing 'You Are Now in Bedford Falls' (the very first thing we see in the film) has been replaced by a screaming neon 'Pottersville'; the friendly Italian bar has become a spit-and-sawdust speakeasy; Bailey Park, the safe-haven housing estate George has founded, has been stripped down and replaced by rows of tombstones. George, panicking according to plan, is the victim of much the same confidence trick as is frequently pulled in *Mission Impossible* on Eastern Bloc Generals, who are remarkably gullible when faced with a bit of sneaky scene shifting. Artifice is, after all, what we're watching: the film's quintessential Christmas landscape was created with truckloads of fake snow in high summer in the San Fernando Valley.

Such manifest artifice quite clearly announces the 'unborn sequence' as a device of persuasion, and thereby entirely subverts its effect – what it reveals is the denial that is necessary if George's visit to Pottersville is not, ultimately, a device for restoring cohesion to a fractured existence, so much as a trauma that introduces an irreparable fracture into the film. It suddenly breaks open a space for all the possibilities that the George Bailey story otherwise excludes – including sexuality, which now blares from every neon sign on Main Street. Violet's apotheosis as a fully fledged bad girl at last expresses the disruptive sexuality that until then has been only implicit in the figure of the small-town flirt.

The anti-Kane

Pottersville jerks us violently out of the familiar Capra universe and into the other American world that exists in parallel to it, the world of *noir* and the psychological thriller. By 1946, those genres had already redrawn the psychic route map of US cinema. A sleepy burgh like Bedford Falls now had to take its place amid the sinister back roads of Edgar G. Ulmer's *Detour* (1945); small-town cosiness had already been exposed as a lethal claustrophobia in Alfred Hitchcock's *Shadow of a Doubt* (1943) and Orson Welles's *The Stranger* (1946), in which Main Street is visited respectively by a serial killer and a fugitive Nazi.

Once the screen is broken that separates Bedford Falls from its dark side, other films and other meanings erupt into *It's a Wonderful Life*. Bedford Falls is no longer a place enclosed in its own little fold of the movie universe, but takes its place in a map dominated by *noir*. Violet's fate is surely to head for the big city to become the sort of hard-bitten dame that Gloria Grahame played in Edward Dmytryk's *Crossfire* (1947) and Fritz Lang's *The Big Heat* (1953). One film touches so many other films: David Thomson used Clarence's dictum as the basis of his 1984 novel *Suspects*, in which characters from crime movies are interlinked in a labyrinthine narrative. Thomson's closing coup is to reveal his sombre narrator as none other than George Bailey, now a fatigued cinephile fantasist with troubled family links to Otto Preminger's *Laura*, and the father of Travis Bickle and Harry Moseby, the doomed hero of Arthur Penn's *Night Moves*.

Pottersville also leads us in the direction of *Citizen Kane*, for what is George Bailey if not the anti-Kane? Welles reviewed the life of a man who made the world in his own image, but whose real effect on it was finally elusive; Capra's film takes the form of a newsreel about an unsung hero who changes the world to its roots. Clarence is Capra's counterpart to Welles's reporter, except that he already knows the truth of George's life and is on a mission to reveal it to him. George has his Xanadu – the old empty house whose windows he smashes wishing for dreams he will never realise, and which Mary turns into the family home. Revisited in Pottersville, the house is a ghost mansion, haunted not by impossible dreams but by cancelled realities. George has his Rosebud too – the petals entrusted to him by his daughter, which signal his return to life, and that life's deepest meaning ('ZuZu's petals!', his wonderstruck exclamation, is surely the strangest thing in the film).

The Pottersville sequence opens out onto Hitchcock, for it also marks the birth of the darker, more fragmented persona that James Stewart would develop in the 1950s. Capra's story of falls is surely Stewart's dry run for *Vertigo*: we can already see Scottie's look of terror, as he dangles from the San Francisco parapet in George's face, filling the screen in harsh chiaroscuro, as he runs from Ma Bailey's Boarding House and heads straight for the camera. Is he looking to us for succour, forcing us to recognise ourselves as his double, or realising with horror that he's a character in a film, the wrong sort of film? Either way, theories on the gaze of the Hitchcockian hero surely have their *ur*-text in this one shot, so violently incongruous within Capra's universe.

Excess of meaning

The last scene of *It's a Wonderful Life* appears to bring a satisfying resolution. George is reunited with his family, the townspeople arrive with money to pay his deficit, and the whole happy community sings 'Auld Lang Syne' – '*Lest old acquaintance be forgot.*' The lesson could not be clearer: remember old friends, observe the ties of community. This theme, community's claim on the individual, is the bottom line of Capra's world,

'Auld Lang Syne' its anthem (it was also the song played to welcome Jefferson Smith to the Senate).

But then Smith was being set up, and so, as we have seen, is George. There is a huge ambiguity in Stewart's face in this final scene – George's look of joy as he returns to the fold seems hysterically overstated, a wild relief that is the forced counterpart to his earlier terror-struck look to camera. We see him at last, hemmed in as family and the entire town cram into his living room. He must know that responsibility weighs on him now more than ever – there is no prospect of reward, rest or escape. Potter, who still has the mislaid $8,000, remains undefeated. The film ends with a strange, unarticulated sense of incompletion.

However, the closing strains of 'Auld Lang Syne' remind us that the film has another theme besides resignation and civic virtue, and that is memory. George's world almost foundered on faulty memory – his crisis was precipitated not by Potter, but by his own benevolent, ruinously forgetful Uncle Billy. And an attentive memory is required if the viewer hopes to unpick the complexities of the film's narrative. At the very start, as the celestial projectionists screen George's life, they warn Clarence, 'Something happens here that you'll have to remember later on.' So in a movie unusually packed with significance, no detail is incidental; the slightest event, as we learn in Pottersville, has continuing ramifications. George saves Harry from drowning, which saves the lives of many airmen, but also leaves him partially deaf. That means that George never hears young Mary's declaration, whispered in a pregnant close-up early on, that she'll love him till the day she dies, and so never identifies her love as a secret thread that holds his life together. Chance remarks rebound in ways that only a second viewing reveals: George jokily refers in passing to 'the old Bailey boarding house', which in Pottersville it literally becomes. No visual detail is lost either, especially that plethora of signs spread around town, which we take for granted until they all suddenly change, usurped by neon and the insignias of Pottersville.

The film buzzes with an excess of meaning, a multiplicity of loose ends which militates against the directness that would be required if the film really were a sermon of good cheer for Good Sams. Just as the never-returned $8,000 is an imbalance in George's economy, so the film's richness and complexity refuse to add up to tally with Capra's declared meaning.

What we end up with instead is something far more complex, indeterminate and stimulating. If the film has a lesson to teach, it is less about citizenship than readership. It offers a lesson in memory, in the difficulty and pleasure in sifting, remembering, interpreting the significant and *potentially* significant details in a story, and in a life. Hence the film's continuing appeal – not as a heart-warmer, but as an intricate, troubling enigma that keeps offering new levels of meaning. On each viewing, different elements are remembered and become newly meaningful; their significances tie up, return and untie themselves, much as they do in *Kane* or, for that matter, in Proust – and the Pottersville episode could not be a more extreme and literal illustration of *le temps perdu*.

Everything in George Bailey's story signifies, down to the last detail, to the point where we might take it as a cue for paranoia – if every moment can affect a life and other lives, how infinite are the choices we must constantly make just to keep afloat?

A pullulating infinity of possibilities opens up to subvert completely the film's ostensible purpose as a warming homily, together with its pious implication that George's destiny is predetermined, scripted in the stars. It may be a wonderful life, but we know it's not the only possible one.

A CHILD'S DEMON

David Thomson

In 1930s Ohio, hard-up father of two Ben Harper (Peter Graves) robs a bank of $10,000, killing two guards. About to be captured, Ben stuffs the loot in daughter Pearl's doll and makes Pearl (Sally Jane Bruce) and her brother John (Billy Chapin) swear they will never tell where it's hidden. In jail, Ben's cellmate Harry Powell (Robert Mitchum), a murderously misogynist preacher in for car theft, fails to get Ben to spill the beans before his death. On his release, Powell starts to woo Ben's widow Willa (Shelley Winters), and he soon announces to John that he is going to become his stepfather. After he moves into the house, Powell begins to threaten and cajole the children into telling him where the money is. When Willa discovers the truth, the children find themselves alone and on the run, with Powell in pursuit.

*   *   *

We are so used to loving the lyric uniqueness of *The Night of the Hunter* (1955) and the big bad greatness of Robert Mitchum, and such willing believers in the hope that two misunderstood actors could still slip a masterpiece into the world, that you might go through life knowing nothing of this.

'Another night he had taken a young mountain whore drunk to his room in a cheap boarding house in Cincinnati and she had passed out naked on the bed and he had taken out the knife and stood by the bed with it unopened in his hand for a while, looking at her and waiting for the Word and when it did not come he pressed the button and the steel tongue licked out, and bending by the bed on the worn rug he delicately scratched a cross in the girl's belly beneath the navel and left her there with that brand so frail and faint upon the flesh that it did not even bleed; and when she woke in the morning alone she did not even notice it, so lovingly and with so practical and surgical a precision had he wrought it there.'

That is Davis Grubb's novel, and it is enough to let you feel the lack of a certain light-handedness in the film. And much as I cherish the memory of Robert Mitchum, as well as the occasion provided by *The Night of the Hunter*, to say to all the idiots, look, he *was* an actor, you have to wonder whether Mitchum had it in him to play that reverie, leaving the cross 'so frail and faint' that not even the whore noticed it. For if there are silent communions between Grubb's Harry Powell and God, could Mitchum's Powell ever let anything stay quiet or inward? That's an odd question, surely, for Mitchum in his own *metier – Out of the Past* (1947), say, or *The Lusty Men* (1952) – was the unspoken actor. He could look, and leave us to notice. But maybe Charles Laughton had arranged the air of his Hunter so that everything had to be loud – like thunder in a play?

Asked to reconsider Charles Laughton's one and only film, I don't want to go back on my old assurance – let alone disown its marvels. For I recall, in the 1970s, in the United States, having to struggle with the natives to persuade them that this was one of their own great things. A lot of smart people then felt it was an aberration, a rather overwrought kids' film. Yet I give some thanks that I was not exposed to cinematographer Stanley Cortez's hound-of-hell night as a child. There are things still to support Pauline Kael's belief that it is 'one of the most frightening movies ever made'. I am thinking of the crucial instant in the night escape, when John and Pearl – tiny in their rowing boat – are about to push off as the demented Powell appears, only a few steps away on the shore. The boat starts to glide and his monstrous reach is stopped only by the quicksand they were too light to sink in. He plunges, the boat clears; but the first time I saw the film I shuddered at the foul grasp so narrowly escaped. And I was 20 or so then. There may have been children marked forever. Except that, at the time of its opening, Kael recalls only a dozen or so seats filled in a theatre made for 2,000. *The Night of the Hunter* was a disaster when it was made, for it was closer in mood to *Ugetsu Monogatari* (1953) than to the hit flicks of its year – *Blackboard Jungle, Love Is a Many-Splendored Thing, Love Me or Leave Me* and even *Rebel without a Cause*.

A bear waiting to be prodded

Where did such an aberration come from? It's tempting to answer, and hope, that the fairytale vision, the pattern of innocence and menace, had always been there in Charles Laughton's soul. But then we'd have to remind ourselves of how often, and with what relish, Laughton had played hideous threats worse than Mitchum's Powell – or monsters held in their own glow of sentimentality. He was a figure of fun by 1955: he had to mix in a Herod and a Henry VIII with the Captain Kidd who met Abbott and Costello. He rarely dominated big pictures as he had in the 30s. He was large, slow, not always well, and often broke. That he had big, vague dreams still is hardly doubted: you can feel that in *Advise & Consent* (1962) as much as in the odd, fatigued Lear he did at Stratford in 1959 (with Ian Holm as his Fool). But he was also a gentle, aimless man, a bear waiting to be prodded. Paul Gregory was that prod.

In 1950, when he introduced himself to Laughton, Gregory was 30 years old, uncommonly handsome, and an agent at MCA. The looks are not just gossip, for Simon Callow in his fond meditation on Laughton believed that the actor – already 51 – may have been infatuated with Gregory. They do not seem to have been lovers, but something like love, or the hope of rescue, may have prompted the great actor whose reputation was in decline. And Gregory was full of bright ideas – he won Laughton over by seeming so intellectual and artistic.

It was Gregory who saw how close to uncastable Laughton had become in conventional works, and who developed the strategy of one-man shows or readings that might earn a fortune. In time, Gregory gave up his agency job to concentrate on being Laughton's manager. And so – from 1951 onwards, with Cedric Hardwicke,

Charles Boyer and Agnes Moorehead – Laughton toured in a version of 'Don Juan in Hell' from Shaw's *Man and Superman*. That was followed by Stephen Vincent Benet's *John Brown's Body* and Herman Wouk's *The Caine Mutiny Court Martial*, both of which Laughton directed and did not act in.

Gregory had given Laughton confidence, for the actor had never before directed. (Famously, his doubts had ruined von Sternberg's *Claudius* project.) And it was Gregory who read the novel *The Night of the Hunter* and recommended it as a movie when the book proved a strong seller in 1953. I wish I knew more about Davis Grubb. He was born in Moundsville, West Virginia (an Ohio River town mentioned in the book and the movie) in 1919. He wrote several novels, though this one was the most popular. Callow says: 'It has not, according to those who know, "worn well".' That's a reference to Charles Higham's earlier book on Laughton, which goes on to say: 'It can now be seen to belong to that odd, hybrid "lyrical" genre that included works like *Dark of the Moon* and *Finian's Rainbow* on the stage. The author aimed at a kind of folksy poetic approach which never quite comes off: a cross between Thomas Wolfe and Sherwood Anderson...'

A voice from the house of childhood

I hope the extract quoted at the start of this essay casts some doubt on that verdict. Davis Grubb writes very carefully – sometimes a touch studiously – but the poetics do not seem laid on. Rather, compared with the tone of the movie (and its sweeping magical realism), there is something both grave and natural in Davis Grubb. Consider the scene, in novel and film, where the fleeing children shelter in a barn loft, and John is woken by the sound of Powell coming through the night, singing. In the movie the barn is a cut-out shape in the foreground, and our eyes go to the far horizon where Powell comes up like a Lotte Reiniger silhouette. It is a great, Grimm scene, presaged by the dissolves that haul the crescent moon higher in the sky, and hugely assisted by the sound of Mitchum singing, a big-chested baritone in a far room of the house of childhood. But Davis Grubb is pretty good, too:

'John had not been sleeping more than an instant until he heard it – faint yet distinct on the barely stirring air. He opened his eyes. The moon had not moved: it stood where it had been when his eyes had closed: half obscured by the beam and pulley which jutted over the aperture. Pearl had not heard, did not stir, asleep in untroubled conscience with her thumb between her pouting lips and the doll cuddled sweetly in the cradle of her arms... It was as clear and distinct now as if the tiny voice were in the mountain of hay at her elbow, and then suddenly in the distance John saw him on the road, emerging suddenly from behind a tall growth of redbud half a mile away: a man on a huge field horse, moving slowly and yet with a dreadful plodding deliberation up the feathery dust of the river road.'

Maybe the most notable thing about this passage is that it comes from an adult book about a child, whereas Laughton elected to make a film as seen and felt from a child's point of view. But that was not his first plan. Laughton and Gregory asked the film critic James Agee to do a script from Grubb's novel. To this day, erroneously, that 'script' is part of the Agee legend. In 1954 Agee was 44, and only a year away from death. Having served for much of the 1940s as film reviewer at *Time* and *The Nation*, he had slipped into screenwriting by way of his friendship with John Huston. Agee worked hard on *The African Queen* (1951) – so hard he had a heart attack to go with chain-smoking and a bottle of whisky a day. He was replaced by Peter Viertel, but esteemed still by Huston for insisting on 'the right, even the obligation, to write and to fuck as much as he can and in the ways he prefers to'.

Agee was given the awesome deal of $30,000 for ten weeks' work on *The Night of the Hunter*. As if sensing a last chance, he moved into the Chateau Marmont hotel and turned the 206-page novel into a 350-page script, full of material about the Depression and its impact on the Ohio River country. His work had been complicated and intensified by a hectic love affair with Tamara Comstock. Laughton was horribly disappointed by the result so he set it aside and began work on a new script of his own that used only a few of Agee's ideas. Instead, it held to the novel's shape; Laughton may even have enlisted Grubb's help. The schedule was delayed and the precarious venture was put in some jeopardy with its financier, United Artists.

Even so, Gregory had worked a modest miracle: a novice director was allowed $700,000 to make an arty project with a good deal of location work. Getting Robert Mitchum as Harry Powell was as vital to the deal as holding Mitchum's creative attention was to the spirit of the film. For already he was among the most indifferent or casual of stars, the proud possessor of the wisdom that all he did was walk through one picture after another, letting himself be photographed. Of course, Mitchum took high risks as Harry Powell (not least in revealing that he could bring an intelligence and caring to bear), and he always said he was adventurous for Charles Laughton's sake. I heard him once in an interview (with his old friend, Niven Busch) where he said he loved working with Laughton, but he never went deeper than that into Powell's nature.

Showing off like crazy

Of course, he didn't need to. Powell is more than the regular Mitchum – given to lengthy, theatrical speeches, moaning like an animal, arching a comic eye at God and generally being extravagant – but in Laughton's concept he is a distorted ogre (half nemesis, half buffoon) as seen by the children. The most remarkable thing about the movie may be that Mitchum – a master of the hard-boiled – so easily catches the flamboyance and fragrance of gothic fairytale. But just because he stands for the children's dread of Powell – the grasp pursuing them – he does not have to ask himself, or show us, much about Davis Grubb's more inward Powell.

Simon Callow notes that Laughton confessed to Mitchum his own homosexuality (he may not have needed to), and wonders – hopefully, perhaps – whether he touched some such buried instict in the frequently surly and very male Mitchum. One never knows, but I find it more likely that Mitchum – intrigued by the part and impressed by Laughton – offered something like a gay comic style in his Powell. In other words, is there something a little swish in this great performance, a gloss that keeps Grubb's more mysterious man at a distance? This may seem churlish – for Mitchum is extraordinary in the film – but I wonder if Robert Ryan, say, might have been truer to Grubb's figure?

Mitchum is so handsome, rather dandyish in his dress, sleek, well spoken and polished – he never gets the shabby, weatherbeaten quality of a real rural wanderer.

Grubb's Powell is less rhetorical, more hurt, and more inwardly wicked in that he finds no comfort in acting out or showing off. Mitchum does not quite seem wicked or past hope – couldn't he go into burlesque, or some other Church, with a chance of being a spellbinder? Yes, Mitchum took a chance with the role, but he showed off like crazy. There was actually a moment in the shooting when Lillian Gish saw the concealed charm he was unloading, and asked Laughton if he shouldn't be more unequivocally evil. The director is supposed to have answered that he didn't want to destroy Mitchum's career. That may be just a movie-set anecdote, but it could also be a sign of the playfulness in Michum's Powell, or the way he is only a child's demon.

More damaging to the film's dramatic potential, I think, is Lillian Gish's serene fairy godmother Rachel, so sturdily pure, so much a mistress of Bible and rifle that no hunting rogue has a chance at the little ones once they are in her protection. Laughton fell in love with Gish, he said, as he studied Griffith's films in preparing for *The Night of the Hunter*. But he was looking at the young woman, a classically threatened figure whose nobility and courage run the risk of death itself. Griffith did not have much time for real, middle-aged women – except as examples of bourgeois hypocrisy. There are glimpses of Griffith in *The Night of the Hunter*: repeated shots of the mother hen and her chicks scampering along the river bank, reflected in the water. But the strangeness of Ohio Valley life, its sense of isolation, comes from Grubb's novel, or from movies about the 1930s, just as Cortez's album-ready photography derives from Germanic imagery of the 1920s.

Cortez excels in the ordeal of the children, even if so many shots – like that of Willa dead in the car on the river bed – feel like set pieces. But once the children have been taken in by Rachel, does anyone doubt their safety? For Rachel is a child's perfect adult: strong, secure, removing all need for responsibility, yet actually child-like herself. The film is so much more worrying when it has adults who are foolish, nasty and vulnerable – like Willa, Icey (Evelyn Varden) and Walt (Don Beddoe), arguably the best thing in the film, and the hapless Birdie (James Gleason). These are adults who cannot reassure the children. Yet at the end of everything, we are asked to swallow the bromide – that little ones abide.

Dark magic

Did Laughton want to believe that? Surely he was too wise and wounded a man to fall for the simplicity. Was he driven to it out of fatigue, as a way of ending the film and settling the dark magic it had brought into being? I don't know the answers, but after years of admiration – and a proper reading of Davis Grubb – I begin to see short-comings in the Laughton film. Yes, it can knock your eyes out. Yes, there is nothing like it. But even when your eyes yield, your mind can find things to worry about, and the greatest of these may be the novel's secret bond between the figure of Powell and the boy John. It's worth adding that, though Laughton's film sides so totally with the little ones, the director could scarcely bring himself to talk to the child actors. That hurt shows in the wary eyes of Billy Chapin.

The Night of the Hunter flopped. François Truffaut, in Paris, was one of the few people who liked it. But before the failure Gregory and Laughton had bought the film rights to Norman Mailer's *The Naked and the Dead*. Laughton and Mailer discussed it together.

A whole script was done – surely worth seeing now, for it may have been *The Thin Red Line* before its time. But when *Hunter* failed the money vanished. Laughton would never direct again. Which may not be the worst thing in the world, for we treasure *The Night of the Hunter* as a solitary excursion.

BRING BACK THE CAT

Kim Newman

Val Lewton, the producer of Jacques Tourneur's *Cat People* (1943) and Gunther V. Fritsch and Robert Wise's *The Curse of the Cat People* (1944), is perhaps unique in US cinema as a producer-auteur whose influence was always beneficial. His 11 films for RKO were made by four directors, written by a small group of scenarists (all extensively revised by Lewton) and drew on the same pool of technicians and contract players, all of whom contributed to the 'Lewton' personality. His approach was not to try to get round his bosses' demands that he make certain types of film, but to make them better, with more imagination.

Vincente Minnelli's *The Bad and the Beautiful* (1952) contains an *à clef* account of the making of the two *Cat People* movies. Ambitious producer Jonathan Shields (Kirk Douglas) is assigned to *The Doom of the Cat Men* (in which he uses shadows rather than monster costumes to terrify the audience, as Lewton and Tourneur had in *Cat People*), but is disgusted when after the successful premiere he is 'rewarded' with his next project, *The Son of the Cat Man*. Most accounts of Lewton's career suggest that this is how he, too, reacted when asked to follow up the great popularity of Tourneur's film with *The Curse of the Cat People*. What he produced – and the secret of the film's greatness – is both a very unusual sequel and an extremely left-field horror movie.

Cat People introduces us to Irena Dubrovna (Simone Simon), a young Serb in New York unable to consummate her marriage to 'plain Americano' Oliver Reed (Kent Smith) because she is terrified she will turn into a murderous black panther if sexually aroused. This eventually drives the impatient Oliver into the arms of Alice (Jane Randolph), prompting Irena to embrace her cat persona, transforming herself several times to menace her rival. Finally kissed by her lecherous psychoanalyst Dr Louis Judd (Tom Conway), she becomes a big cat, and kills the shrink even as he runs her through with a swordcane. Hitherto – apparently at Tourneur's insistence as much as Lewton's – Irena's panther form has been suggested by shadows rather than shown outright, and even in death we don't see the monster she has turned into. However, attempts to read *Cat People* as a study of psychological rather than supernatural shapeshifting are untenable. A privileged shot (seen by the audience but by no screen character) shows us a cat's footprints becoming the marks of high-heeled shoes. As he looks at Irena's corpse, Oliver is forced to conclude: 'She never lied to us.'

By the 1940s any remotely successful horror film was likely to become a franchise along the lines of the *Mummy* movies rival studio Universal was cranking out, reducing the gothic-romantic genre of the 1930s to an assembly line for childish shudder pulps. And even without front-office prompting Lewton had already repeated and elaborated upon *Cat People*, his third film, Tourneur's *The Leopard Man* (1943), is a reworking of elements from *Cat People*: while the masterly *The Seventh Victim* (1943), directed by Mark Robson, is an unacknowledged spin-off, with Tom Conway returning as Dr Judd and another haunted woman (Jean Brooks) rushing to embrace death.

So by the time he told Lewton to make a *Cat People* sequel, RKO production chief Charles Koerner must have known better than to expect him to take one of the obvious routes: to bring back Irena from the dead (as in the sequels to Universal's 'gorilla people' quickie *Captive Wild Woman*, 1943) or to discover a hitherto-unacknowledged descendant (as in *Dracula's Daughter*, 1936). The literature on Lewton suggests that he opted instead to make a movie about child psychology (he tried unsuccessfully to get *Curse* retitled *Amy and Her Friend*), and indeed a great deal of the film is concerned with the sensitive central youngster's troubles with other children and her family, into which Lewton allegedly wove autobiographical elements – like the party invites she posts in a 'magic mailbox' in a hollow tree, resulting in an unattended birthday bash and her ostracism by the uninvited children. However, co-director Wise – originally hired as editor but promoted when Fritsch was deemed to be shooting too slowly – insists that a paramount concern was that the film contain enough thrills to be promoted as 'at least a semi-horror film', while scriptwriter DeWitt Bodeen (who had written *Cat People*) in fact used standard sequel approaches in subtle guise. Irena does return from beyond the grave, and the central character is almost Cat Woman's Daughter.

Made in an era before video, when audience memories were expected to fade a little between films, *Curse* goes out of its way to pick up the threads. Kent Smith and Jane Randolph return as Oliver and Alice, now married and with a daughter, Amy (Ann Carter), while Simon plays a transformed Irena who is perhaps an angelic ghost or perhaps Amy's imaginary friend. Roy Webb's score reuses motifs established in the first film including a lullaby associated with Irena that is vital to the plot. A Goya portrait of a child with cats that decorated Irena's apartment in *Cat People* has been put up in the Reeds' new home: 'It doesn't fit, does it?' says Alice, significantly, 'but it's part of our lives, too.'

Uniquely, *Curse* shows us a couple whose lives have credibly evolved since the first film – the Reeds have moved from New York to Tarrytown and Oliver has advanced from draughtsman to apparently self-employed naval designer who relaxes by making model ships. These characters have been shaped by the events we have seen them live through. Oliver has retreated from an enforced belief in the supernatural and can now tell himself his dead first wife was mentally ill rather than a were-panther. Alice has clearly learned more from the Irena experience and become more sensitive, though her tenacity and conservatism are still evident.

The only fudged linkage is one of time: in the year since *Cat People*, Oliver and Alice have married and had a six-year-old daughter. This is a lot easier to swallow than the 20-year gaps between each of the three *Mummy* movies made between 1941 and 1944, while *The Mummy's Curse*, released eight months after *The Mummy's Ghost*, even sneaks in a locale switch: the mummy drowns in a swamp in Massachusetts and is revived in a Louisiana bayou. Beside that it is almost reasonable that between the *Cat People* films Irena's ethnicity shifts almost subliminally (she sings in French and the name 'Dubrovna' is never mentioned) to align with that of Simon.

Lewton liked to bring back actors from film to film. He stretches the point in *Curse* by casting the striking Elizabeth Russell, the other cat woman encountered eerily by Irena in a Serbian restaurant in *Cat People*, as a new character, the neurotic and tormented Barbara Farren. Since the other actors reprise the same roles, this causes a slight confusion (Russell is in *The Seventh Victim*, too, as yet another glamorous, desperate, doomed woman), though nothing that approaches the way Dwight Frye or Lionel Atwill show up as fresh grave-robber or police-inspector character, in each Universal *Frankenstein* film.

The counter-reading of *Curse* sees it not as a horror film but as a study of a lonely child who takes refuge in a fantasy relationship with an imaginary friend (Simon in fairy-princess form). But those who insist that it should be one 'respectable' thing (a psychological study) rather than something as odious as a horror movie are missing the points that all good horror stories have emotional resonances beyond the chain-clanking, and that the old-dark-house gothicism and magical fantasy garden of *Curse* are literal representations of Amy's world. The film takes care to fulfil its horror remit with gothic atmosphere and suspense sequences far chillier than anything produced at Universal and by deliberately evoking key works of horror literature. Most obviously, in setting the story near Washington Irving's *Sleepy Hollow* and having Amy be terrified by a recital of the legend of the Headless Horseman, Lewton taps into the first great spook story in American letters (soon to be revisited by Tim Burton). There are also elements of Henry James's *The Turn of the Screw* in Amy's relationship with the ghost of a parent figure violently disapproved of by her living father. Throw in a snippet of R. L. Stevenson's *The Unseen Playmate* – which pulls off the trick of presenting the magical world of childhood with enough sinister edge to undercut the sentimentality – and you have almost a themed anthology, *A Child's Garden of Horrors*.

In terms of the film's psychology, Oliver is as cloddish and ineffectual, if well-intentioned a father as he was a husband, his behaviour complicated by lingering feelings for his first wife that are passed on to his daughter. ('She could almost be Irena's child,' he muses.) Alice, who seems to have learned most from the first film, is, as might reasonably be expected, more effectively sympathetic towards her daughter than she was to Irena. But these are still the limited 'plain Americanos' they always were: Alice quivers downstairs on Twelfth Night, at once upset and almost proud that Amy is receiving her first corporal punishment from Oliver. ('A first spanking,' says her schoolteacher friend, 'it's an important occasion.') It is this chastisement that drives Amy out into the snow for a brush with imaginary terrors (the hoofbeats of the Headless Horseman turn out to be the clanking snowchains of a passing car, a classic Lewton 'bus') and the real possibility of death at the Farren house.

The Farren house, site of the film's horrors, is a neighbourhood 'bad place' with precedents that include the House of Usher and descendants in the likes of Hill House in Wise's version of *The Haunting* and the Overlook Hotel in Kubrick's *The Shining*.

Those who don't consider *Curse* a horror film must shut their eyes during these scenes, which display a fine grasp of genre set decoration (Albert S. D'Agostino) and lighting camera-work (Nick Musuraca) and are unmistakably an inspiration for the look and emotional pressure-cooker atmosphere of the Bates house in *Psycho*. Amy is invited in by Mrs Farren (Julia Dean), once a great actress, who terrifies but enchants her with dramatic recitals and tales of long-ago glamour. Mrs Farren's graciousness to this strange child only emphasises her monstrousness in refusing to acknowledge that her daughter is anything but 'just the woman who looks after me' and claiming that her Barbara died when she was Amy's age. In the cruel scenes between the two women is the nugget of a 1960s sub-genre of American gothic horror (see *Psycho* and *What Ever Happened to Baby Jane?*) in which ageing women trapped in decaying houses exact pointless and drawn-out revenge for imagined slights – and, typically, matters are resolved by a death on the stairs.

The finale of *Curse* is truly extraordinary, opting for a way out of the horror few subsequent films have taken. Mrs Farren dies of a heart attack, while on the stairs trying to get Amy to hide from Barbara, prompting the jealous woman ('Even my mother's last moments you've stolen from me') to approach the child with a strangler's hands. Seeing Irena's soft phantom overlaid on the hawk-faced Barbara, which evokes the twinning of Russell and Simon in *Cat People*, Amy appeals – 'My friend, my friend' – and Barbara embraces rather than throttles the girl. The well-lit, modern but folksy Reed home is in contrast with the gothic Farren house with its stuffed cats and inky shadows, but we have seen that the ill-faith that infests the place, which has driven Amy to love a ghost or a conjuring of her own mind, could easily spiral out of control and fester a similarly monstrous, soul-stifling situation.

At the fade-out, just at his last line in *Cat People* confirms that Irena was a real cat person, Oliver claims to see his daughter's imaginary friend (not really meaning it, but trying to forge a connection with the girl), implying that Amy doesn't need Irena any more. Father and daughter go indoors and Irena fades away. This is another privileged shot: as she vanishes, Irena is alone in the garden, which confirms to us that she really was there all the time.

SO GOOD IT HURTS

Amy Taubin

David Fincher's *Fight Club* opens inside the fear centre of its protagonist's brain, although we don't realise that's where we are until we're no longer there. What we see is a semi-dark space that seems both confined and limitless, its details vaguely diomorphic. We are moving though the space at a smooth, regular clip. Our journey is enlivened by flashes of light, pumping music and the film's title, which are superimposed on the brainscape. Just when we might start wondering about what kind of place we're in, we're expelled in a rush and hurtled alongside the body of a gun that's half-way jammed inside someone's mouth.

What's exciting about *Fight Club* is that it 'screws around with your bio-rhythms' – to borrow a phrase from the Chuck Palahnuik novel of the same name which has been adapted with considerable fidelity by Fincher and screenwriter Jim Uhls. Like the novel, the film disrupts narrative sequencing and expresses some pretty subversive, right-on-the-zeitgeist ideas about masculinity and our name-brand, bottom-line society – ideas you're unlikely to find so openly broadcast in any other Hollywood movie.

'Self-improvement is masturbation. Self-destruction might be the answer' is the slogan of Tyler Durden, who is not *Fight Club*'s protagonist but rather the protagonist's significant other, doppelgänger, alterego – all that and more. Tyler is the embodiment of pure id with just enough Nietzsche thrown in to make him articulate. (In the film Tyler's voice trails off after the word 'destruction', which he delivers with a pregnant, upward inflection and Cheshire-cat grin. The alteration to the line is, I suspect, a concession to the MPAA ratings board, which probably gave *Fight Club* an 'R' because its members didn't understand its 'unamerican' social critique.)

Tyler (Brad Pitt) has invaded the life of our protagonist and narrator (Edward Norton) who is nameless in the novel but referred to as Jack in the film, though only when it's absolutely unavoidable. Jack is a depressed wage-slave with terrible insomnia, a corrosive wit and a disassociated perspective on his sterile Ikea life. Tyler encourages him to turn his frustration and bottled-up rage into action. After Jack and Tyler have their first heart-to-heart, Tyler asks Jack to hit him. Jack obliges and Tyler returns the favour. They discover that they are exhilarated by this brute interaction. This is the beginning of Fight Club, a secret society open to anyone who's male and for which Tyler (the self-styled anarchist) lays down the rules. 'The first rule of Fight Club is that you don't talk about Fight Club.'

In Fight Club men strip off their shirts and shoes and go one-on-one with bare knuckles. Everything is allowed short of killing your partner. Fight Club is so seductive as an idea and experience it takes on a life of its own – independent of Tyler and Jack – and soon there are Fight Clubs springing up in basements and parking lots all over the city and then in other cities across the country.

Jack moves into Tyler's house after his perfectly appointed condo is destroyed in a mysterious explosion. Tyler inhabits a dilapidated, decaying mansion on the edge of a toxic-waste dump. Except on Fight Club nights, says Jack, they're Ozzie and Harriet. Which isn't quite true because Tyler has many other ways of disrupting the social contract. A terrorist of the food industry, he works as a waiter in pricey restaurants where he pees in the soup. Moonlighting as a projectionist, he splices single fames of pornography into squeaky-clean family films.

Tyler also sells his own brand of soap to upscale department stores; its secret ingredient is human fat which he scavenges from the medical-waste bags of liposuction clinics. (This last transgression has brought accusations of anti-Semitism on the film, but if you've ever lived in LA, where women have fat suctioned out of their bodies as casually as they go to the hairdresser your first association would not be with Nazi concentration camps. Misogyny, maybe; anti-Semitism, no.) One night as they're making soap Tyler kisses Jack's hand and then burns the imprint of his lips into Jack's skin with pure lye.

If pain is the most expedient route to feeling alive, then the flirtation with self-destruction is what bonds Tyler and Jack – a bond no woman can set asunder, not even Marla (Helena Bonham Carter), a goth queen with the opalescent skin of a heroin addict and the belligerent manner of Judy Garland at the start of a bender. Marla is after Jack but she fucks Tyler while Jack lurks outside the door as if he's a child spying on the primal scene.

It's not Marla who causes Jack to have second thoughts about Tyler; rather, it's that Tyler's tendency to megalomania spins out of control. Without Jack registering what's happening, Tyler transforms Fight Club into Project Mayhem, a guerrilla network that blows up buildings in order to undermine the economic foundations of our credit-card society. When a soldier in Project Mayhem is killed, Jack realises he must break up with the person he's as close to as he is to himself. But Tyler is not easy to get rid of. Which is how Jack winds up where we came in – with a gun in his mouth in an office building that has been targeted for demolition by Project Mayhem. Since Tyler's bombs are as reliable as Jack is as a narrator, this is what you might call, if you think about it carefully, an open ending.

There's a twist in the climax of *Fight Club* that I haven't revealed. No one I've spoken to saw it coming, and the experience of the film is quite different when you know it in advance. Since the twist subverts what for 100 years has been an essential premise of cinema – that it is an index of the physical world – to leave it out of this analysis does the film an injustice. Especially since this premise will become part of ancient history when film is transformed from a photographic medium to a digital electronic medium – and *Fight Club* is nothing if not a glimpse of that future.

Like all Fincher's previous films (*Alien³, Se7en, The Game*) *Fight Club* sets up a conflict with a violent, potentially murderous being who is, as the id is to the ego, the doppelgänger of the protagonist. Weakened by a toxic and perverse society, the protagonist is barely able to hold on to some shred of moral consciousness in the face of this anarchic force. (*The Game*, Fincher's least convincing film, doesn't quite fit this pattern.) Thus Tyler's nihilism and incipient fascism are not the values *Fight Club* espouses, though Fincher complicates the issue by making Tyler so alluring and charismatic. Tyler is posed as an object of desire and of identification – and Pitt, who has never been as exquisite as he is with a broken nose and blood streaming down his cut body, emerges as an actor of economy and control who can rivet attention merely by turning his head.

For the protagonist, who feels emasculated by his buttoned-down, consumerist life, Tyler represents some ideal of free-wheeling male power. He wants to become Tyler or to be taken over by Tyler. There's a blatant homoerotic charge to this identification which the film doesn't shy away from. As in Scorsese's films, the male body is feminised through masochism. You prove your masculinity not by how much pain you can inflict, but by how much you can endure. Shot in a wet-dream half light that films the men's bodies as they pound each other's heads into the cement, the Fight Club sequences are such a perfect balance of aesthetics and adrenaline they feel like a solution to the mind/body split.

But what's most innovative about *Fight Club* is the way, at moments, it seems like the projection of an extremely agile, associative train of thought that can back up and hurtle forward and switch tracks in an instant. The effect is partly the result of a voiceover which is strikingly separated from the rest of the sound and strangely muffled, as if there were a mike inside Jack's head. Fincher has retained the savage humour and manic prose style of Palahniuk's novel, and Norton delivers this interior monologue as if he were making it up on the fly.

In the opening scene, seconds after being ejected from Jack's brain, we hear something about a bomb in the basement and suddenly we're plunged through the window, down 30 storeys, through the sidewalk into the basement, through a bullet hole in the van with the explosives and then out the other side. The sequence, which is digitally created from a series of still photographs, is both astonishing and oddly mundane in the sense that it's a fair representation of the visual component of everyday thought processes. Still, one needs a new vocabulary to describe the vertiginous depiction of space and time in *Fight Club*. Pans and tilts and tracks just won't do.

Fight Club is an action film that's all about interiority. It pushes the concepts of subjectivity and identification to extremes to suggest a male identity that's not only fragile but frangible. Jack is so filled with self-loathing and repressed rage he's desperate to get out of his own skin and into someone else's. And *Fight Club* is not the only recent Hollywood movie to place us inside someone's brain. *Being John Malkovich*, in which the sad-sack protagonist discovers a secret tunnel that leads into Malkovich's brain, is a comic, gender-bent spin on *Fight Club*, though its creepy denouement is more grim than anything Fincher envisions. You also don't have to be a psychoanalyst to deduce from the depiction that the route into Malkovich's brain is through his asshole.

Fincher and Spike Jonze, who directed *Malkovich*, are colleagues in the production company Propaganda Films, so it's not surprising they share an idea or two. And perhaps these films are no more than another turn of the screw in *Frankenstein* or heady variations on *Face/Off*. But it does seem transgressive to put a brain on the screen as an exhibit – especially when the exhibit is connected to the loss of self, in particular the loss of the masculine self. Fincher ends *Fight Club* with the Pixies' recording of 'Where Is My Mind'. That's not all that's gone missing.

*   *   *

Being Brad

'We're making these fucking movies and they're all, like, prototypes,' says David Fincher. 'So you have to find something to start with that you know. I knew who the narrator was because he was me. At some points in my life, I've said, "If I could just spend the extra money, I could get that sofa and then I'll have the sofa problem handled." As I was reading Chuck's book, I was blushing and feeling horrible. How did this guy know what everybody was thinking? And I also know, just from personal experience, that if I could choose to be someone else, it would be Brad Pitt.'

Because he had such a terrible time directing *Alien³* for Fox, Fincher was horrified that Fox 2000 had bought Palahniuk's novel. Nevertheless, he pursued the project. 'I told them that the movie I saw wasn't *Trainspotting*. The real act of sedition is not to do the £3 million version, it's to do the big version. I worked on the script with Jim Uhls for about eight months. He had written a version that eliminated the voiceover because the studio told him it was a crutch. It was like taking the voice out of Dashiell

Hammett. The interior monologue is what gives you some sort of context, some sort of humour. Without the narration the story is just sad and pathetic. From the script we put together a schedule, storyboards, a budget. I went back to Fox with an unabridged-dictionary sized package. I said, 'Here's the thing. $60 million. It's Edward. It's Brad. We're going to start inside Edward's brain and pull out. We're going to blow up a fucking plane. You've got 72 hours to tell us if you're interested.' And they said, "Yeah, let's go."'

Fincher felt the movie needed to move very quickly and to jump around in time and space. 'We didn't set out to leave the audience in the dust, but we wanted to be random access. So we talked about how we could get people to go with this. At the beginning of the book there's a great speech about how the dynamite is wired together and set to go off. How do you show that? Wouldn't it be great if you could see Edward looking at Brad and then just drop 30 storeys, right through to the inside of this van, see what he's talking about, and then go back? So we did tests. We got a Nikon and took photographs looking out of a window down the street. We took them from every floor. And then we mapped them on to simple geometric shapes and did an incredibly fast camera movement over them, and it just drops. And you think, 'Wow, I can make it go as fast or as slowly as I want. I can make it go through the wall.' If you look at it frame by frame, the camera goes through the wall into a janitor's room that has a calendar with naked girls. They literally went in and photographed little rooms the maintenance staff would have used. It's just three frames. It goes by so quickly you'll only be able to see it on the DVD.'

The strange sex scene between Pitt and Bonham Carter was also done with stills. 'We had two cameras, one shooting 1-second exposures and one shooting at 250th of a second. We had this idea of a kind of Francis Bacon version of Mount Rushmore. Because after *Don't Look Now*, there's nothing else to do. I can't ask people to simulate fucking. It's too embarrassing.'

After the shooting of teenagers by teenagers last spring at Littleton High School Fox became nervous about *Fight Club*. The release was postponed; the marketing campaign made the movie look like a goofy comedy. 'Although the book was written five years ago I think the movie is about Littleton in more ways than anyone would care to address. Do I think that people who are frustrated and disenfranchised should blow up buildings? No. Do I care if people who are consenting adults have this Fight Club? I have no problem with that. I'm no sado-masochist, but it seems more responsible than bottling up all their rage about how unfulfilled their lives are. I think the movie is moral and it's responsible. But the scariest thing about Littleton is that two 18-year-olds would think, 'OK. We're going in and we're not coming out. In order to make this statement, we have to give up our lives.' They haven't had a life yet – how can they know they're prepared to give it up? That people would die for such trivial frustrations is scary. And no one wants to look at that.'

FIGHT CLUB
USA 1999
Director: David Fincher

The present. The narrator, possibly named Jack, has a gun in his mouth in a building about to be blown up. Months before, Jack lives in an unnamed US city, has a good job and a trendy flat, but feels empty and can't sleep. Jack takes his doctor's flip suggestion he attend a testicular-cancer support group to find out 'what real pain is' seriously. Moved to tears by the members' plight, Jack's insomnia is cured and he becomes hooked on group therapy. Soon he notices Marla, another 'tourist', and his sleepless- ness returns until they agree not to attend the same groups. On a plane, Jack meets Tyler Durden, who makes a living selling soap. When Jack's flat mysteriously blows up, Tyler offers him a place to stay, but only if Jack will hit him. Tyler and Jack beat each other up for fun. They start Fight Club, at which men can pummel each other with bare knuckles.

Marla calls Jack after taking an overdose; Tyler comes to her rescue and they begin a sexual relationship, much to Jack's disgust. Tyler reveals his soap is made from human fat stolen from liposuction clinics. Meanwhile, Fight Clubs spring up all over the country. Tyler starts Project Mayhem, which involves acts of terrorism against corporations and big business. During one mission Mayhem-soldier Bob is killed. Jack is horrified; Tyler disappears. Jack crisscrosses the country in search of him, only to find everyone thinks he is Tyler. Realising they're right, Jack tries to foil Tyler's plan to blow up several high-rise buildings (credit card companies) at once, but is thwarted. At the primed-to-explode building seen in the opening sequence, Jack shoots himself in the head, only wounding his real body but 'killing' Tyler. Marla, whom he'd put on a bus to safety, is brought to him and they watch together as the bombs go off.

* * *

We know from *Se7en* and *The Game* that director David Fincher likes to evoke enclosed, solipsistic worlds which are also conundrums. *Se7en*'s world is an unnamed, sepulchral US city where it's always raining, and life runs inexorably to the countdown of seven murders. Each killing is a symbolic retribution for a deadly sin and a dreadful tease for the investigating detectives played by Morgan Freeman and Brad Pitt. In *The Game*, divorced financier Michael Douglas's insular life is upended when his younger brother signs him up for an exclusive new entertainment experience devoted to springing scary surprises on its clients. He soon finds himself in urban back-lots, unable to distinguish real danger from the next 'surprise'. *Fight Club* not only fits the pattern of these predecessors like a bloodied rag glove, it also remakes them.

Just as Douglas's character suffers deep ennui at the consumer perfectionism of his existence, so Edward Norton's Jack, an accident investigator for an insurance company, is aghast at his own obsession with the Ikea catalogue. Just as Freeman and Pitt in *Se7en* are made to seem bent down by the weather and emasculated by propriety, so Jack the insomniac seems crushed by the lack of light, adventure and emotion in his life. Society in a Fincher film is an urban nightmare labyrinth disrupted by the seething, denatured and corralled male ego it was built to control. The difference with *Fight Club* is that nearly every other male in the film feels the same way as the protagonist. The Fight Clubs bring all men together, and what they seem to want to do is hit one another, hard, with bare knuckles, to get a sense of empowerment.

Long before we get to the on-screen hitting, though, the movie pummels the viewer with a furious attack of astonishing shots, body-slam cuts and Jack's chewable voiceover aphorisms: 'I felt like putting a bullet in the eye of every panda that wouldn't screw to save its species.' The plot starts with its end – Jack with a gun in his mouth – and shoots off back to the start of his insomnia. Even the sombre, night-time desolation that haunts Jack's first cure for sleeplessness – his slumming in victim-support groups (for Aids, alcoholism, drug abuse, testicular cancer and so on) – is a jagged affair of under-the-chin angles, eyeballing close-ups and shuddering sound effects. The arrival of Helena Bonham Carter as the slinky Marla, another group-therapy cuddle-junkie, ruining it for Jack, is announced with looks and sultry poses that jam into the corners of the frame. This is a movie that makes your skin crawl in a strangely delectable way.

But it's with the inception of Fight Club itself, which begins after Jack meets Tyler and right after Jack's apartment has inexplicably been blown up, that Fincher's most sophisticated conundrum yet hooks us. Tyler asks Jack to hit him in the face, hard. Jack hits him and gets hit back. As Jack and Tyler pound each other, men gather round intrigued and Jack is sure his sleeplessness has gone forever. Soon large groups of white- and blue-collar men file into bar basements and strip to the waist as Tyler expounds the rules: 'The first rule about Fight Club is that you don't talk about Fight Club. The second rule about Fight Club is that you don't talk about Fight Club.' The hitting makes a sly, seductive spectacle of lightweight masochism, homoerotic display and sardonic wit. Later, in one horrific scene of unhingement, it is brutally sadistic. But it remains a baffling, just-plausible compulsion.

Tyler seems to be completely free from any inhibition, able to acquire anything he wants through sheer force of will. Jack's exhilaration at meeting Tyler is undercut by Tyler's immediate sexual success with Marla and then dissipated when he fills their squatted house with Fight Club legions, organised to carry out terror missions. When Jack's grip on his self-control loosens, the film enacts a brilliant twist no caring reviewer ought to reveal. Inventive as it is, however, it also marks an escalation towards the fantastic which loses in conceptual momentum what it gains in dramatic thrills. So *Fight Club* is all of the following: a conspiracy thriller that never leaves the splashy imagination of a paranoid narrator; a value-free vessel that offers conflicting views on Nietzschean ideas about men and destruction; a dazzling entertainment that wants us to luxuriate in violence as we condemn it; a brilliant solution to depicting the divided self as a protagonist; and proof that Brad Pitt, as well as Edward Norton, can really act.

Charles Whitehouse

VANISHING AMERICANS

Michael Eaton

Michael Lesy's *Wisconsin Death Trip* is an archetypal early-1970s artefact. The book juxtaposes a series of photographs taken by Charles van Schaick in the northern Midwest in the 1890s with contemporary extracts from the *Badger State Banner*, the newspaper of the Black River Falls community. The images show the often far from photogenic settlers doing what folk did in front of a camera in those days – hunting, preparing for baptism, getting cheerfully intoxicated, posing with their children, burying their dead – while the text presents instances of their strange deaths and weird psychoses. The newspaper reports, penned by the editor, an Englishman named Frank Cooper, are written in a bland, 'objective', largely adjective-free style which serves to make the 'facts' at issue even more disturbing: 'La Crosse was somewhat agitated last week by an alleged ghost. The spirit manifested itself by the usual symptoms'; 'The Eriksen family had a free-for-all fight and the eldest son, Gustav, struck his father on the head with a trombone, killing him instantly.' *Wisconsin Death Trip* was positioned as an art book rather than a work of social history: the selection and juxtaposition of the images and incidents allowed it to be viewed as a kind of down-home Surrealism, a metropolitan discovery of the bizarre in the rural life of years gone by. But at the time of publication the material had a much more contemporary and political resonance.

In the wake of the ignominious latter days of the Vietnam War and the Watergate revelations of presidential corruption, these baldly stated tales of everyday frontier madness seemed to embody far more than a local dimension. The book connected with a widespread cultural desire to expose the sickness at the heart of American life by looking hard into the gory past to illuminate, if not entirely explain, the brutal present. It was as if the key to unlocking a deep and ongoing psychosis might be located in what these pictures could never quite show and these reports could never quite say: that violence and dementia are as American as apple pie.

It's surprising that this demythologisation should have focused on the frontier, the vainglorious attempt to tame the wilderness that was Americanism's founding myth. If the archaeology of pioneer life reveals the settling of the West to have been not the manifest destiny of civilising white man but a site of atavistic mayhem as destructive to the self as to any others who crossed its path, then surely any attempt to mobilise such values to underwrite the country's self-appointed mandate as policeman of the free world must be exposed as hypocritical at best and genocidal at worst.

This profound scepticism about Horace Greeley's exhortation to 'Go West, young man, and grow up with the country' was also present in films which depicted the moral immaturity of the kind of young men who would once have been heroic Westerners. In *McCabe and Mrs Miller* (Robert Altman, 1971) the protagonist's quest is to establish a brothel in the knowingly named frontier town Presbyterian Church; his madam is an opium addict, the church burns down and he eventually gives up the ghost in an endulging snowdrift. In *Bad Company* (Robert Benton, 1972), a group of cocksure runaway kids empties round after round of their Colt 45s into a hapless jack rabbit. In *Pat Garrett and Billy the Kid* (Sam Peckinpah, 1973, script by Rudolf Wurlitzer) the father of a pioneer family blasts away meaninglessly from their steamboat at bottles thrown by his son into a river; when Garrett joins in the shooting contest uninvited the bearded patriarch suspiciously narrows his eyes and levels his rifle at the sheriff's head until they sail out of range. In *Badlands* (Terrence Malick, 1973 – set in the 1950s but still very much a frontier film) a teenage youth cuts a murderous swathe, his brutal actions immortalised through the uncomprehending diary entries of his female companion. In *The Missouri Breaks* (Arthur Penn, 1976, written by Thomas McGuane) a proud cattleman rides through the vast landscape he owns, lecturing his suitably impressed young companion on his Herculean labours to establish a ranch in this wilderness before we realise he's escorting this rustler to a necktie party.

All these films have in common the cinematically revisionist assertion that the attempt to transform the desert into a garden – the underlying structural principle of much Western fiction – exacted a fatally destructive toll upon colonisers and colonised alike, that it was nothing less than hubristic madness. Maybe there were some places where white feet should never have ventured. *Wisconsin Death Trip* was certainly a book of its time.

Now a feature-length film inspired by Lesy's book has been made by James Marsh for the ever-imaginative BBC2 *Arena* arts documentary series. How can this material speak to us today? Marsh deploys DoP Eigil Bryld's crisp monochrome photography to animate, if not exactly dramatise, a selection of incidents acted out by local performers. Ian Holm's understated voice reads Cooper's prose, interrupted only by occasional breathy extracts from the journal of the director of the local mad-house where many of these individuals ended up.

Already a subtle transformation has occurred: the texts are now married to images that illustrate them rather than allowing seemingly random juxtapositions to create a third meaning. What emerges is a shift of emphasis from the social/political to the individual/psychological. It's now far easier to view Black River Falls as an aberrant gothic liminal zone rather than as a cracked synecdoche for the whole of the Union.

The film presents suicides, abandoned infants, arson, adultery, bank closures, epidemics, witchcraft panics, children who wreak havoc with firearms, depressed mothers who drown their offspring – stories, in fact, of the kind that fill today's supermarket tabloids. But two unforgettable characters weave their eccentric paths through the changing seasons. First, schoolmarm Mary Sweeney: 'The notorious window smasher... was arrested again last week. She had destroyed considerable property with her uncontrollable mania... Mrs Sweeney says she uses cocaine liberally on such occasions because it quietens her nerves.' Second, self-proclaimed diva Pauline L'Allemand, who gets off the train with her son to claim possession of seven acres of worthless land; after she has performed her musical act, compromised by her ill-fitting false teeth, the locals assume she must be a phoney, though in fact she is the erstwhile favourite of the composer Delibes. She too is incarcerated in the asylum; one night she slips away unnoticed and is heard of years later in Chicago complaining of spectral voices from the adjoining room where, it transpires, a ventriloquist has been practising his act. If any producer wishes to develop a feature based on this astonishing material might I offer my services as screenwriter?

Merely to describe these unmakeupable incidents risks overelaboration. Though Marsh's transposition of this Fortean material into cinema blunts any outrage the book might once have provoked, his film connects with what we might call the imaginative British documentary/drama, a hybrid that began its marginal life in the GPO and Crown Film Units of the 1930s and 1940s, and later found a tolerated squat in the peripheral regions of public-service television. I don't think it's too far fetched to glimpse shadows in Marsh's film of Humphrey Jennings's Mass Observation film *Spare Time* (1939) with its bemused but eventually sympathetic delineation of those strange northern working classes at play, or even of Alan Clarke's *Elephant* (1989) with its numbingly deadpan recreations of sectarian murders in Northern Ireland.

This endangered species of film-making is still more alive than the docusoaps and talk shows that have invaded its habitat. Marsh's previous contributions to the genre include a moving account of Marvin Gaye's last days in a Belgian seaside town and an insight into the art and life of Elvis through the carbohydrate-saturated white-trash cuisine he shovelled into his constantly mutating but always iconic body. Without imposing some bogus house-style to confederate 20 years of films unified only by a floating bottle and Brian Eno's theme tune, *Wisconsin Death Trip* is unmistakably a product of executive producer Anthony Wall's *Arena*. The culturally off-centre subject matter, the lack of anchoring voice-of-God commentary, the lateral tracks and pans across the action, the sequences which start on a hard-to-interpret detail before revealing a wider view, the deliberate fracturing of narrative structure – all these tropes have the effect of distancing both the film-maker and the viewer from any easy empathetic involvement with the events and characters depicted and of forcing the spectator to do some interpretative work.

Cooper's words which top and tail the film provide another point of entry. Entirely without irony he says of the unstable community where he too is an immigrant: 'Nowhere can be found a more desirable residence. Our site is not only picturesque ...' The Picturesque implied a natural landscape in which human figures could be placed – working, wandering or musing – a landscape *fit* to be pictured, which held the potential of being in thrall of the figures who could be depicted within it. It's evident this was more of a desire than a realisation – the backwoods had an awe-inspiring effect on the arrivals from northern Europe and the eastern seaboard who attempted to find a secure location there. 'Whatever is fitted in any sort to excite the ideas of pain and danger ... whatever is in any sort terrible ... is a source of the *sublime*, that is, it is productive of the strongest emotion which the mind is capable of feeling' (Edmund Burke, 1757). The Sublime landscape evokes infinite vastness, terrifying uniformity – it dwarfs humanity, crushing the human spirit and driving it to depression and despair. Faced with such terrifying prospects, the third pictorial category, that of the Beautiful – an aspirational classicism based on the perfect proportions of an idealised statue from Ancient Greece – becomes utterly impossible in rural Wisconsin.

The image of humanity that remains after it has been ground in the mills of sublimity must perforce be imperfect, distorted, perverted, literally outlandish – in a word, grotesque. But it is in its fascinated insistence on the grotesque that the film, to my mind, takes its only false turn by depicting the Black River Falls of today. These sequences, shot in colour, seem wearily familiar and cumulatively unilluminating: leafy streets of Lynchian clapboard houses; Diane Arbus kids posing in witchy Hallowe'en costumes while the major declaims that this is a 'real friendly town, a wonderful place to raise children'; the crowning of the Homecoming Queen who has no apparent notion of the sexualised history of her position; the female preacher denouncing the Devil and serving communion wine in individual plastic containers ... then cut to a woman in a bar sculling a shot of liquor; and, most demeaning of all, a barbershop choir performing 'The Star Spangled Banner' to the apparently comatose inhabitants of an old folks' home.

What are these images saying? That folk are still darned strange in the boondocks? That these kids might one day pick up their fathers' handguns and run amok in a fast-food joint? That these born-again communicants might drown their children in an excess of religious ecstasy? That these old people might slash their throats out of unrequited erotic desire? The characters of 100 years ago can reach out from the Phantom Zone only through fading photographs and uninflected prose. But these folk can still speak for themselves. They might even have something to say about their community that conflicts with Lesy's and Marsh's discourses. It would have been better to omit their real presence than to corral them into a caricature parade.

There is, however, a final contemporary sequence which seems entirely appropriate. The local Winnebago Indians live hidden away and have 'never made any trouble worthy of mention to the white settler' – what misery does this phrase repress? We see photographs of the emaciated, pock-marked faces of their children, the crushed drunkenness of erstwhile warriors for whom this landscape was once far from fearfully sublime. But now an idealised sculpture of a Ghost Dance warrior stands in the lobby of a casino run by the Winnebago who are scalping the white conquerors with gambling machines rather than tomahawks. The Vanishing American has returned.

REVIEWS

RED PLANET
USA/Australia 2000
Director: Antony Hoffman

In 2050, as overpopulation on Earth reaches critical levels, the first manned spaceship to Mars investigates the failure of the Terraforming Project intended to render the planet habitable. After a six-month journey under the command of Kate Bowman, the only woman aboard, *Mars-1* reaches orbit but sustains severe damage from a solar flare. The ship's five-man crew crash land on the planet's surface, leaving Bowman in orbit to attempt repairs. One of the crewmen, Chantilas, is fatally wounded; the others search for supplies but find only wreckage from previous missions.

As their oxygen runs out, their co-pilot Santen is killed, but the remaining trio discover the Martian air is breathable. They are being hunted, however, by the expedition's robot AMEE, its controls locked into killing mode. Having restored *Mars-1*, Bowman reports that two of the men might be able to lift off in a Russian probe grounded nearby. One of them, Pettengil, convinced he'll be left behind, sneaks ahead under cover of a storm. AMEE cuts him down.

His body becomes infested with roach-like insects; the bioengineer Burchenal realises they are oxygen producers and potential saviours of humankind before he too is consumed. The remaining astronaut, Gallagher, manages under Bowman's guidance to reactivate the Russian probe, using a battery snatched from AMEE's circuits. Soaring back into orbit, he is rescued by Bowman.

*   *   *

Doubtless in deference to the bewildered explorer of *2001: A Space Odyssey* (1968), the central character of *Red Planet* is called Bowman, a cheerful acknowledgment that the film, which charts a disaster-ridden expedition to Mars, is hardly exploring territory where nobody has gone before. Directed by newcomer Antony Hoffman after more than a decade of prize-winning commercials, with effects supervised by Jeffrey A. Okun (*Sphere*, *Stargate*), the production also employs a number of the talents responsible for *The Matrix*, granting it an unarguable state-of-the-art calibre. Despite this, *Red Planet*, while satisfyingly spectacular, is not out to dazzle with *Matrix*-style acrobatics; apart from a few enjoyable if unnecessary moments inside a robot's head, the film has a persuasive realism in keeping with Hoffman's original training in documentaries. Thanks to the striking choice of desert locations (in Jordan and Australia), Mars itself could hardly look more authentic.

The most prominent recruit from *The Matrix*, in fact, is Carrie-Anne Moss, playing the aforementioned Bowman, the expedition's commander and a recognisable successor to the indestructible Ripley of the *Alien* series. In something of a feminist triumph, it is Bowman's commentary that introduces us to the crew and provides a final summary that leaves no doubt about her plans for the one she has reeled in like a fish on a line. Over-ruling the ship's pleasingly defeatist computer (the evocatively named Lucille), Bowman dodges fireballs and other hazards single-handedly to convert the lifeless mother-ship into usable transportation, to restore contact with Mission Control, and to guide and encourage the stranded crew on the planet below. That she manages it all in a state of gasping panic renders her the more appealing, by contrast with her clumsy male subordinates who focus on a predictable mixture of alcohol, petty feuding and innuendo.

Their leader apart, these wisecracking specialists are a throwback not only to the motley crew of *Alien* but further, to George Pal's chauvinistic space movies of the 1950s. That was a decade which, in the wake of the Pal-produced *Destination Moon*, theorised that astronaut teams would inevitably include one rough-diamond comic, one slightly crazed visionary, one scholarly 'expert', and one or two salt-of-the-Earth expendables. Its personnel lightly reshuffled for *Red Planet*, the purpose of the mission in another Pal-produced science fiction film *Conquest of Space* (1954) is resurrected here in two fundamental respects, apparently unchanged in half a century: to solve Earth's overpopulation problem and to find evidence of divine existence. Aboard ship, both topics are aired ('Science,' they conclude, 'can't answer any of the really interesting questions'), but after the disastrous landing on Mars there is no time for theology. 'What are we going to do?' asks one agnostic astronaut. 'Look out for rocks marked "Made by God"?'

Constructed rather too schematically as a succession of last-minute rescues, *Red Planet* strains plausibility to such an extent that a benevolent intervention from above – at least by the scriptwriter – actually seems the only explanation. It appears unlikely, for instance, that without considerable effort from a *deus ex machina* the plight of an overflowing Earth, at six months' distance away from these astronauts, could be resolved by simple pest-control. Why, in any case, has the creation of a breathable Martian atmosphere by homicidal roaches (whose origin, of course, is a mystery) gone unnoticed by monitors of the Terraforming Project? More immediately, we might be sceptical that the elegantly designed spacesuits of the castaways have no provision for testing the oxygen content of their environment or that the superb sound quality of inter-suit communications appears to cut out immediately when two astronauts get into an argument. There is also a miraculous coincidence when the power-battery of an ultra-modern mechanoid proves to be compatible with the circuitry of a derelict Russian probe.

Its thunder somewhat stolen by *Pitch Black* – which similarly uses a catastrophe in space, livid colours under an alien sky and swarms of lethal wildlife – *Red Planet* is a respectable if simplistic venture, nicely played, and with the extra attraction of the sinuous robot AMEE. An enviable piece of unreliable hardware, cunningly animated, this wanton device is dedicated to cutting men down to size. Naturally referred to as female, she deserves to be long remembered.

Philip Strick

ED GEIN
USA 2000
Director: Chuck Parello

Wisconsin, 1957. Bereaved by the death of his mother Augusta, farm-owner Ed Gein digs up her corpse and attempts to revive her. An habitual grave-robber who fashions clothes and furniture from cadavers, Ed frequents a bar tended by Mary Hogan. Haunted by visions of Augusta, at whose knee Ed and brother Henry learned strict scripture about the whore of Babylon, Ed visits Mary at closing time; he shoots her, and takes her back to his farmhouse. Ed attempts unsuccessfully to swap his expansive farmhouse for a smaller holding to escape the ghosts of the past.

A vision of Augusta instructs Ed to wreak God's vengeance upon local store-owner Collette Marshall whom Ed has failed to seduce. Visiting Collette's store, Ed feigns interest in purchasing a rifle with which he then shoots and mortally wounds

Collette. He takes her body back to his house for dismemberment. The discovery of Collette's disappearance leads the police to Ed's farmhouse where gutted corpses hang from the ceiling. Ed is arrested. In his cell, an older Ed describes his subsequent internment as acceptable, and imagines placing his 'saintly' mother back in her grave.

* * *

As a macabre real-life legend who became known to the public through a combination of outraged newsreels and lurid film fantasies, Ed Gein has always presented a strange marriage of fact and fiction. Arrested in 1957 and ultimately convicted of two killings (for which he was deemed criminally insane), Gein was found to have lived in a farmhouse stuffed with human body parts, the result of years of grave-robbing, a grisly habit he fell into following the death of his mother in 1945. According to author Robert Bloch, the discovery of Gein's misdemeanours shocked America, presenting for the first time the spectre of a monster living unnoticed among a rural community, seeming to be nothing more sinister than an awkward social misfit. The revelation that the misfit was in fact a murderous necrophiliac gave rise to startling urban legends and even twisted children's rhymes. By the time Bloch's novel *Psycho* was published, everyone in America knew that its shy retiring villain was more than just a figure of fiction. Similarly, audiences of Hitchcock's subsequent 1960 screen adaptation can be assumed to have connected Anthony Perkins's twitchy Norman Bates with the real-life figure of Plainfield's most notorious son.

More than a decade later, director Tobe Hooper would turn to his childhood memories of Ed's arrest for inspiration for *The Texas Chain Saw Massacre* (1974), in which the various members of the cannibal family represent fractured aspects of the Gein legend. From here, Ed would go on to achieve cult status as the inspiration for such big-screen figures as the multiple murderer Jame Gumb in *The Silence of the Lambs* (1991).

Considering that Gein is now better known to the public through the fanciful screen characters he inspired than through the grim deeds he committed, the prospect of a biopic that separates fact from fiction seems enticing. Certainly, director Chuck Parello's deadpan appraisal of Gein's life makes much of its factual status; opening and closing with well-worn documentary footage of Gein's arrest, the film attempts to achieve a balance between documentary-style credibility and imaginative poetic licence. It's a difficult balancing act, one which ultimately leaves the viewer frustrated as to the real reasons for Gein's crimes. Dominating religious mothers and violently ineffectual fathers aside, *Ed Gein* does little to move us beyond the abused-dependent-child model which underwrites our 'understanding' of so many modern serial killers.

Ironically, although this may be far less overtly sensational than the previous screen depictions of the 'Wisconsin Ghoul' (the mutilations are seen fleetingly and fairly rarely), Parello's film is also less illuminating, presenting us with a simplified catalogue of compressed events that inadvertently prove only the wild excesses of fantasy can approach communion with Gein's true motives. Closer in tone to an up-market TV movie than a cinema shocker (*Helter Skelter*, the mini-series about the Charles Manson killings, presents the nearest touchstone – not simply because of Steve Railsback's impressive central performances in both), *Ed Gein* takes the audience through a rough tour of the key facts of the case – facts which remain unfathomable, confirming that truth is not merely stranger than fiction, it is also considerably less dramatically involving.

Having cut his teeth on the 1997 sequel to *Henry Portrait of a Serial Killer*, Parello proves himself to be at least an honourable devotee of a higher tradition of horror, eschewing shocks and gore for a degree of intellectual distance and placid remove. He is aided both by Railsback's understated performance, and by an ensemble cast who attempt bravely to keep the tone low-key throughout. Robert McNaughton's off-kilter score maintains an air of ethereal unease while the production design department does an impressive job of recreating Gein's house of bodily horrors. Whether the end result will command the same long-standing affection as, for instance, the 1974 cult shocker *Deranged* (a more *outré* and perversely enjoyable rendering of the Gein story) remains in doubt. For the moment, the 'real' Ed Gein continues to evade entrapment.

Mark Kermode

AUDITION
Japan/South Korea 1999
Director: Takashi Miike

Shigeharu Aoyama, owner of a Tokyo-based video-production company, has to cope with the death of his young wife.

Seven years later, 42-year-old Aoyama lives with his son Shigehiko, who suggests he remarry. Aoyama agrees and seeks the advice of his friend and colleague Yoshikawa. Yoshikawa reminds him of an abandoned feature-film project and suggests that he organise auditions for the female lead to select a suitable wife. Aoyama suppresses his doubts when, among the 40 applications he shortlists, he is struck by the melancholy tone of a letter included by a 24-year-old ex-dancer Asami Yamazaki.

At the audition, Aoyama becomes excited when it is Asami's turn; she appears, demure and submissive. Afterwards, Aoyama tries to resist the temptation to ring her but eventually succumbs and they meet at a coffee bar. Their relationship develops over several meetings but Yoshikawa, checking the details on her résumé, concludes she is not all she seems. Aoyama ignores his warnings and invites her for a weekend at the sea, on which he intends to propose to her and confess his deception. At a remote hotel, they make love and he discovers scarification on her thighs and her preoccupation with pain. When he wakes, Asami is gone.

Back home, Aoyama searches for Asami. He visits the Stone Fish, a bar where she used to work and discovers that the owner has been murdered. At the Shimada ballet school, Aoyama finds Asami's stepfather and remembers her account of the man's mutilation of her inner thighs when she was a young ballet student. At Asami's apartment, Aoyama discovers a mutilated man she has been keeping in a sack and feeding like a dog. Asami breaks into Aoyama's apartment and drugs his whiskey. She returns when he is paralysed but conscious; she binds and tortures him, placing acupuncture needles in his eyes and slicing through his extremities with cheese wire. Shigehiko returns and discovers his dead dog and his mutilated-but-alive father on the floor. In the ensuing struggle. Asami apparently falls to her death down the stairs.

* * *

The first film by prolific and controversial Japanese film-maker Takashi Miike to receive a commercial release in the UK, *Audition* assaults its audience's sensibilities with an unrelenting final-reel sequence of torture, an ending which realises a sadistic breach of contract between film-maker and audience of which Hitchcock could only dream. A recent introduction to the director's work in these pages (*S&S*, May 2000) suggested that Miike uses genre films, which he has been hired to direct, as a starting point for his own aesthetic, thematic and psychosexual preoccupations. In *Audition*, however, genre logic – whether that of the horror movie, or a more generally conceived extreme cinema driven by an urge to shake up jaded audiences – ultimately betrays a fascinating thematic core, which the first two thirds of the movie has built up with meticulous restraint and ambiguity.

Audition attempts to graft the horror genre on to the art movie in its insistence on the unknowable killer Asami as explicitly conjured from the guilty desire of the middle-aged protagonist Aoyama. Asami, unlike most female movie psychos, who, as Carol Clover notes, tend to be motivated by specific moments of (male) betrayal in their adult lives, is apparently driven by her childhood abuse at the hands of her stepfather. But this is conveyed in a phantasmagoric, somewhat reprehensible sado-erotic flashback, which at one point obscures the distinction between Asami as a child and as a woman. Aoyama's obsession with her, on an obvious level, relates to her childlike docility, which suggests, loosely, a critique of traditional male Japanese attitudes towards women. But Aoyama, despite approaching the audition through which he hopes to select his future wife as if he's buying his first car, is no one-dimensional sexist. It is left to his partner Yoshikawa – a chauvinist in all senses – to express dismay at giggling young women enjoying a night out in a bar and claim that Japan is finished 'because there are no good girls left'. Aoyama's wish to find a woman who is 'trained' is also ambiguous because he believes that 'training gives people confidence'. Grief is a significant motivation here – the movie opens with Aoyama in a sun-drenched hospital room at his wife's deathbed, a moving scene which lures us into his mindset. It also dictates the first half of the film's static, sombre aesthetic – all subdued long shots, emphasising expanses of floor, and painfully slow zooms, particularly in Aoyama's apartment, where his Jack Russell is often the only kinetic element (and about whose safety genre-attuned audiences will worry – rightly so – from the outset).

It is Asami's apparent sadness and morbidity that attracts Aoyama, along with her passivity. At the audition – introduced initially in comic montage, in the manner of audition sequences from *Fame* to *The Full Monty* – Aoyama responds, fascinated, to Asami's assertion that quitting dancing was like accepting death and her more general proposition that 'life is what you can't control'. What gives his final dismemberment at the hands of Asami its horrible power – beyond the sequence's unblinking duration – is that it has some dramatic logic if seen as part of Aoyama's guilt-ridden death wish (it may indeed only be his own fantasy); what disappoints is the realisation that Miike has skilfully solicited our empathy for Aoyama, it seems, primarily to create an unforgettable taboo-busting horror sequence.

On the evidence of *Audition*, Miike is clearly a film-maker of great skill and promise. But comparisons with David Cronenberg, whose early films' singular obsession with bodily malaise and authorial inscription created a genre of its own, seem misplaced. From the startlingly effective shot of Asami answering the telephone while an unseen victim suddenly moves in a sack on her floor to the orgy of mutilation at the end, *Audition* rather invokes the David Lynch of *Lost Highway* (even down to the surreal black jokes, here about fish and dogs). Narrative coherence is ultimately sacrificed to wicked postmodern thrills, rendering *Audition* an experience which can fully satisfy only the most conscience-free of gore-hounds and career masochists.

Richard Falcon

Lust for a Vampire (Jimmy Sangster, 1971)

Section 3:
People and Stories

The fantastic cinema has its mythologies. Some are much older than the movies, as Marina Warner proves in addressing the persistence of *Beauty and the Beast*, some have literary roots (like Washington Irving's 'The Legend of Sleepy Hollow'), some interpret literary roots in a distinctive way (like Hammer's 1950s remakes of Universal's 1930s co-options of the gothic canon), some are invented for the cinema and last in popular culture (like Toho's *Godzilla* films), and some spring from the times and the minds of the adventurous. Sometimes, the subject (Godzilla, Nosferatu) can be the star, or even the style (Hammer).

I hope that Thomas Elsaesser's pieces on Murnau/Nosferatu and Lang/Mabuse might provide a context for a reading of the work of Iain Sinclair (a subject rather than a contributor in this instance) and Chris Petit, whose *Asylum* addresses the now and near-future in a way surprisingly close to the approach of the canonical German silent film-makers, deploying elements from science fiction and stretching the definition of a fiction film to explore a catastrophe that is already upon us.

BEAUTY & THE BEASTS

Marina Warner

The first Beast was the god of love, Eros. The many successive versions of the *Beauty and the Beast* fairytale have continued to develop him in this role, and the new Disney *Beauty and the Beast* is no exception.

In the romance the Alexandrian writer Apuleius interpolated into *The Golden Ass*, Eros makes love, invisibly, to a mortal Beauty – Psyche – who rivals his own mother Aphrodite in seductiveness. Psyche is forbidden to see him; her sisters goad her, warning her that her lover must be a monster, a cannibal, whose 'favourite food is a woman far gone in pregnancy'. When Psyche breaks the prohibition, lighting a candle to look at him as he sleeps, he and all his magic surroundings vanish. Her fantasy of his monstrousness proves to be delusory – an important theme in the fairytale, in which later Beauties have to discover for themselves that the Beast's beastliness is an illusion lying in the eye of the beholder. Eros, mysterious, unknown, feared, exceeds all imaginable degree of charm when Psyche does look at him, but her failure to trust, and to obey, costs her his presence and his love. Apuleius' tale echoes stories of Pandora and Eve in focusing on female curiosity as the dynamic of the sex. Punished for her disobedience, Psyche has to prove her love through many adventures and ordeals; finally, this Beauty is reunited with her Beast and adapts him, a god, to the human condition, to society through marriage, and they have a daughter called Voluptas – Pleasure.

The divine Beast offers writers and film-makers a figure of masculine desire, and the plot in which he moves presents a blueprint for the proper channelling of erotic energy in society. It is Psyche, however, who has to strive to that end; the story is her journey, the journey of the soul. This makes her the protagonist, occupying the more usually male role of the chivalrous quester, but it also consistently leaves in place the Eros figure as the object of the soul's quest, again in a reversal of the more expected pattern of chivalry.

As a female pilgrim's progress, a rite of passage with a heroine at its centre, the tale of *Beauty and the Beast* has attracted numerous women interpreters. Linda Woolverton, the scriptwriter for the new Disney animation, follows in a long and distinguished line which includes *ancien régime* rakes, French governesses, English bluestockings, as well as more recently the Surrealists Leonora Carrington and Angela Carter. The earliest writer of true fairytales to tackle the theme paradoxically challenged the very premises of the romance: at the end of the seventeenth century and beginning of the eighteenth, in one famous fairytale after another, Marie-Catherine Jumel de Barneville, Comtesse d'Aulnoy, portrayed her heroines struggling with the conditions of arranged matches and arriving at different stratagems of deliverance from unsavoury suitors. Mme d'Aulnoy herself had been married off in her teens to a notorious libertine, and she and her mother were later charged with plotting to murder him by falsely accusing him of high treason, a capital crime. They were found guilty, but not before M. le Comte d'Aulnoy had spent three years in the Bastille under suspicion. Their sentences were suspended in exchange for spying abroad for the French crown, and when Mme d'Aulnoy finally returned to Paris, she presided over a fashionable salon where the guests played literary parlour games and dressed up in the costumes of characters in fairytales.

The threat of animals at that time was a real and frightening one; in times of scarcity and hard winters bears and wolves would prey on towns and villages, and animal metamorphosis in the tales could consequently pack menace to a degree that can no longer be felt today, when crocodiles and sharks are sold as soft toys and endangered species outstrip the starving Somalians or the Bosnians for relief funds. The various Beast shapes to which the unsavoury lovers are confined in the fairytales embodied Mme d'Aulnoy's and her contemporaries' view of marital union. In *The Ram*, the princess heroine simply leaves the eponymous Beast to die, while she busies herself taking charge of her father's kingdom at his side. In *The Green Serpent*, Mme d'Aulnoy elaborates the Cupid and Psyche story, and the Beast is portrayed as a true-hearted lover cursed with animal ugliness by a wicked fairy; her heroine Laidronette (Little Ugly One) is equally disfigured by an evil spell, but dauntless in her labyrinthine quest. Significantly, when Laidronette comes across a whole circle of hell peopled by men in enchanted animal shape, she discovers that they have been punished for various marital crimes – for wife-beating, rape and so forth – and that their shape corresponds to their offence.

Fairytales, with their generic commitment to justice, often enclose a simple notion of retribution. Francesco Stefani's *The Singing Ringing Tree* (*Das Singende Klingende Bäumchen*), a family film made in the former GDR in 1957 and largely inspired by the Grimm Brothers' early nineteenth-century collection, blended a *Beauty and the Beast*-type tale with another familiar figure: the Haughty Princess who considers herself too good for every one of her dozens of suitors. Her punishment is ugliness: the live-action film animates the grotesque collapse of her beauty and follows her growing, painful lessons in kindness, humility and love as she cares for the magical creatures she once spurned – a giant goldfish, a golden-maned and golden-antlered horse and a flock of doves. Her pilgrim's progress eventually succeeds in freeing her mentor, the Prince, who himself has been changed into a bear by an evil magician. Once she has learned to love, her beauty returns. The Disney *Beauty and the Beast* adapts a similar idea of retributive justice when, at the beginning, it describes how the Prince spurned a beggarwoman who came to his door; for this brutal behaviour, she casts a spell on him that turns him into a brute for all to see. It's a piquant example of concurrence in the area of children's entertainment between the approaches of the old Communist state and the doyen of freemarket cinema; the fun of fairytales for grown-ups often lies in wagging fingers at the young, in a secular, ideological variation on the hellfire sermon.

Moral intentions have influenced fairytales increasingly strongly since the nineteenth century; the Brothers Grimm led the way, as they re-edited and reshaped successive editions of their famous *Household Tales* to clarify their improving message. Their predecessors were less anxious about the possible effect on children of tales of incest, adultery or murder. The earliest fairytale actually entitled *La Belle et la Bête* was written by the French aristocrat Mme de Villeneuve in 1740, and it portrays the Beast as the victim of an ancient and malignant fairy who cursed him when the handsome youth turned down her amorous advances. The story encrypts the corrupt and vicious intrigues of court life, of fortune-hunting and marriage broking, pandering and lust in the *ancien régime*, and, like many of the first literary fairytales, it campaigns for marriages of true minds, for the rights of the heart, for freedom for the true lovers of romance.

The Disney film, of course, has abandoned the cynical combativeness of the tale's first interpreters and remained true to the romantic and idealist yearnings of later tellers. Fourteen years after Mme de Villeneuve's *La Belle et la Bête*, Mme de Beaumont revised it in a polished résumé; it is her version that has become almost canonical, and that inspired Cocteau's film of 1946. Mme de Beaumont was a governess who worked for aristocratic families in England; she collaborated with her charges (she believed strongly in young women's capacities to think and act) on a pioneer pedagogical journal called *The Misses' Magazine*, in which she published conversations, fables, cautionary tales – and fairy stories. It's easy to catch, in her *La Belle et la Bête*, the anxious tones of a well-meaning teacher raising her pupils to face their future obediently and decorously, to hear the hope that inside an undesirable husband might beat the heart of a good man, given a bit of encouragement.

Fairytales' stock-in-trade has become didacticism, but Mme de Beaumont in the mid-eighteenth century was a pioneer in using the form to lead the expectations of the young; in spite of the genre's reputation for happy endings, it tends to teach its audience to know the worst so that they can perhaps deal with it when it happens. The nursery story of *Beauty and the Beast* assumes a female audience (as, it seems to me, does the Disney film) who fully expect to be given away to men who might well strike them as monsters. The social revolution which has established as the norm marriage from inclination has irreversibly altered the reception of such romances, and ironically transformed seventeenth-century women's resistance to their matrimonial lot, as well as eighteenth-century lessons in resignation, into romantic – and materialistic – propaganda for making a good marriage.

When men adopt this material, they often introduce special pleading on their own behalf; Cocteau's film, for all its delicacy and dream-like seductiveness, concentrates on awakening Beauty to consciousness of the Beast's goodness. He does not have to change, except in outward shape; she has to see past his unsightliness to the gentle and loving human being trapped inside. Christian Bérard's designs intensify the Beast's poignancy; he's not an animal, but a hairy anthropomorphic changeling, a Quasimodo, a pitiful Elephant Man who deserves love if only women would listen to the imperatives of the heart, not the eye. King Kong is one of his lineage too, as the last words of the film make plain: "'Twas not the aeroplanes, 'twas Beauty killed the Beast.' This strand in the history of *Beauty and the Beast* consists of variations on the theme of the femme fatale, on men's anguish in the face of female indifference, rather than women's vulnerability to male violence. Ironically, such interpretations make Beauty guilty of fixity, in a story that began as a narrative of a woman's passionate progress.

Underlying the static serenity of Josette Day's Beauty in Cocteau's film lies the Symbolist fetishisation of impassive femininity, as defined by Baudelaire; of Beauty who speaks of herself as '*un rêve de pierre*' (a dream of stone), with a granite breast on which men (poets) wound themselves and discover love '*éternal et muet ainsi que la matière*' (eternal and mute as matter). Psyche-Beauty, as woman, is material, she is flesh, however cool and otherworldly her appearance; Eros-Beast belongs to the spirit world, and his enchanted castle, with its spellbinding moving sconces and speaking furniture, emanates from the higher realm of imagination, the dimension of dream and fantasy, where poets – like Baudelaire, like Cocteau himself – are sent through the love women inspire in them. Cocteau, as a Surrealist, was reinterpreting Symbolist doctrine of the feminine's role in creativity. Not for nothing had the *Dictionnaire abrégé du surréalisme* attributed to Baudelaire its definition of 'la femme': 'She who casts the greatest light or the greatest shadows into our dreams'. The inflexion on 'our' here is obviously masculine. This doesn't prevent Cocteau's *La Belle et la bête* from entrancing a female spectator again and again, but it does divert the story from the female subject to communicate a perceived male erotic hunger for beauty as stimulus to creativity. The ravishing aestheticisation of the film, from the flying laundry at the start to the twilit luxuries of the castle magic, extends the function of the feminine as the Beast's necessary lifeblood.

Cinema, like fairytale illustration, has to display the Beast (the word monster, interestingly derives from Latin *monstrare*, to show). The narrators of earlier versions of *Beauty and the Beast* could avoid giving precise indications of his horrible appearance, and describe his enchanted shape in the most general terms: he is merely so monstrous that anyone beholding him is struck down with terror for their lives. Early illustrators, however, had to wrestle with the problem; and late nineteenth-century printers of children's books pioneered full-colour illustration. At the beginning, mere animal form is sufficient horror in itself: in the Lambs' version, the earliest written for children in English, the artist simply visualised the Beast as a swine, like the victims of Circe's enchantments in *The Odyssey*. But the trend soon moved towards more anthropomorphic-characteristics: two-legged, upright Beasts disfigured by elephant trunks, or boar's tusks, or wart-hog's snouts. The less-than-human took the shape of mammals equipped with natural weaponry. In this, the artists returned to Christian iconography of the devil, multiplying phallic protuberances on face and limbs. But they stopped short, unlike their medieval predecessors, at blazoning monstrous organs in the site of the genitals themselves. It's significant that women artists – fewer in number – tend not to stress the Beast's aggressive arsenal, or to focus on his ferocity, but incline towards characteristics of creatures traditionally classed as lower than mammals, visualising the repellent creature as toad-like, fishy, or lizard-like. From a woman's point of view, the repugnant sometimes looks less-than-masculine, a clammy, flaccid manifestation more like Gollum in Tolkien's *Lord of the Rings* than the male vision of a fallen angel of priapism.

Though the early literature offers different approaches to the Beast's nature, none of it suggests that his monstrousness fascinates and attracts the heroines, that they want to play with the Beast precisely because his animal nature excites them and gives licence to their own desire. The traditional oral material, however, like the Nordic fairytale *East of the Sun and West of the Moon*, does depict the Beast-heroes as captivating in their very beastliness. The Grimms' *Rose Red and Snow White* describes how both the heroines run away screaming when they first set eyes on their suitor, the black bear. But they gradually get used to him, and begin to frolic with him: 'They tugged his hair with their hands, put their feet on his back and rolled him about, or they took a hazel switch and beat him, and when he growled, they laughed. But the bear took it all in good part.' Eventually, the two sisters help to disenchant him from the power of a malevolent dwarf, and he turns out to be a rich prince who marries one of them.

Bears became the most popular manifestation of the Beast, and as the twentieth century advances, they grow less fierce and more cuddly, keeping pace with the new values attached to the wilderness and its creatures as well as with the galloping sentimentalisation of teddy bears. In the Edwardian children's theatre version of *Beauty and the Beast*, bear costumes are recommended; the bear was known, after all, as the 'beast who walks like a man'.

In 1982, a television dramatisation of the fairytale, directed by John Woods, was written by the poet, Ted Hughes. It should be much better known, for it develops the theme, implicit in the classical myth of Eros and Psyche, that Beauty's desire conjures the Beast to her side, and that, after she has lost him, her passion for him brings about their union. The Hughes-Woods version, though made for children, does not scant the heroine's erotic fantasy as the dynamic of the story. It begins with the father crazed with worry that every night his beloved daughter, the Princess, is visited by a monstrous and unnameable terror which takes possession of her; invisible, with a huge voice, this phenomenon occupies her dreams and her bed. Doctors are put to watch by her side, and they too are overcome with horror at what they feel, though they see nothing. Then a wandering musician with a performing bear comes to the palace at the King's request, to entertain the melancholy and even mad Princess – and the bear charms her. She dances with him, and the King, her father, rejoices that the bear seems to have lifted the mad darkness that was oppressing her. But then, as they are dancing, the bear seizes her in his arms and carries her off. When, after a long search, the hunting-party tracks them down, the Princess begs them not to hurt her bear. They wound him, and she weeps – and then, as in other versions, her tears, the proof of her love, fall on his pelt and he stands up, transfigured into a beautiful prince.

Hughes's intuition that Beauty loves the Beast, even when he terrorises her in the night, reappeared in a more definite form in the popular CBS television series (also shown in Britain), in which the Beast never casts off his hybrid form. A roaring, rampaging half-lion, half-human creature, he reigns over the New York subway system as a defender of women and beggars, an urban Robin Hood who was born from an immaculate virgin and the seed of two fathers, the double lord of the underworld, one a good magus and the other a wicked wizard. Beauty in this case works in the DA's office, but communicates secretly with her saviour Beast; their love is passionate, chivalrous and illicit. He is the 'monster of her dreams', and she likes him just as he is.

It would be easy to dismiss these visions of the Beast's desirability as male self-flattery, or even, more seriously, as sentimental justifications of roughness, tyranny and rape. But to do so misses the genuine attempt of the fairytale, sometimes, to face up to the complicated character of the female erotic impulse. The story has always been a great favourite for women: the early writers were followed by Victorians like Mary Lamb, who translated and adapted it for her brother, and Lucy Crane, who worked on it with her brother, the artist Walter Crane. More recently, Leonora Carrington, the Surrealist artist and writer, returned to the theme over and over again in her short stories of 1937–41 and in later images.

Carrington was writing from the age of 19 onwards from the midst of a Surrealist circle centred on Max Ernst, and she responded to Surrealist fantasies about young women – *femmes enfants* – as the innocent, and therefore pure, mediums of erotic power. She voices Surrealist dreams of sexual freedom for men and women, intertwining the macabre English nursery-rhyme tradition with avant-garde flouting of decorum. Her imagery responds to Ernst's own collage novels, like *A Week of Kindness*, in which he imagined savage conjunctions and maulings, as well as celebratory carnal encounters. Carrington conjures equally fierce couplings of her feral heroines and their lovers. In *As they rode along the edge...* the heroine, Virginia Fur, lives in a forest and travels at the head of a procession of a hundred cats, riding on a wheel. She has a huge mane and 'long and enormous hands with dirty nails'. 'One couldn't really be altogether sure that she was a human being. Her smell alone threw doubt on it – a mixture of spices and game, the stables, fur and grasses.' Virginia makes love tempestuously with Igname, a boar, after he has presented himself to her in 'the most sumptuous outfit' – apparel worthy of a wooer; 'a wig of squirrels' tails and fruit hung around Igname's ears, pierced for the occasion by two little pikes he had found dead in the lake. His hoofs were dyed red by the blood of a rabbit. He hid his russet buttocks (he did not want to show all his beauty at one go).'

Carrington's stories throw important light on the development of the *Beauty and the Beast* story in the literature of women, for women. Generally speaking, her Beast represents the energy, hitherto crushed by conventional forces, inside her heroine's spirits. This motive force, in the manner of post-Freudian optimism, is erotic in character: in the wake of early utopian Revolutionaries, the Surrealists believed that the liberation of sexual desire would lead to wider freedom and fulfilment. Angela Carter's short tales, in *The Bloody Chamber*, show an uncannily similar spirit of mischief to Carrington's, even though she cannot have known the older woman's work as it has only very recently been collected. Carter, too, varied her interpretations of the *Beauty and the Beast* theme over and over again: in *The Courtship of Mr Lyon, The Tiger's Bride, The Werewolf, The Company of Wolves*. These are some of the most shivery and sensual tales about women's sexual initiation, and they lift the covers from the body usually concealed in the fairytale. Indeed, Carter herself noted the hypocritical evasions of so many modern versions. In a review of a recent study of the fairytale by Betsy Hearne, she commented caustically that the story was increasingly set to work 'to house-train the id'.

Beauty's attraction to the Beast before his regeneration reflects pulp fantasies about abduction in romance fiction, and even pornography's conjuration of sadism and rape. The territory is heavily mined; one of the reasons Angela Carter's work, in screenplays as well as books, provokes so many contradictory and powerful feelings rises from her plain dealing with erotic dominance as a source of pleasure for men – and for women. But Carter's tales are polymorphous, too, and full of rich contradictions. *The Magic Toyshop* tells the story of a Beast's defeat; the puppet master makes a monstrous swan automaton to assault his niece, but she rejects him, refuses the part in his puppet show and eventually escapes, with the whole family, from his designs. For *The Company of Wolves*, Carter adapted several stories to dramatise a young girl's sexual awakening and the call of the wild. The company of wolves here stirs desire far more profoundly than would the highest pattern of princes.

Linda Woolverton and the team who collaborated on the new Disney *Beauty and the Beast* have clearly seeped themselves in the tale's history, on and off screen; prolonged and intense production meetings, turning over every last detail of representation and narrative, can almost be heard over the insouciant soundtrack. This is a fairytale that's vividly aware of contemporary sexual politics; it has consciously picked out a strand in the tale's history and developed it for an audience of mothers who grew up with Betty Friedan and Gloria Steinem, who have daughters who listen to Madonna and Sinéad O'Connor. Woolverton's screenplay gives us a heroine of spirit who finds romance on her own terms; and beneath this *prima facie* storyline, the interpretation contains many subtexts, both knotty and challenging, about changing concepts of paternal authority and rights, about permitted expressions of male desire, and prevailing notions in the quarrel about nature-nurture. Above all, it places troublingly before our eyes the domestication of feminism itself.

Nevertheless, while the Disney *Beauty and the Beast* ostensibly tells the story of the feisty, strong-willed heroine, and carries the audience along on the wave of her dash, bravery, self-awareness and integrity, the principal burden of the film's message concerns maleness, its various faces and masks, and, in the spirit of romance, it offers hope of regeneration from within the unregenerate male. The graphic intensity given the two protagonists betrays the right of interest: Beauty is saucer-eyed, dainty, slender and wears a variation on the pseudo-medieval dresses of both Cinderella and Snow White, which, as in *Cinderella*, turn into *ancien régime* crinolines cum New Look debutante gowns for the scene of awakening love when she dances with the Beast. Her passage from repugnance to attraction also follows a movement from village hall to castle gate, in the conventional upwardly mobile style of fairytales. The animators have introduced certain emancipated touches: she's dark-haired, walks with a swing, moves with fetching fleetness of gesture, and has a certain graceful carelessness about her appearance – the hook is that she's a bookworm, and the script even contains a fashionable bow in the direction of self-reflexiveness, for Belle likes reading fairytales more than any other kind of book, and consequently recognises the type of story she's caught in.

So Belle is an improvement on Cinderella or Snow White. But, compared to the Beast, she's dull. He has the artists' full attention; the pneumatic signature style of Disney animation suits the Beast's character as male desire incarnate he swells, he towers, he inflates, he tumesces. Everything about him is big, and capable of growing bigger: his castle looms, its furnishings dwarfed by its Valhalla-like dimensions. The candelabra, the clock, the teapot – the three servants who come to life with brio and exuberance – are like Lilliputians lost in a Brobdingnagian's lair. We see the Beast enraged, crowding the screen edge to edge; when he holds Belle he looks as if he could snap her between his teeth like a chicken wing. His body too looks as if it's constantly in the process of burgeoning; poised on narrow hooves and skimpy legs, the Disney Beast sometimes lollops like a big cat, but more often stands erect, rising to an engorged torso, with an enormous, bull-like head compacted into massive shoulders, maned and shaggy all over, bristling with fangs and horns and claws that almost seem belittled by the creature's overall bulk. The Beast's sexual equipment was always part of his charm – hidden or otherwise (it is, of course, dispersed by synecdoche all over his body in the Disney cartoon). When Titania falls in love with Bottom the Weaver, the associations of the ass were not lost on the audience. But the comic – and its concomitant, the pathetic – have almost entirely slipped away from this contemporary representation of virility.

Whereas Bottom, even in his name, was a figure of fun, and the Golden Ass, his classical progenitor, a ruefully absurd icon of (male) humanity, the contemporary vision of the Beast tends to the tragic. The new Disney Beast's nearest ancestor is the Minotaur, the hybrid offspring of Phaedra and the bull and an ancient nightmare of perverted appetite. (It is significant that Picasso adopted the Minotaur as his alter ego, as the embodiment of his priapism, in the vigour of youth as well as in the impotence of old age.) Disney's Minotaur also conveys the rage of the male at experiencing limits: when the Beast is thwarted or disobeyed he lashes out and roars and ruts, but uselessly. Belle fears him, but his violence has no effect on her, or, it seems, on anyone else. He's a prisoner of his own powerful bulk, just as he's a prisoner in his own castle.

The Disney cartoon has doubled the traditional plot by adding a second Beast, Gaston, who personifies another side to the rampant hunk in need of civilising, and refracts the Beast in a second series of mirrors. In French, '*bête*' means 'stupid' when used as an adjective; in Cocteau's film, Jean Marais' Beast can only grunt, though his magical palace breathes caressing words in his erotic baritone to Beauty when she moves about her room. The Beauty who confronts and eventually transforms the Beast though love restores him to culture, civility and language, and in the process, discovers herself. Cocteau's Beast speaks to Beauty through her mirror, for instance, so that she advances towards the knowledge of her desires when she contemplates her own reflection.

The Disney version flatters its heroine with far more profound wisdom; her discovery of the Beast's qualities does not go hand in hand with any needed growth in self-awareness. She knows her own mind from the start. Nor are all Beasts amenable to instruction: Gaston is a killer – of animals – and remains one; he's a lyncher who preys on social outcasts (suspected lunatics and marginals), he wants to breed (he promises Belle six or seven children), and he's capable of deep treachery in pursuit of his own interests. The penalty for his brutishness is death: he falls off a high crag from the Beast's castle. He's the true beast, Calvinist and unredeemed, socially deviant in his supremacist assumptions; unsound on ecology in both directions (he abuses the natural, the forest, and culture, the library). What is significant about this caricature, above all, is that he's a man in a man's shape, a dead ringer for Clark Kent as played by Christopher Reeve. But Supermen are out, and animals are in – witness the success of Robert Bly and his theories of men's need for the wild in *Iron John*.

Splitting the male into the good beast and the bad beast adds needed drama to the story, but it's also a device that helps define by contrast the possibility of a superior, virtuous brand of masculinity, embodied by the Beast. Unlike Gaston, he does not hunt and shoot other creatures; unlike Gaston, he's aware of his shortcomings, and grieves like a good existentialist at his condition; unlike Gaston, he appreciates books and indeed possesses a huge library, big enough to keep even a bookworm like Belle happy for a while. Where Caroline Thompson's *Edward Scissorhands* (1990), the most recent attempt by a woman writer-producer to portray a good Beast, foundered on such a paragon's capacity to survive in the world and sent him back into solitary confinement in his gothic castle, Woolverton's revision cuts its cloth to fairytale's traditional pattern of heroic optimism and presents a Beast who fits the profile of the Bly-style New Man: virile yet tender, natural yet cultivated, in touch with his emotions, connected to the child within yet mature and responsible in his attitude. All he needed was the love of a good woman. Sometimes – though it seems grudging after clamouring for positive feminine representations for so long – such a huge helping of female autonomy, responsibility, self-determination, and powers of salvation add up to a mighty charge for one small Belle to shoulder.

In *Edward Scissorhands*, the heroine also acts quickly, with gallantry and courage, to save this outcast from a mob; but he is fatally hampered by his hybrid form, half way between the automaton and the creaturely: his weapon hands encumber him with man-made technology and cut him off from the desirable aspects of the human, which derive from what is perceived as natural, as animal. The further the cinematic outcast lies from the machine, the more likely his redemption; the beast as cyborg, as in *Terminator 2: Judgment Day* (1991), represents the apocalyptic culmination of human ingenuity and its diabolical perversion. Whereas, to a medieval spectator, the devil was perceived as close to the animal order in his hooved hairiness, and a bloodless angel in gleaming armour approximated the divine artefact, the register of value has since the eighteenth century been turned topsy-turvy and the wild man has come into his own as an ideal. The evolution of the Beast in fairytale, and his portraits in film illustrate this shift in cultural values as well as sexual expectations.

The most significant plot change to the traditional story in the Disney film concerns the role of Beauty's father, and it continues the film's trend towards granting Beauty freedom of movement and responsibility for the action. The traditional fairytale often includes the tragic motif that in return for his life, the father promises the Beast the first thing to greet him when he returns home; as in the story of Jephte in the Bible, his daughter, his youngest and most dear, rushes to the gate to meet him, and the father has to sacrifice her. In the eighteenth-century French fairy story, which focused on the evils of matrimonial custom, the father hands over Belle to the Beast in exactly the same kind of legal and financial transaction as an arranged marriage, and she learns to lump it with her new husband. Bruno Bettelheim, following in the governesses' footsteps, takes a strict line in *The Uses of Enchantment*, where he analyses the story as a lesson in female maturity: Beauty learns to relinquish her Oedipal attachment to her father and discovers her own sexuality with the Beast; furthermore, she should be grateful to her father for making the discovery possible.

Linda Woolverton's script sensibly sets such patriarchal analysis aside, and instead provides subplots to explain away the father's part in Beauty's predicament, as well as supplying Beauty herself with all the determination to make her mistress of her own fate. In the last successful Disney animation, *The Little Mermaid* (1989), the heroine teaches her father, the God of the Sea, to respect her desires, somewhat in the manner of Madonna's song, 'Pappa don't preach'. A few years on, the Disney studio, sensitive to the rise of children's rights, has replaced the father with the daughter as the enterprising authority figure in the family.

The tales in the *Beauty and the Beast* cycle number among the most eloquent testaments to women's struggles – against arranged marriage, towards a definition of the place of sexuality in love. The disenchantment of the Beast has long been a theme in the stories women have made up, among themselves, to help, to teach, to warn. Liking a Disney film doesn't come easily; admitting to enjoying a fairytale cartoon from the same studio that made *Snow White* and *Cinderella*, that held up simpering, gutless, niminy-piminy idiots as paragons and introduced children everywhere to expect malignancy from older women goes against the grain, like accepting all of a sudden that John Major has developed dress sense, or the Pope become a feminist. But this version of *Beauty and the Beast* is funny, touching and lively, and communicates romantic hopefulness with panache and high spirits. It's a true inheritor of a long literary tradition of romance, sieved through the consciousness of 1970s feminism, which asked for plucky fairytale heroines and got this: a Hollywood belle who prefers books to hunks.

BEAUTY AND THE BEAST
USA 1991
Directors: Gary Trousdale, Kirk Wise

France in the eighteenth century. A proud, selfish prince turns away an old woman begging for alms; revealing herself to be an enchantress, she transforms him into a monstrous beast, She gives him a rose, telling him that only if he can be loved before the rose loses all its petals, will he return to human form. Several years later: in a small village lives Belle, the beautiful daughter of Maurice, an eccentric inventor mocked by all. Belle is ardently pursued by the self-important hunter Gaston, but Belle is interested only in reading books.

One day, Maurice sets out for a fair, to display his elaborate new logging machine. Lost in a forest, he arrives at the Beast's gloomy, deserted castle, and is met by its servants, animated household objects: Cogsworth, a clock; Lumiere, a candle; and the teapot, Mrs Potts, and her cup son Chip. But the enraged Beast imprisons Maurice and only agrees to release him when Belle, alerted by her father's horse to his plight, arrives at the castle and promises to stay in his place. Belle is welcomed by the servants, and the assembled kitchen utensils lay on a spectacular dinner-show for her.

Given the freedom of the castle, Belle is told she can go anywhere except the East Wing; spurred by curiosity, however, she disobeys and there, amidst decay, finds the wilting rose. After an outburst by the Beast, Belle breaks her promise and leaves the castle, only to be attached by wolves. The Beast rescues her and is wounded. Belle nurses him back to health and a romance burgeons between them. Back in the village, Maurice tries to tell the villagers about the Beast, but is mocked. Gaston sees a chance to win Belle as his wife, and bribes the asylum keeper Monsieur D'Arque to lock Maurice away, planning to persuade Belle to marry him in return for his release. Looking into the Beast's magic mirror, Belle sees her father ill, and returns to the village with the heart-broken Beast's approval.

As she returns, D'Arque comes to take Maurice away; Belle and her father are locked in a cellar while Gaston sets off with the villagers to kill the Beast. But the pair are released, with the help of the logging machine, by Chip, who has smuggled himself from the castle with Belle. She rushes back to the castle, where the disconsolate Beast is unwilling to offer any resistance to his attackers. The villagers are driven off by the servants, and with Belle's encouragement, the Beast fights and defeats Gaston. The Beast seems on the point of death, but the spell is broken and he turns back into the prince. He and Beauty are united at last, and the castle returns to its former glory, while the servants resume human form.

* * *

Beauty and the Beast has always seemed to be the most double-edged of moral fairy-tales. While it supposedly illustrates the premise that beauty (or ugliness) is only skin-deep, its *raison d'être* hangs on the promise of the Beast returning to his 'real' handsome form – which seems a betrayal of the tale's subversive potential. In this Disney version, as in Cocteau's, the bland prince is given deservedly short shrift – his initial metamorphosis and final 'happy ever after' reward are presented as inexpressively stylised stained-glass tableaux, recalling the chocolate-box flatness of Disney's 1959 *Sleeping Beauty*, of which this tale is after all a direct reversal.

The fable's play on the riddles of surface and depth makes it the ideal vehicle for animation, and directors Trousdale and Wise have achieved a remarkable play-off of two different kinds of depth illusion. On the one hand, there is the traditional Disney technique of rich background and frantically bustling detail (especially in the 'Belle' sequence, where the heroine, Keaton-like, waltzes unscathed through a succession of perils); on the other, the paradoxical solidity of computer animation, which in the ballroom scene achieves a quasi-mystical sense of frozen, impossible space. As the loving couple waltz ecstatically, a glittering hall of swirling chandeliers and marbled flooring whirls around them in modish virtual-reality fashion; the two levels of animation blend brilliantly, but the match is still as unsettling and thrilling as the sight of Dick Van Dyke dancing with cartoon penguins must have been in 1964.

The film's characters and settings refer quite knowingly to their forebears and sources. The French flavour, the village setting and much of the castle atmosphere are a nod to Cocteau; while the nightmare element, the wolves and the massing shadows of the Beast himself refer back to moments like the 'Bald Mountain' sequence in *Fantasia*. The film is shameless about the provenance of its characters, recognising that the more generically rooted they are, the more resonant (after *The Little Mermaid*, which seemed to strain to devise a whole new school of original characters). Belle is half-way between Julie Andrews in *The Sound of Music* and a sexier, sassier Wilma Flintstone. Only the Beast is generally free of such reference. Half bull, half St Bernard, he is most effective early on as a lumbering mass of inchoate shadow; it is only later, preening for the ball, that he takes on shades of the Cowardly Lion in his ribbons and bows.

If these echoes work to the film's advantage, the castle servants are its flaw. The Laurel and Hardy pairing of the pompous clock and the foppish candle is too fussy and facile, and too much a re-run of the mice in *Sleeping Beauty*. More troublesome is Angela Lansbury's annoyingly arch Cockney teapot (mysteriously cursed with an

American-accented child, the repellently cute Chip) – she brings at once an unwelcome touch of the simpering class-consciousness of *Upstairs, Downstairs* and an echo of her own appearance in *Bedknobs and Broomsticks*, a reminder of the old school of 1960s/1970s Disney mawkishness.

If this is very much a film of good and bad bits, that is because of the way the armies of animators (some 600) have been marshalled, with each major character getting his, her or its character animators and clean-up animators. The music, however, is the film's most consistent feature, showing that writers Howard Ashman and Alan Menken – of *The Little Shop of Horrors* – have been studying their Sondheim. The brisk, acidic style of *Into the Woods* dominates the film's first half, which has more of the resonance of the cynical Broadway musical than of the traditional Disney ditty; at his best, lyricist Ashman – who died last year, and was also the film's executive producer – shows dextrous rhyming skill, notably in 'Belle', as the villagers puzzle over the heroine's book-ridden weirdness (given the Andrews resemblance, they could be asking, 'How do you solve a problem like Belle?'). Fragmented as it is, this is the most stylish Disney animation in years, and its satisfying tearjerker ending is marred only by one worry – if all the castle servants have resumed human form, what will the loving couple do for cutlery?

Jonathan Romney

HAMMER'S COSY VIOLENCE

Jonathan Coe

This August's month-long Hammer season at the Barbican Cinema, London, will inevitably revive potent memories among a whole generation of film-goers. For instance, can *you* remember the first Hammer film you ever saw? I can: and, appropriately enough, it's a memory saturated with overtones of transgression and escape. I was only 13 at the time, and in order to sample this forbidden fruit I had to sneak out to a cinema in central Birmingham late one Saturday afternoon, when my parents thought I was safely ensconced at a friend's house. When I saw the same film again on television, more than 20 years later, it fully justified the studio's reputation for uncovering all those darker forces in the British national character that are normally hidden away in shame. It remains, in many ways, one of the most shocking and horrific British films of the past few decades.

No, not *Vampire Circus*, nor *The Plague of the Zombies*. It was, of course, the cinema spin-off version of *Man about the House*.

I only discovered recently that it was a Hammer film at all: a product of their last, floundering years, when the exploitation movies being imported from the continent had started to make the studio's own product look tame, and *The Exorcist* had comprehensively transformed the public's expectations of the horror film. Under these pressures, Hammer was attempting to play increasingly desperate variations on its once reliable themes (*Dracula A.D. 1972*, aka 'Dracula, Chelsea, 1972', aka 'Dracula Chases the Mini Girls' being the most poignant example) while also looking yearningly towards the television sitcom as a supplier of loyal audiences: hence the big-screen versions of *Nearest and Dearest, Love Thy Neighbour* and *That's Your Funeral* – all released in 1973, and all would-be cash-ins on the popularity of *On the Buses* (1971), which was, bizarrely, the most commercially successful Hammer film of all time.

A sad end to the history of a great studio, you might think: but in fact there's a remarkable continuity between these cinematic death rattles and the flurry of modest hits which first gave Hammer momentum in the early 1950s. The history of the studio teaches us, among other things, that the uneasy symbiotic relationship between British film and television – often discussed as if it was a product of the 1980s – goes back a very long way. Hammer was the offspring of two family enterprises, born in the mid-30s when showbusiness entrepreneurs Enrique Carreras and William Hinds pooled their resources to form a distribution and production company. Aside from the Paul Robeson vehicle *The Song of Freedom* (showing at the Barbican on 3 August) their early films were undistinguished, and the company didn't begin to hit its stride until the late 1940s, when it was discovered that cheap adaptations of popular radio shows (such as *Dick Barton – Special Agent* and *The Adventures of PC 49*) could be guaranteed to return a profit. It was only a matter of time before the newer medium was raided for material too: and Hammer's famous breakthrough, into both the international market and the horror genre, came with their adaptation of Nigel Kneale's *The Quatermass Experiment* in 1955.

Although the graphic *The Curse of Frankenstein* (1957) was more overtly influential, while *Dracula* (1958) was probably the best horror film Hammer ever made, it's *The Quatermass Experiment* which somehow embodies everything that is characteristic of the studio's thinking at this time. One of the important things to remember about Hammer is that nobody working there ever had an original idea: everything had to be adapted from a proven formula. With that caveat, however, it has to be admitted that studio heads James Carreras and Anthony Hinds (sons, respectively, of Enrique and William) had something like a genius for choosing subjects which tapped into aspects of the national mood and the public appetite that were not otherwise being catered for. When the mutant creature in this film is finally cornered by Professor Quatermass, for example, the setting for the showdown is Westminster Abbey, a location chosen by Kneale with one eye on budgetary considerations when writing the story for live television in 1953: 'It was the place that remained vividly in the audience's mind from the Coronation a few weeks earlier,' he said, 'and the simplest scenery would act as a reminder.' At the same time he was too intuitive a writer to be blind to its 'symbolic overtones' and admitted, in 1979, that the whole Quatermass scenario was conceived as a corrective to the sentimental optimism of its era: '1953 was an over-confident year. Rationing was coming to an end. Everest had just been climbed, the Queen crowned, and our first Comet jets were being deceptively successful. A sour note seemed indicated.'

Here, then, was the keynote of what was later to become the Hammer project: the smuggling-in of something faintly subversive, a distant recognition of our national vices or secrets or uncertainties, under the guise of a sensational entertainment. And for a while, with these early films, Kneale himself was trying to smuggle in something even more subversive: ideas. This was evident from his *Quatermass* television series, which ended with the big ball of slime being destroyed from within, by the will of the astronaut whose body it had colonised – thereby implying some sort of continuity between human nature and its repulsive mutation. Naturally, such a dénouement was considered far too highbrow for the film version, which has the creature blasted to death with a few trillion volts from Battersea Power Station; but two years later, when Hammer adapted another of his television plays, *The Creature* (renamed *The Abominable Snowman*, and sadly not showing in the Barbican season), Kneale had acquired more clout, and was allowed to write his own screenplay. Here the monsters turn out to be not rampaging freaks but wise, melancholy descendants of the apes, biding their time in hiding until mankind destroys itself: the meek waiting to inherit the earth. Drawing scornful contrasts between the macho aggression of the monster's Western stalkers and the quiet pacifism of their Eastern hosts, this is one of British cinema's most liberal and humane films, and one which reminds us of the civilised literariness that characterised Hammer's output to a surprising degree over the years. (This being a studio which at times provided a commercial refuge for the most unexpected talents, including some of the era's more challenging composers. Companies like Woodfall might have had more intellectual cachet, but while they relied upon the pleasantries of John Addison and Johnny Dankworth, Hammer was offering commissions to such 12-toners as Elizabeth Lutyens and Don Banks – whose 1966 score for *The Reptile* is something of a masterpiece.)

Eyeballs, goo and metaphysics

Intellectualism at Hammer had its decent limits, however. James Carreras's instincts were solidly commercial, and it wasn't *The Abominable Snowman* that pointed the way forward in 1957 but *The Curse of Frankenstein*. Both films were guilty of excesses, but one merely paraded severed heads and pecked-out eyeballs, while the other offered metaphysical ideas – surely carrying things too far. A line had to be drawn somewhere. It turned out that what the public had liked about *Quatermass* was not Kneale's philosophising but the gooey effects (courtesy of Hammer regular Les Bowie, who, as Howard Maxford wittily suggests in his book about the studio, must have had shares in blancmange). And so the new formula was established – quasi-literary adaptations of horror classics, with much gruesome physical detail – and *Dracula*, *The Mummy* and *Curse of the Werewolf* followed rapidly, defining what would come to be recognised as the Golden Age of Hammer.

The reviewer C. A. Lejeune memorably described *The Curse of Frankenstein* as 'without hesitation … among the half-dozen most repulsive films I have encountered'; and indeed, along with its non-Hammer imitators – *Horrors of the Black Museum* (1959), *Circus of Horrors* (1960) and so on – it provoked a groundswell of distaste within the critical establishment that would climax in the opprobrium heaped upon Michael Powell's *Peeping Tom*. Today, of course, post-Dario Argento, and post-*The Evil Dead*, it's hard to see what all the fuss was about. If anything, we've grown so blasé about cinematic gore that we're likely to go to the other extreme to explain these films' enduring appeal: the sense of blanketing comfort which the very (over)familiarity of the regular Hammer ingredients now induces. From 1951–67, the company was based on a country estate at Bray, near Windsor, where the films were made in a close-knit studio environment which irresistibly recalls the heyday of Michael Balcon's Ealing. Here Anthony Hinds and James Carreras built up their family of directors (Terence Fisher, Seth Holt, Roy Ward Baker, Peter Sasdy) and writers (Jimmy Sangster, Tudor Gates, Hinds himself under various pseudonyms), along with production designer Bernard Robinson and editor James Needs, and of course the great repertory company of actors headed by Cushing and Lee. When watching a Hammer film, then, although we are superficially making an excursion into frightening, uncharted territory, this feeling of chilled anticipation is in conflict with the delicious awareness, at a far deeper level, that we know exactly what to expect.

Among the many reassuring pleasures which Hammer films offer us are: the familiarity of the English landscape (just as *Carry On... Up The Khyber* takes us no further than Snowdonia, so the wildest reaches of the Carpathian mountains always bear a suspicious resemblance to Surrey); the familiarity of instantly recognisable genres (for instance, the endless black and white Boileau-and-Narcejac imitations – *Taste of Fear, Paranoiac, Nightmare* – which rolled off the production line during the early 1960s); the familiarity of the television and radio adaptations which begin and end the main Hammer chronology (bearing in mind also that their very last film was a remake of *The Lady Vanishes*); and, most importantly of all, the familiar faces of dozens of British character actors, many of them better known for comedy than anything else. Hammer films are, in short, absolutely typical of English culture in the way they insist that extremes of violence and extremes of cosiness can and must co-exist. This is the literary culture whose most famous twentieth-century investigator of homicide was played on-screen by Margaret Rutherford; and this is the culture in which even a film with a come-on title like *Taste the Blood of Dracula* boasts such sitcom stars as Peter Sallis and Roy Kinnear among its cast.

Timid erotics

You could argue that it was precisely this cosiness that killed off Hammer in the end. Specifically, it offered little room for sexuality; and compared with the full-blooded vitality of the early Draculas and Frankensteins, there's something terribly timid and pale about their later attempts to eroticise the vampire movie. Viewed alongside the models they sought to imitate – Jean Rollin's *Le Viol du Vampire* (1967) and *La Vampire Nue* (1969) – Hammer's 'Karnstein Trilogy' of the early 1970s – comprising *The Vampire Lovers, Lust for a Vampire* and *Twins of Evil* – seems laughably tame. Partly it's the presence of those comedy stars again (how erotic can a scene be when Dennis Price or Erik Chitty of *Please Sir!* is lurking on the edge of the frame?), partly it's British cinema's consistent failure to produce male or female stars with real sexual energy, so that these films have to be populated with faceless Scandinavian nymphets or wet blankets such as Ralph Bates or Michael Johnson. Perhaps by now, at any rate, the American and continental competition had simply become too racy for Hammer, and the very qualities which had once given their product its edge – its literariness, or the odd sense of old-fashioned decorum which prevails even at its grossest moments – were now beginning to look quaint as the cultural climate changed.

Even so, it's those same qualities, I think, that make the Hammer films look fresh and distinctive today, 30 or even 40 years on. The atmosphere of weird domesticity created by Bernard Robinson – surely the real hero of Hammer studios – is exactly right for the Dracula and Frankenstein films, and was completely missed by Coppola's and Branagh's wretched, overblown remakes in their search for pseudo-authenticity. These stories should not be treated as epics because they are, if anything, domestic comedies: tales of enclosure, of what goes on behind the walls of private properties when the rest of the world is looking the other way. *Countess Dracula*, for example, in which Ingrid Pitt attempts to rejuvenate herself with the blood of her own daughter Lesley-Anne Down, is a wonderful allegory of mother-daughter rivalries, and has been favourably compared by at least one critic to Ken Loach's *Family Life*.

Raymond Durgnat once drew a nice pen portrait of Hammer studios, circa 1964, claiming to have had a dream in which he toured the 'script crypt' at Bray: 'There Major Carreras cracked his bull-whip over the sweating backs of the toiling writers, who moaned at their task while an Assistant Producer beat out the typing speed on his kettle drums. The light of the full moon poured in through the gothic windows, and producer Anthony Hinds stared in horror at his hands, as they grew hairy and twitched – another script idea was taking them over, and he was turning into one or another of his dreaded alter egos, John Elder and Henry Younger. [Actually, Younger, screenwriter of *The Curse of the Mummy's Tomb* (1964), was Michael Carreras (Editor's note).] Young Baron Sangsterstein was there ... with fiendish cunning sewing together bits of scenarios from the old Universal book.' And like all good jokes, this one had a solid core of truth. The conditions of production at Bray did have points of similarity with the typical Hammer scenario: a remote, self-enclosed community, a respectable-looking country house which turns out to be full of strangely equipped rooms and bizarre equipment... Above all, in the words of Michael Carreras (son of James), 'It was like a family affair,' and the Hammer films – with their emphasis on secrets, on acts of violence lying long undiscovered, their obsession with sex that can never quite be openly addressed – can themselves be seen as both a portrait and a product of British family life. In that sense at least, they are real 'family films', and among the truest and most enjoyable that this country has ever produced.

GOJIRA MON AMOUR

Ken Hollings

On a recent tour of Toho studios' sound stages in the suburbs of Tokyo, where filming was already under way for *Mothra*, the first in a new series of monster movies aimed at pre-teens, an American visitor enquired whether Godzilla was around.

'No,' the studio guide replied simply, 'He's gone.'

'Gone?'

'He died in his last movie, He's gone.'

Which happens to be true. After a career lasting more than four decades in which he starred in over 20 films, the king of the monsters perished on screen at the end of Toho's 1995 release *Godzilla vs. Destoyah*. No longer able to control the increasing levels of atomic radiation that had been steadily banking up inside him, Godzilla went into a critical meltdown and burned himself up from within, finally succumbing to the very force that had given him life. It was a deeply moving moment, a tribute to all that is monstrous and unpredictable in our world. The flesh literally melted from Godzilla's bones, inundating Tokyo with a poisonous radioactive fallout.

Though Toho reaffirmed its commitment to the *kaiju* genre by running a trailer for *Mothra* after the final credits, everyone feared the worst. It was over. And as if to seal the giant creature's fate, in April 1997 the death was announced of Tomoyuki Tanaka, the man responsible for dreaming up Godzilla and seeing him through all 22 of his productions for Toho.

Born in Osaka in 1910, Tanaka joined Toho while still a young man and stayed with the company for over 50 years, eventually becoming chairman of the board of directors and chief executive producer. Though essentially retired by 1991, he was still credited as Godzilla's main producer to the end, prompting the rumour that he had actually died of a broken heart as a result of the monster's demise. Toho's 1997 release *Mothra II* was dedicated to his memory.

But this was not the end. In March 1993 TriStar placed a huge advertisement in *Variety*. 'Godzilla 1994' was all it said. Ball-park figures were kicked around, budgets discussed and names mentioned. Sony subsidiary TriStar had reputedly paid Toho $1 million for the rights. The movie was happening. Godzilla was go.

TriStar's film is finally set to devastate the nation's multiplexes this summer. The media rampage has already begun in the West, with two expensive trailers making a lot of threatening noises but revealing very little. So will it really be Godzilla we see on our screens this summer or some new incarnation come to destroy our world and demand our respect? Will visitors to his shrine still ask if Godzilla is around, or is he gone for ever? These are questions to be asked only with a certain amount of caution. And a feeling a lot like love.

A roaring in the darkness

Godzilla has always aroused a great deal of strong emotion, frequently of a contradictory nature. Like many horror stars before him, his character is composed of broad, mythic strokes, allowing him to reflect the dreams and fears of his audience. But he owes nothing to the dark European romanticism that spawned some of the genre's traditional figures. Godzilla is the product of a far more recent époque, caught between the public's concern over big science and the demands of the modern studio system.

The 1952 re-release of RKO's 1933 *King Kong* had shown that a giant-monster movie could make money, both at home and abroad. Racking up even bigger ticket sales than it had first time around, Willis O'Brien's stop-motion ape led a first wave of gargantuan creatures out of Hollywood on to the Japanese market. When *The Beast from 20,000*

Fathoms and Disney's *20,000 Leagues under the Sea* managed to spin similar preoccupations with rampaging sea beasts, runaway technology and nuclear explosions into big box office, Tomoyuki Tanaka took notice. Early in 1954 he started a new project, whose provisional title *The Big Monster from 20,000 Miles Beneath the Sea* made no secret of its origins. In collaboration with screenwriter Takeo Murata and special-effects director Eiji Tsuburaya, Tanaka developed a story about an amphibious dinosaur mutated into a powerful monster through exposure to atomic radiation. Also contributing to the script was director Ishiro Honda.

Tsuburaya was a great admirer of *King Kong* and had long wished to make a giant-monster movie of his own. Honda had visited Hiroshima in 1946 and was still searching for a way to capture on film some of the horrifying devastation he had witnessed. Tanaka wanted a successful big-budget production that could stand up to the American blockbusters entering Japan in the wake of the Occupation. The creature who made all these things possible was called Gojira – a name constructed from the Western word gorilla and *kujira*, the Japanese word for a whale. It is also said to have been the nickname of a heavy-set Toho employee – a detail which, true or not, helps illustrate just how much this act of monstrous creation was firmly set in the studio system. Toho sank over $900,000 into what was to become the first Godzilla film at a time when the average Japanese feature cost one-tenth that amount. The result was *Gojira*, a dark and disturbing film that still packs a punch four decades on.

When ships start to vanish in the vicinity of Odo Island, scientists discover traces of a huge reptilian creature which the local fishermen refer to as Gojira after a legendary sea serpent that was once venerated as a god and propitiated with human sacrifices. The Japanese parliament wants to keep Gojira's existence a secret, but this quickly becomes impractical when the giant monster comes wading out of Tokyo Bay, smashing everything in his path. No, only is Gojira indestructible and unstoppable, but he can set whole buildings alight with his radioactive breath. Moved by the suffering the monster causes, an embittered, reclusive scientist Dr Serizawa grudgingly agrees to use his latest discovery upon Gojira. Referred to as an 'oxygen destroyer' in the Japanese script, this transforms the sea into a violent, churning cauldron that eventually claims the lives of both Gojira and Dr Serizawa, who chooses to perish rather than reveal his formula to the world.

A large part of *Gojira*'s power lies in the fact that people get to hear the monster long before they see him. A radio adaptation of the story ran from July to September 1954, preparing the public for the film's release in November. Once the lights went down in the cinema, however, the assault on the audience's ears continued. The heavy pounding of Gojira's footsteps is heard over the opening credits, followed by his angry roaring. To help convey the impression that Gojira is about to smash his way into the auditorium, the monster's roars blend in with the film's title theme: a relentless march composed by Akira Ifukube, another name that became closely linked with Godzilla. Throughout the film, the stark modernism of Ifukube's score complements Honda's spare black and white imagery, amplifying the emotional resonances of a drama whose central protagonist remains a threatening but virtually unseen figure.

The monster is presented first as a series of destructive forces; a blinding atomic flash, a wrathful deity, a nocturnal storm. He gradually takes shape and becomes visible as the film's action moves away from Odo Island and towards Tokyo. Outlined against the flames of a hundred burning buildings, Gojira's presence is at its strongest, and it is only when he disappears back into the ocean, before his destruction at the hand of Dr Serizawa, that it becomes indistinct again. Prehistoric beast and space-age mutant, created out of a nuclear explosion then dissolving into the sea, Gojira is human evolution run backwards. In this sense, he is quite literally what he appears to be on the screen: a man in a rubber suit.

Monster of the century

Gojira was an instant hit, seen by over 10 million people in Japan alone. American rights were picked up by Joseph E Levine, who refashioned the movie to suit mainsteam audiences in the United States. The result was released in 1956 as *Godzilla, King of the Monsters*, a title that carried echoes not only of *King Kong* but also of the poster copy for *The Beast from 20,000 Fathoms*, which billed Ray Harryhausen's animated Rhedosaurus as 'The King of Prehistoric Sea-Giants'.

Levine's Godzilla remained the vast engine of destruction that he was in the Japanese version, but his relationship with the rest of the world was strangely altered. Many of the references to Nagasaki, radioactive rain, contaminated food and bomb shelters were deleted, as was a children's hymn calling for nuclear disarmament, which became a prayer for those killed by the monster. Also played down was any specific connection between Gojira's first appearance and the series of H-bomb detonations being carried out by the Americans in the Marshall Islands.

And what did US audiences get instead of this missing material? Raymond Burr as an American journalist carried along by events, acting opposite body doubles and apologising for his Japanese. Burr gives a strong and creditable performance, but his presence greatly alters the film's central relationships, particularly that between Gojira and Dr Serizawa. It is no accident that the two are destined to die together in a foaming lifeless ocean: both are isolated and lonely figures, aloof from the collective sufferings of humanity. At the same time, both bear the burdens of mass trauma: Gojira has been 'baptised by the H-bomb' while Serizawa lost an eye during World War II. 'If there hadn't been a war, he wouldn't be the way he was,' someone remarks in a scene that was dropped from the US version. Audiences took to Godzilla in a big way, however, making him a star in both Japan and the United States. A rushed sequel, featuring a slimmed-down version of the monster in combat with a four-legged saurian called Angilas, unfortunately went the way of most rushed sequels. Released in Japan in 1955, *Gojira's Counterattack* was quickly surpassed by other Toho *kaiju* and science-fantasy productions, while a confusion over copyright meant that when the film finally appeared in the US it was as *Gigantis, the Fire Monster*.

It would be another seven years before Toho decided to celebrate its 30th anniversary by having Godzilla duke it out with King Kong in his best-known film. Released in 1962, *King Kong vs. Godzilla* was a box-office smash, transforming Godzilla into a celebrity big enough to demand his own film series. It had a similar effect in America when it came out the following year, ensuring a market for dubbed versions of each successive release. Coming at a time when the Japanese film industry had gone into overdrive, its five major studios turning out 547 films in 1961 compared with

Hollywood's 154, Godzilla's return would continue well into the next decade.

But despite his corporate origins Godzilla was still haunted by the lonely ghost of Dr Serizawa. His character unchanged, he remained a vicious renegade. Defeated by King Kong, he went on to be humiliated by Mothra, a giant moth, in 1964's *Godzilla vs. the Thing*. More than a mere force of nature or a technological threat, Godzilla was in danger of becoming the ultimate Japanese nightmare: a team player gone on the rampage. He was turning into a mean and savage loser. Something would have to change.

Godzilla on the beach

In 1965, less than a year after Godzilla's fight with Mothra, a stray meteor hits the earth, unleashing space monster King Ghidorah in a spectacular ball of flames. A winged three-headed golden dragon, King Ghidorah has already destroyed all life on Mars and is soon flying over Japan, blasting everything in sight with lightning-like bolts of electricity from his three mouths. This crowned beast of the apocalypse became Godzilla's saviour as well as his most frequent opponent. The most evidently impassive and 'eastern' of all the Toho monsters, King Ghidorah allowed Godzilla to develop more recognisably human characteristics by displaying none of his own. He was the galactic terror who permitted Godzilla to become the earth's heroic defender. Their first encounter, released in the United States as *Ghidrah, The Three-Headed Monster*, saw the continuing partnership of Tanaka, Honda, Tsuburaya and Ifukube complemented by the on-screen collaboration between Godzilla, Mothra and the 1956 *kaiju* star Rodan, joining forces for the first time to defeat King Ghidorah.

Godzilla was finally on board. Later the same year Rodan helped him rescue the earth from King Ghidorah again in *Monster Zero*, while in 1966 he was seen beating the living daylights out of a giant man-eating lobster as Mothra saved a Polynesian fishing community from a ruthless paramilitary organisation in *Ebirah – Horror of the Deep*. Godzilla's appearance was altered radically to fit the more lightweight fantasies in which he starred in the mid-1960s. Rubber being perishable, the Godzilla costume had to be remade before each new film, offering the chance to give him a subtle but thorough make-over: his head was gradually made to look less flat and reptilian while his eyes were enlarged to give them greater human appeal.

A new creative team was also introduced. *Ebirah – Horror of the Deep* was the first film to be directed by Jun Fukuda and scored by Masaru Sato. Special effects were still handled by Tsuburaya, but the budget was appreciably lower and the emphasis now was on fun rather than horror. With the action focusing on a gang of teenagers stranded on a Pacific island, *Ebirah* was less about urban demolition than about making Godzilla the centre of an extended beach party.

Keeping Godzilla away from the world's major population centres was still company policy in 1967, when Fukuda and Sato collaborated again on *Son of Godzilla*. This time a group of UN scientists gets rescued from Solgell Island while Godzilla defends his new-born son Minya from a gang of giant preying mantises and a monstrous web-spinning spider called Spiga. With eyes even larger than his dad's and an ingratiating leer, Minya is a walking nightmare of cuteness whose sole function seems to lie in establishing Godzilla as a responsible parent. With a child to support and a tropical island time-share, Godzilla had come a long way in a short time. No longer the angry outsider, he was now a committed salaryman destined for bigger things.

This is certainly how he is presented at the beginning of Toho's 1968 *kaiju* classic *Destroy All Monsters.*

* * *

Seen wandering with his son along the shoreline of Ogasawara Island in the Pacific Ocean, where the world's monsters are kept confined in an area known as Monsterland, Godzilla seems strangely at peace. It's hard to imagine that there was once a time when primitive fishermen made human sacrifices in his name. By the end of the movie he is leading Mothra, Rodan, Angilas, Spiga and Minya in an all-out assault on a group of aliens who have established their invasion headquarters at the base of Mount Fuji. Also taking part are such lesser-known Toho stars as Manda, Gorosaurus, Varan and Baragon. King Ghidorah makes his appearance, attempting to defend the invaders and earning himself a righteous stomping in the process. Directed once more by Honda and with a stirring score by Ifukube, this oddly named movie (no monsters are destroyed, not even King Ghidorah) ends with world peace being restored as Godzilla and the gang go back to their island.

Monster Island, as it was later known, represented some kind of prelapsarian paradise which Godzilla should never have inhabited. Toho's 1969 release *Godzilla's Revenge*, in which Minya teaches moral lessons to a young boy with the aid of footage from *Son of Godzilla* and *Ebirah – Horror of the Deep*, appears to take place in a world where atomic science does not exist. Aimed squarely at kiddies, this film also marks the final dissolution of the creative partnership behind the original *Gojira*. Honda was uncomfortable with an increasingly humanised Godzilla and dropped out of the next few projects, as did Ifukube. More seriously, Tsuburaya died soon afterwards, after suffering from ill health.

Things would never be the same again. Produced in 1971, *Godzilla vs. the Smog Monster*, with its dippy anti-pollution message intended for young children and the youth market, is most notable for beginning a period in which the movies came out faster as their budgets grew smaller. In 1972's *Godzilla vs. Gigan* a bunch of aliens plans to destroy Monster Island and replace it with a children's theme park dominated by a hollow replica of Godzilla containing a monster museum in its head. This probably said more than it intended. Tired ideas and recycled footage were increasingly in evidence. *Godzilla vs. Megalon* and *Godzilla vs. the Cosmic Monster*, released in 1973 and 1974 respectively, have all the ritualised predictability of Sumo wrestling while lacking much of its brevity.

One final effort was made for 1975's *The Terror of Mechagodzilla*, which brought Honda and Ifukube together again for the last time. After defeating a mechanical version of himself and an aquatic dinosaur, Godzilla is seen in the closing shot swimming out to sea, a glassy smile of relief on his face. Even he seemed to know it was time to call it a day.

Planet of Godzilla

Anniversaries gain significance in an uncertain world. In 1984, 30 years after *Gojira*'s original release, Japan remained as fragile as ever. Acquiescent to the United States, suspicious of Russia and constantly vulnerable to floods, typhoons, earthquakes and volcanic eruptions, the country was ready for Godzilla to return. Toho's expensive reworking of the first movie saw the US and the USSR trying to violate Japan's non-nuclear policy and bomb a marauding Godzilla back to an irradiated oblivion. Needless to say, much of this was missing from the US release, *Godzilla 1985*. And what did American audiences get in its place? Raymond Burr once again, playing the same journalist as before, plus a bunch of Pentagon generals standing around drinking Dr Pepper. It was as if the 1950s had never gone away.

Despite his still worryingly large eyes, Godzilla was back on fine, building-toppling form and nobody's sweetheart. He had come once more to destroy Japan, not to save it. And a new generation of creative talent promised fresh ideas. The 1989 sequel, the nightmarish *Godzilla vs. Biollante*, paired writer/director Kazuki Omori with special-effects director Koichi Kawakita. Their strong, revisionist ambitions verged on the iconoclastic in *Godzilla vs. King Ghidorah* (1991). This darkly complex time-travel fantasy links contemporary Japan with the closing days of World War II and contains the genuinely disturbing image of King Ghidorah flying over the shattered dome of the Industry Promotion Hall in Hiroshima, thereby breaking a taboo that had been in place since the first Godzilla film.

Times had changed. There was now a waiting list of cities anxious to see themselves being demolished by Godzilla. The national defence forces offered their services free of charge on each new production, grateful for the chance to demonstrate their latest weaponry in the name of protecting Japan. Only one name, aside from Tanaka's, remained to remind cinema-goers of the past: Ifukube, having returned for *Godzilla vs. King Ghidorah*, was persuaded to stay on and write the scores for two further releases – *Godzilla vs. Mothra*, which saw Godzilla losing to the giant moth again in 1992, and 1993's *Godzilla vs. Mechagodzilla*.

Godzilla's appearance continued to alter, his eyes finally growing smaller and darker to reflect the renewed capacity for destruction that lurked behind them. Even so, there was something safe and predictable about Toho releasing a new Godzilla vehicle in December each year. It looked as if he had achieved the ultimate career triumph of becoming a national threat and an institution at the same time. And Toho also took the less than unprecedented step of allowing him to reproduce once again. The results were not quite as alarming as before: Baby Godzilla was cute, but still clearly reptilian. He would later appear as Little Godzilla in 1994's *Godzilla vs. Space Godzilla* and be a witness to his father's death in the final film of the cycle, *Godzilla vs. Destroyah*. [Until *Godzilla 2000* (2000) (Editor's note).]Godzilla Jr's whereabouts are currently unknown.

Except to note that he absorbed enough of the fallout from his father's radioactive flesh both to prevent Tokyo from being reduced to an atomic wasteland and to transform himself into a larger, more fearsome version of his former self. Not a kid any more, Godzilla Jr may well be hanging around a Toho sound stage somewhere. Just in case. Where love and memories are concerned, anything can happen. In December 1996 Dr Yasuyuki Shirota of Hirasaki University announced plans to regenerate the moa, a giant flightless bird extinct for over a century, by using DNA extracts and live chicken embryos. Ultimately, Dr Shirota hopes to recreate a live dinosaur. His inspiration? Watching Godzilla movies as a child.

Godzilla 1998

Ishiro Honda's *Gojira* was an unauthorised semi-remake of *The Beast from 20,000 Fathoms*. But where Ray Harryhausen's Rhedosaurus was brought to life by stop-motion model animation, *Gojira* was a stunt man in a monster suit trampling over detailed miniature sets. Roland Emmerich's *Godzilla*, which mostly abandons model-work and 'suit-mation' in favour of CGI, and switches the locale from Tokyo to New York, seems more like a remake of *The Beast from 20,000 Fathoms* than of *Gojira*. Both films begin with nuclear tests in remote locations, have their monster tangle with ships and offshore islands before clambering ashore at the docks of New York, feature monsters which head instinctively for the Big Apple to spawn, and wind up with their beasts trapped in New York landmarks to be blasted.

Emmerich's monster is one of several rethinks of the Gojira character and the most radical morphing: the upright, pot-bellied, dinosaur creature of 1954 becomes the bent-over, lean, lizard thing of 1998, an Iguana mutated to giant size by more bomb tests. Like the tribbles of *Star Trek* it is asexual but born pregnant, threatening to overrun the world with hatchlings (aka sequels) more like *Jurassic Park* velociraptors than the cute creature of *Son of Godzilla*.

Japanese *kaiju* are explicitly or implicitly anti-American, indicting the US tendency to use Japanese civilians in small- and large-scale experiments with nuclear weapons. This theme has to be expunged from the new *Godzilla*, which looks around for some other nation to blame and seizes with glee on the French. Emmerich opens his movie with grainy bomb-test footage overlaid by the 'Marseillaise', then makes a running joke about Jean Réno's disgust with American coffee and the expendability of his agents, all called Jean-Something. The stalwart and concerned heroes of the Japanese films are replaced by blustering and ineffectual American army officers who do more damage to the city than the monster, while Michael Lerner parodies publicity-conscious Mayor Rudolph Giuliani and a set of Big Apple in-jokes tailors the movie to New York.

An American movie directed by a German and produced by Sony-owned TriStar, the new *Godzilla* has to take into account the Japanese origins if not of the character then of the name. So the first victim of the monster is a Japanese fishing ship, and a sole survivor gasps that they were attacked by 'Gojira', an ancient Japanese fire dragon. Bonehead newsman Harry Shearer mistakenly anglicises the word as 'Godzilla' in a witty approximation of how Godzilla came by his Western name, with Shearer as a parody of the solemn journalist played by Raymond Burr in *Godzilla, King of the Monsters*. The new film thus takes place in an alternative timeline – on an earth where there is a Godzilla but no *Godzilla* movies.

Kim Newman

GODZILLA
USA 1998
Director: Roland Emmerich

The sudden sinking of a Japanese supertanker in the Pacific Ocean is followed by the appearance of enormous footprints in Panama. To analyse the phenomena the United States military assembles a team of scientists including Niko Tatopoulos, an expert in the effects of nuclear radiation on animals who has been studying earthworms in Chernobyl. Meanwhile a group of Frenchmen, supposedly insurance investigators, also track the creature's progress. Niko concludes that the creature is a gigantic reptile, mutated by French nuclear tests in the South Pacific.

The creature arrives in New York, causing panic and destruction. Audrey Timmonds, a television researcher who was engaged to Niko in college, recognises him on a news broadcast. The military wound the creature. Niko tests the creature's blood and realises it is about to lay eggs. Audrey finds Niko and, desperate for a scoop, steals a classified videotape from him. When the footage is broadcast Niko is sacked by the military but is kidnapped by the Frenchmen. Their leader Roaché reveals that they are a unit from the French secret service, keen to destroy the monster. Roaché, his team and Niko (followed by Audrey and her cameraman friend Animal) find the creature's nest inside Madison Square Garden.

The military attack the creature again and believe they have killed it. The hatching eggs release young creatures who kill some of the Frenchmen. However, Niko, Roaché, Audrey and Animal take refuge in the stadium's television studio and manage to broadcast a warning message. The stadium and the creatures are destroyed. Niko and the others escape, but the original creature reappears. They lure it on to the Brooklyn Bridge, where it becomes ensnared in the suspension cables and is killed. In the Garden's wreckage, a final egg cracks open.

*   *   *

As huge and relentless as the creature it is centred on, *Godzilla* has no pretensions to being anything other than a big hunk of dumb fun. On that level it works exceedingly well, fully aware of its own preposterousness and shamelessly skilful in milking every available cliché. The effects deliver, the monster is a star, the plot's nonsenses are largely covered up by pace and noise, and the actors are ruefully aware that nobody has come to the cinema to see them. Given that last point, it would be unkind to complain about Maria Pitillo's profound vapidity or the cartoon mugging of Michael Lerner and Arabella Field, and more constructive to enjoy the performances of Jean Réno and Matthew Broderick. Réno turns in a delightful study of self-parodic Gallic mysteriousness, every shrug and twinkle the sign of a man relishing how much you can earn for doing so little, while Broderick's geeky hero is suitably self-effacing. It's not the first time Broderick has had to underplay in the shadow of a rampaging monster threatening to engulf New York – he was, after all, Harvey Fierstein's boyfriend in *Torch Song Trilogy*.

The most pleasing thing about Broderick's role is how it enables *Godzilla* to back away from the appalling militarism of the same production team's *Independence Day*.

Broderick's Tatopoulos is an unashamed nerd – he wears glasses early in the film, taps on a laptop, and uses such words as 'incipient' and 'anomaly' – and yet he consistently outsmarts the gung-ho military. The kneejerk blow-it-up mentality so celebrated in *Independence Day* is here embodied by Sergeant O'Neal (a clever little performance by Doug Savant), who makes mistake after mistake in the pursuit of the creature. He comes good at the end, of course, but only after he has learned that the brawny jock must sometimes take orders from the brainy weed. In addition, marking a further retreat from *Independence Day*'s flagwaving agenda, the brainy weed teams up with a foreigner, though any critique this suggests of American nationalism is compromised by the way the storyline blames the French for creating the monster in the first place.

As for Godzilla himself, the film sends out mixed messages. The Japanese Godzilla was often an endearing beast, especially towards the end of his career, frequently defending humanity against some other threatening monster, and displaying a particular interest in ecological matters (see *Godzilla vs. the Smog Monster*, for example). Traces of that idea remain here: Godzilla is the product of nuclear foolishness; he attacks only out of self-defence; and his final struggle strains, rather clumsily, after the tragic sensibility of *King Kong* (1933). Indeed, his first rampage through New York is motivated not by destructive malevolence but by sheer clumsiness – he scythes through skyscrapers only because when you're that big you inevitably have a huge turning circle. Any sympathy we might have for Godzilla, however, is undercut once the film switches focus to his offspring. They offer the sheer evil an audience needs in order to cheer on the destruction of the closing sequences, so much so that once Dad re-emerges he's fair game, too.

Although it steals blatantly from *King Kong*, *Jaws*, the first two *Alien* films and, most of all, *Jurassic Park* (if the big creature is T-rex, his brats are a nursery of velociraptors), *Godzilla* lacks the mythic underpinnings that made those films so resonant. Industrious subtext-hunters might want to dwell on the psycho-sexual implications of the creature's ability to be male but still reproduce or on his status as an unwelcome immigrant from the Pacific Rim, and good luck to them if they do, but the film is best enjoyed for what it fundamentally is: an absurdly expensive way of saying 'boo!'

Andy Medhurst

FRITZ LANG: THE ILLUSION OF MASTERY

Thomas Elsaesser

As the Hitchcock industry roars ahead, it is fitting that his centenary celebrations should be followed by a major retrospective of Fritz Lang at London's National Film Theatre. When Hitchcock gave himself a serious film education at Ivor Montagu's avant-garde screenings at the Film Society in London in 1926 and 1927 Lang was an acknowledged influence. Although both directors subsequently ended up in Hollywood – Lang in 1933, Hitchcock in 1939 – there is little evidence they ever met. More likely, they eyed each other at a respectful distance – while Lang admired *Rebecca*, he also envied the younger man's success in the 1950s when his own fortunes were flagging. Their paths might be said to have crossed only in Paris in the 1960s when they became twin pillars of the *Cahiers du cinéma* critics' ideal of 'pure cinema'. Since then, however, the decline of Lang's reputation has been almost as notable as the rise of Hitchcock's. A continuing interest in *film noir*, paranoia movies and the femme fatale keeps some of Lang's American films – *Scarlet Street* (1945), *Secret Beyond the Door...* (1948), *The Big Heat* (1953) and *The Blue Gardenia* (1953) – in repertoire. Meanwhile his German films have suffered from too much muffled deference, with the possible exception of *Metropolis* (1926) which somehow transcended its author to become – thanks to Giorgio Moroder, Freddy Mercury and Madonna – one of the most enduring cult classics of the 1980s.

The case against German Lang has often been made, and nowhere more damagingly than in Siegfried Kracauer's 1947 book *From Caligari to Hitler*. According to Kracauer, Lang's cinema is replete with authoritarian figures projecting conservative-nationalist values. His overblown, mystic-mythical iconography is underpinned by fables offering proto-fascist solutions to economic and social crises. Human relations revolve around power, control and domination and the individual is a mere puppet of hostile forces, malevolent tyrants, master criminals or super-spies. Patrick McGilligan's biography *Fritz Lang: the Nature of the Beast* (1997) added to the charge sheet an obsession with kinky sex and homicidal violence. Sex and violence might open up inevitable parallels with Hitchcock, except that Lang's fixations totally lacked the Englishman's sardonic sense of humour or taste for the frivolous and the absurd. Lang's supreme gift for dramatic irony, on the other hand, has probably always been too cerebral for a genre-based film-maker to become popular, however prized it once was among cinephiles.

A Hapsburg decadent as much as Hitchcock was an Edwardian dandy, Lang had another major handicap throughout his 40 years' stay in California: with his monocle he looked the Prussian officer, his German accent grated on the actors who chafed under his barked commands and he showed a haughty disdain for those who tried his patience – a collection of personality traits Americans all too readily associated with their idea of the Führer, an image ironically derived in part from Lang's own anti-Nazi films *Man Hunt* (1941) and *Ministry of Fear* (1943). Lang did not manage a box-office success after *The Woman in the Window* (1944) and *Scarlet Street*, and these were modest hits by other top directors' standards. To contrast Lang's and Hitchcock's salaries in the mid-1940s is a salutary lesson in the Hollywood class system: Hitchcock, even when a contract director at Warner Bros, was making $250,000 per film whereas Lang's usual fee was $50,000, a pittance by studio standards and embarrassingly little compared with the leading actors in most of his films.

Additionally, there was only cautious commerce between Lang and his prominent Weimar contemporaries during their joint Californian exile. Frankfurt School cultural theorist T. W. Adorno and Lang had frequent contact, though mainly maintained by their spouses; with Bertolt Brecht communication was cordial until they fell out over their collaboration on *Hangmen Also Die* (1943). However, underneath their professional differences there ran a current of mutual esteem because alongside their disgust at Californian-style consumer-capitalism they also distrusted so-called human nature, which is to say they both rejected psychological realism. In Lang's films, even more than evil, it is artifice that triumphs: a fundamentally ironic strategy that earned him the reputation of an anti-humanist.

Looking-glass worlds

The frosty climate of suspicion among the Hollywood émigré community aggravated by frequent humiliations from the studio heads must have pained Lang. Yet his self-protective misanthropy did little to remind Hollywood how prominent he had been in post-1918 Europe. After *Der Müde Tod/Destiny* (1921) and *Dr Mabuse der Spieler/Dr Mabuse the Gambler* (1922) each new film was major international news, and each set itself steep challenges, stylistic as well as technical. *Destiny* showed off some jaw-dropping special effects (the US rights were bought by Douglas Fairbanks, in order to copy the trick photography with impunity for his *Thief of Bagdad*, or so the story goes). *Die Nibelungen* (1924) made a magnificent two-part disaster movie out of the nation's favourite boy's-own epic. *Metropolis* was the most expensive film made in Germany for decades to come. *Spione/Spies* (1928) and *Frau im Mond/The Woman in the Moon* (1929) were blockbusters with advertising campaigns as canny as anything seen today; *M* (1931), cashing in on Weimar culture's morbid fascination with serial killers, became one of the masterpieces of early sound cinema, probing the psychology of the crowd as well as the darker side of the urban flaneur thanks to Peter Lorre's unforgettable portrayal of the cunning child-murderer Beckert. Lang's last film before leaving for Hollywood, *The Testament of Dr Mabuse* (1933), was banned by the Nazis and had to have its premiere in Vienna.

The case for German Lang can be made other than by recalling a technical wizard with an upper-class conservative social agenda. *Metropolis*, an art director's Aladdin's cave to steal from, has always kept the architect in Lang up front. *Spies* strikes one for its acerbic look at conspiracies: criminal ones at the ostensible plot level, but given how much Haghi the master spy is made to resemble Lenin one wonders whether a political parallel was not also intended. *The Woman in the Moon*, despite an all too leaden-footed intrigue about professional jealousy, insipid romance and the quest for gold, manages to incorporate very advanced ideas about jet propulsion and rockets; Lang also claimed to have invented the countdown when trying to figure out how to create a sense of suspense around the launch. His approach to storytelling in that film is that of an engineer: the pieces, pre-formed by pulp fiction and sensationalist cliché, are fitted together with the utmost precision according to a quite beautiful abstract design.

Equally prescient is Lang's ambivalent attitude to surveillance and the cinema's complicity in the militarisation of perception. *Die Spinnen/The Spiders* (1919), *Destiny* and *Die Nibelungen* are complex vision machines full of proto- and pseudo-cinematic apparatuses. In *Destiny* death plays magic lanternist to the hapless bride. The adventure serial *The Spiders* displays its folding mirrors, peepholes and spyglasses as the tools-of-trade of femme fatale Lio-Sha, who doubles as *metteuse-en-scène*. Here Lang makes himself the ironic archivist of the pleasures and dangers of assisted sight. In the epic family saga *Die Nibelungen* Alberich, the guardian of the Nibelungen treasure, plays the projectionist of deferred desire, taunting Siegfried with images of fabulous wealth cast on the smooth stone wall of Alberich's underworld cave. Siegfried, the proverbial Simple Simon, succumbs to the spell of this phantasmagoria, stretching out his hands to grasp at the images. The contemporary audience would have enjoyed the way Siegfried unwittingly mimics the proverbial country bumpkin of early cinema, too unsophisticated to realise these are mere representations. Yet Siegfried is a quick learner: in the event, he wins by deviousness and deception. It is as if Lang had decided to let the whole tragedy hinge on a trick taken straight out of Georges Méliès' box of movie magic, but played out on a stage that foreshadows the looking-glass worlds of Thomas Pynchon's *Gravity's Rainbow* and John Le Carré's Cold War double crosses.

To see, to know, to believe: this is the triad whose contending claims on perception and reason the radical sceptic in Lang plays off against each other. Technologically, in that the trick effects of the early films dazzle us with sights the mind knows are impossible, thrilling us with cognitive dissonance that would have made today's digital images a welcome addition to the Ufa imagineers' arsenal. Politically, in that Lang's German films know everything about advertising and how to build a brand-name image but at the same time let us look inside the mechanism of power and persuasion that make such manufacturing possible.

Lang has often been regarded as the director of appearances that prove to be deceptive, but this presumes to judge these appearances by a standard of reality largely absent from the films. The difficult delights of his work lie in the fact that, strictly speaking, there never seems to be a solid ground from which the realm of appearances might be asserted to be true or false. So thoroughly do Lang's nested narrative and representations suspend unmediated access to the real that each viewer is obliged either to fantasise or metaphorise a meaning into the images and to decide on the frame of reference. One of Lang's keenest critics of the 1980s, Klaus Kreimeier, sees in his German films a vortex of vertigo- and paranoia-inducing images that always cite other images, while behind them loom 'chaos, abyss, hell, death': terms, however, that accumulate in their negative connotations a 'positive' referent – the Nazi regime. Kreimeier then subjects Lang's early adventure yarns of hidden treasures to a Marxist analysis of the world economy and its crises in the late 1920s, against which the director emerges as a political somnambulist, nostalgic for archaic, pre-capitalist notions of money as gold and capital as the hidden hoard.

This lifts Lang out of the narrow proto-fascist groove. But what legitimates the gesture that invokes these historical foils, in order then to critique Lang's reactionary ideology? In Lang there are always several worlds set in contrast, supporting each other only in so far as they comment on each other. For instance, what strikes one about *The Spiders* is how far each episode contrasts the contemporary world of the motor car with the exotic locations of the South American Incas, where aeroplanes pluck the hero from a horse in the pampas or a Chinese opium den is equipped with modern means of telecommunication. Such contrasting worlds comment on each other ironically, each pastiching the other by an act of repetition: the same stories, the same conflicts, the same futility, each time merely in a different fancy dress. *Dr Mabuse*—the first of Lang's trilogy of films completed in 1960—introduces us to several worlds that already look false even before they become real, or rather where the clever fake is that which is most real about reality.

Master of disguises

Dr Mabuse was Lang's breakthrough film in Germany, as well as an early example of a marketing ploy in which the serialised novel and the film became each other's mutual selling points. Announcing itself in its title as a 'portrait of its time' (part one: *The Gambler*) and 'of its men and women' (part two: *The Inferno*) it was loosely based on motifs from Norbert Jacques' tabloid opus, peppered up with topical material by Lang and his then wife, the successful novelist and Germany's top screenwriter Thea von Harbou. The four-hour film starts at a furious pace, with a meticulously timed train robbery leading to a stock-exchange fraud. It then concentrates on Mabuse hypnotising a young American industrialist into running up large debts at gambling, after which the master criminal wins the favours of an aristocratic lady, drives her husband to suicide and eventually kidnaps her. Time and again outwitting the public prosecutor by a mixture of brutality, practical jokes and *agent provocateur* demagoguery, Mabuse is finally cornered in his secret hideout and either goes mad or feigns insanity when he is finally captured.

The film is said originally to have had a pre-credits sequence depicting street battles from the 1919 Spartacist socialist uprising in Berlin, the assassination of foreign minister Walther Rathenau and other scenes of disorder masterminded by Mabuse ('Who is responsible for all this? – Me' was apparently the first intertitle.) Although this opening is now lost or was never made, the various scams Mabuse is involved in (industrial espionage, stock-exchange fraud, forged banknotes) as well as the felonies he perpetrates (he runs a lab manufacturing cocaine, his gang controls gambling and prostitution and plots assassinations) all vividly point to the immediate post-World War I era, especially to Germany's raging hyperinflation between 1921 and 1924 and its black-market economy that pauperised the middle classes while creating a new urban sub-culture of war profiteers, Mafia-like racketeer organisations and vigilante units recruited from the growing army of the unemployed. The political references were not lost on contemporary reviewers or the censors, and even today Mabuse's several disguises seem taken out of a catalogue of Weimar types familiar from the drawings of Otto Dix and George Grosz: stockbroker in a top hat, derelict drunk in a housing tenement, Jewish peddler at the street corner, bearded rentier in a flashy limousine, industrialist with monocle and moustache, pimp, psychiatrist, hypnotist and opium-smoking Tsi-Nan-Fu in a gambling den.

Mabuse was taken to be modelled on Hugo Stinnes, a steel magnate who from humble beginnings amassed a fortune and occupied a key position in the post-World War I rearmament industries (illegal, according to the treaty of Versailles). But Mabuse also doubles as a Houdini-like vaudeville artist, passes himself off as a soul doctor from Vienna and even has a dash of the Bolshevik agitator in the Karl Radek mould. The final showdown was modelled on the famous shoot-out between the police and the

'Fort Chavrol' bankrobbers from a barricaded house in the Parisian banlieue in 1921. In short, Lang's 'portrait of its time' gathers up a fair number of contemporary references.

It was after World War II that *Dr Mabuse* in the eyes of the critics took on a less topical and more overtly metaphoric mien. As indicated, Kracauer ties virtually every significant trend in his diagnostic psychogram of Weimar veering towards totalitarian madness to one of Lang's films: '[*Dr Mabuse*] succeeds in making of Mabuse an omnipresent threat that cannot be localised, and thus reflects society under a tyrannical regime – that kind of society in which one fears everybody because anybody may be the tyrant's ear or arm.' Lang later argued back, pointing out that if he had predicted the rise of Hitler in his films, then Kracauer was pinning the blame for the bad news on the messenger.

Evidently the film's immense popularity at the time and subsequent status as a classic testify to a surplus of meaning, best readable perhaps across the designation of Mabuse as 'der Spieler', meaning the gambler but also the dissembler or pretender. Highlighting both playfulness and risk, a refusal of identity and a slippage of reference, the epithet announces the question of what kind of agency Mabuse embodies as he 'stands behind' events as well as 'fronting' a conspiratorial gang bent on mayhem and mischief. One could call Mabuse a disguise artist, dissimulating both identity and agency, and suggest that he belongs to a rather large family of such creatures in Weimar cinema, whose kinship, but also generic diversity (Caligari and Nosferatu, *Die Nibelungen*'s Hagen and *Spies*' Haghi, Tartuffe and Mephisto), allow some conclusions about the self-analysis of cinema during the Weimar period. Mimicry as metaphor, metaphor as mimicry. If Lang's German films are inventories of styles and if he provided much of the wallpaper for Weimar Germany's national or avant-garde ambitions, he also showed how flimsy it was. Take expressionism, the style intended to create an internationally valid brand name for German cinema in the early 1920s – as Mabuse himself says: 'Expressionism! – it's a game of make-believe! But why not? Everything today is make-believe.' Mabuse both implicates and distances himself, in a gesture that joins mimicry and parody, a mottled person for a mottled ground.

There are many such moments in *Dr Mabuse*. One would be the scene of Mabuse at the stock exchange in which he destabilises both stock prices and currencies by selectively planting information gleaned from the treaty captured during the train robbery. The scene ends with the superimposition of Mabuse's face on the emptied stock exchange, gradually surging from the background like a watermark on a banknote held against the light, as if Lang had tilted the world we have just witnessed and something else had become visible: not the truth, but the recto of a verso. What is left is a kind of hieroglyphic world, barely readable, strange, but consisting of all but the most familiar elements.

A film-maker's mask

Given these meta-levels of meaning, *Dr Mabuse* is a prime candidate for an allegorical approach: the different kinds of *mises-en-abymes* suggest links between Mabuse as *metteur-en-scène* and the *metteur-en-scène* of *Dr Mabuse*, enfolding the director in the schemes of his arch-villain and power-broker. *Dr Mabuse* would then be a cautionary tale addressed to Lang himself about the ambiguous role of the film-maker as master of the machinery of public power fantasies. This is certainly how Lang saw the cinema and photography in several of his American films, from *Fury* (1936) to *Beyond a Reasonable Doubt* (1956).

But Mabuse's reliance on vision and disguise is contradictory, not only because he is finally hoist by his own petard. Mabuse's hard stare resembles a totemic mask, designed to terrify those who look at it. However, the stare is not an expression of power but yet another form of the disguise of power. Often Mabuse dons disguises that make him blend with the urban fabric, becoming a Jewish peddler or a drunken working-class husband berating his wife. At other times his disguise wants to draw attention to itself, as when he plays the buffoon, his clownishness focusing as well as dispersing the onlookers' notice. In such cases one has a kind of Mabuse-Medusa, explicitly in the scenes where he faces down von Wenk at the gambling table and hypnotises him as Dr Weltmann. But as a kind of ritual mask, the rigid face with the piercing eyes can also be a form of disguise that hides the bearer from himself.

In its anthropological sense a mask is designed to ward off evil spirits – it is the bearer's gesture of defence – whereas a disguise that operates as camouflage is the currency the bearer tries to acquire in order to enter into circulation. Disguise in *Dr Mabuse* thus functions in a double system: it absorbs the look of the other in the form of mimicry and camouflage and wards off the look of the other in the form of the mask. Instead of foregrounding the act of looking, as is so often claimed, Lang's cinema captures looking in a set of devices that lend human sight the illusion of new forms of mastery at the same time as they mock its presumptions.

A relay of roles links the spectator, the film, the main protagonist, his disguises and other characters as his dupes – and over this relay presides the director, invisible *metteur-en-scène* of all these roles and impostures. Yet the 'ultimate metaphor' of which Raymond Bellour once spoke would here be Mabuse as *metteur-en-scène* of a world he intends to control, capped by the film-maker Lang ensnaring his audience the more firmly by first arming and then dismantling his hero demonstrating how it is done, while letting complicity trouble the irony. Disguise artist, *Übermensch* and phallic *Übervater* here implicate and complement each other, with the director wearing Mabuse as his own mask, or rather as the stand-in for an all-seeing eye.

Is Lang's cinema, then, the 'ultimate metaphor' because it can speak about the cinema as a locus of power and thus, through the cinema, warn about cinema? It is an idea which, as Bellour has also observed, joins the three Mabuse films: 'The Mabuse series is, within classical cinema, the most important reflection on the cinema ever produced by a director (to the point that, with their 40-year span, the films could be said to mark the beginning and end of the classical period). The three films... deal with the central power of vision and diffusion, defined by the three major phases of the development of cinema: the cinema as such (silent cinema), sound cinema, and cinema confronting video and television' (*CinémAction* 47, 1988).

In this respect Lang's Mabuse films are indeed essays on the social symbolic represented by the new technologies of surveillance as dissembling machines at once fascinating and frightening. The first *Dr Mabuse* makes the homology between Mabuse as *metteur-en-scène* of vision and the cinematic spectacle (at one point the audience witnesses a film-within-the-film which shows a desert caravan riding right through the auditorium). The social dimension emerges in *The Testament of Dr Mabuse* at the very beginning of the sound-film period Lang singles out the human voice via loudspeaker and gramophone to demonstrate how readily it lends itself to the manipulation of presence (a dummy Mabuse, wired up to perform sinister deeds of simulated authority, issues commands and bellows instructions, intimidating his gang into believing him to be the more powerful for being heard but not seen). Finally in *The Thousand Eyes of Dr Mabuse* (1960) it is though the array of television screens, video monitors and other surveillance devices that Lang presses home the notion of a looking-glass world in which sight is not only the sense most easily deceived, but also the one most easily seduced.

The all-seeing eye

At another level the three films figure out what this implies for the political function of cinema as an instrument of social control. And here it also seems as if the direct look is not a look at all, at least not in the sense that it gives access to power. For instance, the opening scene of *Dr Mabuse* has Mabuse facing the audience in an imaginary dressing-table mirror which is, of course, also the screen. So like all the other looks that circulate, Mabuse's own does not finally seem to belong to him, but is 'propped' on some other structure. Yet since Mabuse accedes to power via the look and eventually loses power via the look, these must be two kinds of look: the unmediated, imaginary one and the mediated, symbolic one. His downfall is, classically, the consequence of his rise in that he makes a tragic mistake: the further he rises the more the look he relies on reveals its underside, namely of being a look borrowed from the technologies of vision.

These technologies of vision, however, are blind. The empty look, the frozen stare, the Medusa's gaze – Lang progressively descends into some very cold regions of visuality in which apparently no one is in control and yet everyone struggles for control over others, which suggests that the question of cinema's vision machines poses itself differently: no longer is the look to be thought of as a metaphoric extension of power, but in fact power is that which interrupts the exchange of looks, by which human beings signal their recognition of each other. The cinema, taken to its (techno)logical conclusion, is for Lang the ultimate metaphor not of social control through the power of the look, but proof of the end of this metaphor: the all-seeing eye of surveillance finally sees nothing at all.

One comes back to the apparent contradiction between *Dr Mabuse* as a 'portrait of its time' and Lang's cinema as the 'ultimate metaphor'. It resolves itself if we see Mabuse as a metaphor not of political power – Nazi or otherwise – but of a rebellion against power, in the idiom of imposture, the mask and the disguise, with Lang rescuing his cinema from its all-seeing blindness by aligning it with different modes of 'enlightened false consciousness' (Peter Floterdijk's term for Weimar Germany's different forms of open duplicity). In this sense the original *Dr Mabuse* is a 'pastiche' of (expressionist) revolt, mimicking the make-believe dandy stance of Weimar intellectuals, politicians and artists towards their 'yes-but' democracy. Yet by wanting to stay ahead of the game, the mastermind overreaches himself: Mephistophelean spirit of the metropolis, he descends into the fast-moving traffic in souls and goods, soon lost in a new kind of social agency. Performative yet impersonal, it moulds a space out of sight-lines and architectural prospects, stencilling command-and-control figures out of its technologically assisted theatricality. No wonder postmodern pop likes Lang, always poised to strike the pose.

THE CAGE OF REASON

Kim Newman

'The dominant spirit, however, that haunts this enchanted region and seems to be commander-in-chief of all the powers of the air is the apparition of a figure on horseback without a head. It is said by some to be the ghost of a Hessian trooper, whose head has been carried away by a cannon ball, in some nameless battle during the Revolutionary War, and who is ever and anon seen by the country folk, hurrying along in the gloom of night, as if on the wings of the wind.'

Originally published in *The Sketch-Book of Geoffrey Crayon* (1819–20), Washington Irving's short story 'The Legend of Sleepy Hollow' is a humorous character study, holding up schoolmaster Ichabod Crane as an example of ludicrous superstition, rather than a true horror tale. The spook which pursues Ichabod through the woods is unmasked, Scooby-Doo style, as the ungainly scholar's romantic rival Brom Van Brunt, intent on scaring him away from pretty heiress Katrina van Tassel. Establishing the American order of lusty jock above too-thoughtful nerd, Brom gets the girl and Ichabod is persecuted into fleeing the town. 'As he was a bachelor and in nobody's debt, nobody troubles his head any more about him,' concludes Irving, never guessing that this confident preference for the muscular bully would eventually lead to *Revenge of the Nerds* and even the tragic shootings at Columbine High School. The bluff callousness strikes modern readers as rather chilling; we are now used to stories of worms who turn, sandy-faced weaklings who take Charles Atlas courses and speccy nerds who win the prom queen. The casual dismissal of Ichabod – first archetype of America's nightmare self-image, the loser – is as conceptually frightening to us as a real spectre was to him and would be to later ghost-story writers.

The Headless Horseman is the first truly American addition to the gallery of horror figures which evolved, over 100 years later, into the monster-movie pantheon. Like such comparable British characters as Frankenstein's monster and Dracula, the Horseman is a foreigner, an invader of sacred soil; like that other great bogus ghost the Hound of the Baskervilles, he is such a potent image that many later readers, and all film versions, have regretted he turns out to be a fake. Until Tim Burton's new film *Sleepy Hollow*, the most familiar version of the tale was a Disney cartoon narrated by Bing Crosby in *The Adventures of Ichabod and Mr Toad* (1949) which boasts a flamboyantly animated ghost on a rearing steed, though dotty old Mrs Farren (Julia

Dean) effectively retells the story, with only sound effects, as an aside in *The Curse of the Cat People* (1944) and there is a bland 1979 made-for-TV movie with Jeff Goldblum and Meg Foster well cast as Ichabod and Katrina.

All film and television versions of 'The Legend of Sleepy Hollow' are torn between Irving's smug, rational puncturing of superstition – which he links to Puritan America's witchcraft panic, noting Ichabod's devotion to the works of minister Cotton Mather – and the thrilling visual and dramatic possibilities of the ghost itself. Burton's *Sleepy Hollow* is not merely torn between rationality and superstition, but torn apart by the dichotomy, with each of the film's several significant creators, drawing subtly different, mutually exclusive readings from the material. The project was originally developed by Kevin Yagher, the make-up effects man most famous for the animatronic doll Chucky in the *Child's Play* films and the Crypt Keeper in the *Tales from the Crypt* television series, as a follow-up to his inauspicious directorial debut *Hellraiser: Bloodline* (1996), 'un film de Alan Smithee'. Working with Andrew Kevin Walker, a specialist in exploring more modern American horrors in *Se7en* (1995) and *8MM* (1999), Yagher plotted *Sleepy Hollow* as a low-budget effects showcase with a spectacular murder every five minutes or so and a delight in the process of creating fake monsters that might have led him to sympathise with Irving's Brom – who is, after all the first special make-up effects man in literature.

In the event the film was scaled up to a major big-budget release with several other visionaries involved – though like *Se7en* it remains at heart what Walker once characterised as 'a pretentious slasher movie'. Among the executive producers is Francis Ford Coppola, continuing an attachment to the genre begun with *Bram Stoker's Dracula* (1992) and developed in *Mary Shelley's Frankenstein* (1994). Coppola has been working up a secondary career restoring to the horror genre the literary weight it once had, all the while trying to find ways of retelling old, old stories in new emotional-romantic lights, which may strike unusual chords with contemporary audiences but also work against what we may take as the primary purpose of the horror movie – to be scary. With Walker and Coppola on board, it should be no surprise that *Sleepy Hollow*, though shot in the English countryside, addresses the American roots of Irving's tale.

With the action laid in 1799, and Ichabod Crane (Johnny Depp) raising groans with a speech about how the millennium draws near and a new modern era is to begin, we are only a generation removed from the War of Independence, which created both the US and the Headless Horseman. The Crane who sets out from New York City to the upstate hamlet of Sleepy Hollow is explicitly an American who will interrogate transplanted Dutch and British old folks (the young principals are American actors, the character players almost all British). The hero's commitment to reason is born out of the tension between his Puritan father and witch mother, whose violent clash of beliefs has left him with memory blanks gradually filled in by bad dreams. His reaction has been to reject both their faiths in favour of a scientific method epitomised by Cronenbergian surgical implements and complex optical devices that never enable him to see anything.

This Ichabod is no mere pedagogue but a scientific policeman whose overconcern with matters of detection prompts his superiors to pack him off to Sleepy Hollow to enquire into a series of decapitations that has a symbolic as well as a literal gruesomeness, as the heads of the community are being lopped off. This is the sort of puzzle Walker has specialised in, and Depp's Ichabod merely follows the sleuths of *Se7en* and *8MM* who crack the case but find out more than they want to know about themselves and the nature of the world in the process. There is a flaw in this conception, best understood by looking at *The Hound of the Baskervilles*: though Arthur Conan Doyle was a firm believer in ghosts, he knew the character of Sherlock Holmes could not co-exist in a universe with a genuine supernatural creature and therefore unmasked his hound as a mastiff coated in phosphorus. *Sleepy Hollow* establishes Crane if not as a Holmesian figure then as a clear predecessor of Edgar Allan Poe's ratiocinator Dupin, fussing with his crime-solving chemicals and probing always for motive and means. When faced with an actual apparition he collapses and takes to his bed to conclude his flashback memories and become reconciled to his mystic heritage, symbolised by his consultation of a wood witch and growing attraction to Katrina, who is herself magically inclined. However, there is a curtain behind the curtain, with Ichabod accepting the supernatural only to realise that the killer ghost is acting to a plan under the control of a human mystery villain straight out of Terence Fisher's Hammer film version of *The Hound of the Baskervilles* (1959).

In the end, however, *Sleepy Hollow* is a Tim Burton movie. Taken on after the commercial rejection of *Mars Attacks!* (1996) and the collapse of his long-developed Superman project, material that was already well formed has been thoroughly worked over into something unmistakably the director's own. Depp's Ichabod is his third role for Burton after *Edward Scissorhands* and *Ed Wood* in 1990 and 1994, and his third go as the director's alter ego, again Struwwelpeter-haired and laced into a tight black jacket that makes him scuttle rather than walk. Burton's curious ability to rethink anything from *Pee-Wee's Big Adventure* (1985) through *Batman* (1989) and *Batman Returns* (1992) to *The Nightmare Before Christmas* (1993) as an experiment in expressionist autobiography is yet again in evidence. Ichabod's dreams of his mother (Burton regular Lisa Marie) hauled off to the torture chamber allow the director the *Ed Wood*ian opportunity to regenerate moments from favourite films – conflating scenes with cult actress Barbara Steele from Mario Bava's *The Mask of Satan* (1960) and Roger Corman's *Pit and the Pendulum* (1961) – while imbuing them with an emotional resonance that is as rich and strange as Kenneth Anger's appropriation of drive-in imagery for his own magical purposes.

Brom Van Brunt (Caspar Van Dien) is the latest in a line of bested bullies (Anthony Michael Hall in *Edward Scissorhands*, Jack Black in *Mars Attacks!*) Burton has enjoyed gruesomely killing off. It is a key to Burton's universe that only the truly terrified and alone, such as Michael Keaton's Bruce Wayne in *Batman* or Winona Ryder's goth chick in *Beetle Juice* (1988), can face up to the monsters and earn the reward of romantic fulfilment. Christina Ricci's Katrina, more than answering to Irving's description ('a blooming lass of fresh eighteen, plump as a partridge, ripe and melting and rose-cheeked as one of her father's peaches'), is as devoted to her strange beau (unlike Irving's shallow coquette) as Jack Skellington's sewn-together girlfriend in *The Nightmare Before Christmas* or Ed Wood's succession of supportive helpmates. Ricci seems a natural inhabitant of Burton's world, her broad, child-woman face blank in adoration of her deeply embarrassed swain, credibly witchlike, chaste but not asexual, clearly willing to step into madness if that's what it takes to join the man she loves.

Though the addition of a genuine supernatural creature – wonderfully played, in his headed form, by a wordless Christopher Walken with teeth filed to cannibal points and a Sid Vicious hairdo – is the most striking divergence from the original story, Burton's real rebellion lies in seeing Ichabod Crane not as an awkward weirdo but as an identification figure. As in his earlier freak roles Depp remains a handsome man got up to simulate grotesquery and is never allowed to be the scarecrow geek Goldblum was ideally suited to, most faithfully translated from page to screen in the cartoon version. Given to fainting spells, several times squirted in the eye by jets of blood and thoroughly screwed up by his upbringing, Depp's Crane is a marginalised hero, but a hero nevertheless. Brom is an idiot who blunders pointlessly to his death without helping anyone, but Crane defines that type of courage which involves being genuinely terrified throughout a hideous experience but still getting the job done.

Rarely can a major studio horror film have been the product of so many people who are knowledgeable and enthusiastic about horror as a genre, who take such delight in revisiting the by-ways of its history. There's a real frisson to be had from the cameo casting of the likes of Christopher Lee and Michael Gough, whose genre history goes back to their co-starring roles in Fisher's *Dracula* (1958), though the script gives more weight to such occasional visitors to the genre as Miranda Richardson, Michael Gambon and Richard Griffiths, while finding significant moments for Burton regulars Jeffrey Jones and Martin Landau (decapitated before the credits). The woods through which this Horseman rides look exactly like those stretches of the New Forest Hammer liked to pass off as Transylvania, though there's a tangled CGI hell-tree that evokes Oz and *The Company of Wolves* (1984), and the finale takes place in a burning windmill which is ostensibly a faithful recreation of a set from James Whale's *Frankenstein* (1931) – already homaged as a miniature golf course in Burton's short *Frankenweenie* (1984) – though it might also be a nod towards the more highly coloured locale of Fisher's *The Brides of Dracula* (1960). It's fairly easy to cast a familiar face or drop in a plot reference to a Hammer film, but this is a movie that knows exactly the colour palette of Arthur Grant's cinematography for Hammer or Floyd Crosby's for Corman and works hard to get the mist swirling in the right direction and the precise shade of red for a startling door in an all-white dream church.

Despite Burton's fondness for character comedy and the prevailing Hollywood notion that nobody could possibly take horror seriously, the pleasures of *Sleepy Hollow* come from high style rather than high camp: a scarecrow (another American horror icon, from Nathaniel Hawthorne to the *Batman* villain) which whirls whenever the monster brushes; an animated tendril of ghostly mist snuffing out a row of burning torches before the spectre comes for its next victim; the Hessian motioning two angelic little girls not to give away his hiding place, only to have one calculatedly snap a twig to summon the mob who hack off his head; Richard Griffiths' head spinning on his neck after the fatal slice then tumbling to the ground between Depp's legs to be speared and carried off by the Horseman with a circus-style flourish; the Horseman finally regaining his skull and reattaching it to be covered by sinew and skin in a reversal of the usual monster-movie ending that allows for a wild display of *Evil Dead*–ish effects; the bustle of a 1799 New York street scene in which we see the outlines of the city to come.

Given the nature of the monster's favoured mode of transport, this is a film that has to keep on the move, with thundering hooves and careening carriages. And despite its sometimes mechanical and often broken-down storyline *Sleepy Hollow* is never less than ravishing to look at – courtesy of cinematographer Emmanuel Lubezki and production designer Rick Heinrichs, though Burton's eye is evident in every composition – and manages, when it gets its speed up, to come across as terribly exciting.

What it isn't, and this may be a failing of Irving's conception, is very frightening. Heads are lopped off regularly (the inevitable poster line is 'Heads will roll') and human corruption is everywhere. But Ichabod Crane is terrified for intellectual and psychological reasons we can't really share and Burton has his hero overcome all his fears so he can come up trumps in the extended finale, which combines chase, deduction, confrontation and revelation into one big ball of plot string.

SLEEPY HOLLOW
USA/Germany 1999
Director: Tim Burton

New York, 1799. Ichabod Crane, a young constable, is sent to the upstate village of Sleepy Hollow to investigate a series of mysterious beheadings. Leading citizens, led by landowner Baltus Van Tassel, tell Crane the killings are the work of the Headless Horseman, a Hessian mercenary beheaded during the Revolution who has come back from the grave. Crane does not believe this until he sees the town magistrate killed by the Horseman. Shocked, he collapses, and is nursed back to health by Van Tassel's daughter Katrina with whom he falls in love.

Guided by a mysterious witch, he and Katrina discover that the Horseman emerges from the roots of a tree that seems to be a portal to hell. Crane suspects Van Tassel is behind the killings, then, after Van Tassel is killed, suspects Katrina of witchcraft and decides to leave Sleepy Hollow. Learning from a book she has given him that Katrina's spells are meant to protect him, Crane turns back just in time to save her from her stepmother Lady Van Tassel, the evil witch behind the Horseman. His missing head restored, the Horseman takes Lady Van Tassel to hell. Crane, Katrina and an orphaned village boy Masbath leave for New York City.

* * *

No longer a prodigy at age 41, Tim Burton has now become a problem; I still find myself watching his movies with bemused tolerance, thinking surely he'll be a great director when he grows up. Although it's loaded with pseudo-ghoulish detail and imbued with a distinctive atmosphere – both of which, as usual, seem drawn from a 1970s teenager's comic-book and album cover collection – *Sleepy Hollow* suffers from terminal vagueness and clutter. Its plot is a complicated skein of unrelated fairytale elements and coincidences, punctuated occasionally by balletic beheadings, its characterisation almost entirely haphazard.

There have been several previous film and television versions of Washington Irving's short story 'The Legend of Sleepy Hollow' (familiar to generations of American schoolchildren), and if nothing else Burton definitively captures its mood of wilderness paranoia. His opening scene, in which Martin Landau becomes the Headless Horseman's quarry as he drives a deserted stretch of road, is a classic of gothic terror. As the heads severed by the Horseman twist through the air, we always glimpse in them a moment of horrified comprehension – death (or something that may be worse) has come for them on the lonely edge of this dangerous continent.

Even Burton's vaunted visual sensibility gets him into trouble at least as often as it rescues him. His early vision of Ichabod Crane's Manhattan as a grey, fetid city crawling with crime and fever – where the authorities abuse miscreants and throw them into horrible dungeons with scarcely a gesture in the direction of justice – is so fascinating one feels disappointed when the film abandons it. There's a wonderful moment after Crane arrives in drab, severe, and dead silent Sleepy Hollow, throws open the doors of the inn and enters a crowded party pulsing with colour and gaiety. We understand at a single stroke that terror has driven the town's social life indoors. Burton never returns to this theme either.

Johnny Depp's Ichabod Crane is a man of many parts, never conclusively adding up to a whole. Depp's willingness to push his characters in unsympathetic directions is always engaging, and he plays Crane as a Clouseau-like incompetent, his face a mask of involuntary tics and twitches. His scientific aspirations are portrayed as foolish and grotesque, his bizarre toolkit seems borrowed from Jeremy Irons' mad surgeon in *Dead Ringers*, his goggles make him look like a demon from the *Hellraiser* series. Yet, as we learn in a series of tedious flashbacks, Crane is also another of Burton's damaged naifs, a survivor who finds inner reserves of strength and wins Katrina's love, despite the fact that he is entirely wrong about her, the Horseman and everything else.

Of course Depp and Christina Ricci (resplendent in a lovely blonde wig) make a charismatic pair, smashingly done up in period costumes by Colleen Atwood, and audiences are likely to swallow almost any narrative strategy that sees them united by the film's end. Andrew Kevin Walker's screenplay, which bears little relationship to Irving's story, doesn't offer Katrina much to do beyond gazing at the bumbling Crane with what is meant to be a knowing, tolerant affection. Still, she's better off than Miranda Richardson as Lady Van Tassel, who scarcely appears in the film before being revealed as the wicked stepmother behind it all – and delivering a lengthy Dr Evil-style disquisition on her motives and methods. Similarly, such irreproachable actors as Michael Gambon and Jeffrey Jones make little impression against the scattershot story and Rick Heinrichs's alluring production design. Christopher Walken cuts a fine, fearsome figure in his cameo as the medieval-looking Hessian mercenary, his teeth sharpened to vampiric points.

As ever, Burton quotes from his favourite films – there's an elaborate restaging of the burning-windmill climax in the 1931 *Frankenstein*. Maybe there's something perversely honourable about this; Burton certainly isn't serving plot or character at such moments, just referring to a cherished memory for no particular reason, like a patient free-associating on a therapist's couch. Ever since *Pee-Wee's Big Adventure* in 1985, Burton has been all potential and no delivery (with qualified exceptions for *Ed Wood* and the first *Batman* film). Even with an almost mythic story at its foundation, *Sleepy Hollow* doesn't seem like the work of an eccentric visionary, as Burton has long been labelled. It's more like the good-natured mess produced by a shallow sentimentalist, an undisciplined imitator with a keen sense of style.

Andrew O'Hehir

LUNATICS ON THE PITCH

Kevin Jackson

Asylum, the latest product of an ongoing creative conspiracy between writer-director Iain Sinclair and director-writer Chris Petit, is a long way from your standard terrestrial-channel fodder. So distant, in fact, that even some of the project's principal co-workers were dismayed by what they eventually saw on the cutting-room screen. As Sinclair recalls, 'Our producer, Keith Griffiths, looked at the first, nearly finished cut and said nothing for a long time, and then said, "Wonderful. This is a suicide note for all our careers." Dave McKean, the graphics artist, sat there for half an hour like a dead panda. He didn't utter word. I thought he'd died there on the sofa.'

Such gloom may have been a trifle excessive, though it's fair to assume that *Asylum* won't have the advertising people falling over each other to buy slots for its Channel 4 broadcast. But then, the aesthetically strait-laced quality of much television – and much else in our present climate – is part of what the film sets out to rebuke. As Sinclair puts it: 'I think the whole culture now is down to groups of people who are good at doing meetings and groups of people who are good at putting forward proposals, and out of this chaotic conjunction comes the trash which is the culture.'

Whether or not you find it appealing (and to lay cards on the table, I do), *Asylum* manifestly isn't the sort of beast that is incubated in meetings and pitch sessions. The film begins with a science-fictional prelude, reminiscent in tone if not in detail of Chris Marker's experimental short *La Jetée* (1962). At some time in the future – 'Year Zero plus 14' – an unseen agency recovers a series of film and audio documents from the 'pre-viral' past, variously identified as 'The Project' or 'The Perimeter Fence'.

As the deadpan female narrator explains, an amnesiac plague has swept across the world: 'The virus was terrible. It created itself in the protein soup of bad television with the sole aim of devouring its own memory – the last cultural traces.' Then another voice – labelled 'unidentified male' but unmistakably Sinclair himself sounding his most eerily soothing and quasi-rational – bobs up and down on the soundtrack, spieling about 'a kind of Illuminati, who hold on to the cultural memory of the race... by coming across them you may be able to reach something that everyone else has forgotten.'

These two sci-fi conceits, lightly returned to from time to time, license a series of digressions on a variety of idiosyncratic subjects. There are visits to three members of Sinclair's private pantheon of Illuminated writers: Michael Moorcock in Texas, James Sallis in Arizona and the Black Mountain poet Ed Dorn, dying of cancer, on his last visit to Britain. Marina Warner talks about shadow selves and doubles, a bloke from Margate muses on T. S. Eliot's *The Waste Land* and the film's editor Emma Matthews drifts in and out of the action, microphone in hand, as a sort of secret agent on the trail of the photographer Françoise Lacroix – or more exactly, of her fictional alter ego of the same name, age and appearance who went missing, presumed dead, in the last Sinclair/Petit joint enterprise *The Falconer* (1997).

With me so far? Now it gets trickier. It's not only Lacroix and 'Agent Matthews' who are dragged into the scrambled paranoia: everyone in the film, including Sinclair and Petit in both on- and off-screen manifestations, plays some kind of fictional version of themselves, so Dorn's rants and poems about the Gulf War and Serbia are represented as post-censored fragments of a sometime 'rising star of the [unnamed, obviously sinister] administration'. The visual texture of the film is either roughed up by multiple refilming in the cutting room or smoothed into glossy computer-generated palimpsests of image and text by Dave McKean. The 'dead' Françoise returns and meets her twin sister; Sinclair delivers a screed about ancient Persian mythology and the entire space/time continuum goes belly up. Fade out on shot of (terminal) beach. Roll credits.

As I say, there's not a lot of this sort of thing around nowadays, though there are times when *Asylum* and *The Falconer* put me in mind of Marker's layered film essay *Sans Soleil* (1982) as well as *La Jetée* (a lucky hit: Sinclair and Petit later tell me they watched *Sans Soleil* again before starting work on *The Falconer*). *Asylum* does, however, have certain affinities with developments in other media, and most obviously with Sinclair's multiple interweaving work in novels (such as *Downriver*), poetry (*Lud Heat*) and essays (*Lights Out for the Territory*) – a life's project of research and expression on which he has been engaged for more than three decades with a tenacity and independence of spirit that have bordered on the heroic.

As Chris Petit explains: 'What has interested me in the course of [working with Sinclair] is how you translate writing into images – not making 'the film of the book' but taking something like Iain's style, which is very distinctive, and trying to find a visual equivalent for it.' He remains diffident about the degree to which that ambition has been realised in any of their films: 'I feel at the moment that we're still in the typing pool.'

It's only in the past ten years or so that rank-and-file literati have found themselves obliged to take account of Sinclair, this wise man from the east (Hackney that is), and only in the last three or four – since *Lights Out* became a refreshingly implausible best-seller – that Sinclair has become widely acknowledged as a major hitter in the word game. His status in the image racket is still a lot more tenuous, and *Asylum* bears the self-deprecating, possibly self-defeating subtitle 'The Final Commission' in doleful acknowledgment of their chances of ever being let loose with a proper budget again.

Asylum is the third part of a trilogy that was put together by fits and starts across the course of the 1990s, beginning with *The Cardinal and the Corpse* (1992). Sinclair and Petit had drifted together in the mid-1980s: a period when Sinclair was still working as a second-hand book dealer and Petit, whose career as a feature-film director had run aground, became a regular customer for his specialist list of novels about Soho – Petit being at work on a non-fiction book on the subject. That study was never completed, though the researches fed into Petit's first novel *Robinson*, and his sometime dealer became a friend and collaborator.

Petit: 'I'd nicked a piece about the weather Iain had written for the *London Review of Books* and translated it into a *40 Minutes* documentary for BBC2.' Not one to filch material without some sort of pay-back, Petit recruited Sinclair, who duly 'slid under the carpet some of my collection of lunatics and visionaries, so we'd got [the sculptor] Gavin Jones in his bunker, who was a character in *Downriver*, and a guy called Chris Torrance, a Welsh poet who's the last survivor of a utopian community who's had nothing to do for the last 30 years except make minute notes about cloud fronts and has written an epic poem about the weather, and [the writers] Peter Redgrove and Penelope Shuttle.'

A cast that sat rather uneasily with the film's other materials, from weatherphobes to *Fortean Times* stuff about crop circles and hails of fish. It soon became clear it was time for the two of them to address more directly 'that musty, book-dealing, geezery world' in which they'd first met, and to do so in a manner which – like Sinclair's novels – hopped blithely back and forward between reality, urban legend, myth-making, hyperbole, blague and balderdash. Sinclair: 'The idea was just to go into that world of majorly forgotten figures' – including the novelist Robin Cook, the former rock guitarist and book dealer Martin Stone, and various associates of the Krays – 'and tease out three stories derived from what we knew about them, and let the actors play themselves in their own stories'.

Petit: 'By that stage everyone else had been weeded out and it was just a collection of Iain's freaks.' The two conspirators landed a poverty-row budget ('about 25 grand, I think,' says Petit) from Channel 4 for *The Cardinal and the Corpse* to be produced within the *Without Walls* slot – just enough for a five-day shoot, mainly in and around Brick Lane and City airport. Sinclair: 'I think we evolved an interesting way of working. When we had the crew there Chris would be addressing them and setting up the shots and I would have to deal with the lowlife – be the freak wrangler.'

The end product, which was dressed up with a bit of hocus-pocus from the legendary comic-book writer Alan Moore and Sinclair's old ally Brian Catling (a conceptual sculptor and possibly the only man in the history of British television to be Astoned as 'Gnostic Heretic'), was, it seems, considered revolting by its commissioning editor and dumped out hastily on the airwaves: for further details, see *Lights Out for the Territory*. It took the better part of six years before there was any possibility of a sequel (Sinclair: 'I think both our stocks were dipping away at that point') and *The Falconer* only began to come together in a faltering, happenstance fashion.

Petit: 'Keith Griffiths got in touch with me to say that Channel 4 and the Arts Council were looking to fund low-budget, visionary, blah blah blah Super-8 films, and they were also going to consider doing one or two longer films, so we cobbled together a project called *The Perimeter Fence* and submitted it.'

Sinclair: 'The idea of the Perimeter Fence is that there's an official enclosure of culture, and certain figures have drifted off into the badlands beyond, and we were going off into the territory to get them back... Really it was simply carrying on from *The Cardinal and the Corpse*, but by accident one of the first people we saw was this Peter Whitehead character who grandstanded himself in such a way you realised he'd have to be at the centre of the project – particularly because he arranged a massive heart attack very early on, and rang up from the hospital saying, you've got to get in here, I'm on my way out, I want the cameras in here this afternoon...'

Whitehead, who had himself made a number of films in the 1960s (most famously *Tonite Let's All Make Love in London*), was such an exotic specimen he barely needed fictionalising – not that Sinclair and Petit were inhibited by that, and one suspects that the fictions propagated by *The Falconer* do indeed manage to be stranger than Whitehead's improbable truth. To avoid the possibility of libel suits, let's just say the narratives inside and outside the film include incest, murder, black magic, industrial quantities of cannabis, Howard Marks, CIA sting operations, the Goldsmith family, the illegal trade in falcons' eggs, the royal families of both Saudi Arabia and the United Kingdom, arms dealing and pagan sacrifice.

The completed film met with a variety of responses: at a 'hairy' screening at Leicester University Caroline Coon angrily denounced *The Falconer* as 'an appalling snuff movie about rape and incest'; there was talk of legal action and the threat that Sinclair and Petit would be found guilty of holding a satanic ritual in National Trust property ('Channel 4 was in a state of shock ...'). On the other hand, it won a director's prize at the Edinburgh Film Festival, and the *Evening Standard*'s television reviewer thought it was fabulous, as did critics from more predictable quarters. Most importantly in practical terms, it was singled out for praise by the controller of Channel 4, Michael Jackson.

And so – to simplify somewhat – the path was smoothed for making *Asylum* in the same manner as *The Falconer*: all the footage shot and reshot cheaply on viewcam or Super-8 then treated to rather less cheap graphic retooling by McKean, with whom Sinclair had first worked on a set of related prose fictions entitled *Slow Chocolate Autopsy*. Sinclair sums up the development of the team's working aesthetic like this: 'It's more like poetry this time. I think *The Cardinal and the Corpse* is almost like journalism, like an essay about these people; *The Falconer* is fiction; and this one is moving into poetry and vision and melancholy.'

Why melancholy? 'This one began to feel like the end of things, a rather sad end to the cycle of nature, the end of the cycle of the commissioning process, there was the feeling no one was going to understand...' Sinclair also believes the new film marks something of a return to his exceptionally modest beginnings as a film-maker: 'In the 60s and 70s I used to make endless 8mm films, just records of journeys, a walk or something, and this part [of *Asylum*] which covers the area from Staines down to the river is exactly like a more sophisticated version of those 8mm films... It's as close as I've ever got to the world of Stan Brakhage and that kind of film-making rather than to films with any kind of commercial structure.'

For all this, he's hopeful now that the audience for work such as *Asylum* might well be larger than most people – including himself – have tended to assume. When Petit tells us there's a rumour Channel 4 will want to put the film out fairly late on a Saturday night, Sinclair muses: 'Saturday night would be quite a good slot – people staggering home drunk from the club ... I've shown it to my son, who's a 20-year-old film-maker who thinks what I do is monstrously pretentious, but he had no trouble at all with this stuff. He thought it was perfectly acceptable, almost simple-minded ... just what he and his mates would like to see when they come back at three or four in the morning.'

It remains to be seen whether television will continue to play the role of Maecenas to the Sinclair/Petit axis. Despite the glum prognostication of *Asylum* as the 'Final Commission', Sinclair does think it's possible Channel 4 will put up the cash for a film related to his current non-fiction project, a psychogeographical meander around the M25. But even if the funding dries up, the pair will probably continue, as Petit says, 'to do it ourselves'.

Asylum purports to be a film cobbled together at some point in the hypothetical future. But the specific future form of cinema envisaged as an option by Sinclair, where personal films are made and distributed on micro-budgets – 'like poetry, just the same kind of underground thing to roughly the same size of audience' – is already with us, in a prototype version at least. Both individually and together, Sinclair and Petit have recently managed to shoot, edit and screen a number of extra-curricular projects including a short film inspired by Sinclair's researches into the mysterious East End hermit and autodidactic polyglot David Rodinsky. If television's culture of meetings has no further tolerance for the duo, they've already shown themselves quite ready and able to do the sort of work they need to do elsewhere – out on their own, on the far side of the perimeter fence.

SIX DEGREES OF NOSFERATU

Thomas Elsaesser

'Where do you think you're going?' Professor van Helsing calls after Jonathan Harker in F. W. Murnau's *Nosferatu, eine Symphonie des Grauens* (1922). 'You cannot escape your destiny by running away.' Both the film and Bram Stoker's original novel *Dracula* bear a family resemblance to the 'appointment in Samarra' story of the merchant who came across Death at noon in Bagdad and, panic-stricken, rode to Samarra, unaware that his real appointment with Death was not until the evening – in Samarra. Harker travels to Transylvania, thinking he's selling the mysterious Count a piece of real estate, but what the two also trade when they exchange contracts is the portrait of Harker's fiancée Mina, giving Nosferatu access to and possession of her person – the main reason, at least in Murnau's film, why the Count acquires real estate in the first place. And when Harker manages to escape the Count's castle, making his way home on horseback, little does he know that in the meantime the Count is already sailing ahead to await him in the becalmed port of Harker's native city, ready to land his deadly cargo of plague-carrying rats. Murnau, too, was involved in 'appointments in

Samarra' – for instance, he seems to have undertaken what would prove his last journey in order to evade the very fate that was to lie in store for him. He died on 11 March 1931 in a freak automobile accident near Santa Monica on his way to arrange a steamship passage to New York after having been warned by his astrologer that he should avoid travelling on land.

The making of Murnau's last film *Tabu A Story of the South Seas* (1931), which opened nine days after his death, was similarly ill-fated. Not only did the production, which began auspiciously as a collaboration between Robert Flaherty and Murnau, break up in disarray, but it seems that Murnau himself was proceeding at cross-purposes. According to his correspondence, he actually undertook his South Sea journey to visit not Tahiti, where the film was shot, but Bali, where a long-time friend and former associate had made his home. *Tabu* has often been regarded as Murnau's intimate film diary, the ultimate home-movie: beautiful bodies diving into the deep for pearls, darting canoes, languid and yearning limbs stretched out or embracing. But in its sombre, ominous and uncanny mood, its empty landscapes and restrained framing, *Tabu* is actually a companion film to *Nosferatu*. The old Hindu priest, who impartially but implacably pursues the young couple, fulfils at plot level a function similar to that of the vampire, namely to split up the couple and reclaim the virgin bride. And as in *Nosferatu*, doom in *Tabu* comes in the form of a ship, pushing its way gently into the perfectly framed shot of a peaceful port.

Despite the detailed research of M. Bouvier and J. L. Leutrat, the question of how *Nosferatu* came to be made is still something of a mystery. Virtually the only film produced by Prana-Film – a financial sinking ship whose owners were subsequently taken to court for copyright violations by Bram Stoker's widow despite having changed most of the characters' names – the project owed much to the enigmatic figure of Albin Grau, who signed for the décor and costumes but also seems to have been the driving force behind the production, both financially and artistically. Very little is known about Grau, though a recent article by Enno Patalas depicts him variously as a student of Eastern philosophy, a freemason and master of the 'pansophic lodge of the light-seekers' in Berlin, a fan of Aleister Crowley, a friend of novelist-painter Alfred Kubin and the author of a pamphlet about the use of colour in décor and lighting in black and white films. More predictable collaborators were film-industry professionals screenwriter Henrik Galeen (who co-wrote *The Golem*) and director of photography Fritz Arno Wagner, one of the three top cameramen at Ufa.

Germany in 1921–2 was recovering from the bloodletting of World War I. The spectres that haunted the new republic included the Spartacist uprisings in Berlin and Munich, based on the Soviet model and bloodily suppressed, raging inflation that bled the economy like an internal haemorrhage, and an army of horribly disfigured war cripples. But it was another memorable event that left its echo in *Nosferatu*: in the winter of 1919–20 a Spanish flu epidemic and famine hit Germany, ravaging the country and reportedly killing more civilians than the Great War itself. So the cholera whose origins *Nosferatu* is supposed to record is doubled by several successive disasters befalling a defeated Germany, during which public opinion only too readily blamed the victors of Versailles for not coming to the country's aid. Instead, the French, adding insult and humiliation to injury and penury, insisted on the prompt payment of war reparations and annexed the Rhineland, setting off a chain of events that gave the nationalist right its first electoral successes among the working class.

But the war had left less visible scars and traumas, especially on the veterans. In the run-up to the opening of *Nosferatu*, Grau published a piece in *Bühne und Film* explaining how he'd come by the story and why he'd wanted to turn it into a film. It has to do with the war in Serbia and his experiences as a soldier of the infantry. Dispatched to a remote village as part of what he describes as 'a vermin-extermination commando', he's billeted with an old peasant who tells him the story of his father who, killed in a blood-feud, was buried without sacraments and haunted the village as a vampire. The peasant even shows Grau an official paper about his father's disinterment in 1884, where the body is discovered perfectly preserved except for two front teeth now protruding over the lower lip. The prefect ordered a stake to be driven through the heart of this 'nosferatu' (Romanian for undead), who expires with a sigh.

What comes into view in Bram Stoker's original *Dracula* as much as in Grau's tale and Galeen's unauthorised adaptation for Murnau is Britain and Western Europe's relationship with 'Mittleuropa' and its eastern flank: the Slav peoples in general and those of the Balkans in particular, a world the Germanic West had for centuries studied with fascinated antipathy. And Mittleuropa also encompassed 'the Pale' – the home territories of the eastern Jews whom the collapse of the Austro-Hungarian Empire in 1918 had forced to move westwards. Superimposed in the figure of Nosferatu are several contradictory and conflicting ethnic or racial 'others', making him at once an 'in-between worlds' creature and a babushka doll of 'world-within-worlds'. Put differently, the story prefigures in some sense the imperial coloniser's bad dreams of a reverse colonisation of the mother country by the colonised subjects. The earth Nosferatu brings in his coffins, as well as the name of his ship (*Demeter*, i.e. Mother Earth), give a clear hint of this feared return. That such an influx of the subjugated and exploited should be seen in terms of rats, contagion and contamination speaks volumes: about the unselfconscious racism of the educated classes during the last-but-one turn of the century, but also about 'us', hyper-selfconscious readers of literary texts and filmic discourses, and citizens of 'Fortress Europe', some of whom harbour their own nightmare visions of history's undead heading west from the 'land beyond the trees' and beyond.

Nosferatu is a film about networks of contagion and contamination that are also networks of secret and subversive communication. The lines of attraction and repulsion that link Nosferatu and Harker and Nosferatu and Mina weave a subtle web of interaction and dependency, of transfer and substitution. These different levels of making contact charge the film with the kind of energy that alone gives vampirism its extended metaphoric significance, reverberating, for instance, in the film-within-the-film (a spoof on Ufa's recently inaugurated Kulturfilm documentaries) about nature's own vampires and predators. A mutually sustaining symbiosis mingles passion and revulsion with petrified fascination and drifting abandonment: it takes over the ship, her unfortunate crew and then the burgers of Wisborg, but it's also the subject of Professor van Helsing's natural-history lesson, when he traces a malevolent genealogy from plant life to animal existence, from carnivorous orchids, polyps, spiders and flies, and rats, all the way to the beginning and Mina's playfulness with the cat and her kitten. But a similarly fatal chain of eating or being eaten goes from Mina's anxious possessiveness as Harker sets off, to the servility of the Transylvanian peasants, the dangerous hospitality of Nosferatu, the craven submission of Renfield, the sadistic exploitation of the ship's crew by its master, until it returns full circle with Mina's sacrifice, offering herself to Nosferatu's terrible visitation.

The idea of unpredictable patterns of propagation is perhaps not so dissimilar from what in more recent times has been studied by mathematicians and statisticians under the name of small-worlds syndrome. Small-worlds scientists are trying to understand the dynamics of groups and open systems and the patterns of their interaction, which tend to oscillate between total randomness and total organisation. It's a key issue for biologists (how do thousands of crickets manage to chirp in unison within seconds of starting up?). It's used by economists when predicting global stock-exchange movements or the effects of a particular market's collapse. It's of interest to preventive medicine when looking at the spread of viruses and devising methods of disease control, and it helps designers of mobile communications networks trying to determine the shortest route between two long-distance parties, connecting them by piggy-backing on local data traffic.

To the rest of us, small-worlds syndrome is better known as 'six degrees of separation', according to which everyone knows someone famous across the overlap between one's own circle of friends, acquaintances and associates and the circles of friends of these friends. If we use *Nosferatu* as a template, then the six degrees of Murnau open up intriguing connections.

Born in Bielefeld in 1888 as the son of a textile manufacturer, Friedrich Wilhelm Plumpe adopted the name Murnau as a young adult. The fact that he did so in order to disguise an unflattering surname and in homage to an artists' colony south of Munich already leads to Kandinsky, Franz Marc and other members of the Expressionist group Der Blaue Reiter who used to spend time in Murnau. And Murnau the place is just one of the connections between Murnau the man and Expressionist poet Hans Ehrenbaum-Degele and his circle of avant-garde artist friends.

Albin Grau may link Murnau with Alfred Kubin and such Prague Gothic writers as Gustav Meyrink and Franz Kafka, but he was an outsider to the film industry, while Galeen and Wagner belonged to one or other of the production units that existed at Ufa under Erich Pommer. What's called Expressionist film mainly reflected common tastes and preferences among this remarkably tightly knit community of professionals – no more than two dozen names – who operated as teams and skills networks. With the exception of Fritz Lang, Murnau and a few others, the directors were no more than first among equals, with the set designers probably leaving the most lasting impression on the look of the films.

Murnau's reputation is as German cinema's most exquisite Romantic poet, in contrast with the technophile Lang who had astounded the film world with the trick effects for which Ufa was famous since *The Spiders* (1919) and *Destiny* (1921). In 1915 Murnau was called up and served in the infantry in East Prussia; he hated it and was bored to distraction. The following year he managed to get transferred to the Luftwaffe, where he flew combat missions over France until after an emergency landing during fog he came to spend the remainder of the war as an internee in neutral

Switzerland. Murnau's time as a pilot suggests that this tender soul had nonetheless shown a remarkable appetite for 'storms of steel', blending his high-romantic sensibility with a taste for 'top-gun' technology typical of the aristocratic German dandy in the von Richthofen mould. Indeed, Murnau's obsession with gliding camera movements and intricate spatial set-ups suggests analogies with the perception of pliable space and horizonless vistas experienced by a fighter pilot.

Most cultural-studies approaches to *Nosferatu* (or indeed to Stoker's *Dracula*) have little trouble relating the myth of the vampire to a historically new and politically troubling awareness of female sexuality. The somnambulist Mina and her friend Lucy have been compared to the hysterical females treated by Charcot in Paris at the Salpêtrière, where they were photographed by Albert Londe, thanks to his newly developed chronophotographic cameras, while two young doctors from Germany and Austria, Josef Breuer and Sigmund Freud, looked on. (Stoker has van Helsing support his diagnosis of Lucy's symptoms with a pointed reference to having studied in Paris under Charcot.)

But Murnau's *Nosferatu* is open to another reading of its sexual pathology. Vampires in the movies are usually bisexual, often letting ambiguity hover over the question of whether, say, Dracula's brides are for the Count's ends in themselves, or merely means to an end (as Venus-traps, to attract young men to their rescue who then become the juicier victims). But Murnau's Nosferatu would seem to be the prototype of another gender, not least because of the vampire's many animal features, from his pointed ears and birdlike claws to his rodent teeth, rather than the more usual fangs suddenly bared on an otherwise impeccably gentleman-dandy face and physique (as with Bela Lugosi and Christopher Lee).

The French surrealists admired *Nosferatu* mainly for its eroticism, contrasting the anodyne puppy-love of Mina and Harker with Nosferatu's necrophiliac lust, musty and potent at once, exuding the aroma of dank crypts and leathery flesh. According to Robin Wood, on the other hand, sexuality is branded in Murnau's films as the source of evil: Nosferatu stands for raw carnal desire which must be kept in check in the interest of higher spiritual values, and so Mina, expressing that mixture of desire, curiosity and horror typical of patriarchal culture's depiction of female sexuality, must die along with the vampire. But the love triangles in the film also lend themselves to an interpretation that brings out a more layered structure of sexual attraction and ambivalence. For instance, underlying the secret heterosexual bond between Nosferatu and Mina is the Renfield-Harker-Nosferatu relation. The initial situation suggests that the film superimposes two plotlines, one heterosexual, the other developed around the homosexual relationship between Nosferatu and Renfield doubled by the homosocial story of Harker being befriended by Renfield, whereupon the older man introduces his younger friend to a very 'experienced' queen. Likewise the protagonists of Murnau's *Faust* (1926) – Mephisto and the rejuvenated Faust – could be called a queer couple, especially on their travel adventures to that celebrated destination of homoerotic desire, the Mediterranean, thinly disguised by the excessively heterosexual story of Faust and Gretchen.

Siegfried Kracauer had argued that Weimar cinema obsessively staged anxieties about male self images and male sexuality: his 1966 *From Caligari to Hitler* even ties the theme of damaged masculinity to the vanishing of paternal authority after a lost war. Certainly the preferred stories of Expressionist cinema focus on male identity crises – often signalled by the appearance of a double – and toy with bisexuality by featuring love triangles in which the two males are usually 'best friends' or business associates who show an obvious but rarely openly acknowledged attraction to each other. In this respect Murnau's films are neither an exception or unusually explicit. Doubles abound in Murnau as they do in other directors, whether by way of disguise (*Tartuffe*, 1926) or across a split male character (Faust old and young). Likewise, there are several crucial films where a pure, almost asexual love is threatened or destroyed by the intrusion of another male's predatory attentions – to the man (Nosferatu/ Harker, Mephisto/Faust, Tartuffe/Orgon, *Tabu*'s Hitu/Matahi).

For a novelist such as Jim Shepard, Murnau's homosexuality is crucial to both his films and his life; sorrow and secrecy become the wellsprings of his creative drive, the motives behind a tale of love, longing, guilt and self-abjection. In his fictionalised 1998 biography of Murnau, *Nosferatu in Love*, Shepard makes the twin poles of self-deprecating humour and self-lacerating grief the protective armour behind which the director feeds on lascivious thoughts furtively indulged. For Shepard, the deepest wound the war inflicted on Murnau was the death on the Eastern Front of his intimate friend Hans Ehrenbaum-Degele, on whom he once recklessly cheated. Baffled and hurt, Hans voluntarily enlists and soon gets himself killed, to the undying shame and mortification of Murnau, at least according to Shepard.

It's true that Hans Ehrenbaum-Degele was an Expressionist poet and co-editor of the magazine *Das neue Pathos*. He was the son of a Jewish banker and art-collector, whose mother Mary, a concert singer, virtually adopted Murnau after his return from Zurich at the end of the war. It's also true that the Ehrenbaum-Degele villa in Berlin-Grunewald remained Murnau's home from 1919 until he left for America in June 1926. But Shepard's fictional diary spins its tale around a number of characters and incidents for which there is no evidence in historical records.

There are two other 'degrees of separation' – one that might underpin and the other undermine Shepard's speculations. The first is the suggestion, already made obliquely in the press reports after the opening night, that *Nosferatu* is something of a spoof, the camp interpretation and insider's tale of characters and antics in another castle from that of the film – the private retreat (a castle in Austria) and very public court (the Deutsche Schauspielhaus in Berlin) presided over by the reigning monarch of Berlin's artistic and theatre worlds, Max Reinhardt. (From 1911 to 1914 Murnau was a pupil of Reinhardt's in Berlin, working as an actor and assistant director.) In his brief study of Murnau published in 1977, Stan Brakhage first reads *Nosferatu* as a primal-scene fantasy of Murnau himself, linking it to a homosexual childhood fantasy and the wish to do away with his parents and at the same time play father to his mother. But he, too, links the film to Reinhardt ('Max Schreck') and his circle, where homosexual eccentricity and extravagance were encouraged, and homosexuals with talent and panache found a safe haven and congenial company amid the strict anti-homosexual legislation of the otherwise broadminded Weimar Republic.

Shepard describes these excesses with some gusto by introducing a character called Spiess, who plays the role of seducer, Mephisto and evil genius to the hesitant Murnau-

Faust, and in the end his novelised biography stands and falls by the credibility one is prepared to give this figure. As it happens, a Walter Spies did in fact exist, and was present – the other degree of separation – during the shooting of *Nosferatu*, though he never appeared on any list of credits. But he wasn't the figure depicted by Shepard, and his subsequent life is too important, both to Murnau and to many other histories of dance, music and film, to leave Shepard's account unchallenged.

Although definitely an intimate of Murnau's in the early 1920s – Murnau invited Spies to live with him and asked him to decorate his villa – Spies left Germany soon after the making of *Nosferatu*, disenchanted by the empty frivolity of the film world and its hangers-on. Spies was a painter and musician, born in Moscow in 1895 – another Slav – whose family fled west to Berlin in 1909 and sent their son to study in Dresden with Oskar Kokoschka and Otto Dix. In the ethnological museums of Berlin and Amsterdam he discovered the visual and musical culture of what was then the Dutch East Indies. In 1923 he boarded a ship for Java and settled in Jogyakarta, where he stayed for four years before moving to Bali. His letters to his mother, as well as the few to Murnau, make it clear that Murnau remained his sponsor (he bought several of Spies' paintings) and close friend. A visit to Spies in Bali was on Murnau's mind when, disappointed with his work in Hollywood, he bought a yacht and set off on a voyage on the high seas in the direction of the South Sea Islands and the East Indies. If the prematurely ruptured relationship with Hans Ehrenbaum-Degele made Murnau into something of an undead, a nosferatu in love, then it was certainly not due to Walter Spies. On the contrary, Spies' invisible presence during the shooting of *Nosferatu* makes him a more likely candidate for the haunter, giving another twist to the mystery surrounding the real identity of the central figure.

E. Elias Merhige's recent *Shadow of the Vampire* turns on the idea that Nosferatu isn't played by an actor at all but by a real vampire in disguise, a suggestion first made by Adou Kyrou in *Le Surréalisme au cinéma* (1953): 'In the role of the vampire the credits name the music-hall actor Max Schreck, but it is well known that this attribution is a deliberate cover-up ... Who hides behind the character of Nosferatu? Maybe Nosferatu himself?' The actor-as-star-as-vampire, needing fresh blood and being paid in unsuspecting victims, is in the film business not such a far-fetched metaphor. Many a great star has been known to terrorise the cast with his caprice or turn the set into a bloody battlefield of violated egos and raped reputations. But an even more archetypal movie situation is that of the scientist harnessing the dangerous powers of nature or the unconscious in order to realise his vision at whatever cost to himself and others: every Dr Jekyll trying the serum on himself is a stand-in for the artist-director as sorcerer, no longer in control of the apprentices he has summoned. It's Faust calling on Mephisto, selling his shadow or his soul, an image elaborated in *Shadow of the Vampire* where the director's ruthlessness in sacrificing his leading lady to his vampire-actor for heightened artistic effect is depicted as equal to the vampire's thirst for blood. But with its conflation of actor and vampire, the film only appropriates what lies ready-made in the filmographies not only of Murnau but of German Expressionist cinema in general, with its ubiquitous ventriloquists' dummies, waxworks coming to life, warning shadows, Golems – all caught in the confusion between art and life, or rather of art as more truthful, more youthful and more authentic than life.

Why has this standard type of movie lore made a comeback in recent years. *Shadow of the Vampire* comes right after Neil LaBute's *Nurse Betty*, billed not as camp vampire gore but as a romantic comedy, despite the bloodletting. It, too, focuses on a character whose scary dedication to disavowing the difference between artifice and life is mistaken for method acting. Perhaps it's no wonder that the old problem of realism and art is revived in the digital age, where the fake looks more real than the real thing, but where we're so suspicious of authenticity and the image worlds we inhabit are of such universal duplicity that it's axiomatic that the real thing must be fake.

As with *The Matrix*, *The Truman Show*, *The Cell* or *Being John Malkovich*, the most intriguing questions at the heart of *Nurse Betty* and *Shadow of the Vampire* are philosophical: the (epistemological) problem of 'other minds' and the (ontological) problem of 'other worlds' – in the first case, what would it mean to 'know' what goes on in someone else's mind, and what proof do I have that others actually exist, and in the second, if the world I live in is merely someone else's fiction, where would the 'outside' be, from which I could ever see that it's trapped 'inside', if not inside someone else's inside? These are problems to which the answers are versions of Pascal's wager: the leap into faith (which may be the void) remains the sole cure for such radical scepticism. The vampire movies, as suggested, are more in the line of a Faustian pact than a Pascalian wager, whether entered into out of world-weary longing for youth, love and eternal life, or out of a quest for truth, beauty and the perfection of artifice by ambitious artists or made scientists. Chances are that either way they get more than they bargained for, dying in horrible agony like Oscar Wilde's Dorian Gray or suffering the apparently inverse but in truth complementary fate, namely becoming one of the undead and wishing for mortality: in both cases, ending up as monsters, excluded from the community of ordinary humans and carrying with them an unredeemed or irredeemable surplus.

What is this surplus energy or meaning that brings forth these figures of excessive but also inextinguishable desire? Excess there is, yet is it actually a matter of desire? 'We bring them the plague, and they don't even know it,' Freud is supposed to have said to Jung the day the two of them disembarked in New York harbour in 1908.

The theories of female sexuality woven around Dracula/Nosferatu all suggest that these attractive/repulsive monsters embody the vagaries of desire. But psychoanalysts, especially the Lacanians, might well argue that vampires are drive creatures, not desire creatures, meaning that it's the death drive, the repetition compulsion, the entropic principle of life that animates them, not desire, based on and sustained by lack, renewing itself around the perception and disavowal of difference.

Yet there may be another way of describing both the elements of excess, surplus and residue in these figures and the sense that they're creatures driven not by (human) desire but by some other force and energy – that of our technical revolution, as it has impacted on the domains of information and communication. Dracula may be the only original myth the age of mechanical reproduction has produced. This, at any rate, is the notion of Friedrich Kittler, for whom Dracula stands for the eternal repetition of mechanical inscription which entered the Western world with the typewriter, the gramophone/phonograph and the cinema. But what the myth tells us about these new media is still a moot point.

Kittler, for instance, argues that *Dracula* is the story of how women themselves become media, how their susceptibility and sensitivity are discovered in the middle of the nineteenth century as a resource and raw material. Charcot, Breuer, Freud – for Kittler they all line up as men who 'harvest' the mediatic powers of women, and it's Bram Stoker who calls their bluff, who both exposes the patriarchal mechanisms and offers – as in all good myths – the imaginary solution that allows Victorian society to live with this shocking realisation and its contradictions. In the contrasting and complementary figures of Mina and Lucy, and in the descriptions of their symptoms, Stoker makes hysteria and somnambulism appear as the human equivalents of wireless transmission (invented by Marconi in 1895). On their journey in pursuit of Dracula back to Transylvania, Mina serves the men as both medium and messenger – thanks to her contact with Dracula, she's able to track his global position through the transmissions emanating from him, but also, being familiar with the technically advanced transcription device of the typewriter, she records and fixes the messages he unwittingly sends across the ether, while the posse of pursuers travel towards their appointment in Samarra/Carpathia. As Kittler dryly remarks, women around 1890 had only two choices: to become hysterics or typists. Mina, after the demise of Lucy, is both.

Freud, by contrast, was a notorious technophobe. The only piece of technology he ever pronounced on is the 'mystic writing pad', basically a child's toy and more akin to the wax tablets of the Romans or the palimpsests of the medieval monks than to Edison's, the Lumières' or Marconi's inventions. Freud's refusal to have anything to do with cinema, notably his utter lack of cooperation in the making of G. W. Pabst's *Secrets of a Soul* (1926), is also well documented.

Psychoanalysis and the cinema – born together, but on a collision course ever since. Freud was right: they are antagonists, but they came together against a common enemy it now seems it was their historical mission to kill – literature and the literary author. For the first 100 years, the technological media and psychoanalysis competed over literature's prime task and near-monopoly: representing, that is recording, storing and repeating, individual human experience. Cinema and psychoanalysis translated experience into images and sounds, texts and traces, manifest as physical symptoms or as phantom sensations. Where the cinema does it mechanically, using a synthetic support, psychoanalysis retained the (female) body and the (human) voice as material support. It, too, however, tried to automate the recording process as much as possible through free association as 'automatic writing' and through the analyst as passive recording device. In the process both media produced that famous excess which in various generic formulas (from musical and melodrama to special effects and body-horror) feminism and film studies in the past 30 years have been trying to come to grips with.

In the new century, it's psychoanalysis that's in full retreat, a mere ghost haunting the hermeneutic mills of the humanities. And yet Nosferatu is still with us: the excess energy of the undead is now readable as belonging to the cinema and its eccentric patterns of propagation and proliferation across culture at large. Not only in the way films have deposited their coffins in galleries, museums, schools and libraries, but also thanks to the Renfields – cinephiles turned necrophiles – lovingly restoring perished prints and reviving the 'originals' at Sunday matinees or special retrospectives. Less fancifully perhaps, remakes of cinema's classics and restorations of the cinematic patrimony are also efforts to banish and contain the mysterious forces or lifeforms the sound-image media have brought into human existence. Perhaps the mistake of *Shadow of the Vampire* is not that it fantasises a vampire hiding inside 'Max Schreck', but that the potency of the myth of Nosferatu today speaks less about the making of a movie than about restoration and preservation, so it's perhaps fitting that besides a camp remake we can also enjoy a re-issue (on video and DVD) of a 'brand-new' *Nosferatu.*

SHADOW OF THE VAMPIRE
United Kingdom/USA/Luxembourg 2000
Director: Elias Merhige

Berlin, 1921. Film director F. W. Murnau is shooting the initial scenes of his vampire film *Nosferatu* at the Jofa Studios. Albin Grau, his producer and art director, badgers him for details of the actor cast as the Vampire Count Orlok, but Murnau isn't telling. Together with scriptwriter Henrik Galeen, cameraman Wolfgang Müller and leading man Gustav von Wangenheim, the unit travels to the location in Slovakia.

There Murnau introduces his Orlok, Max Schreck, explaining that the actor, who trained with the Russian theatre director Stanislavsky, will remain in character throughout the shoot and act only at night. In fact Schreck is a real vampire; Murnau has induced him to appear with the promise that at the end of shooting he can sink his fangs into Greta Schröder, the film's leading lady. Given vent to his impulses, Schreck preys on Müller, who falls ill. Murnau flies him back to Berlin and hires a replacement, Fritz Arno Wagner.

The unit flies to Heligoland for the final scenes. Greta, terrified by Schreck, refuses to act with him; Murnau has her pumped full of morphine to play the scene. Eagerly biting her neck, Schreck falls into a drugged stupor. When he wakes dawn is breaking. Realising he has been tricked, he kills Grau and Wagner and advances on Murnau, who calmly keeps filming. Daylight floods in and the vampire disintegrates. Murnau has captured the scene; his film is complete.

* * *

F. W. Murnau's classic silent vampire movie *Nosferatu* (1922) isn't just the first, but by common consent still the scariest Dracula movie yet made. (Murnau changed the title when he failed to gain the rights to Bram Stoker's novel.) Its power derives largely from the chilling presence of the actor Max Schreck, who plays Murnau's vampire. Bald, cadaverous, bat-eared and rabbit-toothed, moving stiffly upright as though still cramped by the coffin he sleeps in, Schreck seems at once terrifying and pitiable in the urgency of his need for blood. Beside him all other screen Draculas, even Christopher Lee, feel crudely overstated.

Given so compelling a performance, it's not too difficult to suspend disbelief in the central conceit of Elias Merhige's film: that Schreck really was a vampire, cast by the megalomaniac Murnau in the cause of artistic verisimilitude and bribed with the promise of his leading lady Greta Schröder's blood. The film blithely disregards historical fact: far from dying during the shoot of *Nosferatu*, producer Grau and cameraman Wagner went on to make more films, as indeed did Schreck. Nor does the loving recreation of early movie-making technique aim at total accuracy: the slow filmstock of the period would certainly have needed far stronger lighting that we see being used, and the 'night' scenes in *Nosferatu* were in any case shot day-for-night.

But accuracy is beside the point. Music-video director Merhige's second feature (his first, the 1991 experimental film *Begotten*, has an impressive cult reputation) is at once an affectionate homage to the silent era and an ironic metaphor: cinema is the vampire, sucking the blood of those who serve it. 'A theatrical audience gives me life,' says Schröder, gesturing with distaste towards the camera. 'This thing merely takes it from me.' Murnau, making what might qualify as the first snuff movie, is far more of a monster here than Schreck; the vampire acts from compulsion, the film director from artistic hubris. Addressed by his colleagues as 'Herr Doktor' and attired in a long white coat and goggles, Murnau often seems to be playing the archetypal mad scientist. Indeed, he even refers to himself and his crew as 'scientists engaged in the creation of memory', and at the film's climax, set on the North Sea islet of Heligoland, we've clearly reached the Island of Dr Murnau.

Willem Dafoe, though a touch too broad in the face, makes an eerily convincing Schreck, and much of the film's humour derives from the mutual upstaging between him and John Malkovich's Murnau. 'I don't think we need the writer any longer,' insinuates Schreck, visibly salivating, to which the director responds, 'I am loath to admit it, but the writer is important.' Dafoe also catches much of Schreck's pathos, mournfully quoting Tennyson ('Left me maimed/To dwell in presence of immortal youth') or voicing his sympathy with Stoker's Dracula. In one of the film's best gags, he breaks off from this heartfelt speech to snatch a live bat out of the air and snack on it like a chocolate bar.

Merhige is at pains to recreate Murnau's atmosphere. Each time Murnau starts filming, colour drains (or should that be bleeds?) from the frame, and it's sometimes hard to tell whether we're watching a facsimile or a clip from the original. What the film misses, perhaps not surprisingly, is the poetry and the compassion that Murnau brought to his material. To some extent Merhige's film is undermined by its own unevenness of tone, so that the ending, with the destruction of the vampire, can't hope to equal the emotional impact of its source. Still, like Bill Condon's rather more accomplished *Gods and Monsters*, *Shadow of the Vampire* stands witness to the enduring iconic potency of the great classics of the horror genre.

Philip Kemp

THE RIDDLER HAS HIS DAY

David Thomson

In a recent interview for American television's *60 Minutes*, Ridley Scott was about as enthusiastic as his gruff, laconic manner (and advanced age) would allow. He confessed that he was having a tremendous time, better than ever, getting up every morning to make movies. Could there be anything more fun in life? In fact, the man is 61; in effect, he seemed half that age. Is that the secret to carrying on in his very tricky business with his energy and panache – and with such pleasing results? Or are we observing a medium that promotes survival if a man acts half his age? And never gives a hint of that betraying defect – growing up – which is the one disqualification worse than growing old?

As one surveys the American film scene, it's hard to imagine that we will find ourselves celebrating 60-year-olds a decade or so from now. Age, experience and maturity are already anathemas; it can't be long before they cease to exist. People will remember Robert Altman as the last of an aberrant strain. More and more, the old are expected to behave like restless colts, or get out of sight. So it's quite remarkable to see the brindled veteran from South Shields rising to what is clearly a fresh peak, with *Gladiator* and *Hannibal* near-concurrent hits.

But don't ask too many awkward questions about how other people are faring in Hollywood as they reach Scott's age. Sixty is the marker looming up for (or already heavy on the shoulders of) Coppola, Lucas, Scorsese, De Palma, Schrader, Bogdanovich and Friedkin. The movie brats are being urged aside by the sheer rampant callowness of so many nerdy new waves. It's easier to recognise the historical perspective that said that any film-maker working past 60 had better be very strong, very determined or blessed with something like rare insight. Hitchcock was that age, more or less, when he made *Psycho* and *The Birds* – but it's an open question whether these were adult films or those of an old man trying to act young. Hawks was 62 when he did *Rio Bravo*. After 60, Huston made *Fat City*, *The Man Who Would Be King* and *Wise Blood*. Fritz Lang would do *The Big Heat* at 62. Sixtysomething Wilder did *The Private Life of Sherlock Holmes*; Fuller made *The Big Red One* and *White Dog*.

Still, I wonder whether those films weren't also green-lit by guys their age. Today, the decision and the funds depend on 35-year-olds who have likely never seen *Rio Bravo* or *Fat City*. Add a footnote: Max Ophuls, Murnau and Lubitsch didn't live to see 60, while Preston Sturges died at that very age after years of being adrift and after a directing fling of less than a decade – if one omits *Les Carnets du Major Thompson*. In short, are we asking too much to expect that anyone spends a career, or even a life, in film? Isn't there time off for good behaviour?

And Ridley Scott? Well, I'm writing a few days after *Hannibal* opened in the United States. The reviews were mixed, but it's reckoned the film earned $58 million in its first weekend – only *The Lost World Jurassic Park* and *Star Wars Episode 1: The Phantom Menace* have beaten that, and one would like to hope that rather more of their customers were innocent babes (an American marketing concept) than parents allowed to see Dr Lecter's cookery class. Above and beyond that, *Gladiator* – which amassed $190 million in 2000 alone – has raked in 12 Oscar nominations, including best picture, directing, script and actor.

Ridley Scott has not yet won a thing. Indeed, his lone nomination hit.terto – for directing *Thelma & Louise* (1991) – lost to Jonathan Demme for *The Silence of the Lambs*. This is the moment to stress – without so much as a trace of guilt – how much I like Ridley Scott's work. Even the sillier projects – such as *G. I. Jane* (1997) and *Someone to Watch over Me* (1987) – are made with relish and a boy's delight in the surface prettiness of things (you could even say that *Someone* is about falling in love with an apartment). I'm never bored or bewildered by Scott (OK – 1992's *1492 Conquest of Paradise* gets very close), in the same way that for a good ten years or so one could count on Michael Curtiz to be entertaining. Don't regard that remark as patronising – just look at *The Adventures of Robin Hood, Angels with Dirty Faces, The Sea Hawk, Yankee Doodle Dandy, Casablanca, Mildred Pierce* and *The Unsuspected* some weekend and recognise the sheer fluency and movie-ish oomph of an old pro. Curtiz directed those seven films in a ten-year span from 1938 in which he made 27 pictures altogether. Scott, so far, in 25 years has made 12.

What I'm trying to say is that there's no shame if Ridley Scott is only as good or as interesting as Michael Curtiz – he simply doesn't get the practice (or live in the same context of competition). That's exactly why I like *Hannibal* more than some people do. It's a very cunning, very adroit retreat – away from impossible horror and camp mockery, towards entertainment – to ensure that a sequel stays watchable instead of advancing down one of the several crazy (and hideous) dead-ends available. If half the stories of its different directions along the way are true – with two strong writers (if you'll excuse that term) and a narrative commercial/aesthetic quandary as to whether Jodie Foster would do the picture (or it could be made right for her) – then Scott deserves all the gratitude of those who hired him. He brought the movie in. It works. It's smart, good-looking, sexy, fun.

But if you took the Demme film seriously, and have ever regarded the Thomas Harris books in that way (and by 'seriously' I mean as if they were receptacles for intelligence, ideas and concentrated argument), then *Hannibal* is to be regretted. I'm more relieved than hurt because I thought *The Silence of the Lambs* was a collection of excruciating tricks unworthy of Jonathan Demme and essentially dependent on torture, cruelty and putting demented behaviour at the heart of the story. Demme was too good to spare us the pain; and the genre and the medium were too greedy to bypass it. *Lambs* was an ordeal to watch and it was harder than ever to suppose that its gouging impact might not disturb fragile, damaged or already dangerous minds – I'm thinking of the kind of people one meets at the movies these days.

No, I'm not saying that *Lambs* might have been cut, censored or banned – no matter that not too many years earlier no one would have dreamed of making it. Censorship is a more reliable evil than the chance of a movie inspiring some unsteady mind. But if you don't think that's a risk *Lambs* takes – with nothing else of a compensatory nature – then I think you're kidding yourself and adding to the peril.

Of course, *Hannibal* is camp, and not just cooked but marinaded first – whereas *Lambs* was raw and terrifying. I give thanks for that relief, and would only note in passing how far it illustrates a dire problem for mainstream narrative cinema: that the story that worked on its own terms, that held its own reality, yesterday, becomes self-parody tomorrow. It's not just that you couldn't do *Casablanca* or *Mildred Pierce* now without making them pastiche. It is, literally, that Hannibal Lecter has become such a household joke that he can't be dreadful again. It seems clear that Anthony Hopkins and Scott saw that, and planned accordingly. That's how the movie was saved. But don't forget how surely this built-in slope is destroying all the main forms of narrative. Talk to children and teenagers today: they believe that all movies are innately silly, self-mocking and ironic. They no longer hear, feel or see a natural gravity – or the chance of it – in movies.

So Scott turned Hopkins loose after a decade in which the actor had had to 'do' Lecter for every boy, dog and talk show he encountered – while finding that sometimes they did the doctor better themselves. So Lecter now is Capote-ish, large enough for cloaks and Borsalino hats, and capacious enough as aesthete, perfectionist and scholarly scold for his disdain to extend over the rainbow. He is the kind of deliciously wicked uncle Clifton Webb promised as Waldo Lydecker in *Laura*. As fruity as summer pudding. Is the character gay? Well, not in any sense that would alarm audiences or befuddle political correctness. But by the code of, say, the 1940s – yes, indeedy.

What's clever about this smuggled perfume is the fragrance it brings to Lecter's feeling – that sniff he gave her once – for Clarice. Demme grasped that straw, and it was alarming ten years ago that Lecter had smelled out something Starling didn't yet know: that she was sexed. What made that thrilling, or menacing, was Jodie Foster's placing of agent Clarice Starling in a sexual out-of-bounds. Her FBI woman was so very numb and unaware, even if she was of legal age. It was when Lecter looked at her that for the first time she got an inkling of what sex could mean. The rest of the world dreamed of cannibalism, but Foster's eyes widened with the sudden vision of cunnilingus. No, not even the vision – the sensation.

I don't know what happened on the road to *Hannibal*. Maybe Ms Foster the actress prevaricated. Maybe she thought to herself that if they needed her they'd have to pay a fortune beyond even producer Dino De Laurentiis's reach. Or maybe she was playing with herself, because something of the Clarice-Lecter intrigue had really shocked and horrified her. Perhaps she guessed that the outrage would turn camp, and counted herself out; she's smart enough to know how limited her humour is on screen.

So Scott went another way – towards an older, more sexually experienced woman. Julianne Moore looks like a handsome hippy 40; she also looks and reacts like a woman with few fears or illusions left about men. In becoming isolated at the FBI because of her professionalism, even her perfectionism (the thing she really shares with Lecter), she's evidently had enough bad affairs to prefer the company of her computer. But Moore saw the old movie, understood the flicker of attraction, and knows Lecter will lead her to the dance. And she's drawn by the prospect, just the chance, of being eaten.

Looked at that way (I could find no other), *Hannibal* is sexy, dirty, naughty, funny and knowing. Indeed, it has enough to let you notice that Lecter and Clarice are a cartoon version of Humbert and Lolita. It's not enough to make the film intelligent or interesting – and Nabokov's novel is all of that. But it keeps a two-hour picture engaging. The laughs and the gotchas are well paced, and it would take a very earnest soul not to be tickled by the hair-raising act that befalls Ray Liotta. Was there ever a cockier look so oblivious to things happening upstairs?

Then there is Italy, or Florence, which Scott does with the empty flourish he has commanded all his career – as if the settings were ready to be eaten. In this instance there could be a vein of comedy in that, a kind of scenery-chewing hungry tic in Hopkins so he can't pass a quattrocento throw cushion without having a nibble. Long ago, in that first, very arresting picture *The Duellists* (1977), Scott showed his total immersion in the visual language of advertising. Indeed, I have seen no evidence since that his notion of beauty extends one inch beyond the urge to depict landscape, buildings, furniture, clothes – come to that, anything – as if it were purchasable. And so in *The Duellists*, just as one was marvelling at the inane, implacable bond of honour and torment that would forever tie Harvey Keitel to Keith Carradine, there was always the intense but irrelevant urge to get oneself a property in the Dordogne.

Let me try to be more precise, and properly angry, about this. The look of advertising is meant to be ravishing and seductive; it is, if you are persuaded by such words, handsome, spectacular, lush, elegant ... rich, expensive, valuable, luxurious, edible. It is not beautiful, for the plain reason that such eye-pleasing attributes as form, balance, chiaroscuro, depth of focus, harmony of colour and so on are all absolutely poisoned by the function of advertising – to make us envious or insecure about not having this golden thing. So when you look at *The Duellists* you want that magic-hour location, whereas when you look at Renoir's *Partie de campagne* you feel the interaction of human nature and nature itself and thus the seasonal round in which all living things must change and wither. It's the difference between a sense of possession and an admission of mortality, or tragedy (for nothing, truly, is possessed for long).

We know very well that Ridley Scott and his brother Tony have had a commercials company for years. Those are details on a professional résumé, and enough to indicate the lamentable thrust of their art-school training. That's their choice, and they're welcome to it. It has surely added to their fortune. But the movies belong to all of us, and someone needs to insist that there's an oceanic gap between the beauty to be found in Renoir, Fritz Lang, Antonioni, Nicholas Ray and Ophuls and the modern lacquer that's glibly described as 'beautiful photography'. Indeed, granted the advances in technology available to photography nowadays, the majority of cinematography we see deserves to be assailed as slick, lazy, anonymous and 'lush' compared with the movie styles of the 1940s. 'Beautifully photographed' is a term that merges characterless proficiency with the kind of buying eye that so undermines Ridley Scott as an artist. For the 'beauty' in Renoir, Antonioni and the others is not just a way of seeing. It's a way of feeling about nature, structure and the lives led in those settings. It's organic, whereas Scott's eye is a decorative coverlet draped over a world the director doesn't trouble to probe.

Scott's cheery ignorance reminds me of an occasion, years ago, when I taught John Berger's *Ways of Seeing* in an introductory course on film, or looking at the world. *Ways of Seeing* was the book that came from a television series in which Berger attempted to analyse the ideologies (or the lack thereof) in modern notions of seeing and attractiveness. I discussed his annihilation of advertising, and I think – with the advantage of his examples – I made a decent job of it. But at the close of the lecture, a student came up to thank me. Prior to that day, he said, he had felt lost and aimless, uncertain what to do with his life. Now the cloud had moved aside. Sun filled his face. He would go into advertising. I'm sure he's there now, with every right and reason to reckon he's one of the elite shaping the world's understanding of itself.

And if it strikes you that *Gladiator*, say, is beautiful – as opposed to just burnished, collectible and in fine condition – so be it. I found *Gladiator* a sumptuously empty film. Monotonous in plot, muddled in action and daft in its ending, it was determined to knock out the eye while neglecting the mind. It was 'about' nothing except a set of clichés of what Rome was like. But it has 12 Oscar nominations and a patina that normally requires centuries of slavery. It's not a film about Rome, but a wallowing in the Roman look.

All too often such disastrous 'stylishness' besets Ridley Scott. Even what I take to be his best and most interesting pictures – *Alien* (1979) and *Blade Runner* (1982) – are as much concerned with the design of their future places as with the quality of their people. Scott has an escape clause there: the more our world adopts his code of beauty, the less human personality will mean – so the intriguing diminution of human character in these two movies fits with the look of things, and especially their mannered shabbiness. Whether that was intended or comes as accidental bonus, you must decide. Whatever the answer, Scott's facile eye is easier to take with imaginary landscapes or décor, so there's something both magical and sinister in the baroque dankness of the future Los Angeles and the fossilised orgy of the dead planet where the alien lurks.

Twice – with Ian Holm in *Alien* and Sean Young in *Blade Runner* – Scott handled the fascination and pathos of a humanoid not quite all there, yet seeming to lead the way for the rest of the 'full' humans who were already enervated or drained. I've never been convinced that Scott is actually the feminist he's credited as, but still he judged the maturing of Ripley (Sigourney Weaver) in *Alien* very well. Yet it seemed typical, at the end, that he saw no reason not to titillate us with Weaver in her sketchy (designer) underwear while also allowing the large intellectual prospect that the alien had fallen for her character. *Alien* is a very tidy, enclosed study in claustrophobia (it ends in the safety of a sleeping tube), and a satisfying film about a heroine in distress. But Scott deserves more praise because he had felt out the ominous sexual charge of the series to come, and captured the ambiguity of loneliness in space.

To argue that Scott sometimes neglects people in his enthusiasm for 'cinema' or entertainment – that he's more interested in shooting things than in revealing depths – is rather as if someone were spoilsport enough to notice that despite the sweet movie-esque coherence of *Casablanca*, its attitude to people is adolescent and superficial, and thousands of miles away from real war and suffering. Was the war ever quite so much fun? And there's always been a trend in film criticism eager to say that doesn't matter. The same enthusiasm saw the real relief of *Casablanca* as the film opened and declared with wide-eyed innocence – the same state of mind ready to think Paul Henreid has been in a concentration camp as opposed to a country club – that surely films did matter and touch history. Whereas, the 'reality' of *Casablanca* is the story of so many strange refugees – with Conrad Veidt and Dalio the real, heroic victims – gathering together under the warm Warner lights to make a romance. Thus the monstrous villain and the droll sidekick were actually actors who had been deprived of their artistic heritage – and in the case of Dalio that world was one of the finest ever known.

All I am trying to suggest here is that Ridley Scott makes romances – and, for myself, I enjoy them very much, at the level I do the best films of Michael Curtiz. His actual unawareness of human depth is regularly masked by his very acute casting instinct. Remember, long ago, that he guessed what Sigourney Weaver might become – saw not just that she was pretty and smart, but tall, lofty, a touch aloof and chilly, with the seed of truculence, like a young woman raised by the military. He knew that in casting such antithetical figures as Keitel and Carradine (the hipster and the obsessive), he might be home already. He relaxed Geena Davis, he discovered Brad Pitt, he had a rapport with Ian Holm, he felt the pain in John Hurt and knew what might be causing it, he knew where Jeff Bridges's rather mortified heroic nature could be found. He casts very well indeed, and reminds us of the old Hollywood adage: if you cast well, you can leave the actors to it.

But it is up to us – I mean the very small resistance movement ready to read or write about film – to argue that this is not enough. In proposing the equality of Ridley Scott and Michael Curtiz, I am seeking to draw our attention to how little of a subject we have left.

HANNIBAL
USA 2001
Director: Ridley Scott

Ten years after the consultations with serial killer Hannibal Lecter that led to triumph over murderer Jame Gumb, FBI agent Clarice Starling is involved with a bungled shoot-out that leaves five dead. Paul Krendler, Clarice's long-time enemy in the bureau, gains leverage over her as she is blamed for the operation. Wealthy paedophile Mason Verger, disfigured by Hannibal, is buying evidence – and law-enforcement officials, including Krendler – in the hope of taking revenge on his mutilator. Hannibal, on the point of being appointed chief librarian in an archive in Florence, writes a letter of sympathy to Clarice, who works on a scent on the paper to track him down.

Florentine cop Pazzi, investigating the disappearance of the academic whose job Hannibal is after, is prompted by the FBI's request for surveillance tapes from a local perfumerie to identify the fugitive. Learning of the huge reward Verger is offering, Pazzi sets out to trap Hannibal, only for the killer to execute him in the same manner as Pazzi's ancestor, who assassinated Juliano de Medici, was despatched. Clarice, who had warned Pazzi not to try to capture Hannibal on his own, continues to work on the case, despite the persecution of Krendler, and becomes aware that Hannibal has returned to the United States. Minions staking out Clarice's home catch Hannibal after he has visited, spiriting him away to an estate where Verger intends to feed him to giant pigs. Clarice is wounded rescuing Hannibal; Hannibal carries her off after encouraging Cordell, Verger's doctor, to tip his patient to the pigs. Clarice wakes up at

Krendler's summer home, where Hannibal serves Krendler's brain for dinner, trying to seduce her into his lifestyle. Clarice traps Hannibal, but he escapes.

* * *

Thomas Harris has now written three novels featuring genius and cannibal gourmet Hannibal Lecter: *Red Dragon* (1981), *The Silence of the Lambs* (1988) and *Hannibal* (1999). The earlier novels were filmed by Michael Mann (*Manhunter*, 1986) and Jonathan Demme (1991), first with Brian Cox, then with Anthony Hopkins (who returns here) as the character who has gradually come out of his cell and become dominant in the overarching narrative that encompasses all three books and their film versions.

One of the strengths of *The Silence of the Lambs* as a novel was that, although essentially a redraft of the plot of *Red Dragon*, it didn't seem like a sequel. Similarly, since *Manhunter* was a slow-building cult effort, Demme's film has rarely been considered a sequel to it. Contrariwise, one of the weaknesses of *Hannibal*, as novel and as film, is that it can only be considered a sequel, and indeed some aspects of the novel – the writing-out, for instance, of a love interest for FBI agent Clarice Starling established in the *Lambs* book but not the movie – suggest Harris was delivering a follow-up to the film of *The Silence of the Lambs* rather than to his earlier book. Ridley Scott's adaptation of *Hannibal*, which comes from *Manhunter* producer Dino De Laurentiis, whose original deal gives him first refusal on any novel featuring the character, is a further shift in this direction, retaining Hopkins for what is now the star role, but acceptably substituting Julianne Moore for Jodie Foster as Starling, to the extent of rerecording some of the Starling-Lecter interviews with Moore doing her own take on Foster's elocutionised cracker accent.

The major change, which perhaps marks a mutation from series into franchise, is that Hannibal Lecter moves centre stage. In earlier incarnations, he was incarcerated, exerting influence on the outside world and flirting with FBI agents; here, he is at large and at something of a loose end. Though he kills people who get in his way, he has discontinued the serial murders of the 'free-range rude' hinted at in the earlier stories. This Hannibal is almost a heroic vigilante, only seeing off people who deserve it, and doing Clarice the favour of making a stir-fry of her office rival's brain as a Fourth of July treat which seems bound to be remembered as this film's most gruesome moment. A problem of this approach, especially with an ending altered but not much improved from the novel's controversial finish (in which Clarice and Hannibal become a couple), is that the script suffers from the familiar marking-time plotting common among middling series entries. There is much running around and new characters are brought on and killed off, but the fade-out leaves the protagonists exactly where they were at the beginning, with only a few emotional and physical scars to indicate any sense of narrative progression.

Working with a blue-grey palette very like Demme's, director Ridley Scott manages to find his own way into Harris's world, and his ad-man's love of animal, especially bird, images seizes upon that vein of the novel. From his brother Tony's repertoire, notably *The Hunger*, Scott takes a lot of fluttering birds and background classical music, with Hannibal characterising Starling (the name is enough, surely) as a 'diving pigeon'. The third major character is a silent-movie grotesque, Mason Verger, a combination of Phantom of the Opera and Bond villain who was once persuaded by Lecter to cut off his own face and feed it to the dog and who relishes his scheme to get even by feeding his tormentor to anthropophagus boars (wonderfully excessive beasts). Gary Oldman, uncredited at the outset like Boris Karloff in *Frankenstein* (1931), is given a pig's snout-like deformed face and made to be the most purely despicable character in the series to date, whose crimes and bad manners have so offended Lecter that he seems to act as an instrument of cosmic justice in punishing him. A fine scene, played to perfection by Hopkins, has Lecter – who has never laid a hand on Verger – persuade a quivering doctor to shove Verger into the pig pit by offering to take the credit for the killing.

The general lopsidedness of *Hannibal* as novel and film is shown by the way the story clumps around the world. The Florence section sets up the interestingly shaded cop Pazzi – nagged into corruption by his wife's insistence he gets good tickets for the opera – as a new opponent for Hannibal in barbed verbal exchanges that draw on the city's twinned traditions of art and violence. But Starling, who is supposedly providing our viewpoint on the events, never makes it to Italy, and her storyline stops dead while Scott stages an elegant, operatic dance of seduction that pays off with Pazzi's gruesome defenestration. When Hannibal is back in America, the plot turns in on itself, makes a knot and finally disappears. By downplaying the police procedural aspects so strong in the earlier films, this becomes a simple *grand guignol* tale of thwarted revenge, and severely limits the directions in which its heroine can go. If the film series is to continue, it may well be time to summon Will Graham, the hero of *Red Dragon/Manhunter*, who has no patience with Hannibal's charm and can still match his darkness with enough daring to bring the supervillain down.

Kim Newman

GORILLA WARFARE

Andrew O'Hehir

Near the end of Tim Burton's *Planet of the Apes* the time comes when Captain Leo Davidson, the twenty-first-century American astronaut played by Mark Wahlberg, must kiss two females goodbye. Davidson has been rescued from almost certain death in the cataclysmic battle between humans and apes by the arrival of an unlikely *deus ex machina* that's one of the most literal-minded uses of that device in film history. Now he can leave the ape-dominated planet and the distant-future era where he has been stranded and make his way homewards through space and time.

One of his snogging partners is a flaxen-haired beauty played by former model Estella Warren, whose appearance suggests that even though the planet's humans are reduced to primitivism and slavery, they still have access to lipstick, eyebrow pencil and other crucial styling aids. The other is a chimpanzee revolutionary named Ari, played by Helena Bonham Carter with an endearing assortment of twitchy, snuffling, louse-picking simian mannerisms. A member of the ape aristocracy whose father is a moderate leader of the Senate (meaning he stops short of advocating the wholesale extermination of humans), Ari has sided with the cause of human liberation against her own kind, out of principled conviction or a prurient interest in Davidson or both.

Of course we in the audience can see the glamorous actress behind the ape mask; this scene goes nowhere near the taboo territory of Nagisa Oshima's *Max mon amour* (1986) in which Charlotte Rampling plays a woman who falls in love with an actual chimp. Still, a ripple of something – curiosity or arousal or discomfort – went through the crowd at the Manhattan preview screening I attended. In the event, both kisses are chaste (and the Warren one rather more lingering). So Burton's film remains indecisively suspended between conformity and transgression, even as Wahlberg speeds off towards the requisite surprise ending. (This one is borrowed from the satirical 1963 novel by Pierre Boulle, rather than from Franklin J. Schaffner's landmark 1968 film, which ended so memorably with Charlton Heston weeping beside the Statue of Liberty's ruined torch.)

Like much of Burton's work, *Planet of the Apes* represents a B-movie aesthetic elevated to the level of mega-budget spectacular and then overloaded with themes, images and references to the point of incoherence. As far as I know, no critic or academic has adequately theorised the process by which a classic genre or exploitation film – *Shaft* or *Planet of the Apes* or *Invasion of the Body Snatchers* (and we'll see about *Rollerball*) – is remade as a mass entertainment, inflated with a pompous sense of its own significance and loses the edge of anger or cynicism or paranoia that made it powerful in the first place. Burton's *Planet of the Apes* is superior in every technical respect to Schaffner's, but it's also more cluttered, less self-assured, more diffuse in its impact.

This doesn't look so much like a reconceived version of the Schaffner film as a later and more sumptuous edition of it; the scrambled classical-gothic-Indian-arabesque design of the apes' planet remains intact but is developed to an exquisite extreme. As advertised, Rick Baker's remarkable ape costumes are in a tangible sense the stars of the production, since they allow actors as various as Carter, Tim Roth, Paul Giamatti and Michael Clarke Duncan to create distinctive, almost operatic-scale characters who are decidedly more interesting than the film's humans. There are impressive action sequences and striking tableaux and, in Roth's sneering General Thade – along with Carter's, the film's stand-out performance – a compelling villain whose malevolent intelligence is devoted to learning every destructive lesson the interloper from human civilisation can teach him. In fact, it's the anodyne Davidson, the apparent hero of the film, and not Thade, who is the story's real vector of evil. Perhaps this makes *Planet of the Apes* more interesting as parable, but correspondingly flatter as drama. Burton never appears interested in Davidson's dilemma, and seemingly abandons Wahlberg to wander around the set gawking at the monkeys. One almost feels the director sees the real story as the struggle between Ari and her ex-lover Thade over the future of ape civilisation, and rather wishes the interfering human – significant mainly as a love object or plot device – would get out of the way.

Indeed, if the 1960s and 1970s *Apes* films were documents of racial guilt – as became increasingly obvious the longer the series went on – this one is a document of species guilt. Burton and his screenwriters (William Broyles Jr, Lawrence Konner and Mark D. Rosenthal) offer a jittery catalogue of millennial anxieties, from the hazards of genetic engineering and the corrupting influence of technology to ecological catastrophe and weapons of mass destruction. Davidson tells his group of ape and human renegades that on his planet (i.e. ours) the great apes have been wiped out in the wild and survive only in zoos or scientific breeding programmes like the one aboard his space station. And in case we haven't got the message yet, Burton also provides a portentous cameo by Heston, as Thade's dying father, telling his son that 'no creature is as devious, as violent' as a human being. (There's a gag of sorts underlying this scene: Heston is the real-life president of the principal gun-owners' group in the US, and his character apparently possesses the planet's only firearm.)

Between the film's sermon on human evil, the spectre of forbidden love and Burton's abiding affection for misunderstood outsiders, embodied here in Carter's human-loving chimp, there seem to be numerous opportunities for narrative tension and conflict. Instead the writers largely rehash the plot of the Heston film, and more generally the standard Odyssean saga of an adventurer far from home in a world turned upside down. A cynic might well wonder whether Broyles et al. had a recent example in mind: you could describe this *Planet of the Apes* as a remake of Ridley Scott's *Gladiator*, with monkey suits as well as centurion armour (not to mention a dose of the Hong Kong-style aerial work belatedly brought to Hollywood's attention by *Crouching Tiger, Hidden Dragon*). Like Russell Crowe's Maximus, Davidson is enslaved by those he once commanded and becomes the nemesis of a usurper (Roth's General Thade in place of Joaquin Phoenix's Commodus) who seeks to wrest imperial power away from a dithering Senate. But unlike Maximus, Davidson is more of a vacancy than a commanding presence, and his struggle to return to his own time and place seems petty amid the chaos and intrigue and overwhelming production design around him.

Wahlberg has agreeably played a series of working-class guys thrown into unusual circumstances in such films as *Boogie Nights*, *Three Kings* and *The Perfect Storm*, but he's strikingly ill at ease with the hero's mantle here. Davidson seems alternately repulsed and bewildered by this brave new world and its creatures, and Wahlberg lacks either the stoical, masculine gravitas that made Crowe the undisputed centre of *Gladiator* or the sheer scenery-chewing histrionics of a Heston or a Kirk Douglas. In fact, it's hard to resist the notion that Burton and the writers have deliberately undercooked the character; we learn nothing about Davidson's life except that he cares about his chimps and that his friends on Earth are having a pool party without him.

We begin in the year 2029, aboard the space station *Oberon* where Davidson is helping train a race of genetically engineered superchimps to serve as deep-space test pilots. (If you suspect this sinister project might have unintended consequences, well, you're nearly as clever as the film-makers.) When one of his prize specimens disappears with a shuttle craft into some kind of electronic disturbance in space, Davidson defies orders and goes after him. Flung several centuries forwards by the same electro-whatsit, he crash-lands in a jungle lagoon on an unknown planet just as a group of the area's wild humans, led by Kris Kristofferson, are being captured and enslaved by the stronger, more agile apes.

Davidson is a desperately dim character; it appears intellectual standards in the US military haven't trended upwards since 2001. He struggles to understand the planet's social order, asking Warren, who plays Kristofferson's daughter, 'What made these monkeys like this?' Reasonably, she replies, 'How should they be?' It takes him most of the movie to grasp what the audience already knows – that he is far in the future and the crew of the *Oberon* and everyone he knows on Earth are dead.

As for the fact that everyone on the planet speaks idiomatic English, Davidson neither seems to notice nor acts surprised. The original *Planet of the Apes* film franchise found an ingenious way of justifying this B-movie convention, of course, since the planet in question turned out to be Earth. (Never mind that the intervening centuries of isolation would have produced a variant of English as distant from our own as Chaucer's was.) Burton's planet is not Earth, although as Davidson laboriously discovers after his escape from captivity and pilgrimage into the desert, there is a historical connection between the two. Still, the fact that the apparent linguistic anachronism is never addressed seems bothersome here in a way it didn't in the earlier films, perhaps because higher production values imply greater attention to detail and less naked allegory.

As Davidson and his fellow prisoners are brought into the ape city in the same rope-lashed wooden carts used to transport Heston, we get a brief, intriguing glimpse of a stratified ape society complete with juvenile delinquents and pot-smoking beatnik musicians. Here Burton strays into the terrain of science fiction as social satire, suggesting George Lucas or Gene Roddenberry (or indeed Rod Serling, co-writer of the first *Planet of the Apes*) at their most sophisticated. As any fan of the films knows, this society has clear caste hierarchies: chimpanzees like Thade and Ari are the intellectual leadership, warlike gorillas (including Duncan and Cary-Hiroyuki Tagawa) provide the muscle, and the buffoonish orangutans focus on business matters. (Giamatti provides a little classic Hollywood comic relief as an orangutan slave trader in the pusillanimous tradition of Bert Lahr's Cowardly Lion: 'One thing you don't want in the house is a human teenager,' he assures a potential customer.)

But the moments when we see what Burton's *Planet of the Apes* might have been only make clear how formulaic and tedious it largely is. The script creaks audibly during a long, slow early patch when we seem to be waiting for the production to catch up with the audience: apes argue tiresomely about whether humans are predisposed to evil or possess souls; Davidson tiresomely explains that on his planet apes are trained to beg for treats. (This echoes Roddenberry and Serling at their most pedantic.) Worse still are the efforts at waggery: 'Extremism in the defence of apes is no vice,' says one character. 'You can't solve the human problem by throwing money at it,' says another.

When Carter appears as Ari, sniffing at Davidson in distinctly erotic fashion, the movie momentarily seems to find a centre and a direction. He holds a knife to her throat and, like the human heroines of entirely too many films, she loves him more for it. But Burton and the writers lack the courage or the foolhardiness to push this interspecies romance too far (even sci-fi bestiality would surely spark Christian boycotters in several US states) and it gets shuffled to the margins of the story. Pursued by Thade, the would-be Prometheus who wants to learn whatever he can about human technology before killing Davidson, the renegade non-couple head out for the territories along with Warren, a few other human escapees and a gorilla warrior turned peacenik (Tagawa).

Planet of the Apes, like most of Burton's films, is full of grandiose imagery that grows wearying before it ought to, perhaps because the elaborate production design and unstable *mélange* of film-making styles seem unconnected to any sense of narrative necessity or economy. As always, some scenes are worth watching on any terms, including the striking night-time battle sequence on a riverbank plane studded with illuminated tents, which recalls the Kurosawa of *Ran* (1985), and a final confrontation between apes and humans in the desert that seems closer to the grand set-pieces of David Lean. There are also faint but plausible echoes of Kubrick's *2001: A Space Odyssey*, along with a dunderheaded rehash of Henry V's St Crispin's Day address to his troops. ('Our history is full of men who did incredible things,' Davidson tells his ragtag band of brothers. 'Sometimes even a small group can make a difference.')

In contrast with the brutal, wordless simplicity of the Schaffner film's conclusion, this movie has numerous puzzles to work out in its last few scenes, with mixed results. What is the significance of Simos, the Shiva-like ape deity to whom superstitious gorillas pray? What are the sacred ruins of Calima, where Davidson's homing beacon leads him? Why does the arrival of Davidson's missing chimp in its spacecraft make all the apes forget about killing the humans? What sense are we to make of the transformed twenty-first-century Earth to which Davidson finally returns? (I think I have figured this out, though it took me several days.) And is there anyone or anything in the whole movie we care about besides Ari, the class traitor who has been branded as a human and a slave and then abandoned by the man she loves?

It's nothing new for a Burton film to be a magnificent edifice of design, a great work of adolescent imagination built around an inconsequential narrative and a hollow central character. As one critic observed on the release of *Batman* in 1989, the title character was three-quarters Batsuit and one-quarter Michael Keaton (which may have been a generous analysis). But at least Batman's alter ego, oddball millionaire Bruce Wayne, like Johnny Depp's dotty detective in *Sleepy Hollow* (1999) recognisably belonged to the Ed Wood–Edward Scissorhands family of eccentric loners who engage Burton's instinctive sympathy. *Planet of the Apes* is less whimsical than *Mars Attacks!* (1996) but it has some of the same pointless, miscellaneous quality and a similar sense that the director may be half-consciously sabotaging his own work.

On one hand it's ludicrous to suggest that Burton is a victim of his own success, since becoming a big-budget Hollywood director was the only thing he ever wanted. Perhaps that's the problem; big-budget Hollywood directors don't have the autonomy they used to, unless their name is Lucas or Spielberg. Burton, one might propose, longed to bring the aesthetic of cult horror and sci-fi fandom to a mass audience, in much the same way as Douglas Sirk once did with romance and melodrama. He wasn't alone in this; David Cronenberg and Paul Verhoeven, to cite the obvious examples, parlayed their hip outsider status into lucrative Hollywood projects that stretched the boundaries of mainstream sci-fi. But that window of opportunity seems to have closed, and both those film-makers have had to choose between diverging paths. *Hollow Man* was standard-issue Hollywood action adventure, easily the most conventional film of Verhoeven's career, while Cronenberg (voluntarily or not) has returned to low-budget Canadian obscurity.

In the era of the global mass audience and CGI effects, mainstream cinema – or at least spectacle cinema – is becoming an increasingly conservative and almost anti-narrative form. This is the kind of pronouncement elitist critics conventionally make, but such summer hits as *Pearl Harbor* or *The Mummy Returns* or *Lara Croft Tomb Raider* make no pretence of offering plot or character beyond a set of reassuring poses and gestures, as familiar as the stock figures of grand guignol were in an earlier day. Stories and characters that don't fit this pseudo-heroic spectacle model are now primarily the province of television, or of the worldwide independent cinema that has accepted its marginal niche and now seems to be thriving; call it the democratic flipside of globalisation and digital technology.

There are, of course, other former independent film-makers who have successfully adapted themselves to Hollywood. Steven Soderbergh is viewed, with some justification, as the reigning prince of mainstream drama, while Gus Van Sant appears to have suppressed every impulse that once made him seem dangerous. But no one wants or expects Burton to make heart-warming, realistic drama. He is supposed to deliver mock-gothic teenage darkness, the flavour of outsiderness and eccentricity without, so to speak, any of the calories.

It would be difficult, and perhaps impossible, for a film-maker of Burton's status to make a reversed-polarities version of *Planet of the Apes* that embraced the damaged and alienated Ari as its heroine (and no truly independent director would get the chance in the first place). So he accommodates himself more or less uncomfortably to his material, squeezing characters or elements that engage his attention into the corners when he can. It may be unfair to blame the Hollywood system, rather than Burton himself, for his predicament. His own shallowness and cavalier attitude towards story are at least partly responsible for turning him into a hired hand almost indistinguishable from Barry Sonnenfeld, an artificer who wraps formula in the trappings of cool. At any rate, he doesn't seem happy about it. Is there a way back to Tim Burton's home planet from here, and does it still exist?

I Still Know What You Did Last Summer (Danny Cannon, 1997)

Section 4:
Case Study – Teenage
Postmodern Horror

In contrast to the section of pieces on 'films', this case study has to cope with a flow of movies. Sub-genres come and go swiftly, and the resurrection of the teenage slasher movie in the late 1990s raced through the traditional cycle – an outrider (*The Craft*) to precede the breakthrough (*Scream*), imitations, sequels, follow-ups, revivals, rip-offs, more works from creators (writer Kevin Williamson is the key figure) associated with the form and, perhaps finally, a low comedy (*Scary Movie*) sending up the conventions of a sub-genre that always had a streak of parody.

Wes Craven, director of *Scream*, originally passed on Williamson's script (initially entitled 'Scary Movie') because it seemed so archetypal as to be not worth making. Craven, of course, was a key figure in at least two earlier slasher cycles, the ferocious (*The Last House on the Left*, 1973, *The Hills Have Eyes*, 1977) and the fantastical (*A Nightmare on Elm Street*, 1984) and, an ex-academic, had already made an extensive argument with his own metafiction in *Wes Craven's New Nightmare* (1994). It seems likely that the success of *Scream*, on a scale that could trigger a cycle, had as much to do with its pitch to a teenage demographic, with the canny (and imitated) use of popular but inexpensive young faces familiar from TV mixed with 70s kitsch holdovers (Linda Blair, Henry Winkler), as with the undoubted skill of its self-aware deployment of horror clichés that audiences raised with video and cable were all too familiar with and Craven's near-unmatched ability to stage and edit suspense sequences.

Like most such cycles, the Screamers burned out like a brushfire. There were mutations as the style was applied to related genres (*The Faculty* is a *Scream* take on *Invasion of the Body Snatchers*, 1956) or even to tart up old properties for a new era (*Disturbing Behavior* is a teen rethink of *The Stepford Wives*, 1974), and the influence was felt in television – in *Buffy the Vampire Slayer* and other (mostly short-lived) high school horror/sf shows (*Roswell High*, etc). It is suggestive of how fast these kids got old that Williamson's directorial debut *Teaching Mrs Tingle* bypassed theatrical distribution in the United Kingdom, which means a review commissioned when it seemed liable to turn up in cinemas makes its debut here to serve as an epitaph for a particular style.

BLOOD SISTERS

Linda Ruth Williams

Try to imagine what *Buffy the Vampire Slayer* would look like if it had been written by Angela Carter and you might get close to the heady cocktail of high-school pubescence and feminist folklore that is *Ginger Snaps*. This is the story of 16-year-old Ginger (Katharine Isabelle) and 15-year-old Brigitte (Emily Perkins), two repressed, weird, goth-styled sisters whose bland Canadian suburb happens to be plagued by a werewolf. *Ginger Snaps* is a sparky, sharp film marked by intelligent dialogue and a complex view of that moment when girls hover on the brink of womanhood but would rather not take the next step. If Carter's Red Riding Hood fell for her wolf and ran off with him in Neil Jordan's *Company of Wolves*, here the bitten girl becomes the wolf. Ginger is attacked on the night she first menstruates, and as the clock of her cycle ticks away to its conclusion on Halloween 28 days later, she metamorphoses into a sinewy, sexualised monster with a nice line in teenage sarcasm.

Ginger Snaps – directed by John Fawcett, whose previous work includes episodes of *Xena Warrior Princess*, and written by Karen Walton – is a radical film in a number of ways, not least in its twist on the economies of punishment that haunt the horror genre. Teen horror pivots on the motif of the sexualised couple punished for their fornication (memorably expounded in such films as *Halloween*, 1978, and *Friday the 13th*, 1980; remorselessly parodied in the *Scream* series), and at first *Ginger Snaps* appears to promote this viewpoint by violating its virgin heroine/monster at the instant her sexual/reproductive functions kick in, suggesting that simply to cross the threshold to womanhood is sufficient to bring the hellhounds to your door. Yet the consequences of feminisation are not so simple. *Ginger Snaps*'s sister heroines are essentially female Peter Pans who have contrived to delay the onset of menstruation for years, masking their terror of adulthood with a performance of supreme adolescent alienation. And who can blame them for not wanting to join the ranks of women? From the school nurse who chirpily explains just what the fertile future holds and the huge wall of sanitary products that confronts the girls at the supermarket to the kooky mother (brilliantly played by Mimi Rogers) who announces to all present at the family dinner table that 'Our little girl's a young woman now' while producing a luridly red celebratory strawberry cake, the choices on offer are hilariously horrifying.

But *Ginger Snaps* also glories in the notion that being a woman is in itself such a crime, one might as well be hanged for a sheep as for a lamb. In one memorable scene in the girls' toilets, Brigitte insists to her sister: 'Something's wrong – like, more than you being just female.' If Ginger's new-found femininity has already 'cursed' her to a life of blood-stained knickers (which Mom finds lurking in the dirty laundry), she might as well immerse herself in a riot of bloodlust and have done with it. 'Can this happen to a normal woman?' a kitsch television commercial queries early in the film. To which the answer – for Ginger at least – is a resounding, 'Yes, precisely because she's a normal woman.'

Yet there are also things one can neither help nor control, the film seems to say. As the pet-dog corpses that litter *Ginger Snaps*'s suburbs remind us, the beast is non-judgmental in his (or her) violence. As in *Jaws*, this is a film in which everyone is potentially meat. One can glory in it or be a victim to it, and Ginger prefers to glory ('I get this ache,' she says, 'and I thought it was for sex, but it's to tear everything into fucking pieces'). Here femininity is a precondition of violence, and violence offers Ginger an alternative to the sexual stereotyping that surrounds her. ('No one ever thinks chicks do shit like this. A girl can only be a slut, a bitch, a tease, or the virgin next door.') An audacious thought indeed for a genre traditionally driven by the testosterone of male adolescence.

But even before the werewolf strikes, Ginger and Brigitte are no ordinary high-school babes. While their contemporaries are going all the way with their boyfriends, these girls prefer the pastime of staging and photographing elaborately grotesque suicide scenes. Part of the film's fun comes from its ability to take a range of grand metaphysical concepts – especially those two great pillars of philosophy and psycho-analysis, sex and death – and run them through the filter of the suburban teenage female mind. What comes out may not be pleasant (the film is visceral and gory), but at least it's interesting.

Ginger Snaps is haunted by stories of high-school massacres (notably Taber and, from across the border, Columbine) which makes its glorious take on a schoolgirl gone (literally) wild a sensitive subject. The film also nods to contemporary notions of sexual morality in its casting of werewolfism as a blood-borne disease that can be caught through the 'consumption' of carnality. Where the early-1990s spate of vampirism-as-Aids narratives figured 'haemosexuality' as a metaphor for STDs (mirroring Bram Stoker's syphilis in the 1890s), here it's werewolfism that's sexually transmitted. As Ginger's external conscience, Brigitte reminds her that violation of the safer-sex code has its consequences: 'You gave it to Jason – you had unprotected sex and you infected him!' But this is just the starting point for a meditation on the biology that defines the condition. Proposing a rational solution to an irrational malaise, the film's Van Helsing figure, drug dealer Sam, retorts, 'Biology! Now there's something you can sink your teeth into ... You're real, your problem's real, the solution's real.' Here Walton's screenplay echoes David Cronenberg in its reference to lycanthropy being 'like an infection, it works from the inside out. It's like a virus.' But if Cronenberg plumps for a poetics of the flesh that finally celebrates the 'world turned upside down' of bodily rule, *Ginger Snaps* refuses to choose. It's a testament to these two young actors' performances that Brigitte's monster-hunting control and Ginger's monstrous derangement are equally sympathetic and alienated.

The arc of the film owes much to John Landis's *An American Werewolf in London* – in particular its buddy story and bleak conclusion which posits that the beast has no sentiment, no room for love and no memory of loved ones. But the questions of identity lost, found, then lost again go further in *Ginger Snaps*. Though the relationship between Ginger and Brigitte is akin to that between twins, the age gap between them pitches them on either side of the pubescent divide. Cinematic twins are often figured as dark and light reflections of each other (from Robert Siodmak's classic *The Dark Mirror*, 1946, to Gregory Hippolyte's kitsch *Mirror Images*, 1991), but the properties of sameness and difference Ginger and Brigitte manifest make them more like Alice and her looking-glass reflection.

When Brigitte deliberately infects herself with Ginger's malaise, she declares, 'Now I am you.' To which Ginger replies, 'I know you are, but what am I?' It's a good question. The 28 days the story tracks show Ginger hovering between a number of identities – human and beast, victim and violator, virgin and whore. All do service to describe the anxious moment of adolescence many a great horror film has tried to articulate (*The Exorcist*, 1973; *Carrie*, 1976) – but seldom with such a strong interest in the point of view of the girl herself. US critic Carol J. Clover once wrote that in our dreams we straddle the divide between monster and victim: 'We are both Red Riding Hood and the Wolf.' Ginger is a girl who walked in the woods and came back as the wolf disguised as a teenage virgin, a wolf in girl's clothing.

REVIEWS

THE CRAFT
USA 1996
Director: Andrew Fleming

Sarah, aged 17, has just moved to Los Angeles with her father and stepmother. She joins St Benedict's Academy, and tries to sit near three girls, Nancy, Bonnie and Rochelle, who freeze her out until she makes a pencil move around on her desk through force of will. A young football jock, Chris, warns Sarah that the three girls are 'the bitches of Eastwick'. In fact the girls have formed a secret coven devoted to witch-craft. They ask Sarah to join them and they visit a shop devoted to the mystic arts.

Having refused to sleep with Chris, Sarah hears he is spreading rumours that she's a lousy lay. Nancy says the same thing happened to her. It is revealed that Sarah's mother died giving birth to her, and that Sarah tried to commit suicide because of nightmares about reptiles. In the woods the four girls perform magic rites and make wishes. Sarah wants to be loved by Chris. Bonnie wants to be beautiful, Rochelle wants not to hate those who hate her, and Nancy wants to absorb the powers of Manon, an evil deity. Their wishes come true: Chris becomes unbearably fixated on Sarah. Bonnie's scars miraculously heal. School racist Laura's hair starts to fall out. Nancy is the only one whose spell apparently isn't working, but later, her abusive stepfather is struck down and killed.

The girls can now change their appearance. Nancy attempts to seduce Chris in the guise of Sarah. Sarah interrupts and Nancy sends Chris crashing through a window to his death. Wanting out of the group, Sarah, who has natural witch powers, performs a ritual to prevent Nancy doing harm to herself and others. She is pursued by the other members of the group in her dreams, urging her to kill herself. She fights them off by invoking the powers of her mother, who was also a witch. Order is restored, Bonnie and Rochelle visit Sarah at home, and Sarah demonstrates that her powers are still intact, while their powers have disappeared. Nancy, however, is in a lunatic asylum.

* * *

Advertised as a cross between Brian De Palma's *Carrie* and the Jane Austen-inspired teen satire *Clueless*, *The Craft*, writer/director Andrew Fleming's second feature (his first was the effective romantic comedy *Threesome*), is spot-on in its essaying of female teenage angst. It evokes a dreamy sensuousness of mood in which the idea of witchcraft is taken seriously, and not just as a metaphor. The script from Peter Filardi is entirely insightful and sympathetic to its young coven of outsiders, Sarah (Robin Tunney), the suicidal teen with real powers, Bonnie (Neve Campbell), who has burn scars, Rochelle (Rachel True) the black girl in school and Nancy (Fairuza Balk), who was abused in childhood.

From the opening storm as Sarah arrives by plane in LA to the final sequence in which her nightmares of snakes, maggots and rats suddenly become real, *The Craft* is drenched in atmosphere. The early scenes in which the four girls experiment with witchery are replete with blood and wine. If some of the standard teen movie twists that their spells then bring about are pure hokum – such as when Sarah makes football jock Chris fall in love with her, or when Nancy 'becomes' Sarah to seduce him – they chime well enough with real teenagers' fantasies of empowerment. And the moment when the coven's powers are unleashed is truly exhilarating, although *The Craft* exhibits its good taste in not pushing the 'nasty' tone too far. For example, when the Rochelle-baiting racist beauty Laura Lizzie's hair falls out we're invited to sympathise, not to gloat.

Thus Fleming never betrays his pact with teen fantasy. When the witchery starts to go horribly wrong, as it must, *The Craft* refuses to put its maverick quartet back on the straight and narrow – they remain committed outsiders, treated with sympathy and considerable indulgence. The closest *The Craft* comes to a conventional morality is through the maternal homilies of Lirio (Assumpta Serna), the mystic shopkeeper. 'Whatever you send out, you get back times three,' she warns them. But the girls have their own pithy tenets. For example, when they're on their way to a shoplifting spree, Bonnie tells a doubtful Sarah that, 'everything in nature steals'.

The Craft is full of gorgeous young actresses – high-school girls have rarely been given such an appealing lustre – but it also has great visuals, sure drama and applied intelligence: a rare combination in horror movies.

Chris Savage King

SCREAM
USA 1996
Director: Wes Craven

Woodsboro, the United States. Casey Becker is pestered by a phone prankster who plays a deadly trivia game with her based on horror films. He murders her boyfriend because she misidentifies the murderer in the first *Friday the 13th* movie, then kills her. The next target of the masked maniac is teenager Sidney Prescott. She is already traumatised by the death of her mother a year ago and is being persecuted by tabloid television reporter Gale Weathers because she may have mistaken her mother's lover for the murderer. When Sidney survives an encounter with the stalker, her boyfriend Billy Loomis is arrested. He is let free after the menacing calls are traced not to his mobile phone but to Sidney's father, who is supposedly on a business trip.

Sidney takes refuge with her friend Tatum Riley, while Gale tries to seduce Tatum's brother Deputy Dewey. During a party at the Riley house, Tatum is murdered. News comes through that the slasher has gutted high-school principal Himbry and hung him on the football field. Most of the teens leave to have a look, while the nerdy horror movie fan Randy, who has explained the do's and don'ts of living in a horror film, watches *Halloween*. Sidney finally surrenders her virginity to Billy, thus losing her invincibility as a horror film heroine. Billy, apparently attacked by the slasher, turns out to be the killer himself, acting in concert with Tatum's boyfriend Stuart. The killers have abducted Mr Prescott, whom they plan to murder as part of the game. Sidney, Randy and Gale confront Billy and Stuart, and despatch them.

⁕ ⁕ ⁕

The initial cinema horror cycle was started in 1931 by Universal Pictures with *Dracula* and *Frankenstein*, and ended by the same hands in 1948 with *Abbott and Costello Meet Frankenstein*, which lampooned the monsters the studio had nurtured for over a decade and half and defused them as figures of fear. The slasher-movie cycle which more or less dates back to *Halloween* in 1978 and *Friday the 13th* in 1980 yielded far more films than the Universal cycle, and fast-forwarded to its Abbott and Costello phase in 1982, when a run of parodies (*Whacko!, Student Bodies, Pandemonium, Saturday the 14th, National Lampoon's Class Reunion*) appeared.

However, the burst of parody did not stem the flow of sequels and imitations, and the form was even revivified in 1985 by Wes Craven's *A Nightmare on Elm Street*, which cannily injected a dose of the supernaturally irrational into the slasher film's cliché-ridden unlikeliness. After a run of *Elm Street* sequels, not to mention an almost unabated flow of returns to *Friday the 13th* and *Halloween*, Craven kicked the form beyond parody into postmodernism with *Wes Craven's New Nightmare*, which was – until *Scream* – the most self-aware, self-reflective slasher ever made. If anything can Abbott-and-Costello the slasher movie, *Scream* may be it: though it offers witty parody, in-jokes like the barely-glimpsed school gardener dressed in a Freddy Krueger hat and jumper, and does not neglect to be genuinely scary, *Scream* is mostly concerned with rigorously dissecting and discussing the formula elements of its sub-genre.

Randy, the video store geek, spouts non-stop slasher movie trivia, most amusingly when the teens' video of *Halloween* is cut into the film proper, so that Randy's comment of 'and now for the obligatory breasts shot' is applicable to Sidney and Billy's love scene as well as P. J. Soles's role in John Carpenter's film. (Craven rather sweetly avoids showing actual nudity in either *Scream* or the extract from *Halloween*.) Moments later, the scene-within-scene sense of infinity applied as Randy shouts 'look behind you' at Jamie Lee Curtis on screen while the madman lurks behind his sofa, a scene simultaneously restaged in Gale's remote-broadcast van as Sidney and a technician watch a feed from a spy camera planted in the house, shouting 'look behind you' at an equally unheeding Randy. This approach allows for likeable cheap jokes, like Randy's 'I never thought I'd be so grateful to be a virgin' as he survives the climax and Sidney's quickfire reaction when Randy says, 'and this is the obligatory moment when the killer comes back from the dead for one last scare'.

There is, however, a bit more depth to the parody, with former English professor Craven and screenwriter Kevin Williamson using the self-referentiality to discuss in quite high-flown tones the interconnectivity of the movies and reality (though the archetypal horror movie town seen here is less convincing as a 'more real' level of fiction than the movie business of *New Nightmare*). The opening sequence, with Drew Barrymore drawn into the deadly game by a phone caller, is an effectively unsettling rerun of the opening of *When a Stranger Calls* (perhaps significantly not referred to in the dialogue), with the killer's first appearance eliciting screams from the audience I saw it with. The finale incorporates some thoughts on the imitation debate, when Sidney accuses the murderers of being influenced by too many horror movies only to be told: 'films don't make psychos, they just make psychos more creative.' She then probes for some motivation and they insist: 'it's scarier when there's no motive … they never figured out why Hannibal Lecter liked to eat people.'

It's a shame that Williamson's superior original title (*Scary Movie*) was replaced with something as generic as *Scream*, though it's possible that the archetypal and not inapt title has been as responsible for the movie's surprise runaway success as its many undoubted assets. Like *Halloween* and *A Nightmare on Elm Street* and unlike *Friday the 13th* and *Prom Night* (lesser known, but a big influence on the whodunit angle), *Scream* has a strong junior cast and benefits from Craven's interest in and liking for the kids. This school body may be convincingly callous about rushing off to get a look at the disembowelled principal and given to acting out tactless jokes with masks and knives, but it's hard not to like the characters as they flirt, joke and talk movies with a video generation familiarity with the conventions ('how about a PG-13 relationship?'). Neve Campbell makes a strong heroine, and the bright Rose McGowan is genuinely in the spirit of *Halloween* in the role of the heroine's about-to-be-murdered (but also to-be-missed) best friend.

A Nightmare on Elm Street – 'the original was okay, but the sequels sucked' declares Drew Barrymore's character – had elements of genuine humour that actually boosted the horror, a lesson forgotten in the wise-cracking follow-ups. This is a funnier movie, satirising tabloid television attitudes and offering a sweet performance from David Arquette as a fumbling young deputy, but it doesn't neglect the shocks and scares. If it never quite revs up the tension as well as it does in the opening scene, it still manages the extraordinarily difficult task of juggling jokes, thoughts and jumps. Craven has never lost his editor's knack of knowing when to cut on a 'boo!' or throw in an eerie image (the scream face reflected in a dead open eye). The real miracle of *Scream* may be that for all its footnotes and cleverness, it plays as a film its Randy the Nerd would love.

Kim Newman

I KNOW WHAT YOU DID LAST SUMMER
USA 1997
Director: Jim Gillespie

The fishing community of Southport, New Carolina. On the night of the Fourth of July, Helen Shivers wins the Miss Croaker beauty contest. She celebrates by going out with her boyfriend Barry Cox, best friend Julie James and Julie's boyfriend Ray Bronson. Because Barry is drunk, Ray drives the group home in Barry's car, but they run over someone on the coast road. Fearing for their futures if they go to the police, the teenagers decide to dump the body. At the last moment, the victim turns out to be still alive but Barry still tosses him in the sea. All promise to keep this secret.

A year later, Julie receives an anonymous letter reading: 'I know what you did last summer.' Barry's first suspect is Max, who has a crush on Julie, and so Barry threatens him. Before long, a mysterious figure dressed as a fisherman kills Max and injures Barry. Julie and Helen visit Melissa, the sister of David Egan whose body was found soon after the accident. The girls get a lead on a possible friend of David's who might be the avenger. The fisherman cuts off Helen's hair the night before she has to ride as the outgoing queen in the Fourth of July parade. He then disrupts the celebrations by murdering Barry, a police officer, Helen's sister Elsa and Helen herself.

Julie realises the body they dumped was not David's but Benjamin Willis's, the father of a girl who was killed in an accident he blames David for. When they hit him, he had just murdered David. For a moment, Julie suspects Ray is the real killer and flees to a boat owned by Willis, who actually survived the accident. Willis menaces Julie, but Ray saves her and Willis is lost overboard. A year later, Julie and Ray have come through their trouble, but Willis has survived and attacks Julie.

* * *

The success of Wes Craven's *Scream*, soon to yield the inevitable *Scream 2*, has clearly given a jump-start to the played-out slasher genre. This adaptation of Lois Duncan's well-regarded young adult suspense novel, scripted by Kevin Williamson – the writer of *Scream* – flirts occasionally with the self-awareness of the Craven movie. Helen and Julie cite Angela Lansbury in *Murder, She Wrote* and Jodie Foster in *The Silence of the Lambs* as they venture out to an isolated farmstead in search of clues, and they take the names 'Angela' and 'Jodie' while posing as stranded motorists and ineptly questioning a woman about her dead brother. However, Williamson is more careless this time round. Here, he displays without irony hackneyed devices such as a corpse which is found in Julie's car boot but then disappears without trace when she brings her friends back. The smart soundbites of *Scream*-style kidspeak tend to be outweighed by clunky lines ('I'll call the cops on your college quarterback ass') and thumping clichés ('Oh my God, this isn't happening!').

Scream's intricate homage-cum-deconstruction approach excused its wholesale pillaging of tropes from other horror movies. Here, the effect is a lot like arrant filching: the shadowy killer in a fisherman's oilskins has been done in the fishing-themed slasher movie *Blood Hook* (aka *The Mutilator*). The small-town celebration backdrop recalls *My Bloody Valentine* and *The Prowler* (aka *Rosemary's Killer*). And the cynically callous finale is a less clever twist on the similar punchline of *He Knows You're Alone*. Any other writer might be able to claim unfamiliarity with such 1980s sub–*Friday the 13th* sludge, but one of the things demonstrated by the *Scream* screenplay is that Williamson has seen an awful lot of slasher movies and has a pretty good recall for detail.

The major disappointment of *I Know What You Did Last Summer* is that the first reel is rather good. Its quartet of kids have genuinely complex relationships, and their potential big futures are sketched economically, suggesting how imperilled they might be. Ray's status as the upwardly mobile son of a fisherman is contrasted with Max, the loser doomed to a life cutting bait. Helen's beauty queen confidence is subtly contrasted with her embittered, abusive elder sister Elsa (the glamorous Bridgette Wilson, cleverly cast as dowdy). She clearly went the same route and ended up running their father's general stores. Even the odious rich jock Barry (whose fault it all seems to be) and the goody-goody lawyer-wannabe Julie are given just enough depth to make their predicament intriguing.

The film starts to drift during the crucial road accident scene which skews the action to exonerate prematurely the four kids. The central section of the film is bogged down by detective work which trots out a great deal of confusing plot information. At least this allows for an evocative cameo by a luminous Anne Heche that shows up the pretty teenage leads. But the shared guilt of the quartet and the *Shallow Grave*–style moral choices they make are eventually revealed to be a false premise.

Furthermore, the elaborate probing of motive and backstory is scuppered when the slasher is revealed as an indiscriminate lunatic, the incarnation of the hook-handed madman of urban legend, who ups the body count by gutting enough of the supporting cast to fill the trailer with gory moments.

Kim Newman

SCREAM 2
USA 1997
Director: Wes Craven

Windsor, Ohio. At a preview of *Stab*, a film about the Woodsboro murders (the story of the film *Scream*), a copycat masked murderer kills students Phil and Maureen. Sidney Prescott and Randy Meeks, survivors of the rampage of Sidney's mad boyfriend Billy Loomis, are at nearby Woodsboro College. Sidney's new boyfriend is Derek; her friends include film students Cici and Mickey and room-mate Hallie. Drawn to town by the new murders are reporter Gale Weathers, whose account of the Woodsboro murders formed the basis of *Stab*, Dewey Riley, an ex-deputy, who is offended by Gale's mercenary exploitation of the events; and Cotton Weary, once unjustly imprisoned for one of Billy's murders.

Randy reasons the new murderer is mounting a 'sequel' to the original crimes and, after Cici is killed, the police give Sidney constant protection. The killer murders Randy and stabs Dewey. After slaughtering Sidney's guards and Hallie, the killer pursues Sidney to the campus theatre. There, he reveals himself to be Mickey and murders the helpless Derek, explaining that he intends to use his trial to test out a defence that he was compelled to kill because of his addiction to violent movies. Mickey is acting in concert with local reporter Debbie Salt, who is actually Billy Loomis's equally mad mother, out for revenge. Sidney and Gale, assisted by Cotton, overcome and execute the killers, and it turns out that Dewey has survived. Sidney allows Cotton, who has wished to exploit his tangential part in the original murders to become famous, to be acclaimed as a hero.

*   *   *

Wes Craven has already delivered the ultimate postmodern sequel in *Wes Craven's New Nightmare*, which withdraws from the frame of the *Elm Street* series to ask questions about what the whole thing means. So he is in something of a quandary with *Scream 2*, which is hipper and slicker than *New Nightmare*, but zooms in rather than pulls back. Though characters express sentiments like 'sequels suck!' and Randy the Movie Nerd is on hand to explain the rules of sequels as he once explained the rules of slasher movies, this pointedly never evokes *New Nightmare* or the underrated *Psycho II*. Instead, it plays riffs not only on disappointing sequels (don't forget Craven's *The Hills Have Eyes, Part II*) and the 1980s run of campus-set slasher movies (such as *The House on Sorority Row*) which co-existed with the high-school-set slasher movies referenced by *Scream*.

There is on the surface quite a lot going on here. *Scream*'s screenwriter Kevin Williamson reunites with Craven to intersperse the scares with jokes that call into question the whole issue of performance. Derek tries to win back Sidney by imitating Tom Cruise's serenade from *Top Gun*. Drama professor David Warner directs theatre major Sidney in an amazingly pretentious student production which has her pursued by a killer chorus in Greek masks. Extracts from *Stab* re-create scenes from *Scream* with worse acting (Tori Spelling plays Sidney) and more obvious horror effects, itself quite an achievement. And one murderer's rant that he intends to use the 'effects' controversy as the basis of his defence is one-upped by his partner's admission that she's killing people for good old-fashioned revenge.

By explicitly setting out the rules by which the story operates within the narrative itself, Williamson borrows a trick from the writer John Dickson Carr, who was wont to drop essays on locked-room murders into his fictions. A less happy debt is to Agatha Christie, who realised that without exactly cheating you could have two apparently unrelated murderers act in concert and thus get away with it by giving them both alibis. As with the out-of-nowhere motivations and heavily misleading set-ups that seem to put all the characters into the frame, this means the finale isn't quite satisfying. As in *Clue*, the film based on the board game, *Scream 2* could have been shot with any number of endings, revealing any of the characters as guilty, so each possible resolution has equal weight.

Though a superbly crafted scare-and-smirk machine, *Scream 2* is ultimately affectless. The early deaths of Jada Pinkett and Sarah Michelle Gellar, staged with flair in the unusual setting of a crowded cinema and the almost insultingly archetypal one of a deserted sorority house, are shocking and saddening, but only because the actresses are so appealing. The film is obliged to spend most of its time with Sidney, who – through no fault of Neve Campbell – is the least realised character in sight. When the ostensible hero is murdered near the end, the show's almost over so there's no point getting worked up about him.

Nevertheless, *Scream 2* deserves points for including so many infallible indices of guilt among its suspect list: Dewey's nerve-damaged handicap (how many crippled villains have risen from their wheelchairs for the finish?); David Warner and Laurie Metcalf's familiar faces in apparently minor roles (Roy Thinnes and Farley Granger had similar turns in horror films and were guilty); Jamie Kennedy's resentment at being a supporting character (an equivalent geek in *The Dorm that Dripped Blood* is the killer). The glee in all this knowingness is infectious, but in cleverness and self-awareness the film becomes all surface. Viewed as a follow-up to Craven's best work – from *The Last House on the Left* and *The Hills Have Eyes* through *A Nightmare on Elm Street* to *New Nightmare* – *Scream 2* is rootless, a picture whose immediately engaging factors are eerily bereft of anything like a subtext.

Kim Newman

HALLOWEEN H20: Twenty Years Later
USA 1998
Director: Steve Miner

The United States. It is 20 years after Laurie Strode was terrorised on Halloween night by her homicidal brother Michael Myers. Since then, she has faked her death, changed her name to Keri Tate and become the principal of Hillcrest, a private school in California. Now a heavy drinker, overprotective of her son John and in a relationship with school counsellor Will Brennan, Laurie is still plagued by visions of Michael.

On Halloween 1998, most of the school goes away on a field trip but John stays behind to be with his girlfriend Molly and his friends Charlie and Sarah. Meanwhile in Illinois, Michael learns of Laurie's new identity and address after he murders Nurse Marion, the assistant of the late Dr Loomis who once treated Michael. At Hillcrest, he sneaks past gatekeeper Ronny, then stalks and murders Charlie and Sarah. Laurie tells Will about her past and produces a gun when she becomes aware of Michael's presence. However, Will mistakenly shoots Ronny before he is himself killed by Michael. Laurie gets John and Molly to safety but stays on the grounds to go after her brother with an axe. Michael is apparently killed in a fall. Ronny turns out to be only wounded and the police arrive to mop up. But, convinced her brother is still alive. Laurie hijacks the ambulance in which his body is stirring. She crashes the ambulance, pinning Michael under the wreckage. The siblings almost hold hands, but Laurie finally decapitates Michael.

* * *

In 1978, *Halloween* was the spookiest kid on the block. After a decade of such increasingly intense, ultra-violent, downbeat movies as *Night of the Living Dead* (1968) and *The Texas Chain Saw Massacre* (1974), John Carpenter's low-budget sleeper rediscovered the fun of horror films. While George Romero, David Cronenberg and others used the genre to dissect a disenchanted post-Vietnam, post-Watergate America, Carpenter was old-fashioned in his commitment to being scary rather than horrific, playful rather than challenging. Wittily written and performed, with an admirable refusal to explain or understand its monster, the film was also technically innovative. Using a then-new Panaglide camera and his own memorably simple score, Carpenter delivered 91 minutes of real suspense, made a new star of embattled babysitter Jamie Lee Curtis and demonstrated that sudden appearances could be more shocking than buckets of gore. Then there were the sequels…

Halloween H20: Twenty Years Later is equipped with an old-fashioned, windy title. But inspired by the recent revival of the slasher cycle in the *Scream* movies (a brief clip from *Scream 2* plays on television in *H20*), it attempts to revive and tie off the franchise for the 1990s. Oddly, though there are *Halloween* snippets in flashback, the storyline is rooted in the revelation of *Halloween II* (made in 1981, the era of 'Luke, I am your father') that Michael is Laurie's brother. (The use of Chordettes' evocative song 'Mr Sandman' dates back to that, too.) Since that disappointing follow-up and the one-off aside of *Halloween III: Season of the Witch*, there have been three more drab sequels which squandered the late Donald Pleasence. The body counts went up as the intelligence quotient came down. On the whole, *H20* ignores those movies – though the last one was made only three years ago – and uses the return of Jamie Lee Curtis as an excuse to pick up where her character, last seen in *II*, left off.

Given how dreary the Michael Myers sequels are, it is hardly much of an achievement that *H20* is the best of them. Steve Miner, who directed parts 2 and 3 of the *Friday the 13th* series (there's a hockey-mask gag in the opening scene), is not up to the John Carpenter of 1978 but shows a tighter grip than the Carpenter of recent years. The mis-step that the sequels took, prompted ironically by the *Friday* series and dozens of other *Halloween* imitators, was in upping the gore effects, emphasising the slashing over the stalking. There are nasty moments here (Sarah's leg trapped in a dumbwaiter) but Miner remembers that the Michael of *Halloween* was more interested in making his victims jump than in killing them.

H20 manages to pull off a great many of those distinctive shocks where someone, either Michael or an innocent party, lurches unexpectedly into the frame, prompting a collective gasp. The fate of Charlie is exemplary. The build-up involves the unfortunate kid retrieving a bottle-opener dropped into a dangerous-looking garbage disposal. The pay-off simply has Michael appear – Charlie's face is reflected in a close-up of the killer's eye – then cuts on Charlie's unexpected reaction ('Oh, hello') without showing us his actual death.

Given that she was the initiator of the project, it is unsurprising that the film is tailored to Curtis's strengths. The first half gives us a credible grown-up version of the girl we saw suffering in her first films, uptight every Halloween and so afflicted by hallucinatory Michael appearances that when he really shows up she blinks and hopes he'll go away. Though Curtis is good throughout, the script is a lot blunter than Carpenter and Debra Hill's original screenplay. Here, the story is hung up on the sibling relationship but no one ever asks why Michael feels a need to murder his family. Curtis shines in a couple of scenes with Adam Arkin which require her to convey exposition with menace. And in a neatly unstressed joke she discusses trauma with *Psycho* veteran (and Curtis's real mother) Janet Leigh ('we've all had bad experiences,' Leigh counsels). Curtis is most on the money, however, in the sustained finale which finds her making an attempt to settle the family business once and for all, paying off with a reversal as Michael finally shows feeling for his sister and Laurie responds by demonstrating that she too has his capacity for ruthless violence.

H2o is brisk (87 minutes), mostly involving and plays expertly on its audience's expectations – delaying the action for a long time, then replaying moments from the original but with different outcomes – but it's still a *Halloween* sequel. Even Carpenter and Hill dropped the ball in *Halloween II*, and a great many of the earlier films' failings are also reproduced here: the comic-relief character of Ronny is annoying; Josh Hartnett carries most dramatic weight but is least interesting of the four fresh teenage faces introduced; the story dawdles for half the film before kicking in; and you can't escape the nagging question of what Michael has been doing all these years and why he is still wearing the outfit (a stolen boiler suit and mask) he improvised in the first film. The final scene seems to offer definitive closure, but a close reading of the last reel reveals a loophole that could allow further sequels.

Kim Newman

THE FACULTY
USA 1998
Director: Robert Rodriguez

Herrington High School, Ohio. After a faculty meeting Principal Drake is attacked by Coach Willis and slashed to death by another faculty member, Mrs Olson. The next morning new student Marybeth tries to befriend Stokely, a moody loner. Class nerd Casey finds a strange organism on the football field, and shows it to the science teacher, Mr Furlong. School-newspaper editor Delilah explores the faculty room with Casey. While hiding in a closet they espy Willis and Mrs Olson implanting an organism in the school nurse, Miss Harper, and find the corpse of another teacher. Casey and Delilah flee, but are stopped in their tracks by a resurrected Drake, to whom they describe what they saw. The police are called, but Miss Harper appears fine while the corpse is gone.

By now, the entire student body is acting strangely – only Casey, Delilah, Stokely, Marybeth, jock Stan and school dope-peddlar Zeke seem themselves. Furlong attacks them but Zeke dispatches him by sticking an ampoule filled with drug powder in his eye. Examining the creature Furlong disgorged in his death throes, Zeke identifies it as an alien parasite that can be killed using his dehydrating caffeine-based compound. Stokely speculates that if the mother alien is killed, everyone will return to normal. Zeke tests the drug on himself and forces the five other kids to take it too: Delilah is exposed as an alien. Soon the other teenagers become aliens, until only Casey and Zeke remain. Marybeth reveals herself to be the mother alien, mutates into a huge gorgon and is finally slain by Casey. Life reverts to normal.

*   *   *

'You're that geeky Stephen King kid. There's one in every school,' sneers class bitch Delilah to bullied misfit Casey in director Robert Rodriguez's sci-fi horror-comedy *The Faculty*. At once you recognise the strange country you're in: it's 1990s pastiche-land, where the citizens are all trash archetypes and the most prominent local custom is tireless self-referentiality. The film marks the historic union of Rodriguez (*El Mariachi*, *From Dusk til Dawn*) and screenwriter Kevin Williamson (*Scream* and *Scream 2*). Perhaps because of the doubling up of such commensurate talents, *The Faculty* effectively cancels itself out. It isn't the least bit scary or particularly involving, but that seems to be the point.

Back in 1976, when Brian De Palma kicked off the whole metatrash industry with *Carrie*, the joke was that something synthesised from scraps of old teen exploitation pictures could still be so affecting. *The Faculty* salutes its great schlock ancestor by casting Carrie's mom Piper Laurie as one of the teacher-aliens (though it's pure synchronicity that the production designer is named Cary White). But the De Palma flick appears the soul of authenticity by comparison. For a radical evolutionary leap has taken place, and the new joke of *The Faculty* is how easily it can do without the traditional suspension of disbelief.

Inevitably, the script offers ample latitude for Williamson's signature conceit: the characters frequently break off their adventures to engage in learned colloquia on the very genre they inhabit. As in the *Scream* films, specialist knowledge of movie clichés becomes a survival tactic: here sci-fi nerd Stokely deduces the existence of a queen-bee alien by remembering *Alien*. Unsurprisingly, the *Ur*-text is *Invasion of the Body Snatchers* (1956), and Williamson even pilfers one of its key lines of dialogue: 'It is so much better. There is no fear or pain.' However, *Body Snatchers* belonged to a world where cultural anxieties found metaphorical expression in pulp. Rodriguez and Williamson have gone beyond all that. Their version of pop cinema cheerfully dispenses with subtext. There's not the faintest pretence that *The Faculty* is about anything but its own sly nudging and winking at the viewer. You aren't seriously meant to care whether these kids succeed in resolving their varieties of teen angst; you're mainly supposed to twig their parodic resemblance to the gang in *The Breakfast Club*. And though the climactic monster puts on quite a bravura show, it doesn't generate a soupçon of primal horror. Instead, you sit there chuckling over the effects and – when the camera ducks underwater for a brief swimming-pool contretemps – the stylistic cribs from *Jaws*.

Rodriguez's entire technique feels similarly hand-me-down. His gratuitous point-of-view tracking provides an ironic gloss on just about every thriller made in the past 20 years. But if *The Faculty* has all the poetic resonance of a round of Trivial Pursuit, at least it manages to be genuinely sportive. One advantage of the movie's elaborate gamesmanship is it demands interactive participation; audience and film-makers enter into a gleeful, knowing complicity. Rodriguez and Williamson assume young viewers these days have racked up considerable expertise in the rules of genre, and *The Faculty* is among other things a nifty meditation on genre mixing. Loosely yoking together creepy crawlies and teen anomie, the film takes as its emblem the cut-and-paste hero Zeke: part nihilist hipster and part brilliant boy-scientist. The script specifies him as a 'contradiction', and indeed the character makes no sense until one realises that his whole purpose is to be a witty bricolage.

The Faculty consistently draws attention to its own ill-joined cracks and seams. There's no telling why alien possession acts as an aphrodisiac on the teachers, yet converts the students into stock zombies (though the latter leads to the film's funniest image: a classroom where every hand is raised). And it's equally useless to fret over the hazy rationale by which some characters get a second chance, while others seem polished off for good. For in a vertiginous postmodern enterprise such as *The Faculty*, cleverness and clunkiness turn out to be the same thing.

Peter Matthews

I STILL KNOW WHAT YOU DID LAST SUMMER
USA/Germany 1998
Director: Danny Cannon

Although she survived an encounter with psycho-killer Ben Willis (now missing, believed dead) student Julie James is still haunted by dreams in which Willis pursues her. At college, she is drifting away from Ray, her boyfriend from back home who also survived Willis. Her room-mate Karla is trying to fix her up with genial Will Benson. When Karla wins a radio contest she invites Julie to come with her and her boyfriend Tyrell on a Fourth of July weekend break on a Caribbean island. Julie asks Ray to make a fourth but he turns her down so Karla invites Will instead.

Changing his mind, Ray drives to Boston but is attacked by a slicker-clad killer who looks like Willis. Ray escapes from hospital, and to buy a gun he pawns an engagement ring he bought for Julie. When they arrive in the Caribbean, the party discover that it's the last day of the season and a hurricane is expected soon. Julie is tormented by messages like the ones Willis used to send, and the hotel's few staff are murdered one by one. Estes, the voodoo-practising caretaker, explains that Willis used to work at the hotel, but left after he murdered his wife. Tyrell is also killed by the murderer, and Will helps Julie to escape only to reveal himself as Willis's son, working with his father to complete the family's revenge. Ray arrives with the gun, and he and Julie are able to overcome and kill the murderers. A year later, Ray and Julie are married, but Willis still seems to haunt them...

* * *

Picking up from *I Know What You Did Last Summer*, in which the heroine seemed to be killed by the mad Ben Willis, this sequel opens and closes with scenes of Julie meekly going about her business when Willis attacks her. Evidently, these shocks are all supposed to be dreams. But they are no more contrived or hokey than the supposedly real scenes they bookend, and have the effect of turning the whole film into little more than a feeble series of jolts. If Julie's death can be revoked at any moment by having her wake up screaming, then there's no point getting too concerned about her.

The original film, itself no masterpiece, at least had a strong premise, from Lois Duncan's novel, and complicated its characterisations by an unusual class awareness. This follow-up briefly evokes the pressures making Julie and Ray break up. The strain stems more from their earlier ordeal than from the fact that she's an A student destined to make it in the big city and he's a fisherman stuck in a small town. And in place of the first film's credible fishing-town setting, this one plays out in an unlikely Caribbean resort which shuts up over the Fourth of July weekend but still rents out suites during the storm season. Director Danny Cannon claimed he wanted to evoke the deserted Overlook mansion of *The Shining*. But this is a cramped hotel and all the settings are anonymous (except in a silly scene in which Julie is trapped on a sunbed as her friends struggle to free her without thinking to turn it off). The hurricane's meteorological threat, meanwhile, proves no more than a stiff downpour.

Having gone from being promising to washed-up without passing through a phase of success, Cannon – who turned down the original film and has pretended not to be humiliated in interviews – here does a job calibrated solely to score enough at the box office in order to make him bankable again after his *Judge Dredd* fiasco. However, this kind of picture is unlikely to impress anyone after the opening-weekend grosses are in. For a moment it seems some satiric point about the dumbness of slasher-movie characters is being made when three college students don't know what the capital of Brazil is. Yet that thread is never picked up and instead, we get a sustained exercise in irritating black stereotyping from Brandy and Mekhi Phifer and thin-faced quivering from Jennifer Love Hewitt.

The self-awareness and 1990s attitude Kevin Williamson brought to the *Scream* films and *I Know What You Did Last Summer* have by now completely washed away. Along with *Urban Legend*, this does its best to seem like an exact copy of such middling slasher films of the 1980s as *He Knows You're Alone*, *The Burning*, *Madman* and *Hell Night*. When Tyrell mocks the panicky Julie by asking her if she saw Jason or Freddy in the shadows, the film overreaches itself. With its father-and-son villain team, it is at once a whodunit and a franchise wannabe that hopes to elevate Willis, with his fisherman's slicker and Captain Hook hand, to the psycho pantheon. In 20 years time, characters in slasher movies won't be invoking Ben Willis the way this one invokes Jason and Freddy. Moreover, given that this sequel is set two years after the supposed crime of the original, and the finale of the first film revealed that Julie and her friends hadn't actually done anything they should feel bad about, even the title of *I Still Know What You Did Last Summer* doesn't bear thinking about.

Kim Newman

DISTURBING BEHAVIOUR
USA/Australia 1998
Director: David Nutter

The small town of Cradle Bay, the United States. Grieving over the suicide of their eldest son, the Clark family arrive from Chicago. On his first day at the local high school, remaining son Steve is introduced to its various cliques by alienated Gavin Strick and his albino friend U.V.: among them are the Blue Ribbons, an exclusive gaggle of overachievers. Later, Steve meets school guidance counsellor and Blue Ribbon-Svengali Doctor Caldicott, and Rachel, another of Gavin's friends. Gavin tells Steve he believes the Blue Ribbons are a murderous cult.

Meanwhile, a Blue Ribbon attacks Rachel in the school boiler room, only to be foiled by janitor Newberry. That evening, Gavin discovers his parents are planning to have him recruited in to the Blue Ribbons. Terrified, he flees. However, the next day at school he appears among the Blue Ribbons. Steve and Rachel steal the school's staff files and learn Caldicott came to teaching from a career in neuropharmacology. They realise the Blue Ribbons are victims of his experiments in mind control. Steve and Rachel are captured be Caldicott, but Newberry intervenes once more, saving the pair in a kamikaze rescue bid which simultaneously wipes out the Blue Ribbons. Caldicott is also killed. Steve, Rachel and U.V. depart the now-deserted Cradle Bay. Weeks later, in an inner-city high school, a new student teacher is introduced to the class: Gavin Strick.

* * *

Although mostly a recasting of Bryan Forbes's overwrought thriller *The Stepford Wives* (1974) as a morality tale for Marilyn Manson fans, *Disturbing Behaviour* nonetheless wastes little time in pillaging stylistic touches from a slew of other sources. Barely a frame goes by without a touch of *Twin Peaks*, a scintilla of *The Lost Boys*, or even – in its hysterical finale – a quick rummage through *A Clockwork Orange* (1971).

However, director David Nutter's primary influence is *The X Files*, for which he directed several episodes, and *Disturbing Behaviour* exudes – notably in the jarring fades to black which pepper the film – an essentially small-screen sensibility. Of course, this approach has its compensations (the pacing, for example, is agreeably brisk). On the whole, however, Nutter seems ill at ease with the physical expansion, and his narrow range of atmospheric panning shots and extreme close-ups of eyeballs only goes so far.

Nutter also hovers nervously around the semi-parodic without ever embracing the downright frothy tropes of, say, *The Faculty*. The dialogue in particular oscillates between one-liners so studied they could almost pass for Gregg Araki ('Self-mutilate this, fluid girl,' remarks one anonymous Blue Ribbon baddie) and impossibly banal, apparently straight-faced moments of exposition ('Neuropharmacology?' quivers Steve, 'You mean *mind control?*'). Ultimately, the same schizophrenic impulse pervades the entire film: it's too pompous to be camp, but too silly to be genuinely engaging.

None of which is helped by the script's reliance on leaden clichés. The characterisation consists mostly of lazily written archetypes – the chisel-jawed hero, mourning the dead brother, the feisty chick sidekick with her barbed-wire tattoos, and, with Gavin before his transformation, the Holy Fool. Yet even dealing with such ciphers, Nutter cannot maintain any narrative coherence amid the series of virtual non-sequiturs which precede the resolution, for instance, we're left wholly in the dark over why the nefarious Caldicott would actually want to brainwash a bunch of pimply ingrates into improving their grades and side-parting their hair. As a consequence, all that remains is a confused paean to a generic notion of individuality, tailor-made for the noble outsider fantasies of perpetual adolescence.

Danny Leigh

SCREAM 3
USA 2000
Director: Wes Craven

Hollywood. Cotton Weary, a talk-show host once unjustly convicted of the murder of Maureen Prescott, is killed by someone masked like the murderers who have terrorised Maureen's daughter Sidney. Producer John Milton is working on *Stab 3: Return to Woodsboro* (the latest film in a series based on the murders that have revolved around Sidney), with music-video director Roman Bridger making his first feature, Dewey Riley working as a technical adviser and actresses Jennifer Jolie and Angelina Tyler cast as real-life figures Gales Weathers, a news reporter, and Sidney.

When actors Sarah Darling and Tom Prinze and a security expert are killed, *Stab 3* is shut down. Gale digs further into the story and Sidney comes to help. It turns out that Maureen was once a starlet at the studio, leaving Hollywood after an orgy at one of Milton's parties. At Roman's birthday party, the killer strikes again, murdering Roman, supporting actor Tyson Fox, and Jennifer and Angelina. Sidney confronts the masked maniac, who turns out to be Roman (who faked his own death), her long-lost half-brother. Having prompted the original Woodsboro killings, he has been taking his rage out on the family he feels cheated out of. Sidney kills Roman.

* * *

In one of the wittiest moments in *Scream 2*, film nerd Randy, explaining the rules of sequels, wound up his argument with 'and if you want your sequel to turn into a franchise, never ever...' only to have his thought cut off before his wisdom could be delivered. Randy pops up again here via a video-diary entry. Explaining what happens when your sequel turns into a trilogy, Randy tells us to expect any character could be the killer and survivors from the earlier instalments will end up dead. Sadly, *Scream 3* is not nearly ruthless enough to go through with this delicious warning/promise.

With original screenwriter Kevin Williamson now pursuing a directorial career, series director Wes Craven is here partnered by screenwriter Ehren Kruger (*Arlington Road*). There's a sense that Craven's emotional investment was in his significantly named 'personal' project *Music of the Heart*, completed last year, leaving this to come together by itself. Has Sidney Prescott been so abused in two *Scream* movies that she has herself become the new killer? Is her dead mother, whose murder kicked the whole thing off, coming back as a ghost to add a supernatural twist? Will Riley and Gale, fake-killed several times in the earlier entries, finally die for real, or get to be unmasked as the secret fiends behind it all? The disappointing revelation here is that a new character with far less dramatic weight than the killers in the first two films is guilty, and Sidney gets to gun him down for a pat wrap-up.

The Hollywood setting allows for a pleasant succession of in-references and gags. Jenny McCarthy has a great set-up-for-death speech as she complains about being a 35-year-old playing a 21-year-old who takes a shower before getting killed, and there's a neat cameo from Carrie Fisher as a studio functionary who claims not have won the part of Princess Leia because she didn't sleep with George Lucas. The best thing in the film is the bickering between Cox Arquette's Gale and Parker Posey as the Method actress who thinks she's better at being Gale than Gale herself. With the exception of a chase through a soundstage, Craven rarely exploits the potential for suspense of his Hollywood setting. Mostly, his visual imagination seems stretched thin; the stalk-and-slash scenes are directed merely with anonymous competence. A warning to the avaricious: if Randy the movie geek has left another video testament, it might well cite *Omen IV* and *Halloween IV* through *H2o* as dire examples of what happens when your trilogy is complete but the producers go back to the well. If you want your trilogy to become a franchise, make something grander than *Scream 3*.

Kim Newman

IDLE HANDS
USA/Germany 1999
Director: Rodman Flender

Bolan, California, a few days before Halloween. The parents of slacker teenager Anton are murdered by a mysterious force, but Anton doesn't notice. He continues to hang out with his dope-smoking friends Mick and Pnub, and fantasise about Molly, the cool girl who lives across the street. Meanwhile, Druid priest Debi is tracking an evil force which takes possession of the lazy and turns them into serial killers.

Anton finds his parents' corpses and calls Mick and Pnub over, only to have his hand – which is possessed – murder them. While Anton tries to get Molly to help, the hand makes advances to her that Anton follows through on. Mick and Pnub come back to life as zombies and suggest Anton consults with heavy-metal kid Randy on the subject of satanic powers. Anton hacks off his possessed hand but it continues to make mischief. Debi hooks up with Randy, who leads her to Anton. They track the hand to the school dance, where more teenagers are killed but Anton saves Molly. Later, Mick and Pnub return from Heaven as angels.

*   *   *

This likeable, if minor, slacker horror comedy is a reworking of the intermittently popular crawling-hand theme, exemplified classically by *The Beast with Five Fingers* (1946), although the splatter-comic elements here also seem inspired by a subplot from *Evil Dead II* in which Bruce Campbell battled with his possessed, amputated hand, a plight closely resembling that of *Idle Hands*'s luckless Anton.

It's an infallibly funny gambit, and Devon Sawa's writhing fingers create a real separate character. There's an undeveloped suggestion that the evil hand is acting out

Anton's desires, as when it gropes Molly, thus landing the timid slacker the girlfriend he would otherwise never have got round to approaching. The film's nugget of irony – based on the proverb 'idle hands are the Devil's playground' – is unforced, but also rather thrown away.

Roger Corman-stable veteran Rodman Flender (director of *Leprechaun 2*) worked previously in television (*Tales from the Crypt, Dark Skies*). He marshals sick slapstick very well, using a Dario Argento-inspired colour palette still unusual in American horror movies. The amiably blank Devon Sawa, credible as a clod who uses a back-scratcher to scoop a remote control when it's out of reach, performs impressive contortions before the evil hand is hacked off his wrist, pulling off the hard trick of approaching Bruce Campbell's skill at battling an apparently rebel body part. Once chopped off and microwaved, the hand is 'played' by Christopher Hart, who handled Thing in the *Addams Family* films. Hart matches Sawa's moves and creates a distinctively different crawling hand from his earlier character. Thing was perky and inquisitive, this hand is sneaky and cruel. Among many horrid japes, the funniest and crassest moment comes during the obligatory teenage backseat make-out scene, as a girl realises her breasts are being fondled by three hands.

As is the fashion with teenage horror films at the turn of this century, *Idle Hands* is more of an ensemble piece than a solo venture. This diffuses its potential for real scariness but also means potential dead spots are filled by scene-stealing supporting players. While Jessica Alba is appealing, most of the work is done by double acts, such as Vivica A. Fox and Jack Noseworthy as, respectively, the Amazonian Druid priestess and the bewildered heavy-metal kid, and especially the vastly underrated Seth Green and Elden Henson as Mick and Pnub, who return from the dead because 'Some voice said, "Walk into the light," but it was, like, really far, so we said "Fuck it."' Raised from the dead, the teens pull a few *Re-Animator* routines: Pnub has to carry around his severed head or jam it back onto his stumbling body with a fork, but the nicest joke is that these zombies would rather lie on the sofa watching MTV eating cheesy snacks than consume human flesh.

Kim Newman

TEACHING MRS TINGLE
USA, 1999
Director: Kevin Williamson

Leigh Anne Watson, the bright daughter of a struggling single mother, needs to graduate ahead of swot Trudie Tucker to become class valedictorian and win a scholarship which will enable her to go to college and escape her small town. To do so, she must get an A on her history project from the fearsome Mrs Tingle, a tyrannical and arbitrarily hateful teacher. After Mrs Tingle has ridiculed her work in class, Leigh Anne is in the gym with her best friend, aspiring actress Jo Lynn Jordan, when class rebel Luke Churner approaches her with a stolen copy of Mrs Tingle's final history test questions. Mrs Tingle catches the three, and indicates that she will tell the principal and that the cheats will all be expelled.

After school, all three kids go to Mrs Tingle's house and fail to reason with her, whereupon they semi-accidentally graze her with a crossbow bolt, then tie her to her bed. Jo Lynn imitates the teacher's voice to call in sick, and the three take shifts holding her captive. When Coach Wardell, a married teacher, comes to the house for an assignation with Mrs Tingle, the kids blindfold him, get him drunk and take blackmail photographs of the adulterous pair. Leigh Anne finds Mrs Tingle's grade book and alters the marks so that she comes out ahead of Trudie, while Mrs Tingle works hard to persuade Jo Lynn that Leigh Anne is manipulating her and cutting in on Luke, in whom Jo Lynn is interested but who has slept with Leigh Anne. In a final confrontation, Mrs Tingle escapes and Jo Lynn pretends to support her in order to save the others, and Mrs Tingle fires the crossbow at Trudie, who is turning up to complain about her grade. The principal fires Mrs Tingle, and Leigh Anne becomes valedictorian.

*   *   *

Teaching Mrs Tingle, more bluntly and mendaciously entitled *Killing Mrs Tingle* until the recent American kerfuffle about homicide in high school, was the screenplay Kevin Williamson sold before his rise to prominence with the *Scream* films, the television show *Dawson's Creek* and spin-offs such as *The Faculty* and *I Know What You Did Last Summer*. In the event, the property has become his own directorial debut and, arriving in concert with the failure of a follow-up television show *Wasteland*, suggests the shelf-life of his brand of media-savvy, self-dramatising teenager has more or less expired. It is typical of Williamson's always-clever but too-often lazy writing that we are supposed to accept Leigh Anne's history project – a re-created diary of an accused Salem witch, written by hand in period ink on period paper in an authentic leather binder – as worthy of an A, even though the single sentence read out from it contains a hideously stupid historical fallacy (in America, witches were hanged not burned) that a real-life teacher as ferocious as Mrs Tingle would have attacked without mercy (instead, the screen character picks over the precise meaning of the word 'irony', which becomes a feeble running joke).

It may be that in his later works Williamson cannibalised rather too many things from this tyro writing piece, and now that it has reached the screen it seems like a sketchier play on them. The three central teens are types Williamson has returned to too often, and none of the performers make much of their standard-issue smart-but-desperate roles. Marisa Coughlan does sustained and pointless imitations of Linda Blair in *The Exorcist* and Marilyn Monroe that use up Williamson's quota of pop culture references. There's no sense, however, that these relate at all to the central theme of the film – which seems to owe something in plot to obscurities such as *Lady in a Cage* (1963) and *3 in the Attic* (1968) – in the way that the discussions of alien body-snatching and slasher movies in *The Faculty* and *Scream* illuminate the current texts. The welcome presence in a tiny role of Molly Ringwald suggests the indebtednesss of Williamson's high-school vision to that of 1980s John Hughes, but he can't match his model in that arena, with Barry Watson's bad boy coming off especially as a xerox of the Judd Nelson character from *The Breakfast Club*. When Mrs Tingle tries to persuade Leigh Anne's friends that they are being sacrificed for her ambition, it might be more interesting if Katie Holmes's performance gave some weight to the accusation but our heroine here is a complete vacuum with an unbelievable dilemma (she could only have come this close to being valedictorian if all her teachers, including Mrs Tingle, had been giving her As for years and it is suggested that Mrs Tingle has always had a down on her) and a borderline distasteful horror of 'wearing a nametag' (the worst future either of the girls can imagine is becoming a waitress).

The film's only really strong suit is a venomous Helen Mirren, cast as a character who might well be the dark doppelgänger of all those committed and passionate teachers in the likes of *Stand and Deliver, Dangerous Minds* and *Music of the Heart.* Instead of working hard to raise disadvantaged kids through education, Mrs Tingle devotes an equal amount of energy to ruining the lives of her charges (though why she likes the appalling Trudie is a plot device left unexamined) and shackling them to small-town misery. Written as a monster about on a level with Miss Elmira Gulch of *The Wizard of Oz*, Mirren plays her as a stony sociopath who is also svelte enough to ply her feminine wiles on her hapless abductors (the subplot with the wasted Jeffrey Tambor's lecherous coach is just misfired farce, however). There are feints to suggest that the teacher herself suffered the same disappointments she is inflicting upon Leigh Anne and Jo Lynn (the names are supposed to sound small-towny) before she grew to be Hannibal Lecter at the chalk face, but these could also be lies deployed in her war with the feeble-willed kids. How much more interesting might the film have been if Mrs Tingle had been the viewpoint character rather than her literally outclassed victim-tormentors is indicated by the few moments when Mirren lets us know what her master manipulator is scheming.

Kim Newman

SCARY MOVIE
USA 2000
Director: Keenen Ivory Wayans

United States, the present. Drew Decker, a senior at B.A. Corpse High School, is pestered by a masked phone prankster who then kills her. The killer's next target is teenager Cindy Campbell, already traumatised because she and her friends – boy-friend Bobby, couple Ray and Brenda, Greg and Buffy – caused the death of a stranger last Halloween. Television reporter Gail Hailstorm arrives and flirts with Officer Doofy to get the inside scoop on the case.

When Cindy survives an encounter with the stalker, Bobby is arrested but released once the killer is seen elsewhere. The killer murders Greg, Buffy, Brenda, Gail and Ray. Cindy surrenders her virginity to Bobby. Bobby, apparently attacked by the slasher, is revealed to be a killer himself, with his secret lover Ray, who turns out to be alive and is embittered because of the cancellation of the Wayans Brothers' television show. The killers have also abducted Mr Campbell, Cindy's drug-dealing father, whom they plan to murder. However, the masked murderer shows up and kills Bobby and Ray before engaging in a martial-arts fight with Cindy. As the police interrogate Cindy, she realises that the clues point to Officer Doofy, who walks away, shedding his disguise. As Cindy rants at the unfairness of it all, she is run over by a car.

* * *

And so cycles turn inevitably to spoof. In the late 1940s, a decade and a half after Universal made a name for itself with a string of horror movies, Abbott and Costello met the studio's pantheon of movie monsters. Then, in the early 1980s, only a few years after the teen slasher genre exploded with *Halloween* (1978) and *Friday the 13th* (1980), a clutch of *Airplane!*-style skits came along: from *Student Bodies* to *Saturday the 14th*. Arriving barely months after the alleged conclusion of the *Scream* series, which it parodies, and far out-grossing its inspiration, *Scary Movie* may well be the most commercially successful spoof yet, as well as the quickest off the mark. Indeed, *Scary Movie* has been such an immediate hit that it must have clicked more with mainstream audiences who appreciate the Farrelly Brothers – whose style of gross-out humour is in evidence throughout – than with the sizeable but cult crowd who saw *Scream*.

A major problem with *Scary Movie* is that it seems to have been made by people who didn't especially care for *Scream*, which was humorously intended in the first place. Director Keenen Ivory Wayans – assisted here by his brothers Shawn and Marlon as co-writers and performers – has previously ventured into parody with the blaxploitation spoof *I'm Gonna Git You Sucka!*. The Wayans' half of the script was developed in two versions, one hewing close to the whitebread conventions of the slasher movie and the other with mostly black characters. In the event, you're left feeling that they would have been happier filming the second script – there are a couple of wry race jokes, notably the cut from the announcement 'white woman in trouble' to the arrival of hordes of police cars – but have been forced to stick with the first.

After the opening riff on the Drew Barrymore killing from *Scream*, *Scary Movie*'s model provides rather thin material for skitting. Some of the parody is so abstruse as to be subliminal: echoing *Scream*'s casting of Henry Winkler, who starred in *Happy Days*, as the school principal, this casts David L Lander from the *Happy Days* spin-off *Laverne and Shirley* in a similar role. Scenes taken from *Scream* – Buffy's sarcastic confrontation with the killer, for instance – are played more broadly than in the original, but actually aren't as funny.

Wayans is on safer ground lampooning *I Know What You Did Last Summer*, a more po-faced slasher than *Scream*, and screws a few laughs out of the hit-and-run victim who keeps insisting he's all right as the teens argue about disposing of his corpse. Otherwise, *Scary Movie* has to yank in bits from other films not so much for parodic effect as for the shock of recognition, cueing limp variations on sequences from *The Blair Witch Project* and *The Matrix* (Cindy riverdancing in mid-air).

The air of desperation is emphasised by the insistence on padding out horror-movie gags with crude Farrelly-style humour: a hairy-chinned gym mistress with dangling testicles, a penis-through-the-brain murder that mimics a moment in *Scream 2* and an ejaculation that splatters Cindy against the ceiling in a rare nod to pre-*Scream* horror (*A Nightmare on Elm Street*). This sort of material initially gets big, shocked laughs but soon wears thin, especially without the Farrellys' streak of sentiment. Indeed, it hardly seems all that daring in a summer that finds a college dean being sodomised by a giant hamster in a PG-12 movie (*The Nutty Professor II*). A rare instance of real humour is the murder of Brenda at the hands of an audience for whom she has ruined *Shakespeare in Love* by talking loudly – and even that's similar to a gag in *Silent Night, Deadly Night Part 2*.

Kim Newman

THE HOLE
United Kingdom/France 2001
Director: Nick Hamm

Rural England, the present. Elizabeth Dunn, a pupil at Brabourne school, turns up after she and three school friends have been missing for some weeks. In interviews with psychologist Philipa Norwood, Liz explains that she was a mousy girl with a crush on American Mike. She prevailed upon her friend Martin to arrange that she and Mike, along with fellow pupils Geoff and Frankie, get out of a school trip by hiding in a disused World War II bunker. Liz says that Martin was jealous of her feelings for Mike and didn't let them out as arranged; in deceiving Martin, who had the bunker bugged, into believing Mike blamed her for their plight, Liz persuaded their captor to free them.

Philipa knows much of this account is fantasy, but the police believe Martin is guilty. During interrogation, Martin claims that Liz was actually a glamorous and manipulative figure in the school and that the four took to the bunker without his help for a party. Liz begins to remember what really happened, especially when confronted by Martin, recently released. She returns to the bunker with Philipa and explains that the party didn't go as planned: Mike was too hung up on breaking up with his girlfriend to pay attention to her; when Geoff and Frankie got together, Mike demanded to be let out. Liz locked them in and concealed the key. Trapped, Mike grew closer to Liz. Ill, Frankie died; Mike then killed Geoff after discovering him with a stash of soft drinks. When Liz revealed that she had the key, Mike became furious and died in a fall trying to escape. Philipa tells Liz that she must clear Martin but Liz has already murdered him and planted the incriminating key on his body.

*   *   *

With its striking opening, as a bloody and bedraggled Thora Birch staggers through a village past the 'child missing' posters that show her smiling younger self, and *Rashomon*-structured flashbacks – alternately fantasies, subjective and honest memories, and horrid revelations – *The Hole* cannily delays until near the end the penny-dropping realisation that this is another entry in that sub-genre of horror movies that centre on a coldly uncaring female killer who'll stop at nothing to get what she wants (cf.: *Fatal Attraction, Basic Instinct*). Indeed, it is the latest in a further refinement of this established sub-genre, one of a growing number of Gidget-gone-bad films that uncover the psychotic potential of ostensibly innocent girls, from the pre-adolescent villain of *The Bad Seed* (1956) to the killer teen queens of *Poison Ivy* (1968) and *The Crush* (1993).

Best known for her role in *American Beauty*, Birch plays Liz, the film's ruthless teenage protagonist who persuades her school friends, Mike, Geoff and Frankie, to spend three days in a disused World War II bunker, only for them to be trapped there for weeks. Managing a creditable imitation of Jenny Agutter, Birch delivers a multi-faceted reading of a role that grows with each plot permutation – the only survivor from the bunker, her explanation of what happened frames the movie. The way her first, utterly mendacious account of what happened presents her – she's slightly withdrawn, an outsider like the character she played in *American Beauty* – is a cunning piece of misdirection. In her fellow pupil Martin's subsequent précis of life at Brabourne, the school they attend, Birch acts like a vampish reincarnation of the teenage bullies in *Carrie* (1976). The most truthful of the flashbacks makes her a deeper, more conflicted character, not thinking too far ahead but resourceful enough to turn dreadful reversals to her advantage and, in the end, a sociopath clearly set for success in life. One might question (as Liz does, putting the words into the mouth of her made-up Martin) why such a powerful young woman is hung up on the dullish Mike; even less credible is the resistance he puts up to her advances – though, again, Liz has ascribed to Martin the truism that the rugby scrums Mike and Geoff take part in are homoerotic ritual, suggesting another reading of the sexual cross-currents of the four teenagers in the hole.

Screenwriters Ben Court and Caroline Ip and director Nick Hamm (*Martha – Meet Frank, Daniel and Laurence*) don't just rely on performance and narrative trickery to get their effects. The first version of what has happened has a fairly light level of suspense, with the partying teens swapping ghost stories at night. The second, extended take is more gruelling, a *Blair Witch*-like exercise in degeneration with the four players convincingly breaking down. The hole itself, cleverly designed by Eve Stewart, is an impressive location that keeps throwing the characters back at each other. There are contrivances around the climax, with the deaths of Geoff and Mike coming through a concealed stash of drink ('I killed my best friend – over a Coke!') and a faulty ladder, but these suggest that even at her most honest, Liz is still lying somehow, slanting events to minimise her guilt. In the end, you're left with the impression that the eponymous setting not only refers to the bunker in which the characters are trapped, but also to the void in the psyche of the protagonist who is aware of her guilt but not so keenly aware that she feels she should take the blame.

Kim Newman

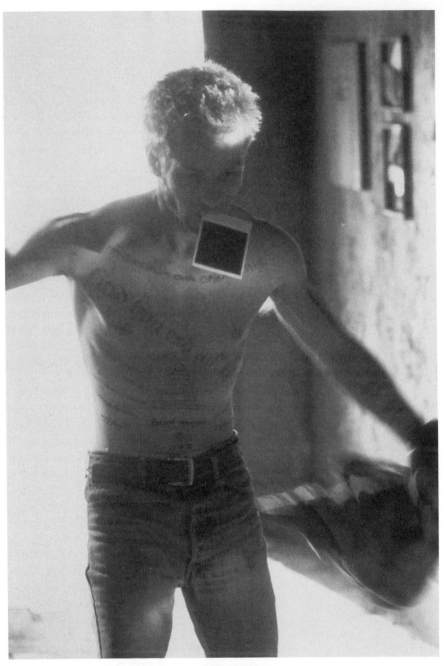

Memento (Chris Darke, 2000)

Section 5:
Case Study – Gamesworlds
and Rubber Reality

Themes of artificial (often subjective) realities and worlds constructed around the rules of games are long-standing staples of written science fiction, appearing often in the works of Philip K. Dick (*Eye in the Sky*, 1957, *A Maze of Death*, 1972), Philip José Farmer (the 'World of Tiers' series), Daniel F. Galouye (*Simulacron-3*, 1964), and many others. Before the advent of computer games, this material wasn't much used in the cinema — though something similar was achieved by the cycle of dream-walking horror movies kicked off by *A Nightmare on Elm Street* (1984). A movie trend which seemed to explode in the late 1990s had actually been a long time a-birthing: it is visible in embryo in such avant-garde efforts as *The President's Analyst* (1967), *Westworld* (1973), *Welcome to Blood City* (1977) and the porn movie *Nightdreams* (1981), not to mention episodes of *Doctor Who* ('The Celestial Toymaker', 1966, 'The Mind Robber', 1968) and *Star Trek* ('The Gamesters of Triskelion', 1968, 'Spectre of the Gun', 1968). The Galouye novel, a fairly minor literary effort in the Dickian tradition, didn't make it to the cinema until 1999, when it was adapted as *The Thirteenth Floor*. But this s-f film was actually a remake of *Welt am Draht* (1973), a trail-blazing German TV adaptation by Rainer Werner Fassbinder. The ideas were around a long time before the special effects necessary to visualise them were perfected, and had to leak into the mainstream via cultural phenomena more visible than garish paperback novels.

Back in 1992, *The Lawnmower Man* was advertised as 'Britain's first virtual reality film', with no more honesty than *Logan's Run* was sold as featuring the first on-screen hologram in 1976. In both cases, what the ad-lines meant was that these new entertainment concepts featured in the films' plots, not that they were an adjunct gimmick like 3-D or Cinerama – though *The Lawnmower Man* did make early use of computer-generated imagery. 'Virtual reality', a meaningless buzz-term, has come to stand for the in-development tech: as explored in near-future efforts like *Strange Days*), featured in the plot of the contemporary thriller *Disclosure* (1994) and domesticated in the 'Holodeck' of the next generation of *Star Trek* (the most self-referential use of the device is 'Relics', 1992, which accepts that the Starship Enterprise is itself a fantasy environment that might be imagined as a wish-fulfilment escape zone). VR also implies a sense of the unreality of the actual, as explored by a run of paranoid movies in which the protagonists come to suspect their whole world is a generated fiction.

Here, we are examining a clutch of disparate films linked by underlying themes, spinning off cultural phenomena like VR, the processing of 'real life' into TV soap, the (ancient) concept that the world we live in is a manufactured illusion, and a profound dissociation from and refusal to accept the mainstream of reality. The group spans satire, s-f, mystery, horror, thriller, psychological case history, juvenile action, intellectual puzzle and glossy star vehicle, and accounts for a range of quality from the excellent to the negligible. This was the theme of the 1990s, and the bubble may burst in the new millennium – *Strange Days*, set in an imagined last week of 1999, is already a quaintly bypassed future-that-never-was – though the co-opting of the 'docusoap' theme via *The Truman Show* and *EDtv*, which were prescient of a wave of TV formats that genuinely have come to pass at the time of writing (early 2001). Computer, video and role-playing games have informed such set-the-counter-to-zero-and-start-again films as *Groundhog Day*, *Run Lola Run*, and *Memento*, which might literally have been inconceivable otherwise, far more than such 'official' game spin-offs as *Mortal Kombat* and *Dungeons & Dragons* (2001), which disappointingly adapt the content rather than the structure of their inspiration. And Mike Figgis's *Timecode* is an experiment with form which will find its real audience on DVD, where it will become genuinely interactive as the viewer can choose which quadrant of the screen to expand and follow, which characters to listen to, which angle to observe.

BUBBLE BOY

Charles Whitehouse

As well as being a pretty big success with American audiences, grossing $100 million at the box office so far, *The Truman Show* has impressed the majority of US media commentators. This is quite a feat for a film which is about trying to break out from the confines of convention. And it's even more impressive that a movie starring Jim Carrey has been praised so much for its intelligent content – after all, isn't Carrey the epitome of dumbing down?

Of course he is, and it's director Peter Weir's masterstroke to cast him as the unwitting star of a 24-hour-a-day soap opera. That is *The Truman Show's* great conceit – Truman Burbank was born into a fake world populated by actors. His emergence from the womb was a massively promoted televisual event, and his world is a huge man-made construction, a bubble somewhere in California containing an island with a fake ocean of gently lapping waves, digitally controlled weather, and a sky projected on a vast white overarching dome. But though *The Truman Show* is set in the future, its town is a 1950s idyll of identical clapboard houses built around a curiously small business centre of corporate buildings and populated by the ideal demographic.

Truman doesn't know any of this, of course, and he is meant to be content with his shrewishly perfect blonde wife Meryl (an actress – played by Laura Linney – who secretly loathes him), his stereotypical best buddy Marlon (Noah Emmerich) – to whom he pours out his heart and soul over a six pack with stunning regularity – and his slightly complicated job as an insurance salesman. The fact that Truman is surrounded by actors is telegraphed to us from the start. As soon as things begin to go wrong, we see them corpsing and looking directly at the camera. These scenes offer us the same kind of pleasures as those gained from such gaffe shows as the UK's *It'll Be Alright on the Night*, or from the self-conscious amateurism of *The Big Breakfast.*

The show itself is watched in the 'real' world by people in bars and by security guards – anyone with time to kill, people 'like us'. They have, through the 30 years or so of *The Truman Show's* history, come to make a huge emotional investment in Truman. And Carrey as Truman Burbank lives up to this by behaving much like a manic version of Dick Van Dyke, or, more pertinently, Dick York in *Bewitched* – a goofy, pathetic husband inured to blandness.

This is Carrey's schtick and the context is perfect for him because here it has a knowing satirical audience complicity to back it up. Audience relaxation is guaranteed by postmodern distancing and the feeling of superiority creatives in the movie business like to engender against the ordinary working stiff. The film works well on a self-reflexive level because it never tries too hard to convince us we are in the realms of the possible – though those commentators who see it as a genuine portent of our future relationship with television would obviously disagree.

The Kafka-inspired allegory of 'real life', though, is pushed to a biblical level, with show creator Christof (Ed Harris) set up as Truman's equivalent to God, a God who loves his own creation but whom Truman must outwit. In this respect it is strongly reminiscent of Patrick McGoohan's television series *The Prisoner* – though screenwriter Andrew Niccol invented a similarly paranoid future world for *Gattaca*, and *The Truman Show* can be seen as a simple inversion of the *Gattaca* story. There, exclusion from the in-crowd was a matter of genetics, and the naturally born hero had to fake his way in. With *The Truman Show*, though, we the audience are the in-crowd, and the unnatural hero has to break out from unwitting celebrity to become one of us.

It is in Truman's transition from mildly suspicious soap dupe to tortured soul in search of an authentic identity that this otherwise well-oiled machine begins to grind a little. For one thing, Carrey can't do deep. As doubt begins to twist his rubbery features into a permanent frown, we see the muscles working too hard, read the face's refusal of emotion. If the film really works with audiences, it's arguably because they can identify with Truman's celebrity powerlessness. Rather than reminding us of our own passivity as consumers, it is its evocation of the myth that stardom is pain that makes *The Truman Show* such an ideal tabloid movie.

But what is it really telling us about television? The movies have a long tradition of demonising their Siamese-twin industry, and there is perhaps no bigger threat to the future of theatrical exhibition than digital widescreen multi-channel television. Assuming that viewers will want to choose between hundreds of channels is to assume a great deal, but let's say that the demand for televisual product continues apace, and the vogue for turning the cameras on to our own lives exemplified in the UK by docu-soaps and video diaries reaches a point where a 24-hour real-life soap becomes desirable. Would there really be a market for the unedited flow of a life? Wouldn't the very repetition of events that dogs current soaps become an exponential problem?

In fact the minute you begin to analyse *The Truman Show* for plausibility it falls apart, and it's probably meant to – it is an allegory after all. This kind of future for television is the purest hokum, perhaps the best ripping yarn Hollywood has produced this year. What's more pertinent about the film's conception is the way it latches on to the same baby-boomer nostalgia so many other of this summer's releases play to. Anti-utopia in *The Truman Show* is all about the same 'little boxes' Pete Seeger sang of, and Carrey's discovery of self is really just another version of the sensitive-boy-escapes-oppressive-suburbia trope that film-makers of the hippie generation return to time and again.

Peter Weir is one of the more talented survivors of that generation, a director who has learned how to make successful 'personal growth' movies such as *Dead Poets Society* (1989) alongside more personal works such as his underrated film *Fearless* (1993), about a man who keeps on trying to cheat death after a plane crash. It's easy to read a subtext into the latter – that it's really about the middle-aged need for experiences that bring you back to a youthful level of excitement. On that level, *The Truman Show* can also be seen as an attempt to re-envision the perhaps simpler problems of the 1960s in a future context. The most modern and relevant aspect of the film is its inclusion of the fictional audience in the text. But crucially, that audience of bar girls and security guards seems not to be watching soap, but something closer to sport.

Just as *The Jerry Springer Show* has turned the chat show into a new form of gladiatorial combat, so *The Truman Show* depicts future soap as a spectacular conflict between a man and his god, a worker and his employer, a 'father' and his son and – if we want to indulge in a little more intertextual metaphor – a star and his studio. As such it remains a dazzling catch-all entertainment that's not quite as clever as it thinks it is. Nevertheless, it is indisputably one of the best Hollywood releases of the year.

GAME BOY

Chris Rodley

eXistenZ. It's new. And it's here. It's a virtual-reality game that's almost indistinguishable from lived experience and it's also the new movie from David Cronenberg. What's more, it's the first wholly original creation from the director since *Videodrome* (1982) – the film his fans regard as his quintessential work because it most effectively captures the alarming nature of the cinema's invasion of the passive self. *eXistenZ* is *Videodrome*'s inverse twin, in which the interactive self invades cinema.

I talked to Cronenberg in London, a city which greeted his last cinema release *Crash* (1996) with an uproar of tabloid outrage. He'd just arrived from the Berlin Film Festival where *eXistenZ* had received its world premiere and its director had won a Silver Bear for 'outstanding artistic achievement'. But there was an air of dread about him. The near-psychotic reaction of some British film critics to *Crash* seems to have scarred him. To Cronenberg, being in London with a new movie feels 'creepy'.

Over the past 17 years Cronenberg has played the symbiotic bug, gleefully infecting other people's texts with his own concerns – novels as diverse as Stephen King's *The Dead Zone*, William Burroughs's *The Naked Lunch* and J. G. Ballard's *Crash.* There's also David H. Hwang's play *M Butterfly* and the rethinking of the 1958 sci-fi movie *The Fly.* Even *Dead Ringers* (1988) was loosely based on the real-life case of identical twin gynaecologists Cyril and Stewart Marcus. *eXistenZ,* however, is completely new.

Shy, sexy Allegra Geller (Jennifer Jason Leigh) is an adored game-devising goddess in a near future in which the inventors of virtual-reality games have become cultural megastars. Her new game, *eXistenZ,* plugs so effectively into an individual's desires and fears that the frontiers between fantasy and reality disappear, leaving the player wandering compassless in landscapes and situations that may or may not be of their own imagining. However, this successful game genius has fanatical enemies – both those who are against gaming and rival gaming companies. After a botched attempt on her life during *eXistenZ*'s first public demonstration, Allegra finds herself on the run with Ted Pikul (Jude Law), a novice security guard for Antenna Research, the hi-tech toy firm with millions invested in the game.

The intense game reality of *eXistenZ* is produced by its unique Game Pod, an organic creature grown from fertilised amphibian eggs stuffed with synthetic DNA. Resembling a kidney with large aroused nipples, the fleshy, pulsating device is connected to each player via an UmbyCord which plugs directly into a Bioport at the base of the spine. Hotwired into the human nervous system, the pod has unrestricted access to personal memories, anxieties and preoccupations. With a $5 million Fatwa on her head from one company or another (possibly her own employers) Allegra, accompanied by Ted, embarks on a synaptic road movie into the virtual heart of her own game where nothing – and this is a gross understatement – is as it seems.

Cronenberg works this game/movie connection into a metaphor so effective that as soon as *eXistenZ* is over you feel the need to 'play' the film again to understand its rules more fully, certain you must have missed something. As one might expect from Cronenberg, *eXistenZ* fuses all the components of cinema – storytelling, acting, production design, sound, images, music – to play with the viewer at the same time as representing the game to them. But what make *eXistenZ* potentially dangerous is its philosophic basis. Like reality, it can bite. Literally. It's a virtual-reality game. And it's a movie.

Techno-prophet

'It came as a shock to me,' Cronenberg says of the idea. 'It wasn't out of desperation, or a feeling of, 'Oh my god, I haven't written anything original for a while and therefore I haven't been true to my flame.' I was just ready to write something original. The spark for it, though, was the Salman Rushdie affair. I had an idea for a sci-fi movie that would have something to do with that situation, which horrified and fascinated me at the same time.'

In spring 1995, while still conceiving *eXistenZ*, Cronenberg was asked by *Shift* magazine in Canada to interview Rushdie. 'I might have had the idea of making the artist character in the movie a game designer even then. Why that should be, I don't know. Maybe I wanted some distance, some metaphorical play that wasn't autobiographical.' During the interview, and unbeknownst to Rushdie, Cronenberg tested his ideas out on the fugitive writer. 'We talked about games and computers. He's had to learn about computers because, being on the run, he needed to work on a laptop. That meeting crystallised things for me, so I posited a time when games could be art, and a game designer an artist.'

With *eXistenZ* Cronenberg has returned whole-heartedly to his most abiding source of ideas – radical developments in bio-technology, and their often disturbing but potentially liberating consequences. As in the telekinetic conspiracy tale *Scanners* (1980) the telepornographic hypnosis conspiracy tale *Videodrome*, the appropriation (or destruction) of these developments by political interests drive the narrative. Indeed, Cronenberg revamps some of *Videodrome*'s notions of 'the new flesh' as technological hardware, confident that some of his seemingly outrageous past imaginings have become reality. For instance, Dr Dan Keloid's 'neutralised' skin grafts in *Rabid* (1976) are now science fact, not fiction.

Cronenberg: 'It's bizarre that something I invented then has come to pass. By using foetal or umbilical tissue they can now make a skin graft that will work on a kidney or whatever because it doesn't know what it is yet. It just says: "Oh, I can be this." But that's a classic sci-fi thing, like Arthur C. Clarke saying, "I invented satellites ten years before they happened." I'm not interested in being that kind of techno-prophet. However, I'm very aware of what's happening with computers and I find it exciting.'

Intel and all the chip makers are now experimenting with animal proteins as the basis for their chips. They can't use metals any more – they have to get right down to the molecular and even atomic level. Imagine the market! People will want it – either on the entertainment or the health front. You have your little case full of different organs that have been designed specifically for game playing. Or organs for things we've never had before. You would have new sexual organs – which I play with metaphorically in the movie. They could be very pleasurable in a way no naturally derived organ has been. People are having surgery for all kinds of frivolous reasons, so why not have it for a really good functional reason?'

Sex you've never even dreamed of

In this bio-degradable anti-metal world, many of the aesthetic signatures Cronenberg's critics love to disparage – deadpan acting, anonymous-looking locations, lack of 'drama' – become virtual virtues. This is not a hand-eye coordination-testing shoot-'em-up world at all, but something that allows the participant to take decisions at their own pace. At a certain point, *eXistenZ* takes the viewer inside Allegra's game, providing a complex Chinese-box structure to the film itself because the game and its framing 'reality' look so similar. Although the 'reality bleeds' continually signalled throughout the movie are not an original device, they presage a massive narrative haemorrhage at the end, so much so that it's impossible to give an in-depth synopsis of the film without literally giving the game away.

'When I started writing it,' says Cronenberg, ' I remember thinking I wouldn't play the game in the movie; that it would be about an artist on the run. I'd allude to the game and you'd see people playing it, but the audience would never get into it. It would be like an elegant frustration. But that didn't last long! Once I'd started, I thought, 'I wanna see what this game's all about!' at that point it became a meditation on the virtual-reality genre and how I didn't want to be part of it. As soon as you do, you're *The Lawnmower Man*, you're *Strange Days*, whatever. Of course we have to be arrogant and assume that we can do something no one else has done.'

And the weight of Cronenberg's recent past – the somewhat solemn debates engendered by his films on the key counterculture novels *The Naked Lunch* and *Crash* – has been lifted in another way. The concern to work at the level of metaphor remains, but there's now a rich vein of black humour. *eXistenZ* is never more hilarious than in the scene where Ted gets fitted with a bioport (he doesn't have one because of a phobia about having his body penetrated) so he can play *eXistenZ* with Allegra in order to assess the damage done to her Game Pod during an assassination attempt. The trouble is, the fitting has to be done off the beaten track in less than hygienic circumstances by a greasy mechanic named Gas (Willem Dafoe, in gleeful, Bobby Peru mode). Ted's virginal fear, a filthy Bioport insertion gun and an explosive 'fitting' – which leaves him face down in agony, legs paralysed, while Gas goes 'to wash up' – are so loaded with sexual content the scene threatens to burst.

eXistenZ is full of such scenes, and Allegra's game works on so many levels that everything the characters say, do or see offers multiple meanings – sexuality being only one of them. 'At Berlin one French journalist wondered if I was aware of the homosexuality in that scene because to him it was totally an anal-fuck scene. So I said,

"Y-e-e-s-s… I can see that now you mention it!" Humour was always there in my films, even in *Crash*, but here it's right up front. The whole middle of the movie plays like a comedy, basically. People sometimes think you decide it's time to lighten up, but it wasn't intentional. There's a ton of sex in the movie, metaphorically speaking, and because it pleased me so much, I didn't want to spoil it with real sex. I'm saying, "This is better sex. This is sex you've never even dreamed of before. Let's just concentrate on this."

eXistenZ was initially developed by MGM, but the studio was concerned that the central character was a woman. 'Their own demographics tell them this kind of movie is going to be attractive to young men – because it's sci-fi and about games – and young men don't want the lead to be a girl. They want it to be them. Suddenly you realise you've not written quite so commercially viable a script as you thought. Feminist so-called paranoia about Hollywood is absolutely justified.'

Cronenberg himself had first conceived of the game artist as male, 'because it's me, Salman Rushdie, whatever', but the script didn't snap into place until he changed the character's sex. 'It's that whole role-reversal thing. If Allegra were a man and Ted a woman, imagine the scene where he has to talk her into getting a Bioport fitted so he can plug into her. It's the guy fucking the girl, it would have been crude. But the punishment came when we tried to find a hot young actor to play a character like Ted, because they don't want to be subservient. Even in unusual movies that same old American macho stuff is still going on.'

Existentialists versus realists

eXistenZ's vision of the near future is set in a countryside littered with old buildings now being used for something other than their original function. This move away from the city comes out of a decision made by Cronenberg with regular collaborators Carol Spier (production designer) and Peter Suschitzky (director of photography) to remove from this world everything people would expect from a sci-fi movie about game playing. There are no computer screens, televisions, sneakers, watches or suits. The result of this multiplication of minor subtractions is perfectly subliminal: you can feel the operation of a 'look', but its exact nature is elusive.

'I removed *Blade Runner*, basically,' admits Cronenberg. 'The production design of that movie has a weird life of its own. It's almost as if that world exists. It's a very interesting phenomenon. Instead, we were replicating some of the style of some video games. If you want a character to wear a plaid shirt, it takes up a lot of memory, so it's much easier if he has a solid beige shirt. So I was trying to replicate the blockiness of the polygon structure of some games.'

Everywhere in the *eXistenZ* world there are game players, game inventors, game doctors and game manufacturers. As Gas declares, he's a garage mechanic, 'only on the most pathetic level of reality'. But the countryside is also home to fundamentalist fanatics opposed to the 'radical deforming of reality' caused by such games. Around this conflict is where Rushdie, the game, the movie, cinema and metaphor that is *eXistenZ* itself fuse so effortlessly. *eXistenZ*'s supporters proclaim 'Death to realism!' and describe its wounded and weary as 'victims of realism'. When Allegra's Game Pod, at one point hopelessly diseased, explodes in a shower of black spores, they are the smothering black spores of 'reality'. This play-off of perceptions is what makes *eXistenZ* such an unexpected meditation on cinema. The characters yelling 'Long live realism!' are not only, on a purely narrative level, the enemy of eXistenZ the game, they are literally enemies of *eXistenZ* the movie – which toys with reality precisely for our visceral and intellectual pleasure.

Humorous as *eXistenZ* is, there's a small scene at the centre that slyly represents the underlying seriousness of the project. Wandering around in a disused virtual-reality trout farm where components for Game Pods are now being bred from mutated amphibians, Ted confesses to Allegra: 'I don't want to be here. We're stumbling around in the unformed world, not knowing what the rules are, or if there are any rules. We're under attack from forces that want to destroy us but that we don't understand.' The game goddess replies: 'Yeah, that's my game.' Ted can only observe sarcastically: 'It's a game that's going to be difficult to market.' But Allegra has the last word: 'It's a game everyone's already playing.'

Cronenberg: 'I'm talking about the existentialists, i.e. the game players, versus the realists. The deforming of reality is a criticism that has been levelled against all art, even religious icons, which has to do with Man being made in God's image, so you can't make images of either. Art is a scary thing to a lot of people because it shakes your understanding of reality, or shapes it in ways that are socially unacceptable. As a card-carrying existentialist I think all reality is virtual. It's all invented. It's collaborative, so you need friends to help you create a reality. But it's not about what is real and what isn't.

'At Berlin I jokingly said the movie is existentialist propaganda. I meant it playfully, of course. But I have come to believe that this is the game we are playing. In Berlin I didn't even get into the discussion about mortality. That's even more basic – the absurdity of human existence. Because it's too short to be able to understand enough, to synthesise enough, to make intelligent choices. So we're blundering around, terrified because we know we're going to die at some inopportune moment.'

TIME MACHINES

Kim Newman

The concept of virtual reality goes back in fiction at least as far as the 'feelies' of Aldous Huxley's *Brave New World* (1932), though it can be argued that the true originator of the idea was H. G. Wells, who in 1896 joined with British film pioneer R. W. Paul to patent a device inspired by his novel *The Time Machine*. Paying customers were to sit in a model of the book's Time Machine surrounded by multi-screen cinema images and various pre-Sensurround effects to convey the impression of journeying into the future. Sadly, this fabulous attraction was never constructed, though rides on its model grace many theme parks.

David Cronenberg's *Videodrome* and *eXistenZ* bracket a boom in film and literary fictions on the virtual-reality theme. But where the real-life touchstones of *Videodrome* were film, cable television and pornography, those of *eXistenZ* are computer games, live-action roleplay and choose-your-own-adventure fictions. The consumer of *Videodrome* was expected to be a passive voyeur, 'patched into the world's missing board' to sample SM and paranoid fantasies, the player of *eXistenZ* is forced to get involved, to shape the narrative into which they have stepped. And it seems that active consumers inspire active rebels, for the world of *eXistenZ* has thrown up a committed, effective 'realist underground'.

A tiny throwaway in the new film – a fast-food franchise called Perky Pat's – is an acknowledgment of a literary pioneer of the territory. Philip K. Dick's 1963 short story 'The Days of Perky Pat' is about Martian colonists who obsessively create 'lay-outs' modelled on suburban American dream homes for their Barbie-like Perky Pat dolls. Throughout his career Dick returned to the notion of Chinese-box realities, each layered inside another and with the most obviously mimetic revealed to be the most contrived. In *The Penultimate Truth* (1964), one of many inspirations of *The Truman Show*, the protagonist's slightly skewed Eisenhower-era reality turns out to be a simulation created in a fantastical future. And the irony of a paranoid who learns he is indeed the focus of a vast conspiracy, set forth in Paul Verhoeven's Dick-based *Total Recall* (1990) – once a Cronenberg project – of course forces the audience to question yet again what is 'real'.

Other remarkable precursors for the game worlds of *eXistenZ* include Lewis Carroll's *Through the Looking-Glass and What Alice Found There* (1871) – which features a fantasy land based on games (chess, cards) – and the violent quest fantasy adventures that serve as entertainment for the jaded in Arthur C. Clarke's *The City and the Stars* (1956) and Brian W Aldiss's *The Eighty Minute Hour* (1974). The games of *eXistenZ*, like the 'dreambeans' of James Morrow's *The Continent of Lies* (1984) and the Holodeck episodes of *Star Trek: The Next Generation* (1987–94), are manufactured narratives, complete with creators, fans, critics, marketing strategies and focus groups. In short, they are (like the Wells-Paul machine) analogues of cinema itself, literal 'feelies' that reach out and embrace their audiences, making them feel part of the story.

Similar in effect are the recorded-experience machines most familiar via the SQUID devices of Kathryn Bigelow's *Strange Days* (1995), which have literary equivalents as far back as Shepherd Mead's *The Big Ball of Wax* (1954) and show up in such films as Michael Reeves's *The Sorcerers* (1967) and Douglas Trumbull's *Brainstorm* (1983), in which new processes for recording and playing back physical sensations are used, predictably, to create bootleg pornography and snuff. Like cyberspace and virtual reality, this trope has been popularised as a frill of 'cyberpunk' fiction by its use in the novels of William Gibson, whose major involvement with the cinema (Robert Longo's *Johnny Mnemonic*, 1995) has only managed to ossify his borrowed or mutated themes into clichés. It is perhaps worth noting that most of these ideas appeared in television episodes of *The Prisoner* (1967–8): 'A B and C' is about recorded and manipulated dreams/memories; 'Living in Harmony' involves a virtual-reality Western. Even Doctor Who visited the Land of Fiction of 'The Mind Robber' (1968), and bested its master in a competition to rewrite the Campbellian uber-story.

eXistenZ can't help but evoke films as minor as John Flynn's *Brainscan* (1994), in which the old horror-story-that-comes-true plot was redone through a satanic computer game, or even the various dumb action pictures based on successful combat or labyrinth games (*Super Mario Bros.*, 1993; *Street Fighter*, 1995; *Mortal Kombat*, 1995). But as with *Videodrome*, Cronenberg shows his true visionary streak by avoiding the situations that have congealed into cliché: cyberjockeys interfacing with their computer screens; sunbed-cum-life-support real-world apparatus; the deployment of archetypal Western or 'B' sci-fi action scenarios as game worlds. Instead, the film plunges us into an alternative reality even earlier than we suspect, and uses it to suggest a larger (but equally bogus) world beyond that which we see. It may be that the final scene of *eXistenZ*, set in the world of *tranCendenZ* and paying off with a question-cum-punchline that resonates out into our reality beyond the cinema, takes this theme as far as it can go, revoking and denying the pay-off of *Videodrome* ('Long live the New Flesh!') by asking whether this is still a game?

RUBBER REALITY

Kim Newman

'What's the matter with you guys,' asked a straight bystander of an acid-hazed Peter Fonda in Roger Corman's *The Trip* (1967), 'isn't the real world good enough for you?' Posed in a film today, that question would still be rhetorical, but the many layers of irony would be more onion-like still. As the Fonda of the 1960s suspected and as so many recent movies reveal, the apparently mundane everyday can sometimes be of even more doubtful provenance than escapist nightmare worlds.

If one cluster of films will eventually be said to have caught the turn-of-the-century zeitgeist, it may be those based on a particular concept of 'virtual reality'. In these films – of which the Brothers Wachowski's new box-office hit *The Matrix* is by far the most extravagant – a quotidian reality that conforms to the conventions of the action movie (or sitcom) is revealed to be a construct designed either to entrap the mass consciousness of humanity or to enslave a single representative specimen.

The form coalesced in the 1990s with Paul Verhoeven's *Total Recall* (1990), a slapdash but epic elaboration on the themes of the sub-genre's prophet, author Philip K. Dick. The protagonist duped into living an ordinary life which disguises something really sinister in Dick's great trope, and the Dick text most often cannibalised for modern use is his 1959 novel *Time Out of Joint*, in which the hero gradually comes to realise that his contemporary reality is an idyllic fake constructed in a hellish future. David Cronenberg was the first film-maker into the *Time Out of Joint* tunnel with the virtual-reality snuff of *Videodrome* (1982), and his *eXistenZ* (1999) suggests the most likely shape of rubber reality for the twenty-first century – elevating gameplaying over *Videodrome*'s pornography as the dominant fantasy mode. Many of Cronenberg's themes were also sketched by Alex Proyas in *Dark City* and Peter Weir in *The Truman Show*.

The Matrix, too, begins inside a fake world resembling a Northern American city and lets the clues drop so the audience starts to question what's on screen before the protagonist does. A stunning action opening sequence has a cadre of fetish-gear fascist cops closing in on hacker outlaw/leather babe Trinity (Carrie-Anne Moss) and being felled by a display of kung-fu gymnastics. In order to escape her pursuers – who are directed by the sharp-faced Agent Smith (Hugo Weaving) – she has to reach a ringing telephone before its booth is destroyed by a truck and, apparently, disappear down the receiver.

Office drone Thomas Anderson (Keanu Reeves), who works by night as a hacker called Neo, is contacted by Trinity. She represents a faction that wants him to throw in his lot with the mysterious rebel leader/terrorist Morpheus (Laurence Fishburne), who has been searching the city for a prophesied saviour known as 'the One'. The narrative feint of the first act suggests this will be yet another film about a cyber-punk hacker on the run from faceless corporate baddies. And it works well considering the risk taken in casting Keanu Reeves as the man on the spot, evoking the dread memory of Robert Longo's bungled William Gibson adaptation *Johnny Mnemonic* (1995). A more focused, trim and haggard Reeves here delivers one of his most committed, gimmick-free performances. (These cyberspace everyman roles are tricky to cast since there's now a genre requirement that the hero must have a mannequin quality, so Reeves sometimes seems stiff when Neo plays stooge to others who can bring him up to speed plot-wise.)

An early twist is a delightful take on *Mad Magazine*'s 'Scenes We'd Love to See' feature: told he has to choose between escaping from a building by clambering around a tiny ledge or surrendering to the *Men in Black*-style goons, Neo refuses what would be for most action heroes a minor bit of daring and meekly lets himself be taken into custody. The 'not in Kansas anymore' feel is strengthened when Neo demands a phone call and the hawk-like Smith takes away his mouth and implants him with a nightmarish creature that is at once an insect bug and a tracker bug.

Quite why a tracker bug would be necessary in an artificial reality maintained by Smith's AI masters is as beside the point as asking why Morpheus' rebels can escape from fake reality via old-fashioned land-line phones but not through the mobiles they carry around all the time. The Wachowskis evidently developed *The Matrix* as a comic book before it was a script, and a great many 'just because it's cooler that way' decisions override the rigours you'd expect from a film based on a novel. Dick would have worked out the levels of reality with more consistency and Cronenberg takes more care with how his characters are affected by their unreal actions, but those cerebral artists could never have delivered *The Matrix*'s non-stop kung-fu action. The sustained chain reaction of climaxes scored to pounding techno (with soundtrack gunshots worked into the music to a precise beat) includes a John Woo set-piece as Neo and Trinity walk through a skyscraper lobby blowing away the guards, Neo and Smith battering each other in a fight scene that sprawls over many locations and the rebels' travelling headquarters being breached by laser-wielding robot-squid sentinels.

Given that the teaser campaign and early scenes revolve around the question-cum-slogan 'What is the Matrix?', it's also a cunning move to reveal the answer at a relatively early juncture. Morpheus snatches Neo from the forces of repression and divests him of his bug, then offers him a choice between two capsules, one which will induce amnesia and one which will reveal reality. Neo takes the reality pill, and wakes up in a tank of goo with a bio-port in the back of his skull. We learn that the real world is two centuries in the future and that almost all the human race are enslaved, living 'batteries' for a vast artificial intelligence which maintains the Matrix, a simulation of 1999 reality that distracts the humans it grows, harvests and uses as an energy source. Morpheus and a crew of like-minded rebels travel the world in a submarine-like giant hovercraft, the Nebuchadnezzar, working against the Matrix on behalf of Zion, an underground city where the last free humans live.

When it gets to 'reality', the film breaks with the cold, monochrome look of the Matrix sections and comes up with a succession of images that could have come from vintage *Metal Hurlant bandes dessinées*: robotic creatures harvesting bubble-grown babies and plugging them into a giant circuit; the Nebuchadnezzar flying through the post-holocaust murk. Unfortunately, characterisation too is at a comic-book level: excellent fight scenes are punctuated by a great deal of kung-fu wisdom (catchphrase: 'there is no spoon'), and the tangle of plot complications is undermined by our knowledge that much of what we see isn't 'really' happening.

The ending as with most previous films in the artificial-reality genre, is a conceptual breakthrough as the world wakes up, but *The Matrix* refrains from depicting the global upheaval that must surely follow Neo's predictable ascension to godhood. Concealed inside the package like a ticking bomb is the decision of Morpheus' crew member Cypher (Joe Pantoliano) that eating pretend steak is better than real-nutrient glop, and Morpheus' musings that maybe most people would prefer the dream to the reality. And while it's hard not to be impatient these days with the rejection of vibrantly colourful Oz in favour of sepia-miserable Kansas at the end of *The Wizard of Oz*, it is also somewhat disturbing that *The Matrix* should embrace a desperate solipsist wish-fulfilment vision which proposes that everything, mundane or magical, is just scene-setting for a kick-'em-in-the-head computer game in which ultimate enlightenment can be attained through skills which have been downloaded from file rather than learned.

RIDDLE OF THE SANDS

Philip Strick

A walk on the seashore, so he said, followed by work on a government survey of sand-flow, provided Frank Herbert with the background for 'Dune World' and 'The Prophet of Dune', two novellas which appeared in the science fiction magazine *Analog* between 1963 and 1965. Combined to form his second novel, the stories were set on the planet Arrakis, known as Dune, where no rains fall and the most valuable commodities are water and sand. Control of both, for reasons mostly relating to sandworms, means control over the entire Universe: science fiction, particularly in the luminous pages of *Analog*, was never inclined to think small. Nor has Herbert's award-winning blockbuster ever, it seems, been regarded with less than awe, admiration and exhaustion from the effort of negotiating the shifting perspectives of its shoreline. Admittedly, serried ranks of publishers turned it down at first. But it became one of the genre's all-time best-sellers.

Quickly recognising that alongside *Dune*'s central narrative, if indeed it contained anything so identifiable, lay the planes and grains of innumerable variations, Herbert wrote five *Dune* sequels and a screen adaptation in the course of the next 20 years, as well as a collection of other novels echoing ideas from the *Dune* saga. Formerly a reporter, jungle-survival instructor, editor, documentary cameraman and political speechwriter, he devoted six years of research and 18 months of writing to *Dune*, acquiring knowledge with a fanaticism worthy of his novel's haunted hero and extrapolating from it with astonishing flights of imagination. Overflowing into several appendices including historical notes, a map of the northern hemisphere of Arrakis, a couple of popular songs and a helpful dictionary of terms and references, he achieved a persuasive density: this is a universe to believe in.

While satisfyingly disguised as a conventional space opera packed with duels, vendettas, battles and interplanetary intrigue, a clear portion of the *Dune* agenda is its concern with the art of manipulation. Herbert's tribal society, in which space travel contrives to be both irrelevant (he hardly refers to it) and essential (it is dependent on the unique Arrakeen spice *mélange*), is dominated by conflicting masterplans. Transcending the needs of individual planets, the groups and families of *Dune*, as if in a galactic expansion of Chicago-style gang warfare, have strategies of calculated immensity, every move, marriage, alliance and confrontation designed over the centuries to achieve some far-distant objective.

From his first published story ('Looking for Something?', 1952), Herbert gave a fresh slant to the alien-invasion theme, his paranoid characters discovering they are mere puppets in the schemas of some unimaginably grander intelligence. At its most brutal in his rather ugly novel *The Heaven Makers* (1968), reminiscent of Peter Weir's *The Truman Show* in its account of the relationship between a 'controller' and his victim, the concept is neatly parodied in Herbert's brief *Occupation Force* (1956) in which the arriving aliens, dapper in top hats and pinstripes, calmly resume their colonialist programme. In *Dune* control at a personal level is simply a matter of using the right tone of voice.

Richly embroidered with worthy topics – including ecology, genetic engineering, evolution and longevity – *Dune* seldom strays from the subject of constant intrusion. The peculiar predicament of its young hero Paul Atreides is that whatever he achieves appears to conform to past predictions, his triumphs and failures guided by some elusive exterior motivation. Even when he acquires the ability to see into the future, the extent to which he can change it is already defined in a variety of alternative universes. The paradox of being a Messiah is that he can only do what has been foretold; wielder of absolute power, with paranormal mental skills, he is in a contradictory state of powerlessness. His arrival is intended to launch a *jihad*, a holy war, but Paul is determined to avert any such catastrophe. Herbert devoted at least two of his sequels to trying to sort that one out.

Ironically, having himself acquired a certain Messianic status among his book's millions of fans ('I get some people looking on me as their guru, asking where they should go next, but I get out of that one very rapidly: be your own guru'), Herbert soon found the *Dune* phenomenon moving beyond his control as other visionaries began to clutch at it. Unlike most writers, who retire wounded as their works are mauled into screenplays, he appears to have derived a solid and hearty enjoyment from guiding and tolerating the various assaults made on his text before he was at last filmed with the clapper-board for the first take of the opening day of shooting for the David Lynch version. And he was a loyal champion of the completed production, calling it 'a visual feast' and 'true to my book even though most of it stayed on the cutting-room floor. If you were disappointed or wanted more, chalk it up to "That's show biz!"'

The story of the filming of Herbert's *Dune* has become a well-known epic in its own right, full of illustrious walk-ons from Orson Welles to Salvador Dalí. It began in 1972 with the purchase of an option on the book by Arthur P. Jacobs (producer of the original *Planet of the Apes*), who recruited Herbert as technical adviser. When Jacobs died the following year the rights were picked up by French financier Michael Seydaux who had been enthralled by charismatic Chilean Alejandro Jodorowsky's dune-filled Western allegory *El Topo* (1971). Jodorowsky proceeded to spend $2 million on artists and designers, including the great comic-book illustrator Jean 'Moëbius' Giraud, special-effects whiz-kid Dan O'Bannon (*Dark Star*) and surrealist painter H. R. Giger. Each artist was given his own planet to conceptualise. 'My planet [Giedi Prime],' reported Giger, 'would be ruled by evil. Violence would run free. Perversion would be the order of the day. In a word, it was my specialty.'

According to Giger, Dalí was to be cast as the depraved Baron Harkonnen (other sources elevated him to the role of Emperor) at a salary of $100,000 an hour. The enormous script – enough for at least four features – culminated in the death of Paul Atreides and the transformation of Arrakis into a sentient planet sharing an intergalactic awareness. Such a crusade for universal harmony was a reasonable extension of the novel's implications, but it threatened an uncontrollable budget. In 1976 Seydaux got out while the going was good, smartly recovering his investment by selling the rights to Dino De Laurentiis.

De Laurentiis commissioned a new screenplay from Herbert himself, but the writer, for whom abbreviation was never a strong point, proved unable to pare down his work to anything manageable. Then came *Star Wars* (1977) with its sandscapes, quasi-mystical theme and teenager with exceptional powers, and science fiction would never be the same again. Recognising that *Dune* would have to be a deliberate counterpoint to the exuberance of *Star Wars*, De Laurentiis turned to Ridley Scott, whose *Alien* (1979) was the stuff of spatial nightmare, and preparations for a fresh *Dune* began at Pinewood. Scott's choice of scriptwriter was Rudolph Wurlitzer, author of the contentious novel *Quake* (described by the *New York Times* as 'as if William Burroughs had written *Lord of the Flies*') and past collaborator with Peckinpah (he wrote, and got shot in, *Pat Garrett and Billy the Kid*). Giger, whose skeletal concepts were the essence of *Alien*, was also redeployed: he designed a spectacular sandworm and some gothic furniture.

Within eight months everything had changed. Not only was the Scott version (budgeted at $50 million) considered too expensive, but the script was said to be wandering into a not-implausible but commercially hazardous story of incest. So Scott went off to make *Blade Runner* and De Laurentiis discovered *The Elephant Man*, whose director David Lynch was in the running to make the third part of the *Star Wars* trilogy, *Return of the Jedi*. Quickly hooked, Lynch consulted with Herbert, Freddie Francis (his invaluable cinematographer on *The Elephant Man*) and designer Anthony Masters (sandblasted veteran from *Lawrence of Arabia*, a strikingly similar tale, and *2001: A Space Odyssey*), coming up with seven script drafts for final approval. 'I tried,' he said, 'to complete things more than the book did – the answers to most of the puzzles are in the movie. Some people say about Herbert that he wrote the greatest unread best-seller in the business; one thing I did want to do was to make the greatest unseen epic in the film business.'

It came close. At last released in December 1984, *Dune* may have unravelled some of Herbert's puzzles but to its mostly baffled audiences it remained crammed with mystery. Explanatory speeches were cluttered with obscure references and unlikely terminology while many of the names seemed to strike even the cast as awkward to pronounce. From his earliest short stories Herbert showed an affection for absurdly named characters (Prester Charlesworthy, Estagién Culoc, Mirsar Wees) which, jolting enough to the reader, translate clumsily to filmed conversation. The sight, for instance, of the Emperor (José Ferrer) nervously demanding Sardaukar (fanatical warriors) like some kind of food additive is cause for irreparable distraction. And while another of Herbert's habits (again from his earlier writings) was to have his characters think in italics, critics complained that when this was faithfully adapted to Lynch's soundtrack it contributed nothing to the film's clarity.

During filming Lynch and his producers were well pleased with each other. De Laurentiis was said even to have permitted the director to film material that would never be used, while Lynch was eager to establish his professional ability to control a crew of more than 1,700. The first rough-cut lasted nearly four hours, but De Laurentiis was adamant that the running-time should be no more than a curiously arbitrary two hours and 17 minutes. The ferocity of the editing process depressed Lynch almost to the point where he abandoned film-making entirely. Plans for two sequels were briskly cancelled. But in two years he was back with another De Laurentiis production, *Blue Velvet*, winning himself an Oscar nomination. In assessments of Lynch these days, *Dune* tends to be discreetly overlooked.

Helping it into obscurity, Lynch took his name off the film when, expanded once more from its 'butchered' theatrical version, it began to find its way into the twilight zone of television and then, packaged with interviews and afterthoughts, into the infinite afterlife of video and DVD. Although it is unavoidably impoverished by small-screen presentation, *Dune* suffers no catastrophic harm in these domestic formats. On the contrary, taken at a moderate pace, with Herbert's text to hand for clarification, they provide a useful opportunity for obsessive observers to spot, say, the tumbling extra in the first 'Navigator' sequence or the moments when blue is strangely absent from Fremen eyes. In September 2000 the appearance of a 177-minute 'Alan Smithee' DVD, complete with a brochure that opens up to a facsimile of the original poster where the Lynch credit remains writ large, served to demonstrate both what Lynch's preferred cut would have been, and why, in disgust, he disowned the whole thing.

The Smithee version starts with a Prologue, its anonymous speaker exuding all the excitement of a heavy smoker propped on a bar stool. With faint, unintelligible echoes in the background of Princess Irulan's original opening speech, the voice whisks us back (maybe that should be forward) to the year 6041, before the reign of the Padishah emperors, when the Universe is ruled by robots (much as, thanks to Asimov and James Cameron, we are increasingly inclined to expect) and the human race has deteriorated into apathy. One may hope that Frank Herbert is the source for all this, but Jaroslav Gebr's accompanying paintings – lurid and cartoonish – are discouraging.

Which said, the Smithee *Dune* redeems itself by explaining with great care the links and rivalries between the Bene Gesserit, the Guild, the CHOAM Company, the Mentats, the Navigators, the Landsraad and the Emperor of the Known Universe, all of which, under pressure, Lynch had to leave in something of a tangle. Unaccountably adding a year to the date, it is surprisingly squeamish when it comes to the excesses of the evil Baron (scant sign of his bathing in slave blood and absolutely no spitting on Jessica) but is punctilious in identifying new characters as they appear and subtly extends and rearranges numerous sequences to their distinct improvement.

The main amendments are listed in David Hughes's just-published *The Complete Lynch*, an invaluable handbook for anyone wondering whether Gurney Halleck (Patrick Stewart) ever got around to playing the baliset, or when Paul's sister Alia was conceived, or exactly how the traitor Yueh (Dean Stockwell) received instructions via corpse-mail. Some might argue though, *pace* Hughes, that the added shots of the Shadout Mapes (Linda Hunt) roaming the dark corridors indicate that rather than committing suicide, she is murdered by Yueh. And Hughes misses out a particularly helpful moment when, having despatched the dreaded Feyd Rautha (Sting), Paul shatters the floor under the corpse by mind-power alone, to the delight of his Fremen followers: thanks to a restored close-up, the previous air of disapproval has been dispelled.

As if the several versions of Lynch were not enough, the story has now been rewritten once again. First unleashed last year on the Sci-Fi Channel, the boldly titled *Frank Herbert's Dune* is already available on video and DVD in three 90-minute chunks, corresponding to the three sections of the novel ('Dune', 'Muad'Dib' and 'The Prophet'). Written and directed by John Harrison with the avowed guarantee that 'whatever we were putting into the movie had its source in the book – nothing has been changed or re-ordered that can't be justified from the original', this adaptation has a certain fascination for its inclusion of all kinds of incident and detail untouched by the Lynch revisions – and for the revelation that they prove to have been expendable anyway. An earnest and largely unknown cast is headed by William Hurt as Duke Leto, underplaying with an impressive if somnambulistic authority, and Ian McNeice, who brings a proper relish to the evils of Baron Harkonnen. The key role of Paul Atreides in taken by newcomer Alec Newman, whose arduous attainment of Messianic adulthood is a melancholy and unshaven ordeal, little helped by the unfocused but obligatory blue gaze imposed on him and his Fremen troops.

A former assistant to George Romero, Harrison wrote the animated Disney success *Dinosaur* but is best known for *Tales from the Darkside: The Movie* (1991), an episodic venture in which he experimented with a different style for each horror story. His contributions to the *Tales from the Crypt* series, notably *Easel Kill You* (1991) featuring Tim Roth as an artist desperately resorting to homicide, indicate a keen eye for striking colour and depth-of-field staging, which duly turn up as assets in his filming of *Dune*. His real stars, in fact, are the Oscar-winning cinematographer Vittorio Storaro, whose fluent use of colour and lighting provides vitality to some otherwise lifeless settings, his regular special-effects supervisor Ernest Farino (some splendid sandworms, premonitory visions, and ominous spacecraft) and above all his Czech designers, headed by Theodor Pistek and Miljen Kljakovic, who prove less steampunk than Lynch's team but still pleasingly outrageous.

The Harrison *Dune*, in this sense, confirms the real purpose behind all the previous assaults on the novel, in which Herbert left appearances mostly to the imagination. Much of the millions spent over the years on developing his work have been devoted not to the script but to the setting, an endless gallery of dream palaces, twin-mooned landscapes and exotic costumes. Harrison has reported, flushed with (moderate) success, that it was sometimes like filming Shakespeare (the chilling assumption of kingship, perhaps, from *Henry IV, Part II*, or the vengeful treachery in the castle corridors of *Hamlet*), and is already embarked on a mini-series sequel based on Herbert's *Dune Messiah* and *Children of Dune*. It is as if Jodorowsky, Scott, Harrison, or Lynch with his 1,700 employees, or De Laurentiis with his mega-wealth, all found the story of Paul Atreides' hunt for leadership and immortality of special and irresistible pertinence – as did Frank Herbert who, way ahead of them, gave due warning. 'Charismatic leaders,' he observed, 'are dangerous people. The errors of the leader are amplified by the numbers of people that follow him. Even if he himself is perfect, he creates a power structure, attracting people who want power for its own sake. And that's when the shit hits the fan.'

THE DREAMLIFE OF ANDROIDS

J. Hoberman

'Stories are real,' insists David, the enchanted robot child who is the protagonist of Steven Spielberg's *A.I. Artificial Intelligence*. David believes that fairytales can come true. Do we? Spielberg the humanist historian is in remission; Steven the regressive mystic has returned, with a vengeance.

An occasionally spectacular, fascinatingly schizoid, frequently ridiculous and never less than heartfelt mishmash of Pinocchio and Oedipus, Stanley Kubrick (who bequeathed Spielberg the project) and *Creation of the Humanoids*, *Frankenstein* and 'The Steadfast Tin Soldier', *A.I.* is less a movie than a seething psychological bonanza. None of the year's Hollywood releases has given US critics more to write about – nor is one likely to. Moreover, given the movie's convoluted provenance and charged subject matter, it's not so much the critic as their inner child who has been responding to Spielberg's provocation.

Opening in the United States in late June, *A.I.* reaped a severely mixed crop of reviews – surely the most varied in its maker's career. *New York Times* critic A. O. Scott hailed *A.I.* as Spielberg's 'best fairytale', as well as 'a more profound inquiry into the moral scandal of dehumanization than either *Schindler's List* or *Amistad*'. Writing in the *New Yorker*, David Denby termed *A.I.* a movie that 'weirdly pours treacle over a foundation of despair...a ponderous, death-of-the-world fantasy'. Adding to the mix have been reports in the trade papers and elsewhere recounting the violent antipathy ordinary audiences have expressed. This disapproval was manifest at the box office where *A.I.*'s grosses dropped 50 per cent and 63 per cent in its second and third weeks. *A.I.* is not the first Spielberg film to be perceived as a flop; it is, however, the first to be more a critical than a commercial success – which is to say, an art film.

If there is a universal personality in contemporary cinema it is surely Steven Spielberg. His movies have ranged from the depths of the ocean to the dark side of Neverland, from the Georgia backwoods to Japanese-occupied Shanghai. Spielberg has brought extraterrestrials down to earth and resurrected the dinosaurs. His sacred texts include not only the Ark of the Covenant but *A Guy Named Joe* (1944). As Walt Disney's invented signature used to emblazon the landscape in the comic books and comic strips produced by his enterprise, so Spielberg has managed to affix his name to the Holocaust, slavery and the European theatre of World War II. In that tradition of aesthetic big-game hunting, he appropriates Stanley Kubrick.

A.I. is adapted from sci-fi writer Brian Aldiss's 'Super-Toys Last All Summer Long', a story first published 32 years ago in *Harper's Bazaar*. Kubrick, who evidently had a long-standing interest in this tale of an artificial child and his human parents, acquired the rights in 1983. Various accounts suggest he was already operating in reaction to Spielberg. Inspired to make *A.I.* by the success of *E.T.* (1982), Kubrick is said to have abandoned the project after he saw the digital effects of *Jurassic Park* (1993). Afraid that by the time he could finish *A.I.* its special effects would be obsolete, he proposed to produce the movie for Spielberg to direct. According to Spielberg, he and Kubrick consequently enjoyed a long-term phone relationship complete with a top-secret fax line dedicated to *A.I.* Having inherited the project, Spielberg worked from the 90-page treatment Ian Watson had prepared for Kubrick, as well as 600 drawings made by comic-book illustrator Chris 'Fangorn' Baker.

A.I. appears then as a curiously hybrid work. One could begin by parsing the title: does the artifice belong to Spielberg and the intelligence to Kubrick? Or is it vice versa? *A.I.* has an unnecessarily complicated yet brazenly irrational premise. The script, for which Spielberg has taken sole credit, more than once becomes bogged down in a hilarious morass of Ed Wood gibberish in trying to elucidate the pseudo-scientific principles by which robots might be imbued with the capacity to love and to dream – to have an unconscious – or the special circumstances under which human beings can be cloned. Why bother? The movie's appeal is not to reason. Its psychological terrain is far closer to the magical realms of Hans Christian Andersen or E. T. A. Hoffman than to sci-fi as we know it.

Spielberg's first exercise in cine-futurism, *A.I.* is set in a vaguely established, remarkably homogenous, bizarrely suburban, post-greenhouse-effect world of strict family planning and robot sex slaves. These humanoids are known as 'mechas', and *A.I.* opens with their benign designer Professor Hobby (William Hurt) informing his devoted band of earth-tone imagineers that he has developed something new, 'a robot child with a love that will never end'. One associate makes an obscure moral objection, but the good professor silences her with an airy wave of the hand: 'Didn't God create Adam to love him?' Yes, of course, and look what happened.

The proto robo-tot will be given to distraught Monica (Frances O'Connor), whose own terminally ill son Martin has been cryogenically frozen pending the discovery of a cure for his disease. The artificial miracle child first appears out of focus, to suggest the elongated embryos who redeemed the world in *Close Encounters of the Third Kind* (1977). Is little David (Haley Joel Osment, scarcely less uncanny here than in *The Sixth Sense*) the baby Spielberg, a holy child with a smooth, open face and limpid blue eyes? Certainly Spielberg's identification with David will seem absolute. Is he a sort of emotional prosthetic device, the Frankenstein's monster of love? Or is this adorable robot child a terrifying metaphor for us all? The acid-ripped runaways and hippies of the Manson Family used to have a mocking chant about the parents they had fled: 'I am a mechanical boy... I am my mother's toy.'

A.I.'s early scenes are exquisitely creepy – perhaps more so than intended. Perpetually smiling and always underfoot, David frisks around Monica like an annoyingly needy pet – even bursting in on her as she demurely perches on the toilet. A psychoanalyst might make something of that scene but it is soon superseded. Once Monica pronounces the magic spell that will eternally bond David to her alone (not, significantly, to the husband who will eventually become David's enemy), the robot boy embarks on the golden road of unlimited devotion. The movie presents a profoundly bleak view of human nature – a child imprinted by and forever fixated on the parent's need. 'Mommy, will you die?' is the newly programmed David's first abstract question, as well as his first use of the maternal noun. Already expressing anxiety, his query does not quite elide the notion that when this slim and pretty woman is a crone of 90, her adoring mecha will still be a child.

David's age is unfixed. He's been described as 11, though he looks three years younger and has the emotional development of a pre-schooler. In any case, his particular instance of arrested development is superseded by the defrosted Martin's return to his now shockingly expanded family. This suspended animation is also part of the fairytale. Given that Spielberg wanted to use the Disneyland theme song for the celestial communication fest that ends *Close Encounters*, it's perfectly appropriate that when Monica visits Martin there would be Disney murals on the walls and Tchaikovsky's *Sleeping Beauty* playing in the background. (Kubrick, for his part, ended *Full Metal Jacket* with a supremely sarcastic use of the *Mickey Mouse Club* marching song.)

Without ever appearing to question the narcissistic assumption that children are put on this earth to love their parents, Spielberg finds his richest material in the family trauma, sibling rivalry and emotional malfunction induced by Martin's return. One thing this future world clearly lacks is the cyborg shrink in a suitcase extrapolated by novelist Philip K. Dick. There is no one to analyse, let alone treat, the rejected David's desire to reclaim his mommy's love or his magical solution that he might do so by becoming a 'real boy'. (This idea had been introduced by the malicious Martin who insists that Monica read her two sons the story of Pinocchio at bedtime.) The mecha quest for an impossible authenticity then becomes the movie's driving mechanism.

A.I. has been designed to terrorise actual children, even as it cannily harpoons the hearts of empty-nest boomer moms and pushes psychological buttons in kids (of all ages) longing for a return to the mother ship. David is Monica's toy – or rather he was. The scene in which a human mother abandons her crying, clinging, pleading robot child in the woods is as supreme a heart-clutcher as anything in *Bambi.* Although curiously glossed over in most reviews of the movie, this long, painful sequence which, as Manohla Dargis pointed out in the *L.A. Weekly,* 'combines Kubrick's aesthetic of cruelty and Spielberg's aesthetic of bathos into a single devastating encounter', is understandably the film's turning point. The hermetic suburban environment of David's family gives way to the garish dystopia of the outside world. Spielberg has always been a master of inadvertent disclosure. One of the most powerful images in his entire oeuvre is that of the obsessed Richard Dreyfus, imprinted by the aliens of *Close Encounters* and constructing a mountain out of his mashed potatoes even as his distressed children look on in terrified amazement at his apparent regression to infancy. What's fascinating is that Spielberg has gone out of his way to characterise *A.I.* as a film made by an indulgent father: 'I am particularly, at this point in my life, somewhat interested in going back a little bit to my past, to tell the kinds of stories I'd like my kids to see. You know, between *Schindler* and *Ryan,* I had a lot of complaints from my kids that I'm not making movies for them anymore ... I think *A.I.* is a movie for my own kids.'

In what sense, one wonders. Does he mean to teach the power of stories? The idea that fantasy is real? Like Spielberg himself in *Close Encounters,* David takes *Pinocchio* as his text, searching the world in the company of Teddy (a sub-Jiminy Cricket 'supertoy') for the Blue Fairy who can grant his wish to become a real child. Unlike the puppet Pinocchio, however, David has no need to demonstrate emotional growth or, indeed, any sort of negativity. He's been designed as a perfect reproach to humanity, hard-wired for innocence. (Thus Spielberg circumvents the moral of the Aldiss story – which is also the pathos of *Blade Runner*–namely that the robots are more human than their creators.)

Whereas Pinocchio's greed led to his being trapped in Stromboli's carnival, blameless David is rounded up by the flying storm-troopers of the Flesh Fair, a heavy-metal demolition derby cum death camp for discarded mechas. (The sequence seems to have been imported wholesale from *Mad Max beyond Thunderdome.*) It's been suggested by some that this bloodthirsty mob represents Spielberg's view of his audience – although, no less than these rabid rednecks, the film-maker evidently loves the effect of the obsolete jerry-built robots running about further decomposing. Actually, in their devotion to so-called reality, the demagogues responsible for the Flesh Fair might equally represent Spielberg's view of his critics. (Rather than the fantasy of *Schindler's List,* these anti-mechas are demanding the documentary *Shoah.*)

Devoted to ritual destruction, the Flesh Fair has a religious aspect: 'We are only demolishing artificiality,' the cult leader explains. Intelligence will come next.

Escaping from the Flesh Fair, David and Teddy team up with (and redeem) a more profane manifestation of cyberlove. Gigolo Joe (Jude Law) is a stiff, absurdly pomaded creature who supplies his own louche soundtrack – a faraway-sounding 1930s version of 'I Only Have Eyes for You' (the very thing surely to guarantee that a lonely repressed spinster will lie back, relax, and lose her inhibitions). Joe's line is no less primitive. 'Once you've had a robot lover, you'll never want a real man again,' he assures a client. Out of concern for his children no doubt, Spielberg resists showing the sex machine in action. (Joe's bionic member is referred to by his timorous partner but, of course, never seen. This does, however, serve to link him to David who in an earlier scene had the functionality – and existence – of his penis questioned by a human playmate.)

As *A.I.*'s resident embodiment of cynical Kubrick consciousness, Gigolo Joe takes David to Rouge City (an elaborate extrapolation of the Milkbar from *A Clockwork Orange*, 1971) to consult the resident oracle, a fragmented babbling holograph. David, of course, wants to ascertain the whereabouts of the Blue Fairy. An impossible dream? At this point readers who wish to protect their own innocence are advised to check out and return after experiencing *A.I.* for themselves.

Sent to the end of the world, a largely submerged New York City, where he is shocked – shocked! – to discover the reification of human relations that mechas represent, little David runs amok. But this single moment of anti-capitalist rebellion is brief. David rejects his creator Professor Hobby to dive from the top of Radio City deep into the maternal vastness of the dream dump.

For an unforgettable moment, I imagined that Spielberg might really leave us with a bizarre and truly despairing image: Pinocchio frozen forever in a world where Jiminy Cricket is mute and Walt Disney dead, praying through all eternity before an inert icon of the irretrievable mother. Not to worry. The shamelessly milked miracle arrives 2000 (and one?) years later, replete with thunderous wonder, appropriate white light and a mother-and-child reunion so obliterating in its solipsism that it bids to split your skull. However sentimental its intent, though, this ending may actually be more hopeless than anything in Kubrick.

As in a Kubrick movie, the humans in *A.I.* are universally shown to be vain, treacherous, selfish, jealous and, above all, cruel creatures. But Spielberg understands that, no less than the robots, we in the audience have feelings – really big ones. What's more, we can dream. Thus the spectators are granted a cosmic fantasy of total symbiosis that combines the everyday mysticism of *2001: A Space Odyssey* (1968), the back-to-the-womb climax of *Close Encounters*, and something akin to the last scene of *Tristan and Isolde*. It's a simulation, which is to say, it's a movie. And though it has been made just for David, there won't be a dry eye in the theatre when, having been treated to his first-ever birthday cake, the ageless cyber-child finally goes to 'that place where dreams are born'. (Some cheeks, however, may be wet with tears of mirth.)

Flattering? The robot extraterrestrials of the future go out of their way to express an insane admiration for the long-gone humanity of which David represents the last 'living' artefact. In somewhat the same fashion, Spielberg imagines himself to be keeping the idea of Kubrick alive. *A.I. is* artificial intelligence. 'I felt that Stanley hadn't really died, that he was with me when I was writing the screenplay and shooting the movie,' the director has said. As *A.I.*'s initial ad campaign put it: 'His love is real. But he is not.'

A.I. ARTIFICIAL INTELLIGENCE
USA 2001
Director: Steven Spielberg

The Earth's melting ice-caps have drowned countless cities, but population control has ensured the United States is still an island of prosperity. Professor Hobby of Cybertronics Manufacturing proposes the ultimate robot, a child-like construction which can experience emotions. The prototype, a robot called David, is placed with Cybertronics employee Henry Swinton and his wife Monica, whose own child Martin has been cryogenically frozen until a cure is found for his terminal illness. The experiment is a success, with Monica and David sharing an ecstatic relationship. Monica even gives him Martin's supertoy Teddy, a mini-robot with superior reasoning. When Martin is cured, David is no longer needed; Martin jealously makes trouble for him. When Monica reads them the story of Pinocchio and the Blue Fairy, David is convinced that he must become a 'real' boy in order to keep his mother's love. After an accident in which David nearly drowns Martin, Monica abandons David and Teddy on a distant wasteland where he is soon captured along with a load of discarded robots. He avoids being destroyed as ghoulish entertainment for the crowds at the Flesh Fair arena. With the help of Gigolo Joe, a 'love robot' who is on the run after being framed for murder, David makes his way to Rouge City, a riotous leisure centre where an omniscient computer tells him the Blue Fairy is to be found at the end of the world, formerly Manhattan.

Dodging the police, Gigolo Joe takes him to the drowned city by helicopter, reuniting him with a delighted Professor Hobby who has been producing innumerable further Davids. In despair at this revelation, David throws himself into the ocean but discovers, far below, a statue of the Blue Fairy and begs her to make him 'real'. Trapped in a sunken helicopter, he remains confronting the statue for 2,000 years until alien visitors release him and decipher his memory. Using a lock of Monica's hair that Teddy has preserved, they are able to reconstruct her for a single day and David at last gets his wish. As the joyful day closes, mother and son fall asleep together as Teddy watches over them.

* * *

For years, rumours emerged infrequently from the Kubrick domain that he was planning a film about artificial intelligence. A safe assumption seemed to be that the story of HAL 9000, the misunderstood computer of *2001: A Space Odyssey* (1968), would in some way be continued. Given the prevalence of pre-programmed, zombie-like characters in Kubrick's work (think *A Clockwork Orange* or *Full Metal Jacket*), an exploration of possible tensions within a part-robotic society seemed an entirely logical route for him to take. We now know that the launch-pad for the project was a Brian W. Aldiss story written in 1969, 'Supertoys Last All Summer Long'. We know, too, that Kubrick, unlike Aldiss, saw this as a version of Collodi's classic fairytale *Pinocchio*, and that he developed it (under the title *Supertoys*) in parallel with what became his final film, *Eyes Wide Shut*. Already hampered enough by other distractions, *Eyes Wide Shut* will be little enhanced by a *Pinocchio* comparison, although the curious odyssey of its frustrated hero, concluding in a Christmas toy shop, is not without its resonances. What appears to overflow directly into *Eyes Wide Shut* from the Aldiss text, however, is both its sense of bereaved passion and, more fundamentally, the question asked by the story's robot three-year-old (aged nearer 11 in *A.I.*): 'How do you tell what are real things from what aren't real things?' To which, at story's end, the all-knowing robot 'supertoy' Teddy replies: 'Nobody knows what "real" really means', a typical Aldiss aphorism. In *Eyes Wide Shut*, the big scene of revelation in which the terrified husband is assured that nothing of the previous night was 'real' casts an overpowering uncertainty across his adventures. And in *A.I.*, illusion and pretence are the only perpetual realities, and fakery is entirely forgivable in direct ratio to the amount of happiness it generates. At heart, *A.I.* and *Eyes Wide Shut* prompt the same questions.

In bequeathing his project to Steven Spielberg, complete with draft scripts and hundreds of futuristic designs, Kubrick found the ideal successor, another Pinocchio fan. As early as his 1972 telefilm *Something Evil*, in which a mother has to rescue her young son from demonic possession, Spielberg was showing us 'lost' children in a persistent battle of the generations that finds its way as much into *Indiana Jones and the Last Crusade* (1989) as such obvious derivatives as *E.T.* (1982) or *Hook* (1991). The most blatant Pinocchio reference prior to *A.I.* can be found in the Spielberg-scripted *Close Encounters of the Third Kind* (1977), where the increasingly childlike father tries to persuade his offspring to see the film he identified with at their age. As he is enfolded into the embrace of the mother-ship after his long quest, a triumphant fragment of the Disney *Pinocchio* theme is briefly on the soundtrack...

Spielberg says he was a different person back then: tackling aliens today (extraterrestrials make a final-reel appearance in *A.I.*) needs a more pragmatic, less idealistic approach. All the same, the primary alien function remains, it seems, to make dreams come true (especially the one about immortality). And combining extraterrestrials with the Blue Fairy (Pinocchio's mother-substitute) produces – as Aldiss feared it would – an uneasy alliance. While it's just about excusable that aliens can be expected to do anything, and would be poor judges of an unstable robot's misguided fantasies, the result unavoidably verges on the ludicrous.

With their wish-fulfilment benevolence, and their matchstick appearance, the aliens of *A.I.* are closely related, in fact, to the thinnest *Close Encounters* visitor. Fascinated by the still-functioning robot-child David, lightly garnished with the accumulated mould of 2,000 years, they can magically reconstruct out of nothing much his 'home' and his 'mother' – but not, of course, his disagreeable 'father' and 'brother' – for an unrepeatable (such are the inexplicable limits of magic) 24 hours. And whatever happened, by the way, to all the other durable Davids – and Darlenes – revealed in Professor Hobby's lair? Hastily reverting to the bedtime-story tones of a conciliatory commentary for a few details of their halcyon day, the film switches itself off at the peculiarly Oedipal final image of artificial repose. It is hard to imagine Kubrick as the Geppetto to all of this, but Spielberg's identification with his marionette couldn't be plainer.

For all Spielberg's loyalty, Kubrick would undoubtedly have filmed it differently. The immaculate corridors and palatial rooms of *Eyes Wide Shut*, furnishings agleam with mellow light, and above all the restless Steadicam patrols, leading and pursuing the performers with an urbane attentiveness, have a magisterial authority familiar from *The Shining* (1980) or *Barry Lyndon* (1975), but find little reflection in the surfaces of *A.I.*. Instead, Spielberg exercises his usual skills – a no-nonsense pace, huge bursts of sound and action, eye-popping special effects – with a nod to Kubrick-style images: the docking scene from *2001*, the smashing of mannequins from *Killer's Kiss* (1955), the plunge into the frozen maze from *The Shining*. The decorative asides to a tale told well, if at some length, are all Spielberg's: the captured Moon hinting at a silhouette or two, the motor-bikes with Jurassic fangs, the use of blazing white to signify angelic innocence, and the affectionate movie reference whereby the 'love robot' Gigolo Joe, with a twitch of the shoulder, summons Dick Powell's romantic ballad (and Busby Berkeley's audacity) from *Dames* (1934).

Of particular note are Spielberg's underwater sequences, replete with the foreboding he has been injecting since *Jaws* (1975). In *Always* (1989) it was a sunken plane and a trapped pilot, in *Amistad* (1997) a line of tethered slaves sinking helplessly, and in *Saving Private Ryan* (1998) a horrific welter of the drowning wounded. In *A.I.* a swimming-pool accident leads to David's expulsion from the family that owns him (a vertiginous aerial shot shows him marooned at the bottom of the pool), while the later scenes of an engulfed New York provide some of the finest ever vistas of that special disaster genre in which Manhattan is always the prime target for submersion. Some future nightmare seems bound to emerge from these murky fathoms. Meanwhile, Spielberg's other triumphs in *A.I.* are in his deployment of the vast gladiatorial settings of the Flesh Fair and the neo-Vegas glitter of Rouge City, reminding us he can handle massive crowd scenes with a touch of skilful artwork and a nonchalant elegance. If *A.I.* is too soft-centred to do little more in the end than *Star Wars* (1977), *Blade Runner* (1982) or *Cherry 2000* (1988) to prepare us for the dubious rewards of robotic integration, at least it restates HAL's case with commendable vehemence and a kaleidoscopic ingenuity.

Philip Strick

REVIEWS

GROUNDHOG DAY
USA 1993
Director: Harold Ramis

Phil Connors, a cynical Philadelphia TV weatherman, is less than happy when he is despatched for the fifth time to the small town of Punxsutawney to cover the annual Groundhog Day ceremony. A snowstorm threatens, too, though he predicts that it will miss the area. The great day – February 2nd – dawns and the groundhog duly emerges from its box. According to the local dignitaries, the rodent seer has predicted six more weeks of winter. Phil's idealistic producer Rita Hanson extols the town's simple virtues, but he remains unconvinced, and when the snowstorm duly materialises to prevent his departure, takes to his bed in disgust. He wakes up next morning to find that it's February 2nd again. At first he is incredulous and seeks help from Rita, from a doctor and from a psychiatrist. The next morning it happens again: it's a new day for everyone except Phil. He gets drunk and ends up in jail after driving a car down a railway track. He wakes up as usual in his guest-house bedroom. Over successive February 2nds, he uses the knowledge he is able to acquire about the town's people and events for sexual and financial gain, seducing women and robbing banks. He devises a devious plan to have his way with Rita, but it consistently fails.

Despondent, Phil steals the groundhog and commits suicide by driving off a cliff. He wakes up as usual to Sonny and Cher on the radio. Having exhausted all possible suicide routes, he manages to get Rita to understand what has happened to him and, after they spend a glorious day together, he tells her that he loves her. Next day, she remembers nothing. After unsuccessfully trying to save the life of an old tramp, Phil starts to use his power of hindsight for the good of the community – catching falling children, performing Heimlich manoeuvres – building up a daily regime of life-saving 'chores'. One Groundhog night he goes to the post-ceremony party that he'd spurned on his first February 2nd. The townspeople treat him like a hero and Rita is so impressed she buys him for the night in a charity auction. Next morning, February 3rd dawns at last for Phil. Blissfully happy, he decides to set up house with Rita in the town he now knows so well.

* * *

Groundhog Day is that rarest of cinematic pleasures – a major studio Hollywood comedy that both delights and surprises. It's based on a story by Danny Rubin, who co-wrote the screenplay with director Harold Ramis, and although it's the original idea that is initially so startling, the inventiveness and delicacy with which it is realised are finally just as impressive. There's not much in Ramis's career to suggest a talent for subtle, character-based comedy – he started out as jokes editor of *Playboy* and went on to co-write *Animal House* and direct *Ghostbusters* (on the plus side, he also made *Caddyshack*). But that, within the framework of a very high concept, is what he delivers.

The idea of the endlessly repeating day is in fact such a high concept – if Samuel Beckett or Philip K. Dick had thought of it, they could have retired early, their work complete – that the film is in danger of catching a nosebleed. The first repetition is crucial; too many big laughs too soon and the film would be over in its first 15 minutes. Ramis wisely gives it time, going for chuckles rather than belly laughs. It is the gradualness of Connors's awakening to the different ramifications of his predicament that is so affecting. Bill Murray's world-weary weatherman redeemed by magic has none of the self-conscious showiness of Steve Martin's character in *L.A. Story*. Murray starts out small and expands the character to fill the space allowed, which, as it turns out, is substantial.

The scenes in which he painstakingly constructs a complete psychological profile of the object of his desire, Rita, in order to get her into bed, only to be repeatedly frustrated, are among his funniest ever. When the material is right, no one can do cheap and deep at the same time like Murray. To their credit, the supporting players never appear bored with their secondary status. Even Andie MacDowell manages to make something worthwhile out of her role as bewildered nice girl, while the townspeople seem to revel in their function as mere pawns.

The film's dark underside (Murray's repeated attempts at suicide are genuinely disturbing) ensures that its humanist message – if forced to stay long enough in the place you most hate, you could come to love it – does not leave a saccharine after-taste. Happily, the streak of misanthropy in Murray's character survives to the end. *Groundhog Day* pays lip-service to Capraesque redemption conventions, but it is refreshing that the weatherman seems to become a better person more out of boredom than anything else. In a way, this film gives the small town due restitution for the savage assaults of the Lynch-mob – instead of peeling away the gloss of a too-perfect façade, it transforms Connors's blistering contempt into admiration.

Ben Thompson

MORTAL KOMBAT
USA 1995
Director: Paul Anderson

In China, martial arts combatants are summoned to take part in a tournament called Mortal Kombat to decide whether Outworld – a ravished alternative universe – and its inhabitants shall be allowed to cross into our world and blight it. Amongst others defending the Earth are Lu, who was raised by martial arts fighting monks, Sonya, a law enforcer and Johnny Cage, an action movie star. They are assisted and advised by a demigod named Rayden. The main contestants representing Outworld are led by Shang, an evil wizard. Under his command are Kano, an English underworld crime boss, Goro, a multi-armed monster, plus Sub Zero and Scorpion, who have unique supernatural powers. The loyalties of the 10,000-year-old Princess Kitana, the rightful heir to Outworld, are more ambiguous.

The forces representing Outworld soon prove their lethal might, but Sonya snaps Kano's neck in combat. Cage battles and defeats Scorpion. Lu draws with Princess Kitana, who surreptitiously gives him advice on his next fight which helps him later defeat Sub Zero. Eventually, Cage beats the seemingly undefeatable Goro. Rayden reveals that he knows each earth's warrior's deepest fears. Shang drags Sonya into Outworld and Cage and Lu follow. There the latter two battle monsters, but are helped by Princess Kitana. Lu challenges Shang to a final bout, and having faced his worst fears (himself, and his destiny) in the process, emerges victorious. Princess Kitana regains the rule of Outworld. Back in our world, the winners' happy reunion with Rayden is cut short when the godlike Emperor emerges on the horizon.

* * *

Many recent action films induce a sense of déjà vu. See one 'concept' and you are more than likely to see it again a few months later. Thrillers set on submarines (*Under Siege,*

The Hunt For Red October, Crimson Tide), men-in-kilts films (*Rob Roy, Braveheart*), and a slew of comic-book based movies drop off the production line. It seems we've only just recovered from the mind-batteringly silly *Street Fighter* when *Mortal Kombat* comes forth to wrest control of the joystick. In their previous incarnations as video games, *Street Fighter* and *Mortal Kombat* were sworn foes, fighting for the forces of Nintendo and Sega respectively. Most consumers tended to agree that *Mortal Kombat*, with more blood and better animation, was the superior game. With elegant cosmic symmetry, *Street Fighter* (actually based on the game *Street Fighter II*) has proved to be the better film, if only for its delightful camp outréness and refusal to take itself too seriously.

The problem with *Mortal Kombat* is its pace. After a striking opening dream sequence in which Lu's brother has his back broken, the first 40 minutes flits peripatetically from location to location. The script presents a lot of overly elaborate back-stories to digest, but they go down awkwardly. When the climax comes with the Mortal Kombat tournament, the fights are so bland and stodgy, a feeling of cinematic dyspepsia never really dissipates. 'Finish him!', exhorts Shang near the end of many of the contests, a catchphrase of the original game. 'Finish it!', you feel like shouting back at the screen.

Director Paul Anderson, whose previous film was the dismal British ramraiding teen-pic *Shopping*, overindulges in slow-motion photography, neglecting to generate a sense of speed to offset the film's many dull stretches. He lacks flair for action, so the overall impression is of watching someone playing the game badly rather than feeling as if you are in the game itself. A nightclub scene, thronged with trendy ravers, provides a nasty flashback to Anderson's previous *Shopping* trip, but there are no new goods on display. Too much energy seems to have been spent designing elaborate sets of leering gargoyles and orientalist clutter that recall Korda's *The Thief of Bagdad*. Yet, nothing spectacular ever happens. There are scenes involving boats, forests, underground taverns and sports arenas, yet everything is so darkly lit and densely decorated it looks like one location.

Several lurid monsters literally rear their ugly heads, often putting in finer performances than the 'living' players. As Rayden, Christopher Lambert reprises his weary immortal act from the *Highlander* films – the lightning bolts from his eyes seem to be the only thing keeping him awake. What most of the cast and stunt people are good at is shouting, kicking, and throwing punches, which they perform admirably. The real stars of this film are the foley artists, who produce the wonderfully realistic sounds of bones breaking and flesh being pummelled. With so many action films coming out these days, all so heavily reliant on these sound effects, one hopes these noble technicians are reaping the financial benefits. They ought to get a share of the grosses.

Leslie Felperin

STRANGE DAYS
USA 1995
Director: Kathryn Bigelow

Los Angeles, December 1999. As the city prepares to celebrate the millennium, ex-cop Lenny Nero hustles the latest illegal attraction: recordings made directly from the brain by the Superconducting Quantum Interference Device (SQUID) which can be worn undetected. On playback, these 'clips' provide total involvement in the recorded experience. Intended for police use only, in Lenny's hands they supply access to any form of vicarious excitement. Lenny's private collection preserves vivid fragments of his past love affair with Faith, a rising pop star now attached to ruthless promoter Philo Gant. Lenny keeps an eye on her through his friend Max Pelticr, also an ex-cop, who works for Philo as a security guard. Lenny's only other friend is Mace, tough woman driver of an armoured limousine.

One of Lenny's contacts, Iris, warns him that Faith is in danger, but has to run from the police before she can explain. At the enormous Retinal Fetish nightclub, Faith tells Lenny to leave her alone and Philo's thugs throw him out. Meanwhile, news that black activist and major pop star Jeriko One has been murdered by unknown killers, raises tensions in the city to a critical level. Viewing a clip sent to him anonymously, Lenny is horrified to find himself participating in the brutal rape and murder of Iris. Recalling that Iris mentioned a message left in his car, which has since been towed away, Lenny and Mace break into the compound and discover a clip in Lenny's vehicle. Two cops, Steckler and Engelman, seize the clip and then pursue Lenny and Mace, setting Mace's limousine on fire. They escape by driving it off a pier.

Having tricked the cops, Lenny plays the recovered clip; it reveals that Iris, wearing a SQUID, was witness to the murder of Jeriko One by Steckler and Engelman. As the massive New Year's Eve celebrations get under way, Faith tells Mace and Lenny that Philo sent Iris to 'tape' an encounter with Jeriko One. Mace persuades Lenny to let her take the clip to the head of the police force, Palmer Strickland. Lenny tracks Philo down only to find him brain-damaged from a SQUID overload administered by Max, who killed Iris to satisfy his own cravings. In a ferocious struggle, Faith helps Lenny to defeat Max while Mace is pursued through the packed streets by the two cops. She manages to handcuff them, but armed soldiers knock her aside; the crowd rushes to her defence and a riot breaks out until Strickland, having checked the clip, orders the arrest of the two killers. Still attempting to destroy Mace, Engelman and Steckler are shot down. As the new century arrives, Lenny realises at last how much Mace really means to him.

* * *

While there can be little doubt that SQUID – a delicate electronic web fitting under the hairpiece so much more comfortably than other parasites we have known – will be with us (by popular demand) by the year 2000, we may well question whether it will be more absorbing than *Strange Days* itself. The breathtaking Kathryn Bigelow style – racing visuals thunderously reinforced by sonic enclosure – may not quite reach the nose or taste buds but it allows little other opportunity for detachment from the experience on show. Largely repeating with its opening number the chase sequence of *Point Break*, when bank-robber, cop, cameraman and audience negotiated an uncut succession of walls, doors, dogs and other obstacles with frantic immediacy, *Strange Days* re-educates us in the share-all process with a subjective burglary, complete with collapsing victims and untimely police arrival, that leaves us plummeting from a rooftop.

Bigelow likes her audiences to plummet along with her protagonists (the least you could say about *Point Break*, for example, is that it sweeps you off your feet), and this vertiginous preliminary flight, a disorienting topple towards impact with the unknown, readies us for the knife-edge of the century's final moments when the villain, too, hurtles to his fate. The same aerial vantage-point, high above the spangled city, that seduced (and, in her nightmares, overbalanced) the rookie cop in Bigelow's *Blue Steel* is again used to introduce the apocalyptic celebrations of *Strange Days*, an astonishing vista of seething crowds and spotlights that punch the sky. Grandeur on this scale is the stuff of instant addiction.

At ground level, the floating camera reverts to discreet third-party participation. While never pedestrian, the drama hustles like its central character, the floundering Lenny, from one beating to another, alternating crisis with shock, mystery with pursuit. The formula closely matches other James Cameron scripts such as *Aliens* or *Terminator 2: Judgement Day*, setting an urgent, escalating pace towards a decisive battle. Compounding the issue, Lenny's path is strewn with bad guys, a bewildering array by comparison with, say, *Blue Steel*, where they were all condensed into Ron Silver, or *Point Break* where – apart from one isolated cluster of gunmen – they weren't really bad anyway. Befitting an updated Chandleresque gumshoe thriller, *Strange Days* sprouts thugs from all sides, a colourful majority to impede Lenny's dogged progress towards some kind of truth.

Part of the fascination of the film's *noir*-ish allegiances is that the streets echo not with the occasional footstep but with blatant warfare, a perpetual carnage of robberies, gunfights, and burning cars, observed as normal by Lenny but staged with an obvious glee by his director who – in one particularly cheerful glimpse – even shows Santa Claus being mugged. That we can hardly take this lowlife inferno any more seriously than Brian De Palma's vision of an incandescent Bronx in *The Bonfire of the Vanities* is confirmed by the explanation stutteringly given by the rapist/killer when Lenny at last confronts him. Filmed from several disjointed angles (signs of indecision on Bigelow's part, or just the visual equivalent of his mental disintegration?), he is all charm and junkie incoherence, confessing to improvisations about death-squads and conspiracies that serve only to exaggerate the chaos. 'Cheer up,' he grins, 'the world has only ten minutes to go.'

Having shoved us to the brink with this vividly substantiated promise, having shown us a *fin-de-siècle* bedlam of intolerable dimensions in the form of the Retinal Fetish nightclub, having implicated us in the foulest uses (albeit necessarily and intriguingly self-censored) of the SQUID, and having finally – in the endless *Terminator*-style duel with killers who refuse to lie down and die – signalled the opening salvoes of a race war that was rehearsed in the Rodney King riots, Bigelow and Cameron stage a tantalising last-minute retreat. The new millennium arrives in a delirium of reconciliation and joy, of relief that the unsolvable can somehow, in this rare dawn, turn out to have been solved by the application of sheer unaccustomed goodwill. Lenny embraces, almost as an afterthought, the woman who has guarded him with muscle and loyalty throughout his erratic quest, and all else miraculously becomes irrelevant. It is the soft centre of the standard Cameron hard sell, a plot twist fashioned from opportunism which hints, as it did in *The Abyss*, at authentic loss and painful rediscovery. In this context, thanks to the impact of *Strange Days* as a whole, it is as welcome as it is unconvincing.

The Bigelow touch, growing surer with each film, imparts Cameron's hit-and-run tactics with an invaluable extra dimension. Her cast may have to tackle some abysmally trite dialogue, but under her guidance they come up with a lexicon of looks and gestures that makes it work. There is little complexity about Lenny (forget about SQUID, think of him as a petty drug-dealer and he becomes the cliché of innumerable straight-to-video quickies), but Ralph Fiennes renders him a clownish romantic – pathetic, stupid, but never dull. As his unnoticed bodyguard, Angela Bassett grabs her chance to play Schwarzenegger with a triumphant display of fistwork, materialism, and glittering impatience while Juliette Lewis, not yet returned from the wastelands of *Natural Born Killers*, more isolated than ever in her private world of unfathomed sensuality, communicates superbly with barely a reference to normal speech. These may not necessarily be the company with which one would wish to greet a new beginning, but a better claim seems unlikely to be staked; as usual, Bigelow and Cameron, in their separate ways, are streets ahead of the competition.

Philip Strick

DARK CITY
USA/Australia 1997
Director: Alex Proyas

In a nameless city, mysteriously frozen at midnight, John Murdoch wakes in a hotel room with a corpse and is phoned by Dr Schreber, who claims to be his psychiatrist. Suffering from amnesia and gifted with telekinetic abilities, he eludes both the arriving police and the Strangers, a race of aliens hiding among humanity by animating corpses. Inspector Bumstead takes over the case from a colleague who has gone mad. John pieces together his former life. He encounters Emma, who may be his estranged wife, and learns that he grew up in a place called Shell Beach, to which no one can direct him.

At midnight, the city stops again. Only John sees the buildings change and the Strangers rearrange the lives and personalities of the inhabitants. Schreber tells John it is all an experiment on humanity; John has been given the past of a murderer to see if he will become one. In a cavern under the city, Mr Hand, charged by the Strangers' leader Mr Book with apprehending John, is injected with a phial that contains John's memories. Hand becomes homicidal. John questions the nature of the world, asking Bumstead why there is never any daytime. He blasts a hole in the wall that reveals the city is floating in deep space. Bumstead and Hand are sucked into the void and John defeats Book in a psychic battle. Advised by Schreber, John reshapes the city, building a sea around it and making the sun rise. Anna, who is Emma with a new identity, meets him at the shore.

* * *

During a lengthy production, Alex Proyas's second feature film metaphorically drew in its horizons: announced as *Dark Universe* and shot under the working title *Dark World*, it has finally arrived as *Dark City*. This last title is as apt as the others, and perhaps less of a give-away of the film's final revelation, while it also evokes numerous *films noirs* (*The Dark Past, The Dark Corner, Night and the City*), particularly William Dieterle's *Dark City* (1950). The strangest thing about the *noir*-science fiction setting which this latest *Dark City* adopts is that it has become such a familiar backdrop for recent movies. There's *Blade Runner* of course, but also *The Crow*, Proyas's debut, which was set in just such a city of dreadful night, a small-scale imitation of *Batman*'s Gotham City.

With its fedoras and trenchcoats, Edward Hopper-cum-Cornell Woolrich hotel rooms and diners, droning snatches of remixed period tunes (Jennifer Connelly wittily gets to sing a verse of 'The Night Has 1,000 Eyes') and morphing buildings, *Dark City* shifts its allegiances slightly, taking much of its visual style from Terry Gilliam's *Brazil*. The underside of the city, where vast clanking machines work huge changes in the upperworld and bald-headed aliens float around in black leather robes, is equally indebted to Fritz Lang's *Metropolis* (1926, with Kiefer Sutherland's psychiatrist Schreber standing in for Rotwang) as well as to Clive Barker's *Hellraiser* and its first sequel. It is hard for *Dark City* to make its own space among its borrowings (there's even a touch of Dennis Potter). But *Dark City* at least has a narrative excuse for the elements deployed purely as stylistic devices by its predecessors. Schreber reveals that the city has been composed out of bits and pieces of humanity's remembered past, and the neverending night is an actual plot point rather than an atmospheric quirk.

Proyas dreamed up the original story but brought in several other writers, including David S. Goyer (*The Crow: City of Angels*) and Lem Dobbs (*Kafka*), to sort it out. The trouble is that the film has a strong premise (reminiscent of the 'conceptual breakthrough' gambits often deployed in 1950s written science fiction), but keeps stumbling over the need to explain itself. Sutherland is too often required to deliver expository speeches, fudging the bits that haven't been thought out. The police investigation seems prominent at first, but later the film concentrates more on suspect-on-the-run John. The parallel business with Richard O'Brien as an alien who learns about humanity when injected with John's memories is hurried through before it can make the quite complex and emotional points the script suggests ought to be covered. Even Jennifer Connelly's role is rather neglected when the film stops for another session of effects. (For example, the city is reconfigured with morphing so that a slumbering slum couple can wake up in a mansion and resume their dinner chat in their new rich personalities.)

If *Dark City* is more interesting than satisfying, it may be that its ambitions to add a little more depth and despair to the comic-book plotting are frustrated by the need to throw in bits of spectacle. Sewell's amnesiac-telekinetic John is an interesting creation, but the revelation that almost nobody in the city has any real identity undercuts the intriguing impossibility of rewriting a decent man as a murderer. A surprising thread of solipsism runs through the film, which climaxes not with the hero finding out who he really is (*à la RoboCop*) but with his readjustment of the entire world to conform with memories that have only been implanted in him. He creates the hometown he falsely remembers growing up in and wins the woman he has been made to imagine was his wife. So although *Dark City* is a definite improvement on the paper-thin posing of *The Crow*, this is nevertheless not quite as achieved a film as it might have been.

Kim Newman

THE TRUMAN SHOW
USA 1998
Director: Peter Weir

Truman Burbank lives in the island community of Seahaven which he never leaves, being afraid of water ever since his father died in a boating accident. Married to Meryl, a nurse, and employed as an insurance salesman, Truman seems content. But he is haunted by the memory of Lauren, a girl he once met who was whisked away by her father to Fiji. What Truman doesn't know is that he was adopted at birth by a television company, run by executive producer Christof, and is the star of an all-day television show, filmed on a huge, enclosed set. Everyone around him is really an actor. Millions of people have watched his whole life on television and even know of his secret longing for Lauren (really named Sylvia, now a campaigner for Truman's freedom).

However, Truman starts to become suspicious of his surroundings. Among other clues, he accidentally glimpses the actor who played his father wandering in a crowd. Christof hastily writes an explanatory reunion for Truman and his father, but Truman's curiosity is not assuaged. He tries to drive away with Meryl, only to be forced back. Truman tricks the cameras by creating a dummy-decoy and sets off in a sailboat. Christof almost drowns him with his computer-controlled weather, but Truman reaches the edge of the set. Christof tries to persuade him to stay, but Truman opens the exit door and leaves for the real world.

* * *

Film critics and preview audiences are occasionally privileged to experience something extraordinary: they get to see a film absolutely cold, before it is written about, discussed, exerpted and trailered into ubiquity, before their friends feel unable to keep themselves from re-narrating the best bits. I feel extremely lucky to have walked into a preview of *The Truman Show* several months ago completely ignorant of its story. By now, most inquisitive film-goers will already know the film's central conceit: Truman Burbank (Jim Carrey), to all appearances an ordinary 30-year-old insurance salesman in a superficially happy marriage, is unaware that he's also the star of a television show.

Consequently, most British viewers seeing it after reports of its summer success in the US and several spoiling articles over here – about how the film has rebranded Carrey as a serious actor, about what the whole thing says about the invasiveness of the media, and so on – will be robbed of the aesthetic bliss of seeing, like Truman himself, the trick revealed piece by piece.

Despite the reservations voiced elsewhere about the film's philosophical depth, there's no denying that director Peter Weir shows his hand and conceals it with charming dexterity. The film gives it all away at the start with an opening 'credits sequence' for the series-within-the-film, but it's easy not to understand what's going on. Truman's wife Meryl, played by Laura Linney with sinister, apple-cheeked irony, calls Truman's existence and her own 'a truly blessed life'. The series' creator Christof

(Ed Harris, dressed all in black like a cross between a coke dealer and a kabuki stagehand) explains that, 'Nothing you see here is faked. It's merely controlled.' (This omniscience recalls the hippie-transcendent notion that 'everything happens at exactly the right time' in Weir's first 1975 feature *Picnic at Hanging Rock*, which now seems like an eerie pre-echo of *The Truman Show*.) Gradually, we begin to realise the extent of this control and that the darkened, weirdly angled shots are not affected cinematic mannerisms from Weir and Co. but subjective views of cameras within the diegesis, planted on the figures passing Truman by, or hidden in houseplants. By the time Meryl is extolling, with an unnatural degree of enthusiasm, the virtues of a slicing-peeling-paring kitchen gadget (which will become a comical weapon later on) many viewers tuned into the insincere, television tone-of-voice that cues product placement will already have 'got it'.

Yet even if you know *The Truman Show*'s big joke, there are many lesser ones to savour. As with the kitchen gadget, the film delights in showing the hidden, evil nature of innocuous props and set dressing: the outsize moon (scale is wonderfully skewed here – look out for the gag about Mount Rushmore) is Christof's observation deck; the too-friendly, floppy-eared dog next door turns into a snarling attacker when the town goes looking for the missing Truman. Echoing the dome that encases this world, much play is made out of circles and cycles and repetitions: a golf ball is used to explain that Fiji, where Truman's true love is meant to have flown, is so much on the other side of the world that, 'you can't get any further away before you start coming back'. Similarly, it's in a revolving door that Truman's rebellion begins.

Of course, a major paradoxical gag is the casting of Carrey in the lead, his character endowed with a first name that's just a bit too much of an allegorical nudge. He is an actor who has built a career on a kind of manic insincerity, which made him perfectly suited if irritating as a lawyer who's jinxed into telling the truth for a day in *Liar Liar*. Here, he's supposed to be the only 'sincere' person in his world, the only one who's not lying (although he later learns deception). And yet, with his gestures large as if he's trying to touch the outsized moon, his smile a row of blank Scrabble tiles, there's a sense even in the earliest scenes that he's performing for the cameras – which would be logical for someone around whom life had been choreographed since he was an infant.

What makes Carrey's self-regarding, class-clown persona so useful to the film is that it buttresses one of *The Truman Show*'s major themes, perhaps its most central: solipsism. Many have read *The Truman Show* as an allegory of how television obsessively watches us, of Bentham-Foucault's panopticon gone digitally out of control. What's more poignant and haunting about this movie is that it's really about how we all secretly want to be on television and see ourselves as the stars of our own home-life movies; it is impossible to leave the cinema after seeing *The Truman Show* and not, at some point, wonder if the world is watching, not experience a flicker of identification with Truman (who has already been rehearsing different roles in front of his mirror every morning before he becomes aware of the plot around him).

This is nothing new. Solipsism is one of the defining tropes of literary modernism, threading through James Joyce's *Ulysses* and most of Vladimir Nabokov's work, Borges' fiction and almost every book by Philip K. Dick (see *Time Out of Joint* and *Flow My Tears, the Policeman Said* for close parallels with *The Truman Show*). But cinema and television have appropriated the theme with problematic results. In a book, be it written in the first or third persons, the reader is always aware that a single authorial presence is playing puppetmaster, writing itself is a solipsistic process. Film's collaborative nature (and the collective way we view it) tugs it into the social realm. What is more, it can seldom comfortably accommodate purely subjective viewpoints. We gradually come to realise that these weird shots of Truman in the beginning are the cameras' views of him, but who is filming Christof in his observatory? What being watches Sylvia watching Truman inside her flat?

Still, *The Truman Show* is a moving exploration of creation-anxiety, of the fear and hope that in a post Darwinian world the only beings with real power are distant public figures and malevolent unknown forces ringfencing our capacity for free will. Solipsism haunts us because it's both a comfort and a terror to think that someone, something has laid all this on for us, but in fiction like *The Truman Show* characters get to make the last moves. I won't give it away here, but the conclusion of the film is both satisfying and chillingly ambiguous: Truman and the viewers get to decide – to paraphrase the series' tagline blazoned on buttons and T-shirts worn by the show's viewers – how it's going to end.

Leslie Felperin

CUBE
Canada 1997
Director: Vincenzo Natali

Two women (Leaven and Holloway) and three men (Quentin, Worth and Rennes) find themselves trapped in a maze of adjoining cubical rooms, many containing deadly traps. Needing to escape before they starve, Quentin, a cop, and Rennes, a jailbreak expert, lead them from room to room, testing each one before they enter it. Despite their caution, Rennes is killed. Leaven, a maths student, works out that the numbers on each threshold indicate which rooms contain traps. Soon they are joined by the autistic Kazan, whose gift for mental arithmetic is later helpful.

When Quentin is wounded in a supposedly 'safe' room, the reliability of the numbers becomes questionable. Worth reveals he's one of the maze's designers; he has no idea who commissioned the structure or why, but he helps Leaven reinterpret the numbers. They find a room with an outside wall, looking out on vertiginous blackness. Making a clothes-rope, they lower Holloway on an exploratory descent. When everything shakes violently, Quentin allows Holloway to fall into the pit below.

Quentin becomes violent, so Leaven and Worth knock him out and abandon him. They find Rennes' body where they left it and assume they have been going in circles. Then they realise that the rooms themselves have been shifting and will eventually return them to the exit point. When they reach the escape room, Quentin attacks them but is crushed between the sliding cubes. Worth and Leaven are fatally injured, but Kazan steps out into the light.

* * *

Much of the fascination of *Cube* derives from its opening, an unforeseeable dice-with-death encounter: an instant fragmentation by a network of razor-wire. Enough to unsettle the audience for a good hour or so, it is an effective warning of what awaits the rest of the cast if they put a foot wrong. It also prompts admiration for a special-effects masterstroke. And what, we may wonder, happens to the residual bits and pieces? Does some kind of room service clean up each cubicle or are the remains left to rot?

If, as we are later led to believe, the giant cube contains hundreds of such slaughter sites shunting and sliding in perpetual rearrangement, they would surely – thanks to their noxious contents – soon become easy to avoid by future explorers. Conversely, since the prisoners we meet in the cube don't find any other corpses, we may theorise that the cruel maze has only recently been put in motion. Clues as to the origin and purpose of the structure are so sparse that *Cube* makes considerable headway as a mystery yarn before it becomes plain that no answer is forthcoming, or even relevant.

Even so, the idea that the cube might be an alien construction, although sensibly dismissed by the prisoners for lack of evidence, does have its attractions, linking the film to a whole range of recent man-versus-puzzle contests in such films as *Contact, Sphere* and *Event Horizon.* There are echoes here, too, of *Alien* and its crew, whittled away by the unknown into the endless anterooms of space, and of the *Star Trek* crew's struggle with the Borg who seek to contain the universe within a malevolent geometry. Adding to the fun, the plot is teasingly tricked out with allusions to three-dimensional Cartesian coordinates, with handy theosophical connections. From this perspective, the only other main 'meaning' for *Cube* lies somewhere between metaphysics, symbolism and sheer bravado.

Vincenzo Natali's first feature extends the theme of an earlier short, *Elevated,* about three people under threat in a jammed lift. Co-written with Andre Bijelic, *Cube* became, Natali states in the press notes, 'a nightmare version of the circumstances of our own lives: we were room-mates entombed in our little apartment'. He likens the characters' experience to that of ants 'in a world of giants', never understanding 'the forces that push and pull you through life'. Interpreted on this basis as existential melodrama, *Lord of the Flies* in the manner of David Lynch, *Cube* heads for its final blaze of white – which could be birth, death or freedom according to taste – with only its players and its visual skills for protection.

Bearing vaguely prison-related labels – Leaven/Worth, Holloway, (San) Quentin – the characters need all the script they can get and earnestly make what they can of the mostly irritable exchanges provided. Although some weight can be expected from the seasoned Wayne Robson (whose screen career began in *McCabe and Mrs Miller,* 1971), and some promise is shown by Nicole deBoer, they hardly achieve more depth than ciphers in a video game. The cop who begins as a confident organiser but who becomes increasingly violent and irrational is a particularly unhelpful illustration of the film's mood of anti-authoritarian complaints.

But if the cast resorts to little better than owlish expressions of disapproval and a great deal of shouting, the assurance with which Natali and his team have turned a single 14-foot-square enclosure into a near-infinite vista of calculated menace deserves plenty of praise. That *Cube* was shot in less than a month is equally remarkable. It feels, appropriately, closer to a lifetime.

Philip Strick

eXistenZ
Canada/United Kingdom 1999
Director: David Cronenberg

North America, the near future. A group of players gather to try out eXistenZ, the latest brainchild of the games world's most notorious genius, Allegra Geller. eXistenZ is an elaborate game in which the players wire themselves up via a bioport – a plug inserted in the spinal column – to a semi-organic game pod, to induce plotted hallucinations. However, as Allegra begins to download eXistenZ, an anti-games assassin opens fire on her.

Allegra is rescued by Ted Pikul, a junior company member. They set off on the run, pursued by bounty hunters, though Allegra is more concerned about her damaged game. She insists she and Ted must play eXistenZ to assess the damage. Initially fearful, Ted agrees finally to have a bootleg bioport shot into his spine by Gas, a roughneck garage man who turns out to be one of the enemy.

They flee to a ski resort where Allegra's colleague Kiri Vinokur replaces Ted's sabotaged bioport so the couple can finally plug in and play. Together, they enter a violent and frequently bloody set of narratives about spies, counterspies and assassins – a story which becomes increasingly confused with events in the outside world. Finally, it emerges that the entire action so far has itself been a game called tranCendenZ; 'Allegra', 'Ted' and all the other men and women are merely players. 'Allegra' and 'Ted' are themselves the true anti-games terrorists. As the lethal couple corner tranCendenZ's inventor Yevgeny Nourish, he asks them fearfully if this is only an episode in a still more inclusive game. They do not reply.

* * *

Fairly or otherwise, two of the critical terms least frequently applied to the Cronenberg oeuvre thus far have been 'fun' and 'cute': a regrettable state of affairs that *eXistenZ* should do much to remedy. First, the fun part: notwithstanding its showstopping metaphysical somersaults between Chinese-boxed levels of reality, *eXistenZ* is in many respects an unexpectedly conventional entertainment. Some of the conventionality is due, we must assume, to the imaginative tastes of Allegra Geller (or, more pedantically, of the transcendental inventor of 'Allegra Geller'), who may be a whiz at bio-tech confections but seems to enjoy an essentially rather banal, if lurid, fantasy life. On the evidence of her taste in adventures, Allegra must have spent her childhood gorging on B movies, Bond films, *The Avengers* and such like, and she's plainly not averse to rescripting herself from a barely articulate wallflower in real life into a devastatingly sexy action babe in eXistenZ life. Somehow, Jennifer Jason Leigh manages to make Allegra into a sympathetic and very nearly plausible character, the single fleshed-out (if that is the apposite term) human being in a gallery of ciphers and caricatures. It's quite a feat.

Next, the cute part. At one point, Allegra notices and smiles at a frisky little two-headed amphibian that wouldn't look out of place in a Disney confection. A few years ago, the *Independent* asked its readers to nominate the least likely combination of director and subject. The winning entry was 'David Cronenberg's *National Velvet*'. Maybe that competition came to the director's notice, and gave him some ideas. Rest assured, the wee beastie meets a literally sticky end, for in most other respects *eXistenZ* is something of a resumé or, less kindly, a puree of just about every previous Cronenberg film, from the mournfully dignified score by Howard Shore to the sombre lighting and preposterous names. Among its equally familiar attractions are furtive visits to the House of Fiction (cf. *Naked Lunch*), a dangerously seductive new form of entertainment (*Videodrome*, the most obvious precursor of *eXistenZ*), crossings of the borderline between biology and technology (*Crash* and so on), lashings of erotic body modifications (*Rabid* and so on) and, of course, a generous portion of the old Cronenbergian red glop.

The red-glop factor is at its highest within the eXistenZ world, particularly when the twists and turns of the game's plot land Allegra and Ted as labourers in a low-rent abattoir-cum-laboratory, where grubby workers hack up frogs and lizards for biotechnological ends, and take their lunch-breaks in a nightmarish Chinese restaurant. Here, Ted orders the daily special, chomps his way through the unidentifiable slippery, slimy horrors he's served, uses the leftover bone and gristle to construct a gun which fires teeth (the very weapon used on Allegra at the beginning) and murders the waiter with a well-aimed molar. At a guess, this is the point of Cronenberg's film at which a lot of younger viewers will find themselves thinking it might be worth saving up for a bioport implant.

But the same qualities which make *eXistenZ* potent for games-world addicts make *eXistenZ* inadequately satisfying for those of us who go in for less all-absorbing forms of diversion, like the cinema. As a thrill-ride in its own right, *eXistenZ* is fine – it's slick, swift and droll. But as an anxious entertainment, which is meant to nag and gnaw at our hunger for surrendering ourselves to surrogate thrills, especially of the disreputable kind that last about two hours (for what, the film keeps nudging us, is *eXistenZ* if not a hyper-real story, and what is Allegra but a Künstler with the *Gesamtkunstwerk* to trump them all?), it's more than a touch half-baked.

eXistenZ tries to make our flesh creep with the insinuation that many of us, if we weren't deterred by the prospect of spinal surgery, would cheerfully invest in bioports and drift away into other people's fantasies. It does its dutiful best to make that Huxleyan thought appear guilty and disquieting. But cheerfulness, or its nastier Cronenbergian equivalent, keeps breaking through the gloom, and the very qualities which make *eXistenZ* watchable also make *eXistenZ* seem like unthreatening fun. Cronenberg has said the film's point of departure was an interview he once did with Salman Rushdie, but as Kim Newman has pointed out elsewhere in these pages, its more compelling literary source is the haunted fiction of Philip K. Dick. Compared to Dick's writing at it ontologically insecure best, though, *eXistenZ* looks as trifling as it is diverting, a little too perky, a little too pat.

Keven Jackson

THE SIXTH SENSE
USA 1999
Director: M. Night Shyamalan

Philadelphia. Psychologist Malcolm Crowe is celebrating his latest award with his wife Anna when former patient Vincent Gray breaks in. Blaming Malcolm's therapy for his dementia, Vincent shoots him, then kills himself.

Months later Malcolm takes on the case of nine-year-old Cole Sear, a disturbed schoolboy living with his mother Lynn. While gaining the boy's confidence, Malcolm begins to have misgivings about his marriage, suspecting Anna of having an affair.

Malcolm enlists Cole's cooperation by telling him about Vincent, and at last Cole reveals his secret: he is visited by dead people only he can see, who plead for his help. Baffled by this delusion, Malcolm despairs of helping the boy, but Cole begs him not to abandon his case. Listening to the tape of his sessions with Vincent, Malcolm suspects a supernatural element and begins to reconsider Cole's claims.

One of Cole's 'visitors' Kyra leads Cole to a videotape that proves to the guests at her funeral that she was murdered. Cole is cheered by his schoolmates, previously his tormentors, for his performance in the school play. Able now to discuss his 'gift' with his mother, who accepts he has special powers, he and Malcolm agree there is no further need for therapy. Returning home, Malcolm recognises that his loving relationship with Anna will always survive Vincent's fatal bullet.

* * *

Constantly on the brink of explanation, *The Sixth Sense* in fact derives most of its fascination from explaining next to nothing. A mass of disquieting details, it takes a number of detours towards a final reversal that throws everything open to question. What was masquerading as one case history gradually becomes several, most prominently that of the psychologist but also those of the mother, the wife, the suicidal psychotic and an ever-widening circle of the troubled and dispossessed.

Inadvertent guide to these lost souls, whether they're alive or in some other limbo, is the bewildered schoolboy Cole. He eventually comes to terms with his power, graduating from crime buster to marriage counsellor while retaining the skills of a seaside-booth medium ('Grandma says "Hi"'). But what kind of future awaits him in the employment of his now-validated gift is left to the imagination.

Director/writer M. Night Shyamalan has been film-making since the age of ten, although primed for a top-grade medical career. Future retrospectives will doubtless reveal to British audiences his 45 short films, his acclaimed 1992 debut feature *Praying with Anger*, and his second film *Wide Awake* (1997). But for now, *The Sixth Sense* (and its huge US box-office success) looks to have materialised almost out of nowhere.

At least we can guess from the available clues that Shyamalan's main concerns are isolation (he took the role of his own 'ghost' in *Praying with Anger*) and the strains and tensions of family ties: *Wide Awake* is about the relationship between a Catholic schoolboy and his grandfather. And generous doses of autobiography can be detected in *The Sixth Sense*, both in the character of the cool headed specialist who finds his career on the wrong path and in that of the child haunted by innumerable dramas in need of an audience.

These traits aside, the film's main appeal is the assurance with which it is made. Studiously versed in art-house classics as much as in Spielberg or Craven, Shyamalan's film is an attention-grabbing fusion of minimalism and overstatement. His horror story is shot as Tarkovsky might have shot it, with briefly glimpsed figures on the fringes and with constant ambiguities of action and attitude. Setting the mood, the opening scene in the wine cellar, the camera hiding furtively behind the racks, would persuade us that an unseen intruder is about to pounce, but he doesn't, and what we've gained instead is a sketch of a highly strung wife along with a timely reminder of the ritualistic status of wine. And then he pounces, in the bathroom where, moments earlier, the psychologist who is about to learn of failure has suggested they consign his latest award.

It fits together so smoothly that one feels that Shyamalan could leave almost anything on the screen for us to assimilate. Since, for instance, he knows Philadelphia, his home town, well, his glimpses of a landmark sculpture plainly add up to something more than the passage of time. But such references are part of the film's attraction as well as its weakness. Keeping us guessing before the full misery of Cole's predicament becomes apparent, there are curiously misleading hints of his paranormal powers, at their strongest in his mother's presence.

Leaving Cole in the kitchen for a moment, his mother returns to find every drawer and door open. Examining family photographs, she finds the same flash of light in each one. Such images have a vivid but unresolved potency, distracting us from more awkward matters. Where does the psychologist go between the Vincent episode and the Cole assignment? If Cole's visitors don't know they're dead, why do they want his help? The enigmas remain, but since another of Shyamalan's accomplishments has been to coax exquisite performances from his cast (including Haley Joel Osment and an intensely introverted Bruce Willis) we are happy to share their bewilderment rather than dismissing it.

Philip Strick

RUN LOLA RUN
Germany 1998
Director: Tom Tykwer

Berlin, 11.40 am. Young tearaway Lola receives a phone call from her petty-criminal boyfriend Manni. He has botched a diamond-smuggling job for homicidal gangster Ronnie, and left DM 100,000 on a subway train where it was picked up by a tramp. If Lola doesn't get to him by 12 p.m. with a replacement sum, Ronnie will kill him. Lola runs to Manni and three contrasting narrative timelines follow.

In the first Lola sprints to the bank where her father is a director, only to interrupt her father's colleague and mistress Jutta Hansen's revelation that she is pregnant. The father turns on Lola, declares that she is not his daughter and throws her out. Lola runs to the phone box just in time to see Manni conducting an armed robbery at a nearby store. When she helps him, she is shot dead by the police.

In the second timeline Lola is tripped by a thug in the hallway. She arrives at the bank after Jutta has told her father that the baby isn't his. Lola robs the bank at gunpoint and escapes. As she arrives in time to prevent Manni from robbing the store, he is run over by a truck.

In the last timeline Lola runs to the bank but this time fails to cause a road accident which in the previous scenarios had prevented her father's colleague Meier from reaching the bank. She misses her father and he and Meier are involved in a road accident caused by Manni chasing the tramp. Lola gambles at a casino and wins the DM 100,000. Meanwhile, Manni has recovered the money and given it to Ronnie. Lola and Manni are reunited.

* * *

Tom Tykwer's supercharged, exhilaratingly hyperactive movie had audiences in Germany and the United States cheering at the screen. Emphasising emotional insecurity and cinematic style as did his earlier work, *Run Lola Run* sets new standards for the cinema of hysteria. It opens with a stylish sequence picking faces out of a crowd which later coalesce to form the title, and which – ironically – looks like a television commercial for insurance or financial services (heroine Lola runs each time to a bank). The voiceover suggests a copywriter's search for the meaning of life ('Who are we? Why do we believe?') but also offers us the answer courtesy of a comically gnomic quotation by Sepp Herberger, the legendary football coach who took Germany to victory in the 1954 World Cup: 'The ball is round, the game lasts 90 minutes… everything else is theory.'

Chaos theory in particular seems to be Tykwer's concern here, for the course of each of Lola's attempts to save her boyfriend Manni is determined by incidental micro-events – whether she is tripped on the stairs, if she causes a man to crash his car, and so on. But there is little of the romantic-comedy irony of *Groundhog Day's* repetitions or *Sliding Doors'* mirrored stories in the crisis that turns into three dramas for Lola. Nor is there an unwavering commitment to the existential crime-plot take on fate and chance that runs from Kubrick's *The Killing* (1956) to Tarantino. So many things have gone wrong by the time Lola receives her phone call – the theft of her moped, a taxi driver taking her to the wrong address in the east – that chaos seems the norm rather than a flaw in a masterplan. The only response is screaming, which Lola duly does, shattering glass like the dwarf Oskar Matzerath in *The Tin Drum* (1979), the benchmark German 'breakthrough film'.

With each repetition of Lola's itinerary we become more familiar with the elements of her environment, as with the levels of a computer game (the film uses a variety of mixed media – animation, video, 35mm stock as well as time-lapse effects and all manner of editing trickery). When Lola dies, she begins her quest afresh. And when she succeeds at the end, we feel, irrationally, that she has earned this for her exertions over the three mutually exclusive stories, none of which is more real than any other. This meticulous representation of chaos is clearest in the asides in which the lifelines of incidental characters flash by in seconds. The extreme alternatives here include car crashes, child kidnapping, unforeseen meetings leading to marriage or sadomasochistic relationships, lottery wins and more. On one level this is slapstick (Tykwer cannot resist showing us the ambulance crashing through the plate glass it narrowly avoided the first time around). But it is also the logic of interactive DVD and of gamesplaying where each decision has potentially disastrous but never mundane results.

With a Hollywood remake likely, *Lola* may, of course, be transformed into a Lara Croft-style digital heroine. What will be lost then, though, is extremely old-fashioned and precisely what makes *Run Lola Run* great: for all its Teutonic version of *cinéma du look* stylisation, pop-video aesthetics and pumping techno which keeps us breathless, we empathise with Lola, whose lover's pillow talk with Manni about love and death links the three narrative strands. That Tykwer maintains our flow of empathy while demonstrating and exploiting the potential of interactive cinema *manqué* is, in itself, an awesome achievement.

Richard Falcon

EDtv
USA 1999
Director: Ron Howard

San Francisco, the present. Cable-station producer Cynthia Topping thinks up a new format to boost ratings: pick an ordinary person and broadcast his activities 24 hours a day. People all over the city send in audition tapes, including boorish Ray Pekurny. Cynthia and her colleagues choose Ray's brother Ed, spotted in Ray's tape. Transmission begins, and Ed's life – working in a video store, hanging out with his friends and working-class family – at first seems prosaic and uneventful. But when a romance unfolds on camera between Ed and Ray's girlfriend Shari (causing a rift between the brothers), ratings pick up and the show is networked across the country.

However, viewers don't warm to Shari and she soon splits up with Ed after humiliating media pressure. Ed starts dating an ambitious starlet Jill, who only wants the exposure. They eventually split up and Ed still hankers for Shari. His long-lost father Hank resurfaces after years of absence, much to the distress of Ed's mother Jeanette and his stepfather Al. Ed begins to tire of life in the limelight and tries to quit the show (with Cynthia's covert support) but television executive Whitaker holds Ed to his contract. Finally Ed appeals to viewers to send in embarrassing material about the station's executives. The blackmail works, and Ed is left alone to reunite with Shari.

* * *

With its Joe Schmo-protagonist the star of a 24-hour cable show that trades for its appeal on the very banality of his life, *EDtv* inevitably suffered on its US release through comparisons with the similarly plotted and critically acclaimed *The Truman Show*. Despite being a self-contained feature in its own right, *EDtv* ended up looking like a pilot for a cheap, sunnily lit sitcom spun off from Peter Weir's film, an impression aggravated by the fact that both its screenwriters (Lowell Ganz and Babaloo Mandel) and director (Ron Howard) cut their teeth on such sitcoms as *Happy Days* (itself a sitcom cloned from the more bleak and brooding *American Graffiti*). In fact, *EDtv* is a remake of a little-known Canadian film, *Louis XIX: roi des ondes*, while *The Truman Show* itself garnered accusations of plagiarism.

In a way, these extra-textual debates about originality are superfluous since both *EDtv* and *The Truman Show* set up their stories' events as springing out of television's ever-increasing problem with format exhaustion. Both Ed and Truman are hailed by their producers as antidotes to the authenticity anaemia of regular programming. The major difference between the two characters is their degree of complicity with their stardom. Ed's willing collusion means *EDtv* is at leisure to make light entertainment from his predicament and turn out a more specifically focused if disposable satire on television.

What you get from *EDtv*, apart from its mild romance, some well-timed comic performances and the debatable charms of Matthew McConaughey on constant display, is more of an insiders' spoof on small-screen shenanigans and a fuller examination of what role television plays in viewers' lives – we see far more of the reactions and opinions of Ed's fans, ranging from Hispanic security guards to camp boys debating the merits of gold-digger Jill's Versace dress. And there's a nice acidity in the portrait of the cable executives' meetings as they worry about their ratings (beaten by a gardening channel, one despairs that, 'people would rather watch soil') and ruthlessly dissect their stars' performances. Like the film-makers themselves, a goodly portion of the cast, from Woody Harrelson to Ellen DeGeneres – got their breaks on television, and there's a sense of scores being settled while they also affectionately salute the medium that made them stars.

Leslie Felperin

TIMECODE
USA 2000
Director: Mike Figgis

Hollywood, the present. A screen segmented into four frames charts the overlapping experiences of a group of movie-business players. The action plays out in real time and pivots around the production offices of Red Mullet films.

Emma leaves her therapy session and travels to the office to tell her partner – philandering executive Alex – that she is leaving him. Meanwhile aspiring actress Rose is being chauffered to the office alongside her wealthy lover Lauren. Convinced that Rose is having an affair, Lauren plants a surveillance device on her and listens in as Rose meets with Alex and has sex in a darkened preview theatre. Struggling cult director Lester is desperately hunting a female lead for his new production. Having unsuccessfully auditioned for the role, actress Cherine leaves the office and meets the distressed Emma.

Returning to Cherine's apartment, the two women share a kiss before Emma is disturbed by the arrival of Cherine's boyfriend and leaves hurriedly. At Red Mullet, Alex brushes off Rose's plea for an audition and is dragged into a meeting with enfant-terrible director Ana. Rose prepares to leave the building but is introduced to Lester, who decides that she is perfect for the lead in his movie.

In a rage, Lauren storms into the building and shoots Alex. Lying wounded on the floor, he is filmed on Ana's digital camera and receives a phone call from Emma who admits she loves him.

* * *

Like a series of lights coming on in an uncurtained building, Mike Figgis's *Timecode* opens at quarter-strength and then builds to full illumination. With the bulk of the screen's physical space still black (though abstracted light sources occasionally streak through or flicker), a window pops up filling the upper right-hand corner. Inside, a young woman (Saffron Burrows) is recounting a dream to her therapist. Midway through their exchange, an adjacent window at the top left-hand comes alive and the viewer sees a power-dressed vixen (Jeanne Tripplehorn) storm down the steps of a Beverly Hills residence and hurriedly let down the tyre of a nearby car. And we're torn. Do we continue to eavesdrop on the low, murmurous confessional in the shrink's sanctum or switch our attention to the more nakedly subversive actions next door? Or do we attempt to keep tabs on both: snooping on the top-right square while playing peeping Tom on top-left. A moment later, two more windows of opportunity have opened up on the picture's bottom storey and we're torn again. Four frames, four narratives. A quartet of options for the discerning voyeur to choose between.

Played out on a quartered screen, in real time, with no edits, *Timecode* is an ongoing fascination. As an exercise in parallel plotting, it's endlessly inventive. As a filmic experiment, it's gloriously audacious. If the closing credits neglect to acknowledge an editor, that's in part because the viewer is implicitly encouraged to fill that role for him or herself: concentrating on the dramas and characters that grab his or her attention and turning out the others. Admittedly *Timecode* falls some way short of attaining the Holy Grail that is the first truly interactive feature film, but it at least has its nose pointed in the right direction.

It also hits something of a high-water mark in Figgis's push towards a more formally ambitious mode of movie-making: a push that began with 1995's award-winning, low-budget *Leaving Las Vegas* and continued through last year's floridly experimental *The Loss of Sexual Innocence*. In preparing *Timecode*, Figgis (a keen musician) composed his film on music sheets, as though scoring a string quartet. He then proceeded to shoot the picture in one continuous 93-minute take. The film's four digital-video cameras (operated by Figgis, James O'Keeffe, Tony Cucchiari and director of photography Patrick Alexander Stewart) were all turned on simultaneously and run on a common timecode, the electronic counter encoded on the tapes. There was no formal script and the blocking was largely improvised. The dangers, of course, in such a no-nets mode of working are manifest. At one stage a tell-tale hand can be glimpsed holding open the door as we trail Salma Hayek's starlet into the washroom while on several occasions where the narratives overlap two frames move into such close proximity that the cameras must be mere inches away from clashing. But on the whole *Timecode* synchronises its high-wire act with aplomb: technically, this is a virtuoso piece of work.

More crucially, the film succeeds on a dramatic level. Figgis has admitted suffering initial qualms over the viability of his split-screen, parallel-plotting device, fretting that *Timecode*'s constant four-way dialogue of sound and visual information would swamp the viewer. He concluded, however, that a diet of channel-surfing and multimedia has made sophisticates of modern-day film-goers, equipping them to process a bombardment of information thrown at them on various frequencies. Where MTV would sate its audience through frenzied editing, Figgis reasoned, *Timecode* would do so through simultaneous, real-time narratives. Formally separate, these two modes of communication are spiritual cousins. The difference is that while the dominant MTV style is traditionally accused of spoon-feeding its public, *Timecode* empowers them. It serves up four dishes and invites us to sample instances of drama from each one.

Undeniably this makes for a tart and appealing diet. *Timecode* revolves around the Hollywood offices of Red Mullet films (the name of Figgis's own production company) and juggles a roster of semi-crazed *Day of the Locust* types with lots of satirical potshots at the movie industry. So we get comedic script pitches ('It's like *Shine* except the guy has a lot more problems'), forlorn mantras ('I am always in the right place at the right time') and duff green-lit projects (a director is auditioning actresses for the star role of a girl 'who's sleeping her way to the top of a public-relations firm in Missouri'). The largely improvised acting is sharp and convincing (particularly from Stellan Skarsgärd and Salma Hayek) and the quartet of stories feed smartly into one another.

But while *Timecode* provides some measure of viewer freedom, this is finally a freedom within limits. Throughout it all, one can never quite escape the godlike hand of Figgis (credited as writer, director, producer and composer) at work behind the scenes. In structuring the film as a piece of music, its creator shrewdly allows some frames to idle while the others combust. In overseeing the sound edit (with no room for a boom, a plethora of hidden microphones were used, following techniques pioneered by Robert Altman on *California Split*, 1974, and *Nashville*, 1975), Figgis elects to keep certain tracks low down in the mix and emphasise the dialogue elsewhere.

He even throws in a mission statement. Near the end of the film, Mia Maestro pops up as Ana, a glacial teenage prodigy who wants to throw out the trusty Eisensteinian montage in favour of a new form of cinematic language. 'Montage has created a false reality,' she proclaims. 'Digital is demanding new expressions.' Her proposed film will be played out in real time, on four cameras, in one continuous take. To Ana, the proposal is revolutionary. To Skarsgärd's anguished executive it sounds like 'the most pretentious crap I've every heard'.

In the end *Timecode* is never pretentious – it's too witty, too sure-footed, too infectiously exuberant for that. But it's not quite revolutionary either. In dispensing with montage, *Timecode* liberates the medium up to a point, but is still constrained by the simple need (perhaps inherent in all drama) to order its material and tell a story. Ergo, *Timecode*'s structure nudges the viewer subtly towards what Figgis regards as the important frames.

Timecode unfolds like a fantastically textured stretch of contemporary jazz. Its segmented interior is maddening, involving, often exhilarating. But there is a strict methodology behind its madness, and what sounds like free-form chaos in the opening bars soon swings into orbit around a central, unifying structure. In attempting to reconfigure the language of film, *Timecode* bends the rules beautifully. Yet it never quite breaks them.

Xan Brooks

THE CELL
USA/Germany 2000
Director: Tarsem Singh

California, the present. Catherine Deane is a psychotherapist employed by the Campbell Center to experiment with a new treatment that permits her to enter the minds of catatonic patients. The technique, involving drugs and an advance cybernetic bodysuit, is being used on a comatose boy who fails to show any signs of recovery. Meanwhile psychotic serial killer Carl Stargher suffers an irreversible neural breakdown following his arrest by the FBI and falls into a coma.

With Stargher's last female victim still imprisoned in his secret cell, which is slowly filling with water, the FBI ask Deane to search Stargher's mind for information about the girl's whereabouts. However, when Deane becomes trapped within Stargher's sadistic inner fantasies, believing them to be real, FBI agent Peter Novak enters the killer's mind to rescue her. Novak also uncovers a clue to the cell's location, and while he rushes to free the trapped girl, Deane invites Stargher into her own mind, where she overcomes his murderous nature, allowing him to die in peace. Equipped with this new therapeutic method of bringing subjects into her own consciousness, Deane returns to treating her young patient.

*   *   *

The latest sign of Hollywood's unconsummated digital affair with virtual reality, Tarsem Singh's directorial debut occupies the hinterland between the deep sensory immersion experiments of the 1990s and a 1960s LSD head trip. 'According to the FBI,' agent Novak remarks to his travelling companion, psychotherapist Deane, after his journey through the inner world of a comatose serial killer, 'you put me through a drug-fuelled mind-bender'. There's little evidence to say he's wrong. The film vibrates with references to psychedelic mental overload, from Howard Shore's resonant score featuring the Master Musicians of Jajouka and dissonant orchestral references to Ligeti and the Beatles' 'A Day in the Life' to the similarity between the vertiginous hallucinatory lightshow that greets Novak's entry into killer Stargher's consciousness and that experienced by astronaut Bowman at the end of *2001: A Space Odyssey* (1968).

The Cell establishes an intriguing correlation between Deane's pad and the serial killer's workshop; the ingenious paraphernalia assembled by Stargher for his sexualised murders finds a direct counterpart in the lush contents of Deane's apartment, where she is shown sitting at her iMac smoking a joint, listening to dub reggae. This attention to detail is typical of Tarsem (he tends to be known only by his first name): a prize-winning director of television commercials and music videos, he loads the screen with a dizzying display of gimcracks and references to such eclectic cultural artefacts as Piranesi's *Carceri* engravings, Oscar Schlemmer's Bauhaus costume designs and Damien Hirst's art-works. There's plenty here to keep the eye busy, but this kind of visual chewing-gum can't completely divert attention from the fact that Mark Protosevich's patchy script – which at times resembles *The Silence of the Lambs* rewritten by Carlos Castaneda – doesn't have much else going for it. With little room for either narrative detail or character development, Tarsem's exploration of a deranged mind soon loses momentum. By the time Deane gets in touch with Stargher's inner child, still tortured by memories of his abusive father, the dense fetishism of the original imagery has given way to camp metaphysical banalities and sketchy plot resolutions.

There's also something vaguely trite about characters having to remind each other of what is real and what is fantasy in a film where the FBI can assemble scores of heavily armed police at a moment's notice and on the flimsiest of circumstantial evidence. However, Tarsem's consummate ability to create small glossy fantasies out of inanimate consumer durables provides *The Cell* with its greatest and most halluci-natory irony. The material world that exists outside the main protagonists' minds has been captured with such close and loving attention to surface detail that every car, helicopter, building façade and interior threaten to take on a life of their own and overwhelm the poorly defined humans that move among them. Beyond computer-generated space, hallucinogenic drugs and violently aberrant psychologies, it seems that television commercials still constitute the ultimate virtual reality.

Ken Hollings

MEMENTO
USA 2000
Director: Christopher Nolan

LA, the present. Since the rape and murder of his wife, former insurance investigator Leonard Shelby has no short-term memory. Having vowed to seek out and kill his wife's murderer whose initials he knows to be 'JG' and whose car-registration number he has tattooed on his body, he writes notes and takes Polaroids to remind him how the investigation is progressing. The story unfolds in reverse chronology.

On the outskirts of town, he accompanies a man called Teddy into a deserted warehouse. After looking at a photo of Teddy on which is written, 'Don't believe his lies. He is the one. Kill him,' Leonard shoots Teddy dead.

Earlier, a woman named Natalie gives Leonard details of the driver she has had traced from the car registration Leonard has tattooed on his body. The owner turns out to be Teddy, whose real name, Natalie reveals, is John Gammell. Leonard writes on his Polaroid of Teddy, 'He is the one. Kill him.'

Earlier still, Natalie tells him she'll get the driver's details for him and meet him later. Leonard has a Polaroid of a man named Dodd, beaten and gagged. Natalie shows him a photo of Jimmy Grantz, a local gangster and her boyfriend, who went to meet a man called Teddy and never came back.

Earlier still, Leonard wakes up in a motel room and finds Dodd in his wardrobe. He and Teddy dump Dodd on the city's outskirts; Leonard goes to ask Natalie what's going on.

Earlier still, Leonard wakes in a bathroom. Dodd walks in. Leonard beats and gags him and takes a Polaroid. He finds a note telling him to get rid of Dodd for Natalie.

Earlier still, Natalie tells Leonard that Dodd beat her up because she didn't have Jimmy's drugs or money. She sends Leonard out to get rid of Dodd. Moments before, Leonard argues with her and hits her, causing bruising to her face which she later blames on Dodd.

Earlier still, Leonard finds a beer mat in his pocket with a message from Natalie saying 'Meet me afterwards.' He goes to the bar and introduces himself to Natalie, whom he doesn't know. Before reaching the bar, Leonard has a car-registration number tattooed on his arm. Teddy tells Leonard that Jimmy Grantz was his wife's murderer.

Earlier still, Leonard meets a cop, John Gammell, and takes a Polaroid of him. Gammell tells him to identify him as Teddy as he's working undercover. He sends Leonard to kill Jimmy Grantz in a deserted warehouse on the city's outskirts. Grantz thinks he's meeting Teddy for a drugs deal and has $200,000 in his car. Leonard kills Jimmy, believing him to be his wife's killer, takes a Polaroid of the body and changes into Jimmy's clothes. Teddy tells Leonard he's a cop who helped investigate the rape of Leonard's wife. Since the police dropped the investigation, Teddy has been finding criminals with the initials 'JG' for Leonard to kill. He tells Leonard that his wife actually survived the rape; it was Leonard who killed her by accidentally administering a fatal dose of insulin. Leonard is distraught. He decides that Teddy is the next man he will kill, writes 'Don't believe his lies' on his Polaroid of the cop and takes a note of Teddy's registration number, which he later tattoos on his arm. Leonard drives off in Jimmy's car, with his gun and the money.

*   *   *

Christopher Nolan's low-budget black and white debut *Following* (1998) was a film to get excited about. A British thriller set in a bleary but recognisable London with not a mockney gangster in sight, it was the work of a film-maker clearly capable of breathing new life into stock *noir* devices. In his LA-shot follow-up *Memento* Nolan continues to invigorate the genre: a remarkable psychological-puzzle film, a crime conundrum that explores the narrative possibilities of *noir*, *Memento* turns its detective hero Leonard Shelby into a surrogate for the spectator, its backward narrative logic forcing us to embark on the kind of investigative work Shelby is engaged in.

Shelby – played utterly convincingly by Guy Pearce as a combination of dogged determination and gaping bewilderment – is a former insurance investigator who since his wife's rape and apparent murder suffers from a condition that makes him unable to form new memories. But despite his severely limited powers of recollection he has vowed to find his wife's killer, whose initials he knows are 'JG'.

While there's a tradition of amnesia narratives in *noir* – from George Marshall's 1945 *The Blue Dahlia* to Scott McGehee's 1993 neo-*noir* *Suture* – Nolan's audacious approach sets *Memento* apart. The opening sequence hints of what's to come: a hand holds up a Polaroid photograph of a murder scene which slowly un-develops, fading to darkness. Nolan follows this with a murder that plays in rewind – the victim's blood seeps up a wall back into his head wound, bullet cartridges spin back into the gun's chamber – erasing the act of killing. From then on, though the film reverts to forward motion, events leading up to this murder are told in sequences that appear in reverse order. We get snatches of scenes which initially make no sense. Only when the film loops out from small details to the larger context does the story begin to form into a cohesive whole.

Nolan pulls off this complicated narrative structure with great flair. Unlike Martin Amis's 1991 novel *Time's Arrow* – which used a similar device to tell the story of a Nazi's life from death to birth – the effect is compelling rather than gimmicky. At heart *Memento* is a detective story, as Leonard makes clear to undercover cop Teddy, who claims to be helping him to track down his wife's killer. 'Facts,' he says, 'not memories. That's how you investigate.' Keeping track of his search with scribbled notes, clues tattooed on his body and sheaves of documents, Leonard anchors his investigation in what he believes are concrete givens. But each time the film reveals the context for his suppositions Leonard is shown to be mistaken.

It's a familiar *noir* trick – pulling the rug out from under the audience. But here Nolan gives the genre's tendency to confound our expectations of a conceptual twist by linking the flow of narrative information to Leonard's condition. One of the ways Leonard attempts to navigate the set of unconnected instants that constitute his experience of time is by taking Polaroids. Each image has scribbled addenda: Teddy's reads 'Do not believe his lies'; the picture of Natalie, the waitress Leonard hooks up with, has 'She's lost someone, too. She'll help you out of pity.' For Leonard – and for us, too – these memory cue-cards are clues in the murder hunt; but there's a wealth of blink-and-you'll-miss-it evidence scattered throughout the film's spiralling narrative structure to suggest that Leonard's 'facts' don't necessarily tell the whole story. On Natalie's Polaroid, for instance, a line has been scribbled out, a detail that instils doubts about her long before it becomes clear she's mercilessly exploiting Leonard's con-dition for her own ends. In the best *noir* tradition, it's hard to trust any of the characters here – from Teddy, played with wheedling shiftiness by Joe Pantoliano, down to the clerk in the motel where Leonard is staying who admits he's ripping him off by booking him into a less luxurious room in the knowledge Leonard will promptly forget the guilty confession.

Leonard's reliance on his remembered past – he claims to recall his life before the murder of his wife – is one of the anchoring elements of the film. Running parallel with the fractured eternal present tense of the protagonist's everyday life is the story of a case he investigated when working for an insurance firm. That of Sammy Jankis, who was afflicted with similar short-term memory loss. In an extended black and white flashback Leonard relates over the phone – to a cop we can only assume is Teddy – how he was suspicious of Jankis who despite his condition could nonetheless administer the correct insulin doses to his diabetic wife. The claim refused, Sammy's wife attempted to snap her husband out of his amnesia by making him repeatedly inject her with insulin shots. But the ploy backfired tragically, leaving her dead and Sammy still adrift in memory-less limbo. Caught like Leonard, in the film's looping reverse narration, we can't help but cling to this flashback as having some kind of authority. It serves as a case history of Leonard's condition and illuminates his attempts to snap out of it – he hires a hooker to help him restage his memories of his last night with his wife, only to nod off and forget about it – as well as adding an emotionally compelling counter-narrative to the chilly formal virtuosity on display. But even this seemingly reliable flashback is undermined: at gunpoint, Teddy tells Leonard he has completely revised his memory of the Sammy Jankis case to avoid facing the fact that his own wife, who survived the assault, died after he over-administered insulin to her. Jankis was a conman whom Leonard, in a state of extreme denial, has reconstructed as a pitiful victim.

While such final-reel revelations – which actually occur at the beginning of the film's story – provide a satisfying explanation of the kaleidoscope of conflicting details, the real pleasure of *Memento* lies in its openness to re-viewing and hence to interpretation. Drawing from the rich metafictional possibilities inherent in the detective genre, *Memento* delivers, in Leonard Shelby, a character who, while he considers himself an investigator, is actually – and all at once – a proficient killer and the perfect patsy: fuelled by his lust for revenge, he'll take out anybody with the initials that fit; dependent on others to provide clues to the identity of his wife's killer, he's also the victim of countless set-ups, the seemingly unwitting cog in the duplicitous manoeuvrings of those around him. At times he's like a wind-up genre automaton who grinds to a halt until the next bout of clues prompts him into action.

Nolan doesn't shy away from the darkly farcical potential of Leonard's condition, having him blunder into scrapes and shoot-outs through misreading his scribbled notes or simply forgetting what was going on a few minutes earlier. But while his amnesia might be exploited by others for greed or revenge, the film's greatest trick is to end by questioning his innocence: 'Do I lie to myself to be happy?' he asks after Teddy has given him his version of his wife's death. 'In your case Teddy, I will,' he tells himself as he writes down the cop's car-registration number, falsely incriminating him as his wife's killer and effectively signing his death warrant. It's a mark of Nolan's achievement that this final scene – which seemingly completes the narrative jigsaw – should cast a cloud over Leonard's motives. It's a stunning tease, a tantalisingly ambiguous note on which to sign off, one that scatters our sense of certainty as we rerun the events of the past two hours in our heads.

Chris Darke

BATTLE ROYALE
Japan 2000
Director: Kenji Fukasaku

Japan, the early twenty-first century. As a reaction to rising unemployment and juvenile delinquency, the government has passed an act allowing the staging of 'Battle Royale', whereby an entire class of 14- to 15-year-olds chosen by lottery are transported to a remote island, fitted with explosive collars that can be triggered by remote control, given supplies and weapons and allowed three days to kill each other off until only one survivor remains.

Class B of Zentsuji Middle School, supervised by embittered ex-teacher Kitano and a cadre of soldiers, includes two 'transfer students' – previous BR winner Kawada and psychopathic volunteer Kiriyama. During the screening of an instructional video that explains the rules of the game, Kitano kills a girl for talking out of turn and detonates the collar of Nobu, a class troublemaker who once assaulted him.

Over the course of three days, the body count rises. Some children opt to commit suicide; Kiriyama obtains an automatic weapon and hunts for sport; Mitsuko, a domineering female pupil, becomes a serial killer; computer-literate Shinji assembles the ingredients for a bomb and tries to attack the game officials; bossy girl Utsumi holes up in a lighthouse with her friends but rivalries within the group lead to a massacre. Shuya, Nobu's best friend, and Noriko, who has always had a crush on him, stick together and form an alliance with Kawada, who claims to know a way that more than one can survive the battle. After Kiriyama has disposed of most of the other survivors, including Mitsuko and Shinji, he is killed by Kawada, who fakes the deaths of Shuya and Noriko. Kitano, who believes Noriko to be the only decent kid in the class, dismisses the soldiers, and allows himself to be killed by Shuya. Shuya and Noriko escape with the mortally wounded Kawada, and return to the mainland as wanted fugitives.

* * *

Made with a cast of 35-year-old cowboys, soldiers or gangsters, *Battle Royale* would be no more shocking than any other post-Peckinpah bloodbath, and many violent dystopian satires – from Peter Watkins's *Punishment Park* (1971) through *Turkey Shoot* (1981) and *No Escape* (1994) to *Series 7: The Contenders* (2001) – have covered roughly the same ground. In this case, however, the kill-or-be-killed situation is Battle Royale, a game backed by a Japanese government of the near future, in which a group of schoolchildren are left on an island and given three days to try to kill each other off. Making the most out of a premise which casts schoolchildren in their mid-teens as killers or victims, *Battle Royale* demonstrates that it is still possible to be transgressive, as roughly 40 uniformed, apparently ordinary kids are murdered in familiar, blood-bursting action-picture manner – riddled with bullets from automatic weapons, throats slashed or blasted out, stabbed, shot with arrows, decapitated with a samurai sword, blown up, gruesomely poisoned.

As in *Lord of the Flies*, an obvious precedent, we are in the territory of allegory rather than a study of real-world child violence. The teenagers of Class B do not represent the likes of the Littleton, Colorado, trenchcoat mafia, the killers of Jamie Bulger or genocidal teenage Khmer Rouge soldiers. Instead they are ordinary kids, representing people we are or might be, and their actions in extraordinary circumstances are supposed to expose the range of human behaviour on the edge of societal madness. The film balances its minx-cum-sociopath and hacker-terrorist with kids who refuse to accept what is going on or simply hide out and hope it'll all go away. A US movie like *The Hills Have Eyes* (1977) posits that we would all become murderers if threatened with murder, but this Japanese film insists that sometimes we would choose to die rather than kill.

The Koshun Takami novel on which the film is based isn't set in the future, but an alternative present (like Stephen King's somewhat similar book *The Long Walk* and the often-misinterpreted *Series 7*), predicated on a Japanese victory in World War II that has created a society in which *Battle Royale* seems to make sense. The script skips over the set-up, with some statistics about unemployment and kid crime that don't sink in, and then delivers a few preliminary jabs, as narrator Shuya comes home to find his unemployed father has committed suicide and soon-to-be-killed tearaway Nobu stabs apparently sympathetic teacher Kitano in the school hallway. Then, on the bus as they are supposedly taken on a school trip, we meet the class who have been selected for this cruel contest, and it is established that they are neither particularly innocent nor especially deserving of this punishment. Nobu, the only guilty party, is killed off quickly, and the chill sets in.

Most other films in this sub-genre are primarily satires at the expense of crass media. This is not an avenue *Battle Royale* chooses to explore – although we do get a hideous moment as a bloodied little girl with braces and a Norman Bates smile is hailed as a celebrity for surviving the last BR, and there is an hilariously perky instructional video for mass murder presented by a pouting Japanese MTV-type hostess. Though monitored by the game officials, and a sad-eyed but brutalised 'Beat' Takeshi (who plays former teacher Kitano), the kids are on their own. An especially horrific aspect of the premise is that the point of BR is not to entertain sadistic mobs, but to teach children a lesson.

The film keeps count of who has died, with print-outs on screen and regular announcements, but with so many characters it can't get close to them all. The obvious central figures, meek Noriko and numb Shuya, are less vivid than some of the shorter-lived characters, and the most effective moments in the film are vignettes: the take-charge head-girl type cheerfully organising her clique to survive, only for everything to go wrong as girls with ordinary grievances ('Why do you have to be the leader all the time?') reach for guns; contrasting moments as boys approach girls on whom they have crushes, with one trying to bully a girl into liking him through death threats and another being shot dead by the girl he has just confessed his love to; the revelation that Kiriyama, sporting a sharp suit and Johnny Rotten hair, has entered the contest for fun; sickle-wielding Mitsuko's assumption of the role of serial murderess, paying back all the real and imaginary sleights she has suffered in school ('I didn't want to be a loser any more').

Perhaps because it's impossible to rationalise the situation as credible, and perhaps because taking it deadly seriously would make the film unwatchably grim, veteran director Kenji Fukasaku mines a seam of very black humour, with the wry, impassive, hard-to-fathom Kitano acting as if this were a normal school activity, as classical music is played over the Tannoy and updates on the class' progress are read out. As the scrambling of character name and actor suggests, Kitano is our anchor in this picture, a familiar presence with an inimitable stance, and his poised, perfect death scene tells us that we must take *Battle Royale* seriously but not literally.

Kim Newman

FINAL FANTASY THE SPIRITS WITHIN
USA 2001
Director: Hironobu Sakaguchi

The year 2065. Thirty-six years ago the Earth was invaded by hostile aliens known as the phantoms; the surviving humans live in cities, which are protected from alien attack by huge transparent shields. Scientist Dr Aki Ross searches an empty New York for the sixth of eight spirits which she believes are the key to ridding the Earth of the phantoms. She is apprehended by a squad of troops, headed by old flame Gray Edwards; they are attacked but escape with the spirit intact to what was Manhattan Island, now Barrier City. Ross's colleague Dr Sid presents his research into these spirits to the Earth Council, the planet's ruling body. He believes every object posesses its own spirit, including the Earth whose spirit is known as Gaia.

Opponent General Hein suggests using the newly developed space cannon on the aliens. The Council reluctantly side with Sid when he reveals that Ross has been infected by the aliens for some time but is kept alive by his research. This infection gives her dreams which she believes are attempts by the aliens at communication. Ross and Edwards' squad head for the Tuscon Wastelands where they find the seventh spirit; they are apprehended on their return by Hein's troops. Held in jail, they realise that the aliens are the tormented spirits of a long-dead race. Hein attempts to coerce the Council into action by dropping the city barrier and letting in the phantoms. As the city is destroyed Hein flees to his orbiting cannon, which the Earth Council invite him to fire. Ross's group escape in her ship, but not before some of them – Neil, Jane and Ryan – are lost to the phantoms. They head for a crater in the Caucasus Mountains where the meteor which first brought the aliens to Earth crashed. Ross and Edwards descend into the crater and locate the final spirit, which belongs to an alien. Edwards is killed; his departing spirit connects with Gaia, triggering an energy wave that destroys the phantom horde.

* * *

Those familiar with *Final Fantasy*, the epic Japanese role-playing videogames from which *The Spirits Within* is derived, will be aware of the theme that runs through them. A party of heroes averts impending global holocaust by drawing on their individual skills, gaining knowledge through challenges and emerging victorious with new-found love and respect for themselves and their companions. It's an old tale and one from which the game's creators, Square, have spun ten multi-million-selling episodes. Those being inducted to *Final Fantasy* through *The Spirits Within* will marvel at the technical expertise of game-producer-turned-director Hironobu Sakaguchi. But they will also wonder how gamers could possibly commit themselves to more than a hundred minutes' playing time (games typically go on for hours) if the confused and cliché-ridden nonsense of *The Spirits Within* is anything to go by.

Despite a promising start, with a shift away from the imaginary worlds of the game series and into a shattered, alien-infested future Earth, the film degenerates into a muddle of visual and verbal clichés during which Sakaguchi plunders recent sci-fi films. References to other works are nothing new for the *Final Fantasy* franchise. But whereas in his games Sakaguchi evokes global mythical figures – specifically in his adoption of such gods as Odin, Shiva and Quetzacoatl – in his film he draws on contemporary Hollywood. We see obvious nods to *Alien* (the extraterrestrial infection of heroine Dr Aki Ross) and the starship chases of *Return of the Jedi*, and we also see clear visual references to familiar actors. Male lead Gray Edwards may have the voice of Alec Baldwin, but he looks remarkably like Ben Affleck, while wisecracking Neil looks, in the right virtual light, like Jason Priestly. The use of mythical figures in the *Final Fantasy* games works because they are recognisable and solid reference points. Jason Priestly – while certainly recognisable – hardly lends the film the same gravitas as *Jason and the Argonauts*.

The strength of *The Spirits Within* is its cutting-edge animation technology. The opening sequence, with its close-up of Dr Ross, showing every pore and strand of hair individually rendered, is the closest we've seen to a believable synthespian. But you can't help wondering whether such technology is yet up to the task. Although CGI is, of course, used extensively in such live-action films as *Titanic* and *Gladiator*, the effects work rarely intrudes on our suspension of disbelief (rather, it adds to the film's texture). Each computer-rendered frame of *The Spirits Within*, however, has to work hard to convince us: every time a facial expression looks unnatural, every time a character's movement seems awkward, our attention is drawn to the film's artificiality. In a film that, unlike, say, *Shrek*, purports to present near photo-realism, this is problematic.

The Spirits Within lacks emotional resonance: characterisation is excessively broad and its script routine. It necessarily lacks the dynamic of player interaction that makes games, in their current form at least, so compulsive. Ultimately, the film is $100 million worth of proof that games and film are not close siblings, but rather many generations removed.

Dan Mayers

The Shining (Stanley Kubrick, 1980)

Section 6:
Case Study – Stanley Kubrick

Though he made three science fiction films, admittedly in completely different sub-genres (near-future nuclear disaster, deep space exploration, dystopia), and one horror film (arguably two, if we count *Eyes Wide Shut*, 1999 – and let's not forget James Mason taking Shelley Winters and Sue Lyon to see *The Curse of Frankenstein*, 1957, in *Lolita*, 1962), Stanley Kubrick is rarely considered a maker of genre films even if he also turned out thrillers (*Killer's Kiss*, 1955, *The Killing*, 1956), war films (*Paths of Glory*, 1957, *Full Metal Jacket*, 1986) and historical spectacles (*Spartacus*, 1960, *Barry Lyndon*, 1975). All his films seem at heart to be icy satires, and the term 'nightmare comedy' (coined for *Dr Strangelove, or How I Learned to Stop Worrying and Love the Bomb*) is apt for his whole oeuvre. We came into this book with *Strangelove*, so it's apt that we should leave with *2001: A Space Odyssey*, *A Clockwork Orange* (in a very revisionary piece) and *The Shining*.

Kubrick is a 'Sight and Sound' type of director – two of these pieces come from a special issue published just after his death and at the time of the release of *Eyes Wide Shut*, while I have dipped back into an earlier incarnation of the magazine for the original review of *2001* by Philip Strick (still a contributor) and a piece on *The Shining* contemporary with its release. The Overlook Hotel (or that room 'beyond the infinite' in *2001*) is a fine model of the way the magazine sees cinema, as a haunted house with many rooms, labyrinths and traps, territory to be mapped, explored, lost in and escaped from.

2001: A COLD DESCENT

Mark Crispin Miller

Dear Mr Kubrick: My pupils are still dilated, and my breathing sounds like your soundtrack. I don't know if this poor brain will survive another work of the magnitude of *2001*, but it will die (perhaps more accurately 'go nova') happily if given the opportunity. Whenever anybody asks me for a description of the movie, I tell them that it is, in sequential order: anthropological, camp, McLuhan, cybernetic, psychedelic, religious. That shakes them up a lot. Jesus, man, where did you get that incredibly good technical advice? Whenever I see the sun behind a round sign, I start whistling *Thus Spake Zarathustra*. My kettledrum impression draws the strangest looks.

Dear Mr Kubrick: Although I have my doubts that your eyes will ever see this writing, I still have hopes that some secretary will neglect to dispose of my letter. I have just seen your motion picture and I believe – please, words, don't fail me now – that I have never been so moved by a film – so impressed – awed – etc. The music was absolutely on a zenith. 'The Blue Danube' really belonged in some strange way, and the main theme with its building crescendos was more beautiful than John Lennon's 'I Am the Walrus', and from me that's a compliment. The story in *Life* magazine, of course, showed the most routine scenes, as *Life* has a tendency to eliminate any overwhelming virtue in a motion picture, and the three best scenes were lumped together and were almost unrecognisable. But lest I run off at the mouth, let me conclude by saying that if the Academy of ill-voted Oscars doesn't give you a multitude of awards in 1969, I will resign from humanity and come a soldier.

Twenty-five years later, Kubrick's fan mail has an unintended poignancy – in part (but only in part) because the letters are so obviously dated. Those fierce accolades are pure 1960s. To re-read such letters now – and Jerome Agel's 1970 *The Making of Kubrick's 2001*, the ecstatic, crazed *homage* that includes them – is to look back on a cultural moment that now seems as remote from our own as, say, those hairy screamers of pre-history, erect with murderous purpose at the water hole, might seem from the low-key Doctor Heywood R. Floyd, unconscious on his umpteenth voyage to the moon.

Privilege and power

The film's first devotees were knocked out, understandably, by its 'incredible and irrevocable splendor' (as another letter-writer phrased it). Others were troubled – also understandably – by the film's disturbing intimation that, since 'the dawn of man' so many, many centuries ago, the human race has got nowhere fast. That subversive notion is legible not only in the famous match cut from the sunlit bone to the nocturnal spacecraft (two tools, same deadly white, both *descending*) but throughout the first two sections of the narrative: indeed, the negation of the myth of progress may be the film's basic structural principle. Between the starved and bickering apes and their smooth, affable descendants there are all sorts of broad, distinctions, but there is finally not much difference – an oblique, uncanny similarity that recurs in every human action represented.

In *2001*, for example, the men feed unenthusiastically on ersatz sandwiches and steaming pads of brightly coloured mush – food completely cooked (to say the least) and slowly masticated, as opposed to the raw flesh furtively bolted by the now carnivorous apes; and yet both flesh and mush appear unappetising, and both are eaten purely out of need. Similarly, in *2001* the men are just as wary and belligerent, and just as quick to square off against tribal enemies, as their tense, shrieking forebears – although, as well-trained professionals and efficient servants of the state, they confront the other not with piercing screams and menacing gestures but by suddenly sitting very still and speaking very quietly and slowly: '... I'm... sorry, Doctor Smyslov, but, uh... I'm really not at liberty to discuss this...' Thus Doctor Floyd, though seated in an attitude of friendly languor (legs limply crossed, hands hidden in his lap), fights off his too inquisitive Soviet counterpart just as unrelentingly as, tens of thousands of years earlier, the armed apes had crushed their rivals at the water hole (which recurs here as a small round plastic table, bearing drinks, and again the locus of contention). Now, as then, the victor obviously wields a handy instrument of his authority (although this time it's a briefcase, not a femur); and now, as then, the females merely look on as the males fight it out. (There is no matriarchal element in Kubrick's myth.)

More generally, the scientists and bureaucrats, and the comely corporate personnel who serve them (polite young ladies dressed in pink or white), are all sealed off – necessarily – from the surrounding vastness: and here too the cool world of 2001 seems wholly unlike, yet is profoundly reminiscent of, the arid world where all began. Back then, the earthlings would seek refuge from the predatory dangers of the night by wedging themselves, terrified, into certain natural hiding places and even in daylight would never wander far from that found 'home' or from one another, even though the world – such as it was – lay all around them. Likewise, their remote descendants are all holed up against the infinite and *its* dangers – not in terror any more (they seem to have forgotten terror), and surely not in rocky niches (their habitats are state creations, quietly co-run by Hilton, Bell and Howard Johnson), but in a like state of isolation in the very midst of seeming endlessness.

Herein the world of *2001* recalls the pre-historic world *before* the monolith gives 'man' his first idea; once that happens, the species is no longer stuck in place. Made strong by their new carnivorous diet, and with their hands now mainly used to smash and grab, the ape-men have already visibly outgrown their former quadrupedal posture (they are *standing* for the first time – when they come back to the water hole), and so are ready to move on. 'A new animal was abroad on the planet, spreading slowly out from the African heartland,' writes Arthur C. Clarke in his novelisation of the film – which, of course, elides that historic episode, along with all the rest of human history, thereby taking us from one great dusk to another. When 'Moon-Watcher' (as

Clarke calls him) exultantly flings his natural cudgel high into the air, that reckless gesture is the film's only image of abandon and its last 'human' moment of potentiality – for, as the match cut tells us, it's all downhill from there.

However, although the film takes us straight from one twilight moment to another, the first *is* very different from the next – indeed, the two are almost perfect opposites. At first humankind nearly dies out because there is no science: no one knows how to make anything and so those feeble simians cannot fight off the big cats, bring down the nutritious pigs, take over fertile territory, set up proper shelters and otherwise proceed to clear away the obstacles and wipe out the extremes, of mere nature – through that gradual subjection turning into men. And yet that long, enlightened course of ours (the film suggests) has only brought us back to something too much like the terminus we once escaped – only this time it is not the forces of mere nature (instincts *and* elements) that threaten to unmake us, but the very instrumentality that originally saved us. In 2001, in other words, there is *too much* science, *too much* made, the all-pervasive product now degrading us almost as nature used to do. The match cut tells us not just that we're on the downswing once again, but that, this time, what has reduced us is our absolute containment by, and for the sake of, our own efficient apparatus. Hence Doctor Floyd is strapped *inside* one such sinking ship, and quite unconscious of it, where Moon-Watcher simply *used* his weapon, and did so with his eyes wide open. That first image of the dozing scientist is a transcendent bit of satire, brilliantly implying just how thoroughly man has been unmade – stupefied, deprived, bereft – by the smart things of his own making: a falling-off, and/or quasi-reversion, that is perceptible only through critical contrast with what precedes it.

Emboldened by hard protein, the apes at once start making war: mankind's first form of organised amusement, Kubrick suggests, and (as all his films suggest) one whose attraction can never be overcome by the grandiose advance of 'civilisation' – on the contrary. In Kubrick's universe, the modern state is itself a vast war machine, an enormous engine of displaced (male) aggression whose purpose is to keep itself erect by absorbing the instinctual energies of all and diverting them into some gross spectacular assault against the other. These lethal – and usually suicidal – strikes are carried out by the lowliest members of the state's forces (the infantry, the droogs, the grunts; 'King' Kong, Jack Torrance) against an unseen enemy, and /or – ultimately – some isolated woman, while those at the rear, and at the top, sit back and enjoy the rout vicariously. There is, in short, a stark division of labour in that cold, brilliant, repetitive world of jails and palaces, hospitals and battlefields. It is the function of the lowly to express – within strict limits, and only at appointed times and places – the bestial animus that has long since been repressed and stigmatised, and that (therefore) so preoccupies the rest of us. Thus Alex's droogs, the grunts under Cowboy's brief command, and the doomed Jack Torrance all revert, as they move in on their respective prey, to the hunched and crouching gait of their first ancestors sneaking towards the water hole.

Meanwhile, it is the privilege of those at the top – 'the best people', as certain characters in *Barry Lyndon* and *The Shining* term them – to sit and (sometimes literally) look *down* on all that gruesome monkey business, sometimes pretending loudly to deplore it, yet always quietly enjoying it (whether or not they have themselves arranged it in the first place). Such animal exertion is, for them, a crucial spectatorial delight, as long as it happens well outside their own splendid confines – at the front, or in the ring, or in some remote suburban house, or in the servants' quarters at the Overlook, or in the ruins of Vietnam.

When, on the other hand, someone goes completely ape right there among them, *that* feral show is not at all a pleasure but an indecorum gross and shattering – whether played as farce, like General Turgidson's clumsy tussle with the Soviet ambassador in *Dr Strangelove* ('Gentlemen, you can't fight in *here!* This is the *War Room!*'), or as a grotesque lapse, like Barry Lyndon's wild and ruinous attack on his contemptuous stepson. Such internal outbursts threaten 'the best people' very deeply; not only by intimating a rebellious violence that might one day destroy them, and their creatures, from without (as nearly happens to Marcus Crassus in *Spartacus*, or as happens to Sergeant Hartman in *Full Metal Jacket*), but by reminding those pale, cordial masters that, although they like to see themselves as hovering high above the brutal impulse, they themselves still have it in them. That rude reminder the pale masters cannot tolerate, for their very self-conception, and their power, are based directly on the myth of total difference between themselves and those beneath them. It is the various troops and thugs, those down and out there on the ground, who do the lethal simian dance, because they are primitives. We who do our work in chairs, observing those beneath us, setting them up for this or that ordeal and then watching as they agonise, and *therefore* beings of a higher order, through this sedentary act confirming our 'humanity'.

Conditioning and castration

Doctor Floyd is just such a 'human' being. If he never appears gazing coolly down on others as they suffer, as do the generals in *Paths of Glory* or the Ludovico experts in *A Clockwork Orange*, that omission does not connote any relative kindliness, but is merely one reflection of his total separation from reality: Doctor Floyd never callously looks down on suffering because, within his bright, closed universe-within-a-universe, there is no suffering (nor any physical intensity or emotional display of any kind) for him to look down on. For that matter, Doctor Floyd never really looks at anything, or anyone, until the climax of his top-secret visit to the moon, when he looks intently at the monolith, and even touches it (or tries to). Prior to that uncanny action, the scientist's gaze is, unless belligerently opaque (as it becomes in his brief 'flight' with Smyslov), consistently casual, affable and bored, the same pleasant managerial mask whether it confronts some actual stranger's face, the video image of his daughter's face, or that synthetic sandwich.

Although he floats, throughout, at an absolute remove from any site of others' gratifying pain, Doctor Floyd is nonetheless inclined, like all his peers in Kubrick's films, to see himself as definitively placed *above* the simian horde – which is, in his case, not just some cowering division or restive troupe of gladiators, but his own planet's entire population. As he would presume himself in every way superior to the proto-men of aeons back, so does he presume himself – and, of course, the Council, which he represents – far superior to his fellow-beings way back 'down' (as he persists in putting it) on earth. Those masses, he argues, need to be protected from the jarring news that there might be another thinking species out there – hence 'the need for absolute secrecy in this'. 'I'm sure you're all aware of the extremely grave potential for cultural shock and social disorientation contained in this present situation,' he tells the staff at Clavius, 'if the facts were suddenly made public without adequate preparation – and conditioning.' That last proviso makes it clear that Doctor Floyd is, in fact, ideologically a close relation to those other, creepier doctors at the Ludovico Institute; the whole euphemistic warning of 'potential cultural shock' betrays his full membership of that cold, invisible elite who run the show in nearly all Kubrick's films, concerned with nothing but the preservation of their own power. Surely, what Doctor Floyd imagines happening 'if the facts were suddenly made public' would be uncannily like what we've seen already: everybody terrified at first, and then, perhaps, the smart ones putting two and two together and moving, quickly, to knock off those bullying others who have monopolised what everybody needs – 'the facts' having instantly subverted those others' ancient claims to an absolute supremacy.

The film itself is thus subversive, indirectly questioning Floyd's representative 'humanity' through satiric contrast with his grunting antecedents. At first, the safe and slumbering Doctor Floyd seems merely antithetical to the ready, raging apes. Whereas those primates – once they have tasted meat, then blood – were all potential, standing taut and upright at the water hole, their leader fiercely beckoning them forward, Doctor Floyd is placid, sacked-out, slack: as smooth of face as they were rough and hairy, as still as they were noisy and frenetic, as fully dressed (zipped up and buckled in) as they were bare – and, above or underneath it all, as soft as they were hard. If they were the first exemplars of the new and savage species *homo occidens* (and only secondarily, if at all, fit to be entitled *homo sapiens*), the scientist, unconscious in his perfect chair, exemplifies the old and ravaged species *homo sedens*. As he dozes comfily, his weightless arm bobs slow and flaccid at his side, his hand hangs lax, while his sophisticated pen floats like a mini-spacecraft in the air beside him. It is a comic image of advanced detumescence – effective castration – as opposed (or so it seems) to the heroic shots of Moon-Watcher triumphing in 'his' new knowledge of the deadly and yet death-defying instrument: his sinewy arm raised high, his grip tight, his tool in place, he seems to roar in ecstasy as he pulverises the bones lying all around him ('Death, thou shalt die!'), and the pigs crash lifeless to the ground, as limp as Doctor Floyd looks minutes later.

The seductive waltz

Although seemingly so different from the simians, however, Doctor Floyd is not only their enfeebled scion but also, deep down, their brother in aggressiveness: a relation only gradually perceptible in his various muted repetitions of the apes' outright behaviours. As his subdued showdown with the Soviets recalls the frenzied action at the water hole, so does his mystified authority recall Moon-Watcher's balder primacy, the scientist relying not, of course, on screaming violence to best his enemies and rally his subordinates, but on certain quiet managerial techniques (body language, tactical displays of informality, and so on). His inferiors are just as abject towards him as Moon-Watcher's were towards *that* head monkey, although the later entities display their deference towards the manager not, of course, by crouching next to him and combing through his hair for nits, but just by sucking up to him. Placating him with nervous, eager smiles and stroking him with witless praises: 'Y'know, that was an excellent speech you gave us, Heywood!' 'It certainly was!' 'I'm sure it beefed up morale a helluva lot!' In such dim echoes of the apes' harsh *ur*-society we can discern the lingering note of their belligerence – as we can still perceive their war-like attitude throughout the antiseptic world of their descendants, who are still cooped up in virtual fortresses and still locked into an arrangement at once rigidly hierarchical and numbingly conformist, the clean men as difficult to tell apart as were their hunched hairy forebears.

Thus is the primal animus still here; indeed, it is now more dangerous than ever, warfare having evolved from heated manual combat to the cool deployment of orbiting atomic weapons (one of which sails gently by as 'The Blue Danube' begins). Yet while the animus has taken on apocalyptic force, its expression among human beings is (paradoxically, perhaps) oblique, suppressed, symbolic, offering none even of that crude delight which the near-anhedonic simians had known: the thrill of victory (as the sportscasters often put it), and, inextricable from that, the base kinetic entertainment of (as Alex often puts it) 'the old ultra-violence'. Such overt and bestial pleasures have been eliminated from the computerised supra-world of the Council and its employees (although not from life back 'down' on earth, as *A Clockwork Orange* will, from its very opening shot, remind us). Just as the animal appetite has, in those white spaces, been ruthlessly denied, so have all other pleasures, which in Kubrick's universe (as in Nietzsche's and in Freud's) derive straight from that ferocious source. In the world of Doctor Heywood Floyd, it is only the machines that dance and couple, man having had, it would appear, even his desires absorbed into the apparatus that, we thought, was meant to gratify them.

As 'The Blue Danube' starts to play, its old, elegant cadences rising and falling so oddly and charmingly against this sudden massive earthrise, the various spacecraft floating by as if in heavenly tranquillity, there is, of course, no human figure in the frame – nor should there be, for in this 'machine ballet' (as Kubrick has called it) live men and women have no place. Out here, and at this terminal moment, all human suppleness, agility and lightness, all our bodily allure, have somehow been transferred to those exquisite gadgets. Thus the hypnotic circularity of Strauss's waltz applies not to the euphoric roundabout of any dancing couple, but to the even wheeling of that big space station. Thus, while those transcendent items sail through the void with the supernal grace of seraphim, the stewardess attending Doctor Floyd staggers down the aisle as if she's had a stroke, the zero gravity and her smart 'grip shoes' giving her solicitous approach the absurd look of bad ballet.

Her image connotes not only an aesthetic decline (Kubrick had idealised the ballerina-as-artist in his early *Killer's Kiss*), but a pervasive sexual repression. With the machines doing all the dancing, bodies are erotically dysfunctional – an incapacity suggested by Kubrick's travesties of dance. In *A Clockwork Orange* he would again present a gross parody of ballet: in the scene at the Derelict Casino, where Billy-boy's droogs, getting ready to gang-rape the 'weepy young devotchka', sway and wrestle with her on the stage, their ugly unity and her pale struggle in their midst suggesting a balletic climax turned to nightmare. There, eros is negated crudely by male violence. In *2001*, the mock ballet implies no mere assault on the erotic but its virtual extirpation, its near-superannuation in the world of the machine. Here, every pleasurable impulse must be channelled into the efficient maintenance of that machine, which therefore exerts as inhibitive an influence as any fierce religion. Stumbling down the aisle, the stewardess looks, in her stiff white pants-suit and round white padded hat (designed to cushion blows against the ceiling), like a sort of corporate nun, all female attributes well hidden. And so it is appropriate that, as she descends on the unconscious Doctor Floyd, her slow approach does not recall, say, Venus coming down on her Adonis, but suggests instead a porter checking on a loose piece of cargo, as she grabs his floating pen and re-attaches it to his oblivious trunk.

Hermetic spaces

The stewardess dances not a fantasy of some delightful respite from the waking world, but only further service to, and preparation for, that world. Likewise 'The Blue Danube' refers not to the old sexual exhilarations of (to quote Lord Byron) the 'seductive waltz', but only to the smooth congress of immense machines. As Doctor Floyd slumps in his chair, the flight attendant re-attaching his loose implement, the very craft that holds them both (a slender, pointed shuttle named *Orion*) is itself approaching, then slides with absolute precision into, the great bright slit at the perfect centre of the circular space station, the vehicles commingling as they do throughout the film – and as the living characters do not, as far as we can see. *Orion* having finally 'docked', the waltz comes to its triumphant close – and Kubrick cuts, on that last note, to an off-white plastic grid, an automatic portal sliding open with a long dull whirr. There first appears, seated stiffly in the circular compartment, another stewardess, a shapely and impassive blonde dressed all in pink and manning the controls, and then, two seats away from her, there again is Doctor Floyd, now wide awake and holding his big briefcase up across his lap like a protective shield. He zips it shut. 'Here you are, sir,' she says politely (and ambiguously). 'Main level, please.' 'Alright,' he answers, getting up. 'See you on the way back.'

The human characters are thus maintained – through their very posture and deportment, the lay-out of the chill interiors, their meaningless reflexive courtesies – in total separation from each other, within (and for the sake of) their machines, which meanwhile interpenetrate as freely as Miltonic angels. And yet there is a deeply buried hint that even up in these hermetic spaces, people are still sneaking off to do the deed. 'A blue, woman's cashmere sweater has been found in the restroom,' a robotic female voice announces, twice, over the space station's PA system just after Doctor Floyd's arrival. That abandoned sweater may well be the evidence of the same sort of furtive quickie that takes place in General Turgidson's motel room in *Dr Strangelove*, or that, in *A Clockwork Orange*, a doctor and nurse enjoy behind the curtains of a hospital bed while Alex lies half-dead nearby. Given Kubrick's penchant for self-reference, it may be that, in conceiving that aside about the cashmere sweater, he had in mind the moment in *Lolita* when Charlotte Haze, speaking to her wayward daughter on the telephone (the nymphet having been exiled for the summer to Camp Climax), querulously echoes this suspicious news: 'You lost your new *sweater*?... In the woods?'

Such details reveal yet another crucial similarity between the simian and human worlds of *2001*. For all the naturalness of their state before the monolith, we never see the apes attempting sex, although we see them trying to find food, to get some sleep, to fight their enemies. That gap in Kubrick's overview of their condition is surely not a consequence of prudishness (no longer a big problem by the mid-1960s), but would appear deliberate – a negative revelation of the thorough harshness of the simians' existence. The apes are simply too hungry, and too scared, to be thinking about sex, which would presumably occur among them only intermittently, in nervous one-shot bursts – much as in the world of Doctor Floyd, where everyone is much too busy for anything other than a quick bang now and then, and where there's not a decent place to do it anyway, just as there wasn't at 'the dawn of man'.

Afloat in the 'free world'

Doctor Floyd's deprivation is not merely genital, however. If, in his asexual state, he is no worse off than his simian forebears, in his continuous singleness he is far more deprived than they. For all their misery, those creatures had at least the warmth and nearness of one another – huddling in the night, there was for them at least that palpable and vivid solace. For that bond – too basic even to be called 'love' – there can be no substitute, nor can it be transcended: 'There are very few things in this world that have an unquestionable importance in and of themselves and are not susceptible to debate and rational argument, but the family is one of them,' Kubrick once said. If man 'is going to stay sane throughout [his] voyage, he must have someone to care about, something that is more important than himself'.

Sacked out on the shuttle, Doctor Floyd is the sole passenger aboard that special flight: literally a sign of his status and the importance of his mission, yet the image conveys not prominence but isolation. The man in the chair has only empty chairs around him, with no company other than the tottering stewardess who briefly comes to grab his pen and, on the television screen before him, another faceless couple in another smart conveyance, the two engaging in some mute love-chat (Doctor Floyd is wearing headphones) while the viewer sleeps and the living woman comes and goes. Here too the machine appears to have absorbed the very longings of the personnel who seemingly control it – for even those two mannequins, jabbering theatrically at each other's faces, have more in common with the huddling apes than does Doctor Floyd or any of his colleagues.

Whereas the apes had feared and fed together, here everyone is on the job alone. Efficient service to the state requires that parents and children, wives and husbands all stay away from one another, sometimes forever, the separation vaguely eased, or merely veiled, by the compensatory glimpses now and then available (at great expense) by telephone. For this professional class, the family is no sturdier within the 'free world' than it is under Soviet domination. 'He's been doing some underwater research in the Baltics, so, uh, I'm afraid we don't get a chance to see very much of each other these days!' laughs the Russian scientist Irina, a little ruefully, when Floyd asks after her husband. Although (the unseen) Mrs Floyd is, by contrast, still a wife and mother first and foremost, with Heywood the only wage slave in the family, their all-American household is just as atomised as the oppressed Irina's. As we learn from Floyd's perfunctory phone chat with his daughter ('Squirt', he calls her), the members of his upscale ménage are all off doing exactly the same things that the apes had done millennia earlier, although, again, the simians did those things collectively, whereas Floyd's 'home' is merely one more empty module. Mrs Floyd, Squirt tells her father, is 'gone to shopping' (charged, like Mrs Moon-Watcher, with the feeding of her young), while Floyd himself, of course, is *very* far away, at work (squaring off against the nation's foes, as Moon-Watcher had done). Meanwhile, 'Rachel', the woman hired to mind their daughter in their absence, is 'gone to the bathroom' (*that* primal business having long since been relegated to its own spotless cell), and Squirt herself, she says, is 'playing' (just as the little monkeys had been doing, except that Squirt – like her father – is all alone).

Every human need is thus indirectly and laboriously served by a vast complex of arrangements – material, social, psychological – that not only takes up everybody's time, but also takes us all away from one another, even as it seems to keep us all 'communicating'. In the ad-like tableau of Doctor Floyd's brief conversation with the television image of his little girl, there is a poignancy that he cannot perceive, any more than he can grasp the value of his coming home, in person, for her birthday party. 'I'm very sorry about it, but I can't,' he tells her evenly. 'I'm gonna send you a very nice *present*, though.' In offering her a gift to compensate for his being away, Doctor Floyd betrays the same managerial approach to family relations that enables him to carry on, with his usual equanimity, this whole disembodied conversation in the first place; as far as he's concerned, that 'very nice present' will make up completely for his absence, just as his mere image on the family telescreen ought to be the *same thing* as his being there. She, however, still appreciates the difference. When he asks what present she would like, with a child's acuity she names the only thing that might produce him for her, since it seems to be the sole means whereby he checks in at home: 'A telephone'.

For all its underlying sadness, the scene is fraught with absurdist comedy: for that telephone is inescapable. It is not just the bright tool through which the family 'communicates' but also the very content of that 'communication'. Here the medium is indeed the message – and there's nothing to it. 'Listen, sweetheart,' says the father, having changed the subject, or so he thinks. 'I want you to tell Mummy something for me. Will you remember?' 'Yes.' 'Tell Mummy that I telephoned. Okay?' 'Yes.' 'And that I'll try to telephone again tomorrow. Now will you tell her that?'

The sense of profound emptiness arising from that Pinteresque exchange persists throughout the film, but – once the story shifts to the *Discovery* – in a tone less satiric, more elegiac. The mood now becomes deeply melancholy, as the two astronauts – a pair identical and yet dissociated, like a man and his reflection – eat and sleep and exercise in absolute apartness, both from one another and from all humankind, each one as perfectly shut off within his own routine and within that mammoth twinkling orb as any of their three refrigerated crew-mates. Aboard that sad craft, every seeming dialogue – save one – is in fact a solitudinous encounter with the Mechanism: either a one-way transmission from Earth, belatedly and passively received, or a 'communication' pre-recorded, or a sinister audience with the soft-spoken HAL, who, it seems, is always on the look-out for 'his' chance to eliminate, once and for all, what Dr Strangelove calls 'unnecessary human meddling'. That opportunity arises when the astronauts finally sit down, in private (or so they think), and for once talk face-to-face; an actual conversation, independent of technology and therefore a regressive move that HAL appears to punish, fittingly, by disconnecting his entire human crew – one sent careering helpless through the deeps, the three 'sleeping beauties' each neatly 'terminated' in his separate coffin, and the last denied re-admittance to the relative warmth and safety of the mother-ship. Thus HAL fulfils the paradoxical dynamic of the telephone: seeming to keep everyone 'in touch', yet finally cutting everybody off.

Too busy for erotic pleasure, as the apes had been too wretched for it, and much lonelier than those primal ancestors, Doctor Floyd is also much less sensitive than they – a being incapable of wonder, as opposed to the wild-eyed monkey-men. This human incapacity becomes apparent as the scientist very slowly, very calmly strokes – once (and with his whole body in its plastic glove) – the black lustrous surface of the monolith, thereby both repeating and inverting the abject obeisances of his astounded forebears, crouched and screaming at its solid base and touching at its face again and again, hands jerking back repeatedly in terror at its strangeness. The same profound insensitivity is already apparent in that first satiric tableau of the unconscious scientist, who in his (surely dreamless) slumber is as indifferent to the great sublimity around him as the tense simians were heartened by its distant lights and stirred by its expanses. Whereas the most adventurous among them might sometimes look beyond their own familiar niche (as Clarke's epithet 'Moon-Watcher' implies), those now in charge take that 'beyond' for granted, watching nothing but the little television screens before them.

On the phone to Squirt, Doctor Floyd pays no attention to the great home planet wheeling weirdly in the background, just outside the window. Here, as everywhere in *2001*, the cool man-made apparatus has lulled its passengers into a necessary unawareness of the infinite, keeping them equilibrated, calm, their heads and stomachs filled, in order to ensure that they stay poised to keep the apparatus, and themselves, on the usual blind belligerent course. Thus boxed in, they calculate, kiss ass, crack feeble jokes about the lousy food – and never think to glance outside. As the moon bus glides above the spectral crags and gullies of the lunar night, and seems to glide on past the low and ponderous pale-blue earth, three-quarters full, the atmosphere sings eerily, exquisitely, in dissonant and breathless ululation. That is until the point of view shifts into the bus completely, with a dizzying hand-held shot that slowly takes us back from the red-lit cockpit, back into the blue-lit cabin, where one of Doctor Floyd's subordinates first fetches a big bulky ice-blue spacesuit), then heaves it slowly back to where Doctor Floyd (likewise besuited) sits in regal solitude, perusing documents, with Halvorsen, his second-in-command, attending him (and dressed the same). As that shot settles us well into this snug artificial space, the atonal shrilling of the quasi-angels gradually gives way to the tranquillising beeps and soporific whoosh of the smart bus itself, and to the (necessarily) stupid conversation of its passengers.

Within that ultimate cocoon, those wry little men are disinclined to think on what had come before them, or on what might lie ahead of them, but concentrate instead on their own tribal enterprise, and on their own careers (and, at some length, on those sandwiches), trading bluff banalities as to the mystery awaiting them. 'Heh heh. Don't suppose you have any idea what the damn thing is?' 'Heh heh. Wish to hell we did.

Heh heh.' Such complacency endures until their instrument, the hapless 'Bowman,' is yanked out of their cloistral world of white and goes on his wild psychedelic ride 'beyond the infinite', ending up immured again, but only temporarily – and in a state promising some sort of deliverance from the human fix. At first shattered unto madness, as opposed to the others' blank composure, and then quickly wrinkled, turning white, as opposed to their uniform boyish smoothness, he finally, from his sudden deathbed, reaches up and out towards, then merges with, the great dark monolith, thereby undergoing an ambiguous 'rebirth'.

Lonely at the top

In 1968 the 'futuristic' world Kubrick satirised so thoroughly was not, despite the title, some 30 years away. The changes the film foretold were imminent. Within a decade *2001* was already getting hard to see – and not just because ever fewer theatre managers would book it, but because its vision was starting to seem ever less fanciful and ever more naturalistic. In other words, the world that Kubrick could confidently satirise in 1968, looking at it – as an artist must – from a standpoint well outside it, would soon begin to look so much like the world that the delighted mass response of the late 1960s would soon give way to reactions cooler and less comprehending. Now viewers were less likely to feel 'so impressed', so 'awed', and more likely to reply, 'So what?' – an indication not of the film's datedness, but of its prescience.

Within a decade of the film's release, the crucial spaces of the human world – where people live, work, shop, see movies, talk about them – had begun increasingly to look like the arid mobile spaces where the people 'live' in *2001*. The long white sloping corridors of the space station with their sealed windows and fluorescent glare, their hard red contoured chairs and small white plastic tables, now no longer anticipate some eventual trend in architecture but reflect, as if directly, the unilinear vistas within countless shopping malls (which began to dominate the American landscape – urban and suburban – in the late 1970s), 'business parks' and corporate headquarters. Likewise, those over-bright, hermetic confines, so carefully designed to withstand both the great external vacuum and any possible internal breaches of 'security', now seem oddly imitative of the recent condos, hospitals, hotels and dormitories of the West, all of them likewise built *against* the threats of nature and the human swarm. That implicit militarisation of our various homes has surely had profound and imperceptible effects on us – effects that might pertain to the recent invisibility of *2001*. The film's first undergraduate devotees were also members of a student generation likely to assemble in protest – a social tendency soon systematically disabled by the sponsors and practitioners of the New Brutalism, which, as applied specifically to campus architecture in the 1970s, was intended to pre-empt further insurrection by eliminating all common spaces, openable windows and any other points or means of mass agitation or discussion. Thus today's student audience, taught and housed within the quieter system, would tend much less to sense, looking at Floyd's hushed domain, that there's something wrong with it.

If it were re-released today, *2001* would be diminished by the multiplex not just because of the smaller screen and poor acoustics, but because the very setting would implicitly subvert the film's subversive vision. Even if it were brought back to some quaint old movie place, however, *2001* still could not exert its original satiric impact because the mediated 'future' it envisions is now 'our' present, and therefore unremarkable: a development not merely architectural but ideological. The world of Doctor Floyd (like the new dorm, mall or hospital) is a world absolutely *managed* – the force controlling it discreetly advertised by the US flag with which the scientist often shares the frame throughout his 'excellent speech' at Clavius, and also by the corporate logos – 'Hilton', 'Howard Johnson', 'Bell' – that appear throughout the space station. In 1968, the prospect of such total management seemed sinister – a patent circumvention of democracy. Today, within the ever-growing 'private' sphere the movie adumbrates, that 'prospect' seems completely natural.

Whereas audiences back then would often giggle (uneasily, perhaps) at the sight of, say, 'Howard Johnson' up there in the heavens, today's viewers would fail to see the joke, or any problem, now that the corporate logo appears *en masse* not just wherever films might show, but also in the films themselves, whose atmosphere nowadays is peculiarly hospitable to the costly ensign of the big brand name. We might discern the all-important difference between what was and what now is by comparing Kubrick's sardonic use of 'Bell' and 'Hilton' with the many outright corporate plugs crammed frankly into MGM's appalling 'sequel' *2010*, released in 1983. Whereas the (few) plugs in Kubrick's film were too weird – and the film itself too dark and difficult – to make those corporations any money, in the later film the plugs were so upbeat and unambiguous (the advertisers actually helped out), and there were so many of them, that the whole complex of deals was hailed by advertising mavens as a break through in the commercialisation of cinema. '*2001* is a case of how product placements in the movie are becoming a springboard for joint promotions used to market films,' exulted *Advertising Age* before the film's release, noting the elaborate plugs for Pan-Am, Sheraton Hotels, Apple Computer, Anheuser-Busch and *Omni* magazine. (Those outfits evidently liked the insane revisionism of *2001*, which ends with the ecstatic news that what those dark monoliths portended all along, in fact, was the emergence in our heavens of a second sun – so that *night will never fall on us again!*)

As such colossal advertisers have absorbed the culture since the early 1970s, they have helped obscure *2001* by celebrating and encouraging the very drives Kubrick satirises. Indeed, the impulse to retreat from nature, to lead a life of perfect safety, regularity and order in some exalted hi-tech cell, and to stay forever on the job, solacing oneself from time to time with mere images of some beloved other, is – one might argue – the fundamental psychic cause of advertising. So it makes a certain sense that some of Kubrick's most ironic images should keep popping up uncannily – that is, without the irony – on billboards and television screens, in newspapers and magazines. 'AHH. IT'S LONELY AT THE TOP.' Thus TWA and American Express extol the very state that Kubrick questions – the same unconsciousness and isolation, the same complacency, with the advertisement relying on an image strangely similar to Kubrick's mordant tableau of the flaccid Doctor Floyd. We likewise recall him in glancing at an ad for Continental, which promotes 'a big, comfortable electronic sleeper seat with adjustable headrest, footrest and lumbar support; two abreast seating; and a multi-channel personal stereo entertainment system with your own five-inch screen'.

Such come-ons offer the busy manager a range of artificial substitutes for the warmth he's left behind – as in *2001*, where it is not only the 'electronic sleeper seat' that is meant as compensation, but, as we have seen, the vivid image of a 'loved one' made as if available by Bell. That satiric moment too has been much repeated, and completely neutralised, by advertisers. In a television spot for MCI, a father talks as warmly to his daughter's image on a tele-screen as if the girl herself were there before him (MCI's point being, of course, that there is no difference). In an ad for Panasonic, Mom's voice rising from the answering machine, and forming a protective shield between the needy little girl and her strangely droogish 'brother', itself seems as protective as Mom herself would be were she only there. Whereas Kubrick's telephone is an uncanny instrument – like HAL, a means that would itself dictate the end – Bell's ads deliberately promote the instrument's displacement of its human users, offering the telephone itself as your closest 'friend'.

Thus has the satiric prophecy of *2001* been blunted by its own fulfilment. And yet there is still more to it than these brief speculations would imply. The fatal human tendency to shut oneself off, wall oneself in, has been accelerated since the film's release, not only by certain architectural trends, nor simply by the great commercial conquest, but – primarily – by the rise, or spread, of television, which has facilitated that great conquest, enabled (and been all the more enabled by) those architectural developments, and which has at once vindicated Kubrick's satire and practically extinguished it.

Frankly 'wide-eyed', 'thrilled', 'so very lifted' and blithely venturing impassioned and detailed interpretations (with many a bold foray into numerology), Kubrick's ardent first fans seem as anachronistic today as, say, the earnest maiden devotees of the Pre-Raphaelites, now that television has universalised a spectatorial attitude so much more jaded and less demanding. The vision that so awed those first several million viewers is now more likely to leave audiences cold – or to get them snickering, since a certain blasé knowingness pervades the global culture of television as fully as a certain blissed-out recklessness prevailed within the original cult of LSD. The apparent high solemnity of Kubrick's neo-epic – and the immediate recognisability of its most famous bits – would seem now to require the same sophisticated chuckling that so often greets the *Mona Lisa*, say, or Kane whispering 'Rosebud', or Marion Crane screaming, or any other much-remembered 'classic' clip. Even while *2001* was still showing up in theatres, its most vivid touches were already being neutralised by parody – the motif from Strauss's 'Zarathustra' recurring as an automatic joke in numerous commercials (and in Mike Nichols's *Catch-22*), the famed match cut inspiring bits among stand-up comics, in *Mad* magazine and (brilliantly) in *Monty Python's Flying Circus*. Today most big releases are immune to parody, since – like mass advertising, countless television shows and virtually every candidate for public office – they come at us already (gently) parodying themselves (and/or their exhausted genre), so as at once to pre-empt any spectatorial ridicule and to solicit the cool viewers' allegiance by flattering them with an apparent nod to their unprecedented savvy. Every viewer has become a watchful ironist; and in this nervous, jokey atmosphere Kubrick's genuinely cool and wholly uningratiating film must seem, in spite of its Nietzschean subtext, as archaic and austere (and as hard to follow) as the Latin Mass.

Artificial voices

Yet while television's most devoted ironists probably could not enjoy the film, in their plight they also prove the chilling prescience of *2001* – for that pastime is just one more technological absorption, sold as a nice cold substitute for the warmth of actual others. On Comedy Central, 'the only all-comedy cable channel', there is a very hot new show called *Mystery Science Theater 3000*, which features hours and hours of bad old movies, 'watched' by a man and his two robots, who, appearing in silhouette along the bottom of the screen as if a row ahead of you, wisecrack throughout the dated spectacle. 'A New Thanksgiving tradition,' proclaims a recent ad in *TV Guide*. 'Watching 32 straight hours of a human and his robot cohorts rag on cheesy movies while your relatives argue over the white meat.' Thus those born since the release of Kubrick's film are jeeringly invited to surrender utterly to the machine. Like Frank Poole playing chess with HAL (and losing), and like Doctor Heywood Floyd, who also thinks he knows it all already, they would approach the future in their chairs, alone, needing no friends, since they have those artificial voices – and the sponsors – 'there' to crack the jokes, and to laugh along.

2001: A SPACE ODYSSEY
United Kingdom 1968
Director: Stanley Kubrick

Already, it seems, there exist third-generation computers so complex that they have had to be constructed and programmed by other computers, in turn developed by comparatively primitive man-made originals. Isaac Asimov has foreseen a future in which this growing family of artefacts will take over our planet completely, replacing with cold logic the expendable and inefficient human race. On one level at least, Stanley Kubrick's *2001: A Space Odyssey* (MGM) follows this extrapolation to the point at which man becomes at best an outmoded spectator of laws and forces spectacularly beyond his comprehension.

More sinister still, Kubrick also extends the theory retrospectively by showing mankind in its simian infancy being indoctrinated by possibly the identical omniscient slab that is later to confront and confound us on the enigmatic surface of Jupiter. This imputation that man could not have invented even as pedestrian a robot as, say, a traffic light without the aid of a hefty nudge from superior beings has not surprisingly been the source of considerable pleasure as much to the UFO-spotters as to the Bible-readers in Kubrick's audiences. Whatever one's theory of evolution, however, the Kubrick–Clarke screenplay doesn't really bear analysis any too well.

The film begins unexpectedly with the title 'The Dawn of Man', and ends equally unexpectedly with a sequence which implies that the opening label was an ironic one. As an interplanetary dawn breaks somewhere over Jupiter, contemplated by the staring eyes of a foetus travelling in its own fixed orbit, we are supposedly now present at the *real* birth of human knowledge. The trouble with this line of thought (assuming it's the right one) is that if man was so dim initially that it would take a few million years of prompting to make him realise merely that he is an unborn child before the mysteries of the universe, one can't help wondering why any outside force, however benevolent, would have bothered to take on his schooling in the first place. Boredom, perhaps. Or the need for an appreciative audience? Worse, if it's Man's *natural* progress that is being accelerated by carefully timed appearances of the singing monoliths, the haste of this spoon-fed rush to maturity is scarcely justified by the film's conclusion that we've not yet begun. If, on the other hand, the suggestion is that man would never have developed at all without outside help, the film is reducing us to mutant freaks, purposelessly nurtured and cultivated.

Perhaps it is being too severe on *Space Odyssey* to submit it to this type of *reductio ad absurdum*. Yet thematically, however one looks at the film's four linked episodes, the efforts of its characters emerge as singularly futile. Given the brainwave of using a bone as a weapon for food, the apeman's first act is to club one of his own kind with it. Given the facility of space-travel and the awesome splendour of the solar system, the twenty-first-century man dozes, gossips, makes banal remarks about sandwiches, and takes snapshots. Given the technology to create a superhuman computer that does all but scratch the astronaut's back while controlling his entire spaceship, the human discovers nevertheless that he has to dismantle the thing in order to survive at all. And finally the blazing display of alien concepts reduces man to an inarticulate embryo. Kubrick has always pushed men to extremes in his films, finding them in the last resort incapable, and with the immense canvas of *Space Odyssey* he again appears to be expressing that vote of no confidence which has been, after all, the constant theme of most written science fiction.

Granted this gloomy forecast, however, the film manages to come out as irrationally optimistic on another level – that of the sheer audacity of the human race. It once took man 10,000 years to double his store of knowledge, but only 15 years ago the rate of doubling was one decade and today it is expected that a mere seven years should cover the same process. Whether the first spark came from elsewhere or not, the film demonstrates a wholehearted human eagerness to take full advantage of this innate human ability, summarised particularly stunningly by the shot of a ball-like spaceship sinking majestically into its landing bay in the surface of the moon while tiny figures supervise calmly from a hive of observation points.

A signal from another planet finds a group of men quickly ready to respond, hibernation techniques and all; an astronaut adrift in space is tracked down and collected with hardly a second thought; and a berserk, seemingly inviolable computer is demolished as a result of the quicksilver ingenuity of its intended victim. The opportunism of man is undeniable, even if so much of his effort is wasted on banalities, and *Space Odyssey* demonstrates his resilience convincingly enough for one to interpret the film's final hint of rebirth as heralding a challenge that at long last will be worth the challenging.

What really undermines the film's whole thesis of man's dependence upon other-worldly forces is, of course, the film's own existence. As Arthur Clarke has said, if the next space picture is going to be better than *Space Odyssey* it will have to be made on location. With a battery of special effects designed by Kubrick himself, the universe has been astonishingly recreated and further, populated: no strings, no visible backdrops, and only a few, almost indistinguishable touches of process work. With his multi-million dollar investment, the entire resources of the MGM British studios and some of Shepperton's as well, his 90 tons of specially dyed sand, and his 36-foot high centrifuge, Kubrick has won the ultimate technical triumph in that his film is beautiful to watch from start to finish.

If there were any doubt that space travel will be the most spectacular adventure of mankind's future, *Space Odyssey* is the definitive affirmation that every last coin spent on the space race will be worth it. His camera dances in an unrestrained love affair with the planets and with the curious knobby craft that will forage between them. Floating exuberantly through the light-years to the obsessive, formal, and startlingly appropriate tune of the 'Blue Danube' waltz. His interiors are equally breathtaking, from the sheer white of the space-station dotted with its stark red furniture to the huge circular room where the Jupiter-bound astronauts indulge in callisthenics that literally include the ceiling, or watch themselves being interviewed on flat television screens set into the lunch table beside their dishes of synthetic food-pastes. Best of all, there is a sense of fun that never obtrudes – the helmeted stewardesses who calmly turn upside down, the zero-gravity toilet with its immense list of essential instructions, the astronaut who is more concerned about his salary increase than about the significance of his voyage, and that splendid invention, HAL-9000, the talking computer who admits, with a complacent flicker of equations, that it enjoys working with people.

It could all too easily have been invalidated by some conventional narrative, a touch of spacesuit melodrama, a tidy ending. The strength of *Space Odyssey* is that it pinches the best from Arthur Clarke's original short story 'The Sentinel' and makes no ill-considered attempt to overload it – despite touches of padding in the not quite wholly successful first sequence (the apemen are acceptable enough until one sees their chimpanzee offspring) and in the amusing but ultimately slight second.

One realises afterwards that one has been almost hypnotised by the visual magnificence of the film, gliding on a roller-coaster of colours until the unclassifiable landscapes of the Jupiter surface and the total dislocation of our arrival in the exquisitely furnished rooms haunted by a dying Keir Dullea fling us, as Kubrick has cannily intended, headlong into what feels like a new dimension altogether.

Only afterwards, as the magic recedes, comes the suspicion that all the artifice has simply been used to disguise what was an artificial premise to begin with. Like that curious cut from a bone falling in slow motion to a spaceship hovering among the stars, the eyes are tempted to accept without question what the mind would be equally tempted to refuse. Kubrick's greatest achievement has been to persuade us to believe him.

Philip Strick

REAL HORRORSHOW

Kevin Jackson

1. **Tolchock** to hit or push; blow, beating

In 1987 Anthony Burgess adapted his cacotopian fable *A Clockwork Orange* for the stage in a semi-musical version intended for production by amateur groups. On the last page of the published text, just before a valedictory chorus sung to the tune of Beethoven's 'Ode to Joy' ('Do not be a clockwork orange/Freedom has a lovely voice ...') is a striking stage direction: '*A man bearded like Stanley Kubrick comes on playing, in exquisite counterpoint,* Singin' in the Rain *on a trumpet. He is kicked off the stage.*' 'Exquisite counterpoint,' I suspect, may hark back 15 years or so to friendlier days. When Burgess first visited Kubrick at the director's then home, Abbot's Mead, he had taken pleasure in bashing away at the piano, illustrating the harmonic affinities – entirely serendipitous, because it was Malcolm McDowell who brought the song to Kubrick's film during production – between 'Singin' in the Rain' and 'Freude, schöne Gotterfunken, Tochter aus Elysium ...'

In 1990 Burgess revised his musical play for an RSC production directed by Ron Daniels, republishing it as *A Clockwork Orange 2004*. (Hard to believe the added 2004 isn't meant to one-up, or three-up, Kubrick's global franchise on 2001.) Here the savage indignity visited on the Kubrick surrogate is prudently excised. It seems fair, however, to infer that the stage direction was more than just a cheeky wink at the man whose film had bestowed on Burgess the vexed gift of worldwide fame, or notoriety.

Burgess was a man of prodigious talents and boundless energy; a man whose artistic career, though begun late in life, would eventually run to some 60 books of fiction, criticism, biography and linguistics, many film and television scripts, dozens of musical compositions (including three symphonies and a musical version of *Ulysses*), countless articles and the creation of a prehistoric language for Jean-Jacques Annaud's *Quest for Fire* (1981). And yet from 1971 onwards talk-show hosts and newspaper straplines would inevitably introduce this astonishingly fecund, polyglot, polymathic opsimath as: 'Anthony Burgess, author of *A Clockwork Orange*'. Better to be recognised in an insultingly limiting way than not at all, perhaps, but it's easy to see why Burgess's feelings towards Kubrick might be less than fulsomely grateful. (Imagine that everywhere you went, people introduced you by referring to some best-forgotten squib from your salad days: 'Kevin Jackson, author of "What I did on my summer holidays".') For a time novelist and director were on pretty good terms – friends, almost, if not quite droogs. More often, Burgess had his doubts. His problems with Kubrick began well before the film was released.

2. **Razrez** to cut, rip, tear

It seems that Kubrick first encountered *A Clockwork Orange* during the filming of *2001*, when Terry Southern – a fan of Burgess's work – gave him a copy of the book. Unfortunately, from Burgess's perspective, the edition Kubrick read was the US one, published by W. W. Norton. In its earliest British version *A Clockwork Orange* is divided into three parts, each of seven chapters, giving a total of 21: seven for the seven ages of man, 21 for the traditional age at which maturity is reached. (Burgess, a devotee of Joyce, cared about numerology and other shaping principles.) In the 21st chapter Alex reaches the ripe old age of 18 and starts to grow up, seeing his former life of tolchocking and ultra-violence as a classic juvenile disorder, and the state of youth itself as 'being like one of these malenky toys you viddy being sold in the streets, like little chellovecks made out of tin and with a spring inside and then a winding handle on the outside and then you wind it up grr grr grr…' Like clockwork, in fact.

Burgess often told the story of how this final chapter was deleted from the US edition at the insistence of Norton's vice-president Eric Swenson, who felt its hints of a happy ending – a happiness severely qualified by its horrendous vision of a cycle of adolescent mayhem going on and on unstoppably until the end of the world – amounted to a cop-out. America was tough enough for the tough ending. Burgess, uneasy but far too short of cash to object very strenuously, acquiesced. (It's only fair to add that Swenson doesn't agree with this version of events; as he recalled in an interview with my droogie David Thompson, '[Burgess] said "You're absolutely right" – I remember those words. "Take it out," he said. "My British publisher wanted to have the ending so I wrote them one, but you're right to take it out…"'

According to John Baxter's *Stanley Kubrick: A Biography* (1997), the director was a good four months into work on the film when he found out the author had intended a radically different ending. Kubrick brusquely dismissed it as 'completely out of tone with the rest of the book' and carried on regardless. The completed film ends with Alex's silky voice-over purring 'I was cured all right', and a vision of himself naked and copulating with a half-naked damsel, while grey ranks of establishment mannequins – refugees, as it might be, from the 'Ascot Gavotte' sequence of *My Fair Lady* – applaud his thrashings with genteel enthusiasm. Deliciously worldly, if you relish such worldliness, but a conscious distortion of the book's deliberate focus-pull to the wider, sadder perspective of the adult world.

One of Burgess's motives in adapting *A Clockwork Orange* for the stage was to give back to theatre-goers the palinode readers had long been denied – for many years even the standard Penguin text ended movie-style, so you couldn't read Chapter 21 unless you hunted down an early edition. (And even today, neither of the Penguin editions – one of which is given away with this issue of *Sight and Sound* – supplies the epigraph Burgess has said he would have liked, from *The Winter's Tale*, III, iii: 'I would there were no age between ten and three-and-twenty, or that youth would sleep out the rest; for there is nothing in the between but getting wenches with child, wronging the ancientry, stealing, fighting…')

3. **Slovos** words
Burgess had three stories to tell about the origins of *A Clockwork Orange*, and all three involve violence or the threat of death:

4. **Zheena** wife
The first happened in 1944. Burgess, stationed with the British army in Gibraltar, received a letter from Sonia Brownell (soon to marry a man who, by the end of that

decade, would himself write a well-known dystopian satire – George Orwell) in London, telling him his wife Lynne had been set upon late one night by four GI deserters, who punched and kicked her to unconsciousness. Lynne was pregnant, and aborted, and suffered from that time on with attacks of dysmenorrhoea – vaginal bleeding. The Burgesses would never have children.

In Chapter 2 of *A Clockwork Orange* the unnamed writer ('Mr Alexander' in the film) who is beaten and forced to watch while his wife is raped is at work on a social polemic entitled *A Clockwork Orange*.

5. **Dratsing** fighting

The second happened in 1959 and 1960. Burgess had been invalided home from his job as a teacher in Brunei and told he had an inoperable brain tumour and only a year to live. Instead of going on a drunken binge, he went on a work binge, and wrote five and a half novels. The half-novel began with nothing more than a title – *A Clockwork Orange*, which Burgess often described as an old Cockney phrase denoting 'queerness', not necessarily sexual. (Though no Londoner I've ever asked, of any vintage, can recall the phrase; he may have invented it.) Compulsive worksmith and polyglot that he was, Burgess saw the Malayan word *orang* (man) lurking inside the English 'orange', and that set him thinking of mechanical men, behaviourism, B. F. Skinner and Pavlov, and of rumours about the forcible reconditioning of habitual offenders.

As a recently returned expatriate, he was surprised by the new strut and arrogance of British youth, incarnated in the 'Edwardians' or Teddy Boys and the Mods and Rockers whom he had seen ritually beating the hell out of each other one summer afternoon in Hastings. It reminded him of the Elizabethan apprentice riots of the 1590s and he began to compose a novel set in that period before realising that foresight might be more artistically productive than hindsight. He then relocated the action to a suitably distant future: 1970 or thereabouts. But he found the novel was proving difficult so he set it aside for more than a year.

6. **Govoreet** to speak, talk

The third happened in 1961, when Burgess and Lynne went on a holiday to Leningrad. Before they travelled Burgess taught himself to speak Russian. A notebook from the time, now housed in the Burgess Centre at the university of Angers, shows precisely how he did it: by inventing funny little mnemonics and cartoons. Thus next to the translation and transliteration of the Russian word for 'man, person, fellow' – *chellovek* is a doodle of a cello with a man's face. He realised he now had an answer to the problem which had stumped him: how to write a book full of teenage slang when such slang by its very nature becomes outdated in a matter of months. Simple: by inventing a slang, using mostly a modified Russian vocabulary – 'rooker' for *ruka* or hand, 'noga' lifted directly from *noga* (leg and foot), 'horrorshow' from *khorosho*, the neuter form of the word meaning good.

By the time they set sail for the USSR Burgess was a good way into the novel's second draft. Leningrad helped to confirm his instincts, offering the spectacle of a drunken riot by young *stilyagi*. Adolescent hooliganism, it appeared, was not a social disease peculiar to capitalism but a plague of the late twentieth century. Burgess duly christened his artificial argot Nadsat, from the Russian suffix meaning teen.

7. **Viddy** to see, look

The first time *A Clockwork Orange* was put on screen was in May 1962. The producers of the BBC current-affairs programme *Tonight* brought Burgess to the studio to be interviewed by Derek Hart, and dramatised part of the book's first chapter – 'very effectively', Burgess thought. It has been estimated that some million people watched this broadcast, but it had a minimal effect on sales. According to the archives of Burgess's publisher Heinemann, the novel sold just 3,872 copies in its first year. (His previous novel, *Devil of a State*, had managed some 15,000.) The BBC has not preserved this programme in its archive.

8. **Messel** thought, fancy

Extract from an unwritten reference book on British cinema in the 1960s: '*A Clockwork Orange* (1967, UK). Directed by Michael Cooper. Produced by Sandy Lieberson, Si Litvinoff. Screenplay by Michael Cooper and Terry Southern, from the novel by Anthony Burgess. Starring Mick Jagger as Alex, with Keith Richards, Brian Jones, Bill Wyman and Charlie Watts. Score by Jagger/Richards, performed by the Rolling Stones...'

It almost happened. As Sandy Lieberson recalls, it all began when his photographer friend Michael Cooper, who had shot the Peter Blake cover for *Sgt Pepper*, introduced him to the novel. 'I thought, "My God!..." I had to go back and read it a couple of times, but I was stunned by the power of it, so I made enquiries into the rights.' Burgess's agent put Lieberson on to Si Litvinoff, who at that time was Terry Southern's lawyer, and who had optioned the book with his business partner Max Raab for just a few hundred dollars. 'I knew Si,' Lieberson continues, 'so I approached him and said, look, I'd like to put a film together with Michael Cooper as writer and director.'

For a while things proceeded swimmingly. 'We decided where it was going to be shot, it was going to be almost all Soho – there was a rawness to Soho at that point which doesn't exist today. We had picked out the site for the Korova Milkbar, which was some weird kind of Chinese restaurant-bar. It certainly felt possible to recreate the atmosphere of the book in a much more gritty, dirty way, more realistic than Kubrick's approach... I also think that our instinct was that the language had an importance as great as the visual.'

But the Stones couldn't find time to make the film. By the time Kubrick stepped in and picked up the option – Warners handed over $200,000, plus 5 per cent of the profits – everyone had moved on. Lieberson finally collaborated with Jagger on *Performance*, and gave Burgess some work rewriting Sandy Mackendrick's screenplay about Mary, Queen of Scots. Michael Cooper committed suicide in his early 30s, thus depriving the world, Lieberson believes, of an exceptional visual talent. Would the Cooper *A Clockwork Orange* have been as successful?

'It certainly would have been unusual – it wouldn't have looked like any other film of that time. I think it would have been good. But if you have to lose a film, thank God it was Stanley Kubrick we lost it to, and not some... some jerk.'

9. **Strack** horror

In other alternative universes *A Clockwork Orange* was directed circa 1968 by Ken Russell, who took a serious interest in the project for a while before turning to Aldous Huxley and *The Devils*, and/or by another hip young photographer, David Bailey.

10. **Malchick** boy, youth

A final speculation: maybe the Stones would have come to *A Clockwork Orange* anyway, by another route. Their callow Svengali, Andrew Loog Oldham, was a great fan of the book; his sleeve notes for the group's 1965 album *The Rolling Stones, Now!* are written in a pallid approximation of Nadsat, replete with internal rhymes: 'It is the summer of the night London's eyes are all shut tight all but twelve peepers and six hip malchicks who prance the street...

'This is The Stones new disc within. Cast deep in your pockets for loot to buy this disc of groovies and fancy words. If you don't have bread, see that blind man – knock him on the head, steal his wallet and lo and behold you have the loot if you put in the boot, good. Another one sold!'

Pressure was put on the Stones' record company, Decca, when someone actually bothered to read this thin gruel and realised what it was recommending, tongue in cheek or not. Oddly enough, though Burgess hated pop music with all the cold fury of a thwarted composer in the Western classical tradition – the figure of Yod Crewsey in his novel *Enderby Outside* is in some measure a caricature of John Lennon – he was ungrudgingly well disposed to Mick Jagger: 'I admired the intelligence, if not that art, of this young man and considered that he looked the quintessence of delinquency.'

11. **Horrorshow** good

When I first saw the film I was 16 – just a year older than Alex at the book's start. (Malcolm McDowell was pushing 28 when he played the role.) Violating the 'X' certificate code was about the most spectacular crime of my own adolescence, and added to the excitement. Naturally, I thought it was a masterpiece.

12. **Cal** faeces

I watched a laserdisc of *A Clockwork Orange* again this week, now being older than Kubrick was when he shot it. The film has its virtues, undeniably, and the greatest of them is McDowell's performance – demonically sexy and arrogant, bristling with malicious intelligence: splendid. Otherwise...

It strikes me now as a mean-spirited exercise in dim sarcasm, and, for long stretches, egregiously dull. Every character save Alex is a caricature worthy, at best, of 1970s sitcom (Alex's pathetic 'pee' and 'em' – the em plainly too far gone in years to be his biological mother – would not look out of place in *Are You Being Served?*). Example: in the novel, Alex's correctional adviser, Mr Deltoid, is quite enough of a pompous fool for anyone's comic gratification. Kubrick, obedient to the aesthetic principle that if a thing's worth doing it's worth overdoing, not only makes Deltoid a crotch-grabbing, predatory homosexual but rounds off his big scene with a punchline about accidentally drinking from a dentures glass.

In his lengthiest addition to the book Kubrick films Alex's induction to prison in wearisomely complete detail, delighting in showing what a jumped-up, anally retentive berk the warden is: *Porridge*, in other words, without Ronnie Barker to humanise the poor wit. (The novel, far swifter, just jumps forward a couple of years.) It's almost a textbook example of how to milk a feeble joke until it's stone dead. But Kubrick's greatest crime against the art of acting is the performance he extorts from

Patrick Magee, the great interpreter of Samuel Beckett, as Mr Alexander. I believe the technical term is 'chewing the carpet'.

To indulge the sitcom comparison one last time: it's a film Rik from *The Young Ones* would adore for its sneering attitude towards the grown-up world of 'straights'. Alas, the terrible reality is that the straights had at least one good argument in their otherwise hysterical campaign against Kubrick's film. Compare it point by point, scene by scene, tolchock by tolchock with Burgess's book and it really does, as they claimed, jollify, prettify and generally render titillating its ultra-violence – turning Alex's brutal rape of two ten-year-olds into a fast-motion sex romp, turning the ancient cat-lady Alex murders into a much younger, foul-mouthed health freak, and fastidiously or timidly cutting away from any hint of true horror. There's not a frame in the film to compare with the ghastliness of the original: 'The writer veck and his zheena were not really there, bloody and torn and making noises.'

The issue isn't the hoary one of fidelity to the letter, but of truth to the spirit of Burgess's work: Kubrick's reading amounts to a sustained dilution and vulgarisation. Moreover, a couple of brisk, bravura set pieces aside – Alex's Beethovian visions, the gang-ballet with Billyboy's droogs – the film is cut and staged at a numbingly slow pace. Kubrick had seen the future, and it limped.

His decision to withdraw the film from British circulation in 1974 may well, as his biographers suggest, have been motivated by his fears of attacks on his family, but it is also the shrewdest thing he could have done for its maverick reputation. Kubrick's film may be a cinematic legend, oh my brothers, but it is also, frankly, a load of cal.

13. **Groodies** breasts
One of the many notes that help to make Kubrick's film a spiritual cousin of Benny Hill is its mammary obsession: the milk-dispensing dugs of the Allen Jones-inspired statuary in the Korova, the pendulous bosoms of the girl being raped by Billyboys' gang (again, she was a little girl in the book), Adrienne Corri's breasts, the breasts of the concubines in Alex's biblical reverie, the breasts in the Ludovico films, the breasts of the nurse who is screwing Alex's doctor...

14. **Bolshy** big, great
Asked to give his full name to the prison authorities, Alex replies: 'Alexander Delarge'. The name seems to have been derived from the passage in which Alex rapes the innocents: 'This time they thought nothing fun and stopped creeching with high mirth, and had to submit to the strange and weird desires of Alexander the Large...' But if you look closely at the montage of newspaper reports about Alex's release later in the film, you'll see he is referred to as 'Alex Burgess'. Is this a rare instance of Kubrick letting his attention wander? Or some half-hidden dig about Burgess's identification with his terrible hero?

15. **Yeckate** to drive
In the early 1950s Burgess was a teacher at Banbury Grammar School, and took an active part in local amateur dramatics. One of the youngsters who acted for him was Martin Blinkhorn. The proud owner of an open-topped sports car, a rare luxury in

those years, Blinkhorn would also act as Burgess's chauffeur. When the pubs closed they would speed wildly through the countryside, and Burgess, ripped on deep draughts of cheap cider, would stand up in the passenger seat and bellow into the night wind–passages from Chaucer, from the Elizabethans. Years later, when Blinkhorn saw *A Clockwork Orange*, he thought he recognised the autobiographical origins of the scene in which Alex and his Droogs barrel through the night in their stolen Durango 95.

Burgess was a peaceable man, a decent man–hard-working, kindly even to fools, unfailingly generous with time and effort and praise, gentle and uxorious. Yet there may have been more of unregenerate Alex in his nature than he liked to acknowledge: 'I was sickened,' he once wrote of his novel's violence, 'sickened by my own excitement at setting it down.'

16. **Crast** to steal, rob; robbery
At various times both Burgess and McDowell were furious with Kubrick for treating himself to what they regarded as a greedy solo credit for the screenplay. All Kubrick had really done, they recalled, was to bring a copy of the book on set, look at the scene in question – 'Page 59. How shall we do it?' – spend hours discussing and rehearsing, shoot the result (often in a single take), then go home and type up the improvised dialogue. Burgess once snarled to one of his friends about the aptness of Kubrick's selection from Rossini for his soundtrack: *The Thieving Magpie*.

17. **Cluve** beak
Even so, Burgess pointedly did not name Kubrick in the lawsuit he brought against Si Litvinoff, Warner Bros and others on 9 May 1973 for 'conspiracy to defraud' him: *Variety* reported that, 'Burgess claims misrepresentation by Litvinoff led him to relinquish valuable rights to the novel.' He won the case and was awarded some percentage of profits.

18. **Starry** old, ancient
At about the same time as this lawsuit Burgess wrote a short, funny novel entitled *A Clockwork Testament* in which his long-term alter ego, the dyspeptic, ageing poet Enderby, is caught up in media rows after writing a screenplay for a scandalous film based loosely on Gerard Manley Hopkins's 'Wreck of the Deutschland'. It isn't his most subtle novel, but it catches wonderfully some of the folly in which he was engaged when he agreed to go on the US publicity circuit on Kubrick's behalf, leaving the director to 'pare his nails' back in his English country house, a *Deus absconditus* happy to have created a naughty world and then withdraw from it. Kubrick's reaction to the novel is, so far, unrecorded.

19. **Sloosh** to listen
Apart from Alex's vicious crooning of 'Singin' in the Rain', the only popular music in *A Clockwork Orange* is Erika Eigen's inane ditty, 'I Want to Marry a Lighthouse Keeper'. The auditory world of Nadsat trickles with the sweet orange juice of Purcell and Beethoven and Rossini, rendered clockwork by the Moog synthesiser of Walter Carlos.

Yet the film's effect on pop culture has been abiding. David Bowie would use the Purcell for Queen Mary's Funeral Music as a prelude to his concerts, and the word 'droogie' can be caught in his song 'Suffragette City'. The 1980s band Heaven 17 lifted its name from the book. The highly literate Elvis Costello is rumoured to have been building up a collection of first editions; the rather less literate Paul Cook, drummer for the Sex Pistols, once boasted of having read just two books – a biography of the Kray twins and *A Clockwork Orange*. Damon Albarn and the other members of Blur dressed up as droogs for the video of 'The Universal'. One good argument for the rerelease of the film in the wake of Kubrick's death is that it might put an end to all this malenky malarkey.

20. **Droog** friend
The dedication to Burgess's novel *Napoleon Symphony* is shared by the novelist's second wife Liana and one 'Stanley J. Kubrick', who is addressed as *'maestro di color'*. When I first read this in the mid-1970s I was quite ignorant of Italian and assumed it meant 'master of colour'. A few years later, sweating my way through Dante in the original, I found that Burgess was tacitly alluding to a celebrated phrase from *Inferno*, IV, i. 131: *'vidi il maestro di color che sanno'* (I saw the Master of those who know). Dante was referring to Aristotle. Respectful; very respectful. And yet, as Burgess was well aware, the man at whom Dante is gazing is a long-term resident of Hell. Dante was not the only writer who knew about settling grudges in literature.

21. [Deleted]
With many thanks to John Baxter, Sandy Lieberson and David Thompson

THE OVERLOOK HOTEL

Paul Mayersberg

Jack Torrance applies for the job as caretaker at the Overlook Hotel high in the Colorado Rockies during the winter months. Jack is warned that a man can get very lonely up there. He laughs it off. He is also told, if not actually warned, of a murder by a previous winter caretaker, Mr Grady, who apparently went mad and killed his wife and daughters with an axe. Jack smiles and says that nothing like that will happen to him.
    What follows when Jack brings his wife, Wendy, and his small son, Danny, to The Overlook, is not the unfolding of a narrative so much as a series of glimpses into the real and imagined lives of Jack, Wendy and Danny. And also the lives of previous inhabitants of the hotel. A sequence of events suggests that Jack Torrance is going mad. But this is not quite true. Jack Torrance is crazy by the time he gets to the hotel. He is crazy for choosing the caretaker's job. Like an updated Henry James story, *The Shining* depicts a state of mind in which 'the story' is as much a figment of the character's imagination as it is of ours.

Events that seem to take place in the present may be re-enactments or simply memories of the past. To take *The Shining* at its face value is a mistake. It has no face, only masks, and it has no value, only implications. *The Shining* belongs firmly in the tradition of *The Turn of the Screw* and *The Beast in the Jungle*. If the setting of the film had been an hotel in Yorkshire or a deserted winter retreat in Maine, the nature of the piece would be even more apparent.

The film opens with an extraordinary shot. An island, apparently in the middle of a lake or a river, seems to be moving towards us, floating on the surface, perhaps driven by an unseen machinery. It is an optical effect. In fact the lake is so still that the camera moving towards the island makes it look as if the island itself is moving. This unsettling image sets the tone of the film. The following sequence of aerial shots, tracking Jack's car up into the snowy rockies, is equally disorienting. At one point the camera sweeps away from the road, literally over the edge of the mountain. At precisely that moment the main title of the film appears, just when we are lost over the edge.

Over the edge, and over the top is Jack Nicholsons's performance as Jack Torrance. But not really. Shelley Duvall's performance as Wendy Torrance, like Nicholson's, shows very little true development. This is not an oversight on the part of the director or actors. Jack and Wendy arrive at the Overlook Hotel with their personalities fully formed. They are like two characters picked off park benches. One look at them and you know they're nuts. Pinter's plays are peopled with similar caretakers.

The Shining is not about internal character development. It questions the extent to which a character shapes his environment or to which the environment shapes him. Does the place drive you crazy or are you crazy to live in the place? Are these people ghosts already dead, having been driven to crazy deaths? Or are they ordinary folk infected by the frightening past of the monster hotel?

Jack claims to be a writer. To be a writer is a way of escaping mundane reality. He wants to write a project, not a book. His life seems to have amounted to nothing. He's a modern man. People turn to writing as they turn to astrology when they don't know where they are going. Jack is deeply frustrated. He is obviously intelligent, some of his phrases are quite vivid, his silences are either empty or profound. When it comes to the act of writing he has no discipline. This is a reflection of his past; he clearly could never stick at any job. His writing project is vague, that is to say he has no idea what to write about.

In the past he has turned to drink. The hotel is dry. Jack's visits to the bar and his conversations with the ghostly barman are banal. Jack is a lost soul. When he orders the first drink of the day it's 'The hair of the dog that bit me.' He is doomed to repeat himself. 'I'd give my soul for a drink,' he says. And so he does. Then he confesses his life as drunks confess to their barman. It seems that in a fit of drunken anger Jack has beaten his young son, Danny. It is obvious that he will do it again. The answer to a drink is another drink.

Jack Nicholson's performance is a splendidly gothic reworking of Ray Milland's in *The Lost Weekend*. All alcoholics see things that aren't there. They say things they don't mean. They become people they are not. At least on the face of it. Perhaps, though, alcohol is a way of becoming the man you think you ought to have been.

In the loneliness of the Overlook Hotel Jack Torrance becomes an earlier inhabitant of the place. But not exactly. Grady, the earlier caretaker, killed his daughters and wife with an axe and shot himself. When Grady 'visits' Jack, 'accidentally' spilling a drink over the revenant, he takes him to the men's room, a blood red airport lounge. Grady goads Jack, as the new caretaker, to kill Wendy and Danny in the correct Overlook manner, that's to say with an axe. Jack reasons with himself that this must be the correct procedure. His contemporary frustration must be answered with tradition. Later, Jack, ever conventional, gets a fireman's axe and goes about his business. But Jack does not succeed and nor does he shoot himself as Grady did.

So the parallel with the past, real or imagined, is deliberately inexact. Why? Because the world has changed. This is the comment of *The Shining* on the facile convention of horror writing and film-making. In most films the present reproduces exactly the past. But not in *The Shining*. As in life, things turn out quite differently in this horror story.

Jack never 'sees' Grady's two doll-like daughters and no one ever 'sees' Grady's wife. The daughters are 'given' to Danny, the little boy who has the shining, as 'friends' of his own age. The little girls beckon him and tease Danny in his psychic state. Like Danny, Jack absorbs from the hotel what is appropriate to his own age and his own life. Wendy sees nothing. She does not even understand until very late just how dangerous Jack is, when he actively attacks her, or just how psychic her son is until he writes the word 'Redrum' on the door of her bedroom knowing that when she wakes she will see it in the mirror as 'murder'.

Everyone has certain psychic powers. The limitations are within our own personalities. Even in a psychic sphere we see only what refers to us in our own situation. Only with difficulty can we see what is beyond us. Danny sees an elevator door leaking and then flooding with blood. This staggering image has no relation to any scene in the film. But why should it? Danny has had a glimpse of the future. The flooding of blood has yet to come. As everyone knows who has visited a clairvoyant, the past, the present and the future are often indistinguishable. We are impressed by observations about the past, but often mystified by portents of the future.

The Overlook Hotel will continue its life as a building after our characters have left. The floating furniture in a sea of blood is a scene from the never-to-be-made *The Shining 2*.

The psychic powers of young Danny and of Hallorann, the black cook, who leaves the hotel at the start to go to his home in Florida, are genuine. The two recognise each other from the first. The act of recognition, the act of one person seeing in another what he understands, is crucial to our understanding of the characters in *The Shining*.

Danny has an imaginary friend called Tony. Tony is represented by Danny's index finger wiggling, like a seductive come-on. Tony also has a voice, which seems to come through Danny's mouth. The joking reference to *The Exorcist* is one of many in a film that satirises horror movies. Tony is the ventriloquist's dummy who may eventually come to control his young master in the manner of *Dead of Night*. Tony warns Danny and also entices him. Is Tony out to destroy Danny? We cannot tell.

In one scene, after Danny has gone into the forbidden room 237 and he appears like a ghost before his parents during a terrible row, it is never certain how Danny acquired the bruises on his neck and arms. Wendy blames Jack because Jack has already attacked his son. We blame whoever it was in room 237. Danny won't speak about it.

Jack says, 'Maybe he did it to himself.' That is the least credible explanation but it is possible that Tony did it. Or do we do it all to ourselves in the end?

As Danny stands watching the terrible argument between his parents it is as if he is watching their first encounter, not the primal sexual scene, but the primal psychic scene. In any case, Danny is silent about his visions and adventures. He cannot express himself in words, perhaps because he is too young, perhaps because his experiences are non-verbal. Apart from Tony, the only person who understands Danny is Hallorann, two thousand miles away in Florida. When Danny becomes most frightened that his father will attack and perhaps kill him, Hallorann, in his strange, long apartment in Florida, shines in. Hallorann then flies back to Colorado and drives through the blizzard to get to the Overlook Hotel. His shining costs him his life.

It seems that Hallorann is impelled by his relationship with Danny. But there is another level to Hallorann's perceptions. He is presented from the start as an asexual Negro. He lives alone, but in his Florida apartment he has a photograph of a naked black girl on the wall facing his bed, and another nude over his bed. It so happens that the scene which drives Hallorann finally back to Colorado is not what happens to Danny in room 237, but what happens to Jack in 237 when he visits the room afterwards.

Forced by Wendy, Jack fearfully goes alone into the room. Its colours are ridiculously garish, dominated by a sensual purple. Jack goes into the bathroom. He becomes aware that behind the shower curtain in the bath is a figure. The figure pulls back the opaque curtain and stands up. It is a naked woman. She steps out of the bath. Jack smiles, no terror here, as the woman walks towards him and puts her arms round him. They kiss. As he pulls back from the embrace he sees that he has been clutching an old woman covered in marks that are a cross between leprosy and tattoos. The old woman laughs at him. Jack is horrified. A trick with time: somehow the old woman is still in the bath as Jack is embracing her across the room. When Wendy asks Jack about room 237, he replies that there was no one there.

This is the strangest scene in the film. It has no reference to earlier events, and it seems completely unconnected with any of the characters. Yet it serves as an important link between all the characters in this psychic drama. It would be wrong to insist on a single interpretation of this scene, but in looking at it it exposes the heart of Kubrick's method in the film.

First, it is a rewrite of the shower scene in *Psycho*. In *Psycho* it is the lady in the shower who is threatened by the monster outside. In *The Shining* this is reversed. Jack is the 'monster', scared by what might emerge from the shower behind the curtain. This reversal of well-known horror conventions is one of many in the film. Later there is a reference again to *Psycho* when Jack menaces Wendy by climbing up the stairs. It is Wendy who has the weapon in her hand, the baseball bat, but it is she who is backing away, frightened by the empty-handed Jack. Underlying many sequences in *The Shining* is a critique of the whole genre of horror movies. The character of Jack Torrance himself is presented as the innocent, not knowing what he is getting himself into, whereas he is in fact the threatening element.

Secondly, the woman turning from slim youth to grotesque age is perhaps symbolic of everyone's most feared destiny, growing old. To watch your own body over a period of years disintegrate before the mirror is an essential horror story for all of us. Fear of old age grips Jack Torrance by the throat as does fear of losing his mind. Growing old and losing your senses, time passing, is a frightening notion that is inescapable.

Thirdly, it is the only overtly sexual scene in the movie. *The Shining* is a strangely chaste horror story. Part of this comes from Jack's sexual indifference; he is always glancing at women, including his wife, but he never actually does anything to them. Lack of sexual drive is characteristic of a paranoid personality. The young naked woman also seems asexual. She looks like one of those models who pose in seedy lunchtime photographic clubs.

Fourthly, the marks on the old woman's body, which so repel Jack, are difficult to identify. When she rises out of the bath in a shot that seems to refer to Clouzot's *Les Diaboliques*, she seems diseased. Then the marks look as if they had been applied like paint. There is also a hint that this woman has come from another world or an earlier civilisation.

All these interpretations have a certain validity without getting near totally to describing the scene. It may come down to the simple fact that the scene in room 237 is no more nor less than a nightmare of its creator. But one of the extraordinary aspects of *The Shining* is the way the simplest events in bright light conjure dark fears, guesses and portents. The movie is constantly ironic, if not down right satirical. The humour of *The Shining* puts it close to *Lolita* and *Strangelove* in Kubrick's work. As in much of Hitchcock and Buñuel, and to some extent Polanski, there is an underlying crazy comedy which is also deadly serious.

The central horror of *The Shining* is family life. For a child there can be few characters more frightening than his angry father. Danny, despite his stoicism, is terrorised by his father. Wendy is terrorised by her violent husband. Jack is frustrated to the point of rejection and violent aggression towards his family. It is a nice picture of American home life.

The Shining, the least admired major American film in the past year, is an accidental but none the less effective reworking of *Kramer vs. Kramer*, one of the most admired films of the past year. Both treat the collapsing single child family. Kubrick makes no attempt to deal with this subject from the social point of view. The psychology is dealt with in broad strokes; the characters, with the exception of Danny, are grotesque masks. There are, of course, real people behind the masks, but who they are is like saying what will they become. The three people alone in the overlit Overlook Hotel are similar to the three characters in Sartre's play, *Huis Clos*. They are in the hell of each other. Danny sees his father as an eye-rolling lunatic. Jack sees Wendy as a weak, whining housewife, and Wendy sees nothing. Until the end of the story she seems completely devoid of psychic power. It is almost as if *The Shining* is showing that bright people are more capable of understanding telepathically than less bright people.

The family hierarchy, Dad, Mom and kid, is very strong. The equivalent hierarchy in the Overlook Hotel itself is the idea of the maze in which they are lost, both inside and out. The more intelligent you are the easier it is for you to solve the puzzle of the maze. The only character who can get out of the maze is Danny. Not because of his psychic ability but because of his high intelligence. They seem to go together in Kubrick's behaviourist view. The maze is not treated in the manner of *Marienbad*. In *Marienbad* the labyrinth of the hotel is a philosophical question. It cannot be solved. It can only be apprehended and interpreted. In *The Shining* the maze is a Sunday morning puzzle, and the most intelligent member of the family will always come up with the correct solution first.

There is a sense in the Overlook Hotel that it represents the world after the bombs have gone off; the loneliness, the incredible store of food, ways to survive.

The Shining may be the first film of the post-nuclear age to come. A bizarre follow up to *Strangelove*. The music of Penderecki, the *Dies Irae* of the Auschwitz Cantata, creates an exactly post-Apocalyptic tone. The music of Ligeti and Bartók is music for the world that followed the Second Vienna School of Strauss and Mahler. The Ligeti has a mocking tone as if laughing at all past music and at people with notions of fixed values. The Bartók is wonderfully lyrical, but who, among ordinary filmgoers, would hear the strong music of Bela Bartók and think instinctively that it is lyrical and dance-like? But there was a time when Beethoven's *Grosse Fuge* was considered unacceptable and esoteric by his own publisher.

The Shining has a lot in common with post-war music. It seems technically brilliant and yet fundamentally heartless. It seems deliberately clever and yet remains enigmatic. Kubrick has tried to bridge a gap which has occurred in the language of film. How can you express dissonance and fragmentation, the essential features of our present lives, in a manner which respects traditional harmonies? Can disorder ever be expressed in an orderly way? Kubrick has reached the limits of conservative film art in *The Shining*. It used to be thought that the antonym of art was nature. But this Shakespearian opposition is no longer true. Art and nature are both by definition devoted to order. The opposite of art is enigma.

The Shining is not an enigmatic film. It is actually about enigma. That is why Kubrick is instinctively drawn to technology in his work, camera technology in particular. The machine is better able to cope with enigma than the human hand. Most enigmatic paintings from Cimabue's Crucifix to de Chirico's piazzas somehow suggest the presence of a machine. *The Shining* is about this machine that cannot be seen. It is, if you like, the machine in the ghost.

Shining denotes the ability to communicate telepathically, to see backwards into the past and forwards into the future. *The Shining* is nothing more nor less than a metaphor for the cinema itself. Film has the shining. Danny is probably the director of the movie. He is certainly identified with the camera. The Steadicam tracking shots through the hotel corridors and then in the maze evoke the exhilaration of a small boy racing about on his tricycle. He imagines himself to be a machine.

In *The Shining*, Kubrick plays with the Steadicam like a toy. It is essentially childlike. He wants to find out all the things he can do with his latest acquisition. Danny's visions are represented in cuts, in montage, so the boy is not only the camera he is also the movieola. The director-child is seeing his own parents and the world around him. In a way the hotel becomes his doll's house, like the model in Albee's *Tiny Alice*, and his father and mother are turned into his neurotic children. If they go crazy from time to time he can still control them with his superior intelligence and visionary ability. Film, after all, is the art of seeing and showing from a fresh point of view. But the boy is not an artist. He is before art, and after it. Picasso said it took him ten years to draw like Raphael and a lifetime to draw like a child. There is the child in all of us. There is the artist in all of us, and to varying degrees we are all capable of shining.

If the cinema was born around 1900 then he is 80 years old today. *The Shining* reminds us how far the cinema has come and how much it has stayed the same. It shines bits of an enigmatic film future which in the last image turns out to be a still from the past. There is no immutable order of experience when the past becomes a picture of what might have been.

RESIDENT PHANTOMS

Jonathan Romney

The best place to enter a labyrinth is through its exit. So let's start with the famous final shot of Stanley Kubrick's *The Shining* (1980). Jack Torrance (Jack Nicholson), the ill-fated winter caretaker of the Overlook Hotel, sits statuefied in the snow, having met his frozen fate at the heart of the Overlook's maze, while his wife Wendy and son Danny (Shelley Duvall and Danny Lloyd) are long gone in the snowmobile. The Overlook is quite empty now, apart from its resident phantoms and, in case we've forgotten, the corpse of chef Hallorann (Scatman Crothers), the only person Jack has succeeded in killing during his Big Bad Wolf rampage (but then, that's for the management to worry about when the hotel re-opens the following spring – and, presumably, for the next caretaker to worry about too).

So, amid the quiet – broken only by ghostly strains of a 1920s dance tune – the camera tracks slowly towards a wall of photographs from the Overlook's illustrious history. It closes in on the central picture, showing a group of revellers smiling at the camera, and then, in two dissolves, reveals first the person at the centre of the group – Jack himself, smiling and youthful in evening dress – and then the inscription, 'Overlook Hotel, July 4th Ball, 1921'. Cue credits, cue shudder from audience.

Just what makes this chilly pay-off so uncanny? It appears to reveal something, the final narrative turn of the screw, or perhaps an explanation of the story's ambiguities – but really it reveals nothing for certain. What's more, the last thing we see is not an image but an inscription – hardly the chilling *coup de théâtre* we expect from a horror film. But *The Shining* is a film that, while it uses written language sparingly, is very much concerned with words: not just the words of the literary *chef d'oeuvre* Jack attempts to write, but also the film's frequent intertitles, and the fetish work 'REDRUM' (murder in mirror-writing) that preoccupies Danny.

The closing inscription appears to explain what has happened to Jack. Until watching the film again recently I'd always assumed that, after his ordeal in the haunted palace, Jack had been absorbed into the hotel, another sacrificial victim earning his place at the Overlook's eternal *thé dansant* of the damned. At the Overlook, it's always 4 July 1921 – although God knows exactly what happened that night. In fact, Jack Nicholson's likeness literally has been absorbed into the picture: collaged into a 1920s archive shot and matched to the photographic grain of the original.

Or you can look at it another way. Perhaps Jack hasn't been absorbed – perhaps he has really been in the Overlook all along. As the ghostly butler Grady (Philip Stone) tells him during their chilling confrontation in the men's toilet, 'You're the caretaker, sir. You've always been the caretaker.' Perhaps in some earlier incarnation Jack really was around in 1921, and it's his present day self that is the shadow, the phantom photographic copy. But if his picture has been there all along, why has no one noticed it? After all, it's right at the centre of the central picture on the wall, and the Torrances have had a painfully drawn-out winter of mind-numbing leisure in which to inspect every corner of the place. Is it just that, like Poe's purloined letter, the thing in plain sight is the last thing you see? When you do see it, the effect is so unsettling because you realise the unthinkable was there under your nose – *overlooked* – the whole time.

However you interpret the photographic evidence with which the film singularly fails to settle its uncertainties, this strikes us as an uncanny ending to an uncanny film One of the texts Kubrick and his co-writer, novelist Diane Johnson, referred to when adapting Stephen King's novel was Freud's 1919 essay 'The 'Uncanny'. The essay, which examines the troubling effect of certain elements in life and supernatural literature, defines the uncanny as 'that class of the frightening which leads back to what is known of old and long familiar'. Or as Freud puts it, quoting Schelling, the uncanny is 'something which ought to have remained hidden but which is brought to light'. The hidden brought to light: a theme common to ghost stories and one you'd expect to be prominent in a film called *The Shining*.

The final scene alone demonstrates what a rich source of perplexity *The Shining* offers. At first sight this is an extremely simple, even static film. A family move into a Colorado hotel for the winter so Dad can write his great literary work in peace while performing his function as caretaker. But the ancient blood-soaked visions recorded like old movie scenes in the hotel's walls emerge, and Jack is possessed, driven homicidal. Or perhaps he's crazy to begin with: the film's central question, as Paul Mayersberg put it in a 1980 *Sight and Sound* article, is: 'Does the place drive you crazy, or are you crazy to live in the place?'

It all seems simple enough – the Big Bad Wolf storms around with an axe, the Little Pigs (his snarling sobriquet for Wendy and Danny) escape. At the time of the film's release many critics were unimpressed by this schema – Kubrick had put so much effort into his film, building vast sets at Elstree, making a 17-week shoot stretch to 46, and what was the result? A silly scare story – something that, it was remarked at the time, Roger Corman could have turned around in a fortnight.

But look beyond the simplicity and the Overlook reveals itself as a palace of paradox. There's an unsettling tension about the film's austerity on the one hand (there's something positively Racinian about the unities of this grand-scale chamber piece) and dizzying excess on the other. Kubrick's apparent disdainful detachment from the horror genre shows itself in the systematic flouting of a key convention: instead of an old dark house, a modern, brightly lit one. But when Kubrick does lay on ghoulie business it's almost farcically extreme: a festering bogey-woman in the bathroom, a courteous blood-soaked reveller, and instead of the time-honoured scarlet drips, tidal waves of gore burst from lifts and flood corridors (and what rich, dark claret it is). Then there's the acting – perfectly naturalistic and restrained at the start, building towards animal eye-rolling, as Duvall becomes the shrieking incarnation of panic, and Nicholson, in a performance that has defined him for life, snarls, grinds his jaw and occasionally tempers his Neanderthal psychosis with tics that look like Oliver Hardy impersonations (check out his first scene at the haunted bar).

Even if the drama appears straightforward, there's the matter of the unearthly stage it's enacted on – the hotel itself, with its extraordinary atmospherics. Hotel manager Ullman (Barry Nelson) welcomes Jack by telling him how a former caretaker, Charles Grady, went crazy and chopped up his family: the problem was cabin fever, the result of confinement in isolation. Not only do the Torrances suffer cabin fever but Kubrick wants us to as well. *The Shining* makes us inhabit every corner of the painstakingly constructed hotel sets, and the way the film guides us along corridors, around corners, up staircases – thanks to Garrett Brown's revolutionary new gizmo the Steadicam – makes us feel we know every inch of the place, even (especially) the sound of it silences.

The Overlook is no less a maze than the leafy one that stands in its garden: the whole film is informed by a disorienting inversion of inner and outer spaces. The spacious Colorado Lounge is steeped in daylight – suffused at first with autumnal glow, then later, in the unnerving shot of a snarling, transfixed Jack, with the same cold blue light we've seen outside in the snow. The most unsettling of these inversions comes when the camera follows Wendy out through the hotel door and into the snow outside. But it feels instead as if she's entering a giant freezer like the one she's already visited in the hotel's kitchen – and, of course, it's just that, a huge snowscape set constructed at Elstree, itself bounded in isolation.

Then there's the eerie sense of things closing in, reducing, paring themselves to the essential. We feel it in the film's time scheme, which seems elastic and amorphous but is mapped out more and more precisely in a succession of intertitles: 'A Month Later', 'Tuesday', 'Sunday', '4pm' and finally the last shot, which brings us to a specific but eternal moment outside time. A further sense of reduction comes from Kubrick's treatment of Stephen King's baggy, prolix novel (416 closely typeset pages in the current NEL paperback – not bad for a book about writer's block). Kubrick and Johnson have stripped out swathes of King's references to the outside world including much exposition of Jack's and Wendy's unhappy family histories and Jack's alcoholism, disastrous teaching career and uneasy relationship with a benevolent patron. They also lose copious specifics about the various deaths, scandals and murders that mark the Overlook's history, not to mention many of King's supernatural sideshows such as the animated topiary animals, replaced (ostensibly because the special effects were unworkable) by the maze. In the film, events happen largely behind closed doors, and the backstory – and the import of Danny's telepathic 'shining' – have to be inferred. (Anyone with a taste for more literal King spookery is referred to the laborious, FX-laden television mini-series adaptation of the novel, directed by Mick Garris, which King, frustrated by Kubrick's treatment, wrote and produced.)

A further reduction is the film's own curious shrinkage. It was first shown in the United States at a running length of 146 minutes, but in the early weeks of release Kubrick excised a two-minute sequence from the end, in which Wendy was visited in hospital by Ullman. By the time the film reached the United Kingdom it had lost another 25 minutes including a tableau of cobwebbed skeletons discovered by Wendy as she wanders through the hotel towards the end of the film. The cut referred to in this article is the extant UK version currently available on video. This version seems to be *The Shining* stripped to the bone, and the elision and spareness are surely what make the film so effective – there's a tangible sense of things closing in towards the essential, just as the closing shot tracks in on its final revelation.

The dominating presence of the Overlook Hotel – designed by Roy Walker as a composite of American hotels visited in the course of research – is an extraordinary vindication of the value of *mise-en-scène*. It's a real, complex space that we don't just see but come to virtually inhabit. The confinement is palpable: horror cinema is an art of claustrophobia, making us loath to stay in the cinema but unable to leave. Yet it's combined with a sort of agoraphobia – we are as frightened of the hotel's cavernous vastness as of its corridors' enclosure. When Jack attempts to write in the huge Colorado Lounge we wonder what's getting to him more – being imprisoned in his own head or being adrift at his desk as though at sea. Wendy's reaction on arrival is 'Just like a ghost ship, huh?', and the Gold Room full of revenant party-goers is the very image of the Ship of Fools, still carousing while the boat goes down in a tide of blood.

The film's subtexts resonate in the vastness as in a sound box. It's the space itself that allows so many thematic strands to emerge from an ostensibly simple narrative, whether or not they are explicitly delineated. The copious critical literature on *The Shining* reads it variously as a commentary on the breakdown of the family, the crisis of masculinity, the state of modern America and its ideologies, sexism, racism and the dominance of big business. But what gives the film its curiously resistant, opaque feel – which makes it possible for critics to conclude that *The Shining* is really about nothing at all, simply a botched genre job – is the fact that this is a film about the experience of watching *The Shining*. The subject is not only possession but film as possession seeing the Torrances in their different ways bewitched by the Overlook, we can't help wondering what's happening to us as we watch them. Are we as sceptical of the hotel's legends as Jack seems to be when first told of the Grady killings? Or are we transfixed, eyes gaping like Danny? A recurring question in horror cinema is how our reactions are affected by seeing other people in the grip of terror: are we terrified out of empathy, or do we distance ourselves with cool scepticism? (Wes Craven's *Scream* films are entirely about this question.)

The film does a lot to discount its more conventional horrors. Hallorann describes the Overlook's lingering images of past horrors (photographs or metaphors?) with disarming domesticity, as being 'like burned toast'. The first such picture Danny sees – in a famous shot that echoes Diane Arbus's photographs – is of the two murdered Grady girls, who invite him to come and play 'for ever and ever and ever'. This image is intercut with shots of the girls lying dead and blood-stained, but we're immediately warned to take there horrors lightly; Danny's guardian spirit Tony tells him, 'It's just like pictures in a book, Danny. It isn't real.'

Kubrick by turns discredits the visions and has them startle us out of our wits: one minute throwing them at us in a sudden cut or shock zoom, the next denouncing them as a mere magic-lantern illusion (the little girls, like the blood-steeped *bon viveur* who raises his glass to Wendy, are first shown dead-on frontally, as if projected on a screen). Wendy's bizarre vision of a dapper toff caught in *flagrante delicto* with a figure in a dog costume is framed in a doorway – another picture rather than a manifestation integrated into the real. In a sequence shortly afterwards, in the US version only, she comes upon a group of seated skeletons in a dark, cobwebbed lounge apparently lit by moonlight from outside – inexplicable and incongruous lighting since the rest of the Overlook is suffused with a warm, brownish glow, eerily suggestive of dried blood. It's as if, in this scene, the house itself has gathered together its dustiest genre props for a conventionally spooky haunted-house tableau (*mort* rather than *vivant*).

The shining – the telepathic power to perceive and project – minimally belongs to Danny, but is shared by the Overlook itself, as much a cinema as a hotel, its gold and orange corridors suggesting the ambience of an archaic movie palace. (As Johnson said in a 1981 *Positif* interview: 'In a certain sense, it's the hotel that sees the events: the hotel is the camera and the narrator.') But the Overlook is also a place where people come to let their imagination run riot, to make movies in their head – and sometimes to transmit them into the world. Jack attempts that in his writing, but Danny does it much more successfully. Whether or not Danny's telepathy brings the Overlook's spectres to life, what's certain is that the boy is actually able to transmit them. The film's big horror routine – Jack's encounter in Room 237 with an etiolated vamp turned suppurating hag – might not really be happening at all (Jack subsequently tells Wendy he's seen nothing in the room), but may in its entirety be a hyperimaginative boy's visual metaphor for the urgency of events. There's stark difference between the shots of Danny wide-eyed in shock elsewhere in the film and the images of him here, in a dribbling trance, not so much transfixed as in a state of extreme concentration, as if he's at once composing the images and sending them. We already know Danny is an adept of television culture – he is first seen watching Roadrunner cartoons, a role model for his evasion of Jack's Coyote.

Wendy is somewhat sidelined in this dynamic – a screaming, gawping bystander who never gets the measure of what she sees. The thoroughly bad deal she receives is due in no small part to Kubrick's difficult on-set relationship with Duvall, resulting in what seems an unfairly punitive attitude to her character. In the minutes missing from the UK version Duvall fleshes out Wendy's character considerably: she has a number of key scenes with Danny, a nervous soliloquy musing about escape from the hotel and a scene back in Boulder where she tells a doctor (Anne Jackson) how Danny was once injured by a drunken Jack. Duvall's twitchy, pained performance here, evoking a complex mixture of confession, guilt and denial, makes it clear how much energy Wendy devotes to keeping the household together. With these scenes cut she is effectively landed with the role of the naïve movie-watcher, one who never learns to see through the shoddiness of horror images but just screams uncritically at everything she's shown: she's 'a confirmed ghost-story and horror-film addict', Jack announces, and for those viewers Kubrick shows only disdain. (*The Shining* was made at a time when consumption of horror was most often thought to turn viewers into credulous rubes, rather than to hone their critical skills as it is today in the intertextual age of *The Faculty*.)

It's tempting to read *The Shining* as an Oedipal struggle not just between generations but between Jack's culture of the written word and Danny's culture of images. The written word comes off pretty badly. It's understandable that writers often get a bad deal from cinema: offering the possibility of madness and distraction, *not writing* (cf. *Barton Fink*) is a more fruitful movie theme than writing. The prospect of generating meaningful words seems hopeless in *The Shining*, perhaps as a corrective to King, who accumulates all too many.

Much has been said about Jack's agonised travails as an image of Kubrick himself, and about the Overlook as a Kubrickian fortress of solitude like the space-stations and rococo bedroom in *2001*. But you can't help wondering what Jack's writing actually entails. He's not necessarily there to create anything so mundane as a novel or a play – he's 'outlining a new writing project', he tells Ullman. A new form of writing? One that isn't necessarily limited to words carrying meaning? As he snarlingly informs Wendy, whether he's typing, or not typing, or whatever the fuck he's doing, he's writing. And maybe the work gets done, despite appearances. The film's most shocking moment is Wendy's discovery of his slab of completed text – a stack of sheets typed with the words 'All work and no play makes Jack a dull boy' over and over again in countless permutations: neatly double-spaced, organised in chunks, blocks, script form, verse form. Who's to say this isn't Jack's definitive oeuvre – a Mallarmé-esque supertext that transcends literal content but creates meaning in strictly typographic form, in the performance of writing? What is it but a muscular and entirely accurate portrait of Jack, a faithful recording of his being?

Jack also uses the written word to more mundane purpose – to sign his 'contract' with the Overlook. 'I gave my word,' he says, which we take to mean 'gave his soul' in the traditional Faustian sense. But maybe he means it more literally – by the end of the film he has renounced language entirely, pursuing Danny through the maze with an inarticulate animal roar. What he has entered into is a conventional business deal that places commercial obligation – the provision of services – over the unspoken contract of compassion and empathy that he seems to have neglected to sign with his family. Jack's the loser: it soon becomes clear that the Overlook has reneged on its part of the deal from the start and conned Jack into doing a job he hasn't bargained for.

The Overlook doesn't want a neat caretaker, let alone a resident writer. It likes to reduce clever people to menials: look at Grady the butler, clearly a cultivated man through and through. The Overlook wants Jack as a clown, an entertainer for the bored spooks wintering up there alone. The privileges Jack is accorded (tolerance from Lloyd the sepulchral barman, limitless credit from the management) are the sort of deals given the in-house cabaret act. The ghouls are assembled to watch Jack wrestle with his demons and lose: this is effectively Kubrick's second gladiator movie, after *Spartacus* (1960).

Hence Jack's reward, after his defeat: a central place among who knows how many other doomed variety acts on the Overlook's wall of fame. He's added to the bill on the Overlook's everlasting big night back in 1921. And, having done his stuff, he deserves an acknowledgment from us too as we get our coats and go. And that's exactly what he gets. The last thing we hear in the film – although we're probably half way to the foyer by then – after the echoing strains of 'Midnight with the Stars and You' is a round of polite applause over the end credits, which then dies down as the ghouls too leave the theatre.

Index

*Page numbers in **bold** refer to in-depth analyses or special features; those in italics refer to illustrations*
r = review